Barney Dalgarno

Spatial Learning in Virtual Environments

Barney Dalgarno

Spatial Learning in Virtual Environments

An Exploration of the Distinguishing Characteristics of 3D Virtual Environments and the Contribution of these Characteristics to Spatial Learning

VDM Verlag Dr. Müller

Impressum/Imprint (nur für Deutschland/ only for Germany)
Bibliografische Information der Deutschen Nationalbibliothek: Die Deutsche Nationalbibliothek
verzeichnet diese Publikation in der Deutschen Nationalbibliografie; detaillierte bibliografische
Daten sind im Internet über http://dnb.d-nb.de abrufbar.
Alle in diesem Buch genannten Marken und Produktnamen unterliegen warenzeichen-, marken-
oder patentrechtlichem Schutz bzw. sind Warenzeichen oder eingetragene Warenzeichen der
jeweiligen Inhaber. Die Wiedergabe von Marken, Produktnamen, Gebrauchsnamen,
Handelsnamen, Warenbezeichnungen u.s.w. in diesem Werk berechtigt auch ohne besondere
Kennzeichnung nicht zu der Annahme, dass solche Namen im Sinne der Warenzeichen- und
Markenschutzgesetzgebung als frei zu betrachten wären und daher von jedermann benutzt
werden dürften.

Coverbild: www.purestockx.com

Verlag: VDM Verlag Dr. Müller Aktiengesellschaft & Co. KG
Dudweiler Landstr. 125 a, 66123 Saarbrücken, Deutschland
Telefon +49 681 9100-698, Telefax +49 681 9100-988, Email: info@vdm-verlag.de
Zugl.: Wollongong, University of Wollongong, 2004

Herstellung in Deutschland:
Schaltungsdienst Lange o.H.G., Zehrensdorfer Str. 11, D-12277 Berlin
Books on Demand GmbH, Gutenbergring 53, D-22848 Norderstedt
Reha GmbH, Dudweiler Landstr. 99, D- 66123 Saarbrücken
ISBN: 978-3-639-06981-5

Imprint (only for USA, GB)
Bibliographic information published by the Deutsche Nationalbibliothek: The Deutsche
Nationalbibliothek lists this publication in the Deutsche Nationalbibliografie; detailed
bibliographic data are available in the Internet at http://dnb.d-nb.de.
Any brand names and product names mentioned in this book are subject to trademark, brand or
patent protection and are trademarks or registered trademarks of their respective holders. The use
of brand names, product names, common names, trade names, product descriptions etc. even
without
a particular marking in this works is in no way to be construed to mean that such names may be
regarded as unrestricted in respect of trademark and brand protection legislation and could thus
be used by anyone.

Cover image: www.purestockx.com

Publisher:
VDM Verlag Dr. Müller Aktiengesellschaft & Co. KG
Dudweiler Landstr. 125 a, 66123 Saarbrücken, Germany
Phone +49 681 9100-698, Fax +49 681 9100-988, Email: info@vdm-verlag.de

Copyright © 2008 VDM Verlag Dr. Müller Aktiengesellschaft & Co. KG and licensors
All rights reserved. Saarbrücken 2008

Produced in USA and UK by:
Lightning Source Inc., 1246 Heil Quaker Blvd., La Vergne, TN 37086, USA
Lightning Source UK Ltd., Chapter House, Pitfield, Kiln Farm, Milton Keynes, MK11 3LW, GB
BookSurge, 7290 B. Investment Drive, North Charleston, SC 29418, USA
ISBN: 978-3-639-06981-5

Acknowledgements

I would like to thank Barry Harper for his supervision and guidance throughout the study. His exceptional knowledge and experience, his generosity in the provision of time and his ability to intuitively judge an appropriate scope for the study, have been invaluable. I would like to thank John Hedberg for his supervision through most of the study. His insight into technology-facilitated learning and his uncanny ability to trigger the development of my own ideas, were of great assistance. And I would like to thank Sue Bennett for her supervision in the final stages of the study. Her exceptional editing skills and her ability to see the different ways in which something might be read and interpreted has contributed greatly to the quality of the thesis.

I would like to acknowledge the contributions of Kerrie Cullis to my emerging knowledge of statistical analysis techniques, and of Andrew Rigney and Andrew Wilkinson to the development of the Virtual Laboratory. I'd also like to thank Andrea Bishop and Danny Bedgood for their cooperation in allowing their students to participate in the study, and the chemistry laboratory staff at Charles Sturt University for their support during the development of the virtual laboratory.

Lastly, I'd like to thank my partner Val for her support and encouragement and my children Ben, Ellie and Lucy for bringing me back to reality when I have come home with my head full of ideas.

Abstract

Three dimensional (3D) technologies have revolutionised computer games to the extent that virtually all new games are based upon 3D graphics. Some might claim that it is only a matter of time before 3D environments become the norm for other types of software, such as business systems, desktop computer task managers and online learning resources. On the surface it would appear that 3D environments have great potential in educational contexts as they provide the possibility of rich learner engagement and allow learners to explore, construct and manipulate virtual objects, structures and metaphorical representations of ideas. This thesis argues that the potentially unique contribution of such environments to learning depends on their ability to facilitate spatial learning. Specifically, it is argued that the ability of such environments to facilitate spatial learning is an implicit assumption in applications of 3D learning environments, whether they are based on models of real or metaphorical objects or spaces.

In order to explore the degree to which 3D environments have unique advantages over alternatives such as video or interactive multimedia in facilitating spatial learning, it was necessary to first identify the distinguishing characteristics of 3D learning environments. The study identified seven characteristics of 3D learning environments that distinguish them from other types of multimedia learning resources. These are realistic display, smooth update of views, smooth display of object motion, consistency of object behaviour, control of view position and direction, object manipulation, and control of object model and simulation parameters.

Having identified the distinguishing characteristics of 3D environments, the study explored the contribution of these characteristics to spatial learning. Investigating the contribution of all of these characteristics was considered to be outside the scope of a doctorate. Consequently, the contribution to spatial learning of smooth display of view changes, smooth display of object motion, user control of view position and direction, and object manipulation were investigated. Additionally, the study explored the effect of learning task design within a 3D environment on spatial learning.

Versions of a 3D environment modelled on a chemistry laboratory were developed for use as research instruments, each with the inclusion or exclusion of some of the identified distinguishing characteristics. Participants in the study used these environments and then undertook tests to determine the degree to which they formed a spatial cognitive model of the laboratory and its apparatus. Quantitative data analysis techniques were used to compare their test performances. This allowed conclusions to be reached about the contribution of each of the identified characteristics to spatial learning.

Three phases of investigation were carried out. The first, a pilot investigation, used qualitative methods to explore the usability of the virtual environment and to explore aspects of the learning that occurred through its use. In the first major investigation, three groups of participants were used. One group explored a version of the virtual laboratory with smooth view changes, smooth display of object motion, user control over view and object manipulation. A second group explored a version of the virtual laboratory without user control over view or object manipulation capability. A third group explored the real laboratory. In the second major investigation, three groups of participants were again used. One group again used a version of the virtual laboratory with all of the identified characteristics. A second group explored a version of the virtual laboratory without user control over view or object manipulation capability. A third group explored a version of the virtual laboratory without user control over view or object manipulation capability and without smooth display of view changes and smooth display of object motion. Additionally, the task carried out by the first group was varied in this second investigation in order to explore the contribution of learning task design to spatial learning.

Smooth display of view changes was found to contribute to spatial learning in some but not all circumstances, and user control over view position and direction was found to contribute to spatial learning only when the task carried out in the environment was closely aligned with the desired learning. The results provided little support for the contribution of smooth display of object motion or object manipulation to spatial learning, but there were limitations in the complexity of the objects explored and the range of object manipulations carried out.

The results have implications for educational designers considering the development or use of a 3D learning environment and needing to make a decision between this and alternatives such as static images and video. The advantages of such environments over video depend on the degree to which the environments allow tasks to be performed that directly align with the desired learning outcomes. If such tasks can be identified then learning advantages can occur, but only if learners are explicitly advised to undertake these tasks either through guidance provided within the environment or as part of supporting materials. The free exploration of a 3D environment with no explicit task advice is unlikely to lead to learning advantages over video or interactive multimedia.

Table of Contents

Certification iii
Acknowledgements...v
Abstract..vii
List of Figures xiii
List of Tables xv

Chapter 1. Introduction..1
  1.1 Background to the Study 1
  1.2 Research Questions 3
  1.3 Overview of the Study...4
  1.4 Significance and Limitations...6
  1.5 Thesis Structure...7

Chapter 2. Literature Review and Theoretical Analysis...............................9
  2.1 Introduction 9
  2.2 3D Environments...10
  2.3 Learning Theory..25
  2.4 Constructivism, Computer Assisted Learning and 3D Environments 28
  2.5 Spatial Perception and Cognition 45
  2.6 Spatial Learning in Real and Virtual Environments 53
  2.7 Distinguishing Characteristics of 3D Learning Environments................55
  2.8 Researchable Issues...58
  2.9 Related Work...60
  2.10 Summary 64

Chapter 3. Methodology and Research Design 67
  3.1 Introduction 67
  3.2 Methodology Background..67
  3.3 Research Design 77
  3.4 Development of the Environments...169
  3.5 Summary 184

Chapter 4. Pilot Investigation 185
  4.1 Introduction 185
  4.2 Method...185
  4.3 Results 194
  4.4 Discussion 221
  4.5 Conclusion...229

Chapter 5. Investigation 1...231
  5.1 Introduction 231
  5.2 Questions Addressed by This Investigation 231
  5.3 Method...232
  5.4 Results 245
  5.5 Summary and Discussion 272
  5.6 Conclusion...280

Chapter 6. Investigation 2 .... **281**
6.1 Introduction 281
6.2 Questions Addressed by This Investigation 282
6.3 Method 282
6.4 Results 300
6.5 Summary and Discussion 348
6.6 Conclusion 354

Chapter 7. Conclusions and Discussion **355**
7.1 Overview of the Study 355
7.2 Main Findings 357
7.3 Additional Findings 364
7.4 Discussion 370
7.5 Limitations of the Study 382
7.6 Further Research 385
7.7 Conclusion 386

References **387**

Appendices **401**
Appendix A. Laboratory Structures and Apparatus Included in Virtual
Laboratory 401
Appendix B. Pilot Study Training Tasks 403
Appendix C. Pilot Study Virtual Laboratory Task Worksheet 406
Appendix D. Pilot Study Laboratory Manual Task Worksheet 410
Appendix E. Pilot Study Test 413
Appendix F. Pilot Study Questionnaire 422
Appendix G. Pilot Study Information Statement and Consent Form 431
Appendix H. Investigation 1 User-control Command Summary 437
Appendix I. Investigation 1 Task Worksheet 439
Appendix J. Investigation 1 Test 441
Appendix K. Investigation 1 Information Statement and Consent Form 450
Appendix L. Investigation 2 User-control Command Summary and Practice
Exercises 457
Appendix M. Investigation 2 User-control Task Worksheet 460
Appendix N. Investigation 2 Dynamic Views and Static Views Task Worksheet ... 463
Appendix O. Investigation 2 Test 466
Appendix P. Investigation 2 Laboratory Task Observation Notes 473
Appendix Q. Investigation 2 Questionnaire 476
Appendix R. Investigation 2 Information Statement and Consent Form 479
Appendix S. Contents of CD-ROM and Installation Instructions 483
Appendix T. VRML Prototypes 484

List of Figures

Figure 2.1 This researcher's model of spatial knowledge 48

Figure 3.1 The virtual laboratory from outside (version used in Investigation 1) 85

Figure 3.2 Looking across the virtual laboratory (version used in Investigation 1) 87

Figure 3.3 Cupboards, drawers and apparatus in the virtual laboratory (version used in Investigation 1) 89

Figure 3.4 Screen layout of the pilot investigation version of the virtual laboratory with menus shown 93

Figure 3.5 Screen layout of the pilot investigation version of the virtual laboratory with menus hidden 95

Figure 3.6 Screen layout of the Investigation 1 User-control version of the virtual laboratory 99

Figure 3.7 Screen layout of the Investigation 2 User-control version of the virtual laboratory 101

Figure 3.8 Screen layout of the Investigation 1 Dynamic Views and Static Views versions of the virtual laboratory 109

Figure 3.9 Screen layout of the pilot investigation version of the virtual laboratory after picking up a conical flask 113

Figure 3.10 Screen layout of the Investigation 1 version of the virtual laboratory after picking up a Bunsen burner 117

Figure 3.11 The process of connecting objects together using the Investigation 2 User-control version of the virtual laboratory 121

Figure 3.12 The pipette filler lever and dial 125

Figure 3.13 The burette tap 127

Figure 3.14 A held object in the Investigation 2 version of the virtual laboratory 131

Figure 3.15 Topological map of the virtual laboratory 147

Figure 3.16 Images making up a panorama provided in test Part G in Investigation 1 153

Figure 3.17 Example question from test Part B in Investigation 1 157

Figure 3.18 Example question from test Part B in Investigation 2 161

Figure 4.1 Screen layout of the pilot investigation version of the virtual laboratory....189

Figure 5.1 Screen layout of the Investigation 1 User-control version of the virtual laboratory 235

Figure 5.2 Screen layout of the Investigation 1 Dynamic Views version of the virtual laboratory 239

Figure 6.1 Screen layout of the Investigation 2 User-control version of the virtual laboratory 287

Figure 6.2 Diagram of apparatus provided for test Part C in Investigation 2 295

List of Tables

Table 1.1 Research summary and timetable..6

Table 2.1 Applications of 3D learning environments and implicit assumptions 42

Table 2.2 Visual depth cues...46

Table 2.3 Distinguishing characteristics of 3D learning environments 58

Table 3.1 Characteristics of pseudoscience, from Reeves (1995), along with arguments
for why this study does not exhibit each 75

Table 3.2 Research summary 80

Table 3.3 Frame rates achieved by the version of the virtual laboratory used in each
major investigation 104

Table 3.4 Development timetable..178

Table 4.1 Pilot investigation summary and timetable 187

Table 4.2 Number of participants correctly answering each multiple choice question
(out of five participants in each group) 195

Table 4.3 Number of participants correctly able to identify each item of apparatus (out
of five participants in each group)...196

Table 4.4 Number of participants correctly able to indicate the position of locations
within the laboratory (out of five participants in each group)...............................197

Table 4.5 Number of participants correctly able to indicate the position of items of
apparatus and equipment within the laboratory (out of five participants in each
group) 198

Table 4.6 Average group scores on procedural description questions 199

Table 4.7 Observed problems with the task design 200

Table 4.8 Observed problems with the menu and information display..........................200

Table 4.9 Observed motion and view control problems...201

Table 4.10 Observed object manipulation problems..202

Table 4.11 Observations of unexpected usage 203

Table 4.12 Observed limitations of the 3D model 204

Table 4.13 Observations during laboratory session 205

Table 4.14 Summary of structured interview responses to questions about participants'
general impressions of the virtual laboratory 206

Table 4.15 Summary of structured interview responses to questions about participants'
impressions of specific aspects of the virtual laboratory 208

Table 4.16 Summary of structured interview responses to questions about apparatus
already able to be identified by the participant prior to the study.........................212

Table 4.17 Summary of structured interview responses to questions about apparatus
procedures already familiar to the participant prior to the study 212

Table 4.18 Summary of structured interview responses to questions about the usefulness
and ease of use of aspects of the virtual laboratory...213

Table 4.19 Summary of structured interview responses to questions about proposed
changes to the virtual laboratory 216

Table 4.20 Identified changes not implemented 225

Table 5.1 Allocated time for each task in Investigation 1...232

Table 5.2 Participants in Investigation 1 233

Table 5.3 Items of apparatus and small equipment included in Investigation 1 versions
of the virtual laboratory..242

Table 5.4 Items of furniture and landmarks included in Investigation 1 versions of the
virtual laboratory (number of occurrences bracketed) 242

Table 5.5 Performance on spatial learning test by gender 247

Table 5.6 Chemistry experience levels within each group...249

Table 5.7 Performance on spatial learning test by prior chemistry experience 250

Table 5.8 Performance on Part A of the test, requiring identification of apparatus
(number of items correctly identified) 253

Table 5.9 Performance on Part A of the test, requiring identification of apparatus
(percentage of unfamiliar items able to be identified) 254

Table 5.10 Performance on Part B of the test, requiring recognition of apparatus
structure..255

Table 5.11 Performance on Part C of the test, requiring drawing of a map containing
laboratory furniture, doors and windows 257

Table 5.12 Performance on Part D of the test, requiring drawing of a map given a list of
laboratory furniture, doors and windows to include 258

Table 5.13 Performance on Part E of the test, requiring indication of position and direction of given views of the laboratory..259

Table 5.14 Performance on Part F of the test, requiring indication of location of items of apparatus on laboratory plan 261

Table 5.15 Performance on Part G of the test, requiring location of apparatus within laboratory photographs..262

Table 5.16 Responses to questions requiring self-report of spatial ability by group 264

Table 5.17 Responses to questions requiring self-report of spatial ability by gender...264

Table 5.18 Pearson's Correlations (PC) between questions on spatial ability and performance on spatial tests 266

Table 5.19 Responses to questions on sense of presence by group...............................269

Table 5.20 Responses to questions on sense of presence by gender..............................270

Table 5.21 Pearson's Correlations (PC) between sense of presence and performance on spatial tests 271

Table 6.1 Allocated time for each task in Investigation 2..283

Table 6.2 Participants in Investigation 2 284

Table 6.3 Apparatus and furniture listed on task worksheets.......................................290

Table 6.4 Apparatus manipulation tasks 291

Table 6.5 Apparatus manipulation test carried out in real laboratory 299

Table 6.6 Statements included in questionnaire 300

Table 6.7 Interactions identified in Investigation 2..301

Table 6.8 Performance on spatial learning test by gender 302

Table 6.9 Performance on real laboratory apparatus usage test by gender 304

Table 6.10 Performance on real laboratory apparatus location test by gender 305

Table 6.11 Chemistry experience levels within each group..306

Table 6.12 Performance on spatial learning test by prior chemistry experience 308

Table 6.13 Performance on real laboratory apparatus usage test by prior chemistry experience..311

Table 6.14 Performance on real laboratory apparatus location test by prior chemistry experience..313

Table 6.15 Performance on Part B of the test, requiring identification of apparatus (percentage of items correctly identified) 314

Table 6.16 Performance on Part B of the test, requiring identification of apparatus (percentage of unfamiliar items able to be identified) 315

Table 6.17 Performance on Part B of the test, requiring identification of correct model of apparatus (percentage of items, for which the correct model was able to be identified.) 316

Table 6.18 Performance on Part C of the test, requiring description of apparatus usage procedure (number of steps correctly described). 317

Table 6.19 Performance on Part C of the test, requiring description of apparatus usage procedure (number of identified critical steps correctly described)......................318

Table 6.20 Performance on Part D of the test, requiring the drawing of a plan of the laboratory including all furniture, doors and windows (number of correctly positioned items) 319

Table 6.21 Performance on Part E of the test, requiring indication of position and direction of given views of the laboratory...320

Table 6.22 Performance on Part F of the test, requiring recall of apparatus location (number of items correctly placed) 321

Table 6.23 Performance on real laboratory apparatus usage test by group...................324

Table 6.24 Performance on real laboratory task requiring location of apparatus (number of items correctly located)...326

Table 6.25 Performance on real laboratory task requiring location of apparatus (total time taken in seconds) 327

Table 6.26 Responses on question requiring self-report of spatial ability by group.....328

Table 6.27 Pearson's Correlations (PC) between question on spatial ability and performance on spatial tests 329

Table 6.28 Spearman Correlations between question on spatial ability and performance on real laboratory apparatus usage task..331

Table 6.29 Pearson's Correlations (PC) between question on spatial ability and performance on real laboratory apparatus location task...331

Table 6.30 Pearson's Correlations (PC) between question on spatial ability and questionnaire responses..332

Table 6.31 Responses to question requiring self-report of spatial ability by gender 332

Table 6.32 Responses to questions on sense of presence by group 334

Table 6.33 Pearson's Correlations (PC) between sense of presence and performance on spatial tests 335

Table 6.34 Spearman Correlations between sense of presence and performance on real laboratory apparatus usage tasks 337

Table 6.35 Pearson's Correlations (PC) between sense of presence and performance on real laboratory apparatus location test...338

Table 6.36 Pearson's Correlations (PC) between sense of presence and questionnaire responses 339

Table 6.37 Responses to questions on sense of presence by gender...........................340

Table 6.38 Responses to questions about enjoyment and ease of use of virtual laboratory by group...343

Table 6.39 Responses to questions about usefulness of the virtual laboratory by group 344

Table 6.40 Questionnaire responses by gender 347

Table 7.1 Contrast of methods and results in this study for exploring user control with those used by Peruch et al. (1995) and Christou and Bulthoff (1999) 371

Table 7.2 Contrast of methods and results in this study for exploring static and animated display with those used by Peruch et al. (1995) and Christou and Bulthoff (1999) 379

Chapter 1. Introduction

1.1 Background to the Study

Computer facilitated learning has been around for four decades and the potential for the use of computers to assist with many aspects of the learning process is well accepted. Research in computer facilitated learning has been driven both by developments in computer technology and developments in theories of learning.

The key developments in computer technology have been the miniaturisation and mass-production of computer components that led to the widespread availability and affordability of micro-computers in the early 1980s, the widespread adoption of graphical user interfaces which made these computers useable by a much wider range of people in the early 1990s, and most recently, the rapid development and widespread use of the Internet. A development that has occurred alongside the Internet and which has been very significant in the computer games industry has been enormous improvements in personal computer graphics capability, allowing for the exploration of highly realistic virtual environments based on three dimensional (3D) geometrical models. This last development is particularly important for this research.

Alongside the developments in computer technology there has been a gradual adoption of new approaches to teaching and learning driven largely by learning theories that fit within the broad theoretical base called constructivism. Constructivism is a term that means different things to different people and consequently needs clear definition if it is to be used in a meaningful way. Section 2.3 discusses constructivism in more detail. The slant on constructivism taken by this research is one that draws heavily on Piaget's stage independent theories of learning. These theories focus on individual knowledge construction through cognitive activity.

Research on the role of computers as tools for active knowledge construction, consistent with Piaget's theories of learning, was probably the most active area of computers in learning research up until the mid 1990s (see for example Papert, 1993; Jonassen, 1991; Harper and Hedberg, 1997). From the mid 1990s an explosion in the use of the Internet tended to shift the focus to the use of computers as information search tools and as tools for communication within learning communities. This research, however, focuses on the use of computers, and in particular 3D environments, as tools for knowledge construction.

A key example of the way computers can be used as tools for knowledge construction is the use of simulations or microworlds. These tools allow the learner to explore, manipulate and construct representations of real or abstract entities, in order to develop their own individual cognitive representation of the knowledge domain. A number of CD-ROM based educational multimedia systems have been developed that incorporate such tools, including for example, Investigating Lake Iluka (Harper, Hedberg & Brown, 1995). The consequences of various interpretations of constructivism for computer assisted learning have been explored in earlier work by this researcher (Dalgarno, 2001) and are discussed further in Section 2.4.

The developments in graphics capabilities, and particularly 3D rendering capability, on personal computers provide enormous opportunities for improvements in the degree of realism of these simulations and microworlds. The enormous popularity of computer games based on the use of 3D virtual environments, particularly amongst children and young adults, suggests that this increase in realism has the potential to lead to a huge increase in the degree to which the learner will be engaged and motivated by the learning resource. Consequently, many have concluded that learning resources based on computer game technologies should be the ultimate goal of educational developers. However, there are a number of untested assumptions implicit within this conclusion.

It is argued in Section 2.4.5 that it is the spatial representation of the ideas and through this the facilitation of spatial understanding that 3D learning environments are particularly suited to. It is argued that this is the case regardless of whether the knowledge domain is one encompassing real entities or abstract concepts. The potential of such resources, however, depends on an implicit assumption that spatial learning can occur from the exploration of a computer-generated 3D environment and that such environments provide for superior spatial learning to alternatives such as videos, animations or static images. Research carried out to date has not yet provided clear evidence for this assumption and it is this gap in the existing research that is addressed by this study.

In order to explore the degree to which 3D environments have unique advantages over alternatives such as video, animation or static images in facilitating spatial learning, it was necessary to first identify the characteristics of 3D learning environments that distinguish them from such alternatives. Seven characteristics that distinguish 3D environments from other types of learning resources were identified. The study then explored the contribution of a set of these characteristics to spatial learning in 3D environments. One such characteristic, for example, is the ability of the learner to modify their viewpoint within the environment by controlling their own movement. If this characteristic is not important for spatial learning then a video would be just as effective. It is generally much cheaper to make a video of an environment than to produce an interactive 3D environment. A second such characteristic is smooth transitions between viewpoints, equivalent to panning a camera. If this characteristic is not important for spatial learning, a set of still images, for example as part of web pages, might be just as effective. Again, it is much cheaper to take a series of photographs than to produce a video or an interactive 3D environment.

An important aspect of the design of any computer facilitated learning resource is the design of appropriate learning tasks. This is particularly the case within a simulation or virtual environment, where very different learning can occur depending on the tasks undertaken. An additional focus of this study was the effect of the design of the task undertaken by learners in a virtual environment on the learning that occurs.

1.2 Research Questions

The background theory and associated research that have led to the research questions is discussed in detail in Chapter 2. The questions are presented here to give the reader a sense for the overall direction of the research.

Firstly, the overall focus question was:

> **What are the distinguishing characteristics of 3D learning environments; does each characteristic contribute to spatial learning; and does the design of the learning task contribute to spatial learning in such environments?**

The specific questions addressed were as follows:

Question 1. Does smooth display of view changes in a 3D learning environment contribute to spatial learning?

Question 2. Does smooth display of object motion in a 3D learning environment contribute to spatial learning?

Question 3. Does user control over view position and direction in a 3D learning environment contribute to spatial learning?

Question 4. Does object manipulation in a 3D learning environment contribute to spatial learning?

Question 5. How does the design of the learning task within a 3D environment affect the spatial learning that occurs?

1.3 Overview of the Study

The study consisted of the development of various versions of a 3D environment, each with the inclusion or exclusion of certain characteristics; the use of these environments by participants; and the testing of these participants' spatial learning. Quantitative data analysis techniques were used to compare the spatial test performance of participants using the various environments in order to determine whether the included or excluded characteristics contributed to spatial learning.

Specifically, a 3D environment based on the Charles Sturt University undergraduate chemistry laboratory in Wagga Wagga was developed. From this point on, this environment will be referred to as 'the virtual laboratory'. A number of versions of the virtual laboratory were developed, with certain characteristics included or excluded from each version. After carrying out tasks in a version of the virtual laboratory, learners undertook written tests as well as practical tests in the real laboratory. The performance on these written tests and real laboratory tests provided the main research data.

Three phases of investigation were carried out, a pilot investigation and two major investigations. Additionally a number of phases of usability testing were carried out prior to each investigation as part of the iterative design and development of the virtual laboratory.

The pilot investigation used qualitative methods to explore the usability of the virtual environment, and to explore aspects of the learning that occurred through its use. It involved the observation of participants as they explored the virtual laboratory, using think-aloud protocols (Ericson & Simon, 1993) to understand their cognitive processing, as well as interviews and questionnaires.

In the first major investigation, three groups of participants were used. One group explored a version of the virtual laboratory with smooth view changes, smooth display of object motion, user control over view and object manipulation. A second group explored a similar version of the virtual laboratory, but without user control over view or object manipulation capability. This version consisted of a series of animated displays showing a similar sequence of views to that likely to be seen by participants in the first group. A third group explored the real laboratory.

In the second major investigation, three groups of participants were again used. One group again used a version of the virtual laboratory with all of the identified characteristics. A second group explored a version of the virtual laboratory without user control over view or object manipulation capability, that is, a version consisting of a series of animated views. A third group explored a version of the virtual laboratory without user control over view or object manipulation capability, and without smooth display of view changes and smooth display of object motion. This version consisted of a series of still images.

In order to explore the affect task design has on spatial learning in 3D environments, the task undertaken by learners in the second major investigation was changed substantially so that it was aligned much more closely to the spatial learning outcomes that were the subject of the tests. Specifically, in the first investigation the task involved exploration of the laboratory with a goal of locating each item on a list of apparatus. In the second investigation learners were required to locate the apparatus, carry them to a workbench, set the apparatus up for an experiment and then put each item back where it belonged.

A questionnaire was also completed by participants in the second major investigation, which included questions about the virtual laboratory's ease of use and effectiveness and about the participants' enjoyment of the experience.

Table 1.1 shows a summary of the research method and the timetable followed in the study.

Table 1.1 Research summary and timetable		
Date	**Investigation**	**Explanation**
February 2002	Pilot Investigation	Ten first-year undergraduate chemistry students were observed using the virtual laboratory, completed a spatial learning test and undertook a structured interview.
May 2002	Investigation 1	Thirty-four undergraduate information technology students were divided into three groups. One group carried out a task in the virtual laboratory. A second group viewed a series of animated displays generated from the virtual laboratory showing a similar sequence to the first group. A third group carried out a similar task in the real laboratory. Participants undertook a written test on their spatial learning.
February/March 2003	Investigation 2	Ninety-two undergraduate chemistry students were divided into three groups. One group carried out a task in the virtual laboratory. A second group viewed a series of animated displays generated from the virtual laboratory showing a similar sequence to the first group. A third group viewed a series of still images corresponding to the displays viewed by the second group but without the animated transitions between views. Participants undertook a written test on their spatial learning and a week later undertook tasks within the real laboratory. Participants also completed a questionnaire.

1.4 Significance and Limitations

By addressing the research questions identified in Section 1.2, the study has the potential to contribute to 3D learning environment research in a number of ways. Firstly, identifying whether 3D environments have advantages for spatial learning over alternatives such as interactive multimedia resources incorporating video, animations or static images, which in many cases will be cheaper and easier to develop, will provide clear advice to educational designers and developers who need to choose appropriate technologies for their educational contexts. Additionally, providing a clear indication of the characteristics of 3D environments that contribute to spatial learning will allow designers and developers of 3D learning environments to focus their efforts on those aspects that are likely to lead to learning benefits.

It is recognised, however, that there are limitations in the use of quantitative research methods in education due to issues of internal and external validity. It is always very difficult to control all of the potential independent variables in an educational study to ensure that the effects being measured are the only ones that contribute to the results. For example, in this study the spatial ability of the participants, their prior experience in laboratories, their age, their gender and their motivation to achieve the intended learning outcomes could all contribute to the learning that occurs. Using a sample size sufficient to ensure an even spread of abilities, experience and motivations is difficult because undertaking of tasks in a virtual environment can be time consuming and requires supervision and assistance from the researchers. Consequently, there may be questions about the internal validity of the study. This study has attempted to address these issues by selecting participants with a similar background within each investigation. Specifically, Investigation 1 used undergraduate information technology students as participants and Investigation 2 used undergraduate chemistry students as participants.

However, selecting participants with a particular background can affect the external validity of the results. For example, undergraduate students tend to have a relatively narrow age range and information technology and chemistry students may have particular aptitudes and abilities that are not representative of the population as a whole. Consequently, there may be questions about the degree to which the findings can be generalised to other learners. Further studies that attempt to replicate the findings with other cohorts of learners will be necessary to provide more definitive and generalised conclusions.

Despite these potential limitations it is the view of this researcher that clear findings in relation to the identified research questions will add substantially to knowledge about learning in 3D environments. The issues related to the internal and external validity of the study are discussed further in Chapter 3.

1.5 Thesis Structure

Chapter 2 begins by setting the context of the research with a discussion of background theory and research in the areas of 3D environments, learning theory and computer facilitated learning. Research and theory relating specifically to 3D learning environments is also presented, and the key assumptions and primary research questions are derived. An overview of research on 3D technologies is presented as a precursor for a more detailed discussion in Chapter 3.

The research method is described in Chapter 3, beginning with a justification of the methods chosen, leading to a detailed description of the methods used in each investigation, with reference to relevant literature. The design of the versions of the virtual laboratory used in each investigation is also described and justified in Chapter 3. The design of the 3D model, and the user interface for motion control and object manipulation are presented in the context of relevant literature. An overview of the technologies used in the development and the development process followed is also included in Chapter 3.

Chapter 4 describes the pilot investigation, which used primarily qualitative techniques to explore spatial learning using the virtual laboratory and to explore the usability of the virtual laboratory. Learning tasks in the virtual laboratory were also tested during the pilot investigation along with some of the spatial learning test instruments. Changes to the design of the environment, to the learning tasks and to the spatial test instruments as a result of the pilot investigation are discussed.

Chapter 5 describes the first major investigation, which compared spatial learning through free exploration of the virtual laboratory with learning from undertaking a virtual tour and with learning from exploring the real laboratory. The chapter begins with an overview of the research methods employed. The results of the investigation are then presented, followed by a discussion of their implications.

Chapter 6 describes the second major investigation, which compared spatial learning through task directed exploration of the virtual laboratory with learning from undertaking a virtual tour with animated transitions between viewpoints and with learning from a similar tour but without animated transitions. The chapter begins with an overview of the methods employed. The results are then presented followed by a discussion of their implications.

Chapter 7 discusses the overall conclusions and the consequences of the results for educational developers. Possibilities for further research are also discussed.

Chapter 2. Literature Review and Theoretical Analysis

2.1 Introduction

This chapter begins with a review of background literature in the areas of 3D environments and learning theory. This background is intended to clarify the scope of the study and provide definitions of key terms that are used throughout the remainder of the thesis. Potential learning applications of 3D environments, consistent with a constructivist view of learning, are then discussed, and classified according to the interpretations of constructivism each is consistent with. References to published descriptions of 3D learning environments are included in this discussion.

The range of potential applications of 3D learning environments is then summarised in a table and the pedagogical assumptions implicit within each are identified. A recurring assumption is that using a 3D environment can lead to the formation of a spatial cognitive model. In order to explore this assumption, the nature of spatial learning is examined with appropriate references to the literature, followed by a review of studies of spatial learning in 3D environments. This review concludes that 3D environments can contribute to spatial learning.

Having ascertained that 3D environments can contribute to spatial learning it then becomes important to identify the specific aspects of such environments that contribute to spatial learning. In order to do this the distinguishing characteristics of 3D learning environments need to be identified. After reviewing various researchers' conceptions of what the distinguishing characteristics might be and after demonstrating that there is a commonality to the various ideas, it is proposed that the fidelity of the representation, along with the possible learner activities, distinguish 3D learning environments from other learning resources. The sense of immersion or presence is seen as being a consequence of the fidelity and the learner activity rather than as being an additional distinguishing characteristic.

Having identified distinguishing characteristics of 3D learning environments, a set of specific questions is identified, which address the importance of each characteristic for spatial learning. It is argued that the answers to these questions are of interest to educational designers who need to make a decision about whether to use a 3D learning environment or whether to use an alternative such as a Web site or a video. Research addressing aspects of these questions is then reviewed. It is argued that although research has been undertaken that addresses some aspects of the questions identified, the results are unclear, and consequently there is a clear need for the research undertaken in this study.

2.2 3D Environments

2.2.1 Definitions

The term '3D environment' used in the title of this thesis was chosen in preference to a number of other possible terms, including 'virtual reality' and 'virtual environment'. Wann and Mon-Williams (1996) claim that the term virtual reality is "an oxymoron that is misleading and unnecessary" (p. 833). They say that the term implies that we are trying to simulate every aspect of reality, when in fact we should be trying to simulate a sub-set of the real world sufficient for communication of information. Macpherson and Keppell (1998) suggest that the term virtual reality refers to the experience rather than the hardware or software. They define virtual reality as "a state produced in a person's mind that can to varying degrees, occupy the person's awareness in a way similar to that of a real environment" (p. 63). Bryson (1995) concurs, differentiating between the term virtual reality, which he uses to refer to the overall experience of the user, and virtual environment, which he uses to refer to the environment itself:

> *Virtual reality is the use of various computer graphics systems in combination with various display and interface devices to provide the effect of immersion in an interactive three-dimensional computer-generated environment in which the virtual objects have spatial presence. We call this interactive three-dimensional computer-generated environment a virtual environment. (p. 3)*

The media hype during the early 1990s about virtual reality has tended to make the use of the term clichéd and it is now used in the research literature much less frequently than the term virtual environment. This is evidenced by a survey of the titles of articles published in 2002 in the journal 'Presence: Teleoperators and Virtual Environments' and papers presented at the 2002 Association for Computing Machinery (ACM) Virtual Reality Software and Technology (VRST) conference. Out of 75 papers, 18 included the term virtual environment or the initials VE in their title, and 7 included the term virtual reality or the term VR in their title.

The term virtual environment, though widely accepted in the Human Computer Interaction (HCI) literature, is problematic within the educational community because the term 'virtual learning environment' is now widely used in relation to Web-based learning resources which do not include any form of visual simulation. Such environments typically consist of pages of text and 2D graphics supplemented by tools allowing for synchronous or asynchronous text communication. For example, Ryan and Hall (2001) state that the four elements that a virtual learning environment would usually contain are courseware, support materials, online assessment and online support. A search on the Educational Resources Information Centre (ERIC) database returned 19 papers published between 2000 and 2003 containing the term virtual learning environment, of which only one used the term to describe a 3D environment. The remainder referred to online learning resources like those described by Ryan and Hall.

Consequently, the term '3D virtual environment', or '3D environment' for short, has been chosen because the inclusion of '3D' clearly differentiates the environments that are the subject of this work from text-based environments. Nevertheless, most definitions of virtual environment taken from within the HCI literature describe the types of environment that are the focus of this thesis.

The definition used by Wann and Mon-Williams (1996) describes the main aspects of a 3D environment, stating that such an environment "capitalizes upon natural aspects of human perception by extending visual information in three spatial dimensions and may supplement this information with other stimuli and temporal changes" and that "a virtual environment enables the user to interact with the displayed data" (p. 833).

Wilson (1997) defines a virtual environment as "an environment other than the one in which the participant is actually present" (p. 1057), and then suggests that a more useful definition is that "it is a computer-generated model, where the participant can interact intuitively in real time with the environment or objects within it, and to some extent has a feeling of actually 'being there', or a feeling of presence" (p. 1057-1058). Ellis (1991) provides a definition of virtualisation, which puts less emphasis on the feeling of presence, and thus extends to virtual objects. He says that "virtualisation may be defined as the process by which a human viewer interprets a patterned sensory impression to be an extended object in an environment other than that in which it physically exists" (p. 913). Wilson, Foreman and Tlauka (1997) note that:

> two principle features distinguish virtual environments from other forms of visual imaging such as video. First, the user can control the viewpoint on the environment with six degrees of freedom. Second, the user can interact with objects within the environment. (p. 526)

Drawing together the elements that make up the definitions quoted above, it can be concluded that three-dimensionality, smooth temporal changes and interactivity are the most important defining features of a 3D virtual environment. It is these features that distinguish 3D learning environments from other types of virtual learning environments.

2.2.2 Technologies

Early interest in virtual environments focussed primarily on technologies that allowed for the development of 'immersive virtual environments'. The term 'immersive' is normally used to refer to environments explored using special hardware, such as a head-mounted display, along with special interaction hardware, such as a data glove (Robertson, Card & MacKinlay, 1993).

Morton Heilig's 'Sensorama', developed in 1962, was one of the earliest attempts at an immersive virtual environment experience (Lefcowitz, 2003). It used a cinematic projection with a display that restricted the user's view to the environment, supplemented by "binaural sound, wind and odours effects" (Ellis, 1991, p. 921). The first head-mounted display system was developed in the mid 1960s by Ivan Sutherland (McLellan, 1996). However, the graphics capabilities available at the time were very primitive and consequently a great deal of work on fundamental graphics algorithms and hardware implementations carried out over many years was required before head-mounted displays and associated graphics systems that could be used to simulate a real environment were available (McGreevy, 1993). The first of these was the Virtual Visual Environment Display system (VIVED), developed in 1984 at NASA (McGreevy, 1993). More recently there have been substantial increases in pixel density allowing for very high resolution head-mounted display systems (Hopper, 2000).

There are three important features of head-mounted displays (HMDs) that distinguish them from desktop or projection displays. Firstly, they are mounted on the head and restrict the user's view to the virtual environment. That is, they prevent the user also looking around the real environment. Secondly, they normally use two separate image projections to provide a stereoscopic image, which means that the image provided to the left and right eyes differs, simulating the fact that the two eyes are in slightly different positions in space. Lastly, many head-mounted display systems also include head-tracking, which means that the user's head movements are tracked and the view direction within the virtual environment is modified to simulate the effect of the user turning their head to look around the environment.

For a number of reasons, new input devices were required for interaction in immersive environments. Firstly, because a head-mounted display restricts the user's view to the virtual environment, it is not possible to use a traditional keyboard. Secondly, unconstrained movement and object manipulation in a virtual environment require a device with much more than the two degrees of freedom provided by a desktop mouse. One example is the data glove, which allows for complex hand gestures as well as virtual grasping of objects (Fisher, 1990). Another example is the six degree of freedom mouse, which is held in the air and allows for movement in any combination of the three planes as well as rotation about any combination of the three axes (see for example Frohlich & Plate, 2000; Ware & Osborne, 1990; Xiao & Hubbold, 1998). More recently there has been a growing interest in force feedback devices (see for example Massie & Salisbury, 1994; Stevenson et al., 1997).

Although immersive virtual environments captured the attention of the popular media and many researchers in the 1990s, research into 'desktop virtual environments' which can be explored using desktop computers, was carried out in parallel, and became increasingly important as the graphics capabilities of standard desktop computers began to improve dramatically. These improvements, primarily driven by the demands of the computer games industry, have allowed for richly detailed 3D environments to be delivered at realistic frame rates and with very high response rates (Kelty, Beckett & Zalcman, 1999), and have meant that mainstream use of virtual environments has become possible. Additionally, it is now possible with simple PC hardware to produce spatial audio. Spatial audio system vary the volume from each speaker depending on the user's proximity and orientation to the source of the sound in the environment.

An alternative to the use of desktop displays or head-mounted displays is to use a large projected display. Systems that project the view of an environment onto one or more walls of a room are sometimes termed 'semi-immersive systems'. Early inspiration for such systems may have come from Myron Krueger's 'Videoplace', developed in the 1970s, which was a screen-projected virtual environment using two-dimensional (2D) video with superimposed computer graphics generated in response to object manipulation (Krueger, 1993). Probably the most advanced projection system is the 'Fakespace CAVE', in which the virtual environment is projected in stereo onto three walls of a room with the participant wearing 3D glasses and a location sensor (McLellan, 1996).

Photographic panorama environments, such as those provided by Apple's QuickTime VR software, provide an alternative to the use of 3D technologies for desktop virtual environments (Apple, 2003). They are developed by 'stitching' together a series of photographs to create a 360 degree panorama. This panorama is presented on a desktop computer as a virtual environment in which the user can interactively 'pan' around. Through the use of hot-links to panoramic images taken from other locations, the user can interactively 'jump' to other viewpoints (Norris, Rashid & Wong, 1999). Interaction in these panoramic environments is quite limited when compared to 3D virtual environments because it is not possible to move the viewpoint freely or to manipulate objects. It is also not possible to include objects with simulated behaviours within such environments.

Another recent development is the use of multi-user collaborative virtual environments (CVEs). These environments allow multiple users to explore an environment concurrently, with each user represented within the environment by an 'avatar', which is a 3D representation of that person. Users' computers can be either co-located, connected through a local area network (LAN), or located at geographically remote locations connected using the Internet. Typically an interface is provided allowing either for text-based chat or for audio communication between users (see for example Active Worlds, 2003). More advanced systems allow for cooperative object manipulation (Ruddle, Savage & Jones, 2002).

The focus of this study was single user (non-collaborative) 3D environments that can be explored using standard PC hardware, that is, desktop virtual environments. Aside from the accessibility advantages of desktop environments, there are also significant usability advantages. For example, Robertson, Card and MacKinlay (1993) argue that desktop environments can be easier to use than immersive environments because people are already familiar with controlling the desktop computer. Additionally, they argue that such environments rarely subject the user to simulator sickness, the physical and psychological stress often associated with immersive environments. Wilson (1997) also notes the problems of simulator sickness frequently encountered by users of immersive virtual environments. In evaluating immersive environments as part of the ScienceSpace Project, Salzman, Dede, Loftin and Chen (1999) found that of thirty participants, "several experienced symptoms of simulator sickness, including oculomotor discomfort, nausea and disorientation" (p. 24). In a subsequent study where an immersive environment was compared with a traditional 2D multimedia resource, participants in the immersive environment "experienced significantly greater simulator sickness symptoms ... and had more trouble using [the environment]" (p. 32).

Early virtual environment research tended to play down the importance of desktop environments. For example, Winn (1993, p. 2) notes that "desktop VR does not meet the four necessary conditions for immersion ... and therefore does not engender presence" and "although this kind of non-immersive VR has a great many potential uses in education ... it offers no more than a few modest extensions of computer graphics programs". However, a number of researchers have noted that there is a difference between physical (or objectively measurable) immersion and psychological (or subjectively reported) immersion (see for example Hedberg & Alexander, 1994; Whitelock, Brna & Holland, 1996). Researchers into psychological immersion in 3D environments use the term immersion to refer to an objective measure based on the technologies being used, and the term presence to refer to a subjective measure of the degree to which the user experiences a sense of 'being there' (Slater, Usoh & Steed, 1995).

Robertson, Card and Mackinlay (1993), argue that psychological immersion is in fact possible in desktop environments. They say that:

Full immersion is often seen as a major advantage. But our experience and the
experience of others suggest that, for many applications, the same effect is possible
with proper 3D cues and interactive animation. As the user controls the animation
and focuses on it, he or she is drawn into the 3D world. Mental and emotional
immersion takes place, in spite of the lack of visual or perceptual immersion. Anyone
who has played a good video arcade game, many of which are examples of
nonimmersive VR, knows the truth of this. (p. 81)

It is the view of this researcher that psychological immersion or the sense of presence is of more interest to educators than physical immersion and that appropriately designed desktop virtual environments can engender a sense of presence. Additionally, a sense of presence is only one of the characteristics of a 3D environment and the argument that it specifically contributes to learning is not clearly supported by the empirical evidence available to date. For example, in a study comparing exploration of a real building, a virtual building and static images, no significant correlation was found between reported presence and performance on route-finding or configuration knowledge tests (Witmer, Bailey & Knerr, 1996).

Results of studies exploring the learning benefits of physically immersive environments over desktop environments are unclear. For example, Winn (2002) found that learners wearing a head-mounted display demonstrated significantly greater learning than learners who explored a similar environment using a desktop computer. However, a number of studies have found no significant difference between desktop environments and physically immersive environments in the spatial cognitive model formed as a result of virtual environment exploration (see for example Patrick et al., 2000; Ruddle, Payne & Jones, 1999). Hunt and Waller (1999) also argue that the greater sense of presence in physically immersive environments does not necessarily lead to greater spatial learning. They note that:

The acquisition of configural information depends upon the conceptual interpretation
of information about the environment, not perceptual interpretations of that
information. This result has implications for theories of spatial orientation. It also
has implications for the design of training in spatial orientation. For the purposes of
environmental learning we may not need a Star Trek® holodeck -- a desktop
computer will do fine. This conclusion runs counter to the considerable effort to
create realistic (and expensive) immersive VR, on the grounds that the sense of

involvement accompanying an immersive VR experience should produce better
learning. (p. 71)

Cutting and Vishton (1995) carried out an analysis of the relative importance of visual depth cues available in the real world. They identified 13 such cues (see Table 2.2) and of these only binocular disparity is available in immersive environments but not desktop environments. They found that binocular disparity is only of primary importance for objects within a few metres (or virtual metres) of the viewer and becomes of negligible importance once objects are more than about 10 metres away. This would suggest that for many virtual environments there would be no advantage in a binocular display. It should be noted, however, that features of physically immersive environments other than the binocular display, such as head tracking, and the fact that the participant's visual field is restricted to include only the virtual environment, may contribute to spatial learning.

In addition to the fact that the spatial learning benefits of physically immersive environments over desktop environments are unclear, immersive environments have been found to cause a number of ergonomic problems for some users. Wilson (1997) in discussing the ergonomic issues related to virtual environments notes that "it is interesting that developer companies in the forefront of [head-mounted display based] VR are increasingly emphasizing the desktop or wallscreen versions of their systems" (p. 1063) and goes on to say that "it is increasingly likely that many applications may be best served with the majority of participation with the VE via a desktop system but with a HMD being worn … for certain significant activities" (p. 1067). In a study comparing spatial learning through virtual environment navigation using a head-mounted display (HMD), a large projection display and a desktop display, it was found that the degree of simulator sickness as reported in a questionnaire were significantly higher for HMD participants (Patrick et al., 2000). In a study comparing route-finding performance after learning an environment using a desktop and a head-mounted display (HMD), three out of twelve HMD subjects had to withdraw through sickness, and all twelve reported at least two "slight" side effects (Ruddle, Payne & Jones, 1999). Wilson (1997) discusses a series of 12 experiments involving 223 subjects using HMD environments for various lengths of time. He notes that "approximately 80% of subjects across all experiments reported some increase in symptoms; for most the symptoms were mild and short-lived but for 5% they were so severe they had to end their participation" (p. 1072).

This section has discussed the 3D learning environment technologies available and has noted that the two main sets of technologies are physically immersive technologies, which include head-mounted displays and special purpose input devices, and desktop environment technologies. A rationale for the decision to study desktop technologies has been presented. This rationale, drawing on evidence from a number of sources, is based on usability problems and other human factor issues with immersive environments and the lack of clear evidence that immersive technologies provide significant advantages for spatial learning.

2.2.3 Applications

This section discusses existing applications of 3D virtual environments. The focus is on non-educational applications, although some training systems are also discussed. This section has been included because an understanding of non-educational applications of 3D environments can help identify potential applications in education. Educational applications are discussed specifically in Section 2.4.

Vince (1995) divides applications of virtual reality technologies into four groups, based on the application domain: engineering, entertainment, science and training. Earnshaw, Vince and Jones (1995) use a similar categorisation in presenting a series of case studies of virtual environments, under the three headings of science and engineering, simulation and training, and visualization. Wilson (1997) categorises virtual environment applications in terms of the ways in which the technology is used, identifying four distinct types of application: visualisation, user editable environments, tele-operation; and communication.

Wilson's categorisation is most useful here because an appreciation of the different ways in which the technology can be used is necessary for identifying the potential educational applications of virtual environments. However, Wilson's visualisation category is a little too broad because it includes both the exploration of environments modelled on the real world and the exploration of abstract environments, such as those that represent scientific data. The following sub-sections, then, discuss the applications of virtual environments within each of Wilson's categories, but with the first category further divided into real environments and abstract environments.

2.2.3.1 Simulation of Real Environments and Objects

Ellis (1991) distinguishes between the focus of 'media artists' who want to create the experience of a synthetic place, including sight, sound, touch and smell, and the focus of 'simulator designers' who focus only on aspects of the real environment that are necessary for specific training goals. In some applications a realistic visual model is required, but very little interactive capability is necessary. The virtual gallery described by Ramires-Fernandes, Pires and Rodrigues (1998) is one such example. On the other hand, in many training applications, visual realism is not as important as appropriate interactive behaviour of the system. Additionally, some systems consist of a 3D model of an environment in which the user can move around, but with little or no interaction with objects, whereas others contain objects with simulated behaviours or which change their properties as a result of user action.

Training through simulation of hazardous environments is one of the most discussed potential applications of 3D environments. Vince (1995) mentions surgery, air-traffic control and nuclear power plant control as examples for which such training environments have significant potential. According to Ellis (1991), the need for training simulators for piloting aircraft, vehicles and ships provided stimulation for the early research into virtual environment technologies. Training simulators for pilots are one of the most sophisticated examples of virtual environments. Typically they include a physical cockpit-like workspace, with a 3D model projected onto the pilot's cockpit window. The controls provided match exactly the controls for a particular type of aircraft and the display is dynamically modified in response to the pilot's actions. 3D environments modelled on some of the world's major airports are available for these simulators (Vince, 1995). Vince also describes a system developed by Electricitié de France (EDF) which models a nuclear power plant and allows an operator wearing a head-mounted display to carry out simulated tasks within the environment, with a display showing the radiation levels.

Another potential application of early interest was medical diagnosis and training. For example, the construction of computer generated 3D models of anatomical structures based on 2D slices from CAT, PET or MRI scans have significant potential for improved diagnosis (Ellis, 1991). More recently the use of force-feedback input devices (see Massie & Salisbury, 1994; Stevenson et al., 1997) have been of interest in surgical training because the sense of touch is very important in carrying out surgical procedures. Stevenson et al. (1997) argue that the process of inserting a needle into human tissue is one that requires sensory feedback. They describe the development of a training simulator based on the 'PHANToM' haptic device, allowing for different levels of resistance as the user inserts a virtual needle through each layer of tissue within a simulated environment.

McGreevy (1993) describes work at NASA towards the development of 3D terrain models of planets such as Mars. These models allow astronauts and scientists to develop an understanding of what it might be like to walk around on one of these planets to a much greater extent than, for example, satellite photographs.

One of the most important recent applications of 3D environments, especially desktop environments, is in the entertainment industry. 3D games began to emerge in the early 1990s with DOOM (Id Software, 2004) being one of the first truly 3D games to obtain widespread use. Since then the use of 3D technologies has become so widespread that nearly all new games are now based on a 3D environment (Rouse, 1998). More recently, a number of multiplayer games have been developed, which include complex team-based strategy games and team-based first-person shooting games that are played over the Internet. One of the most successful of these has been Ultima Online (Fisher, Fraser & Kim, 1998).

The likely convergence of digital TV and broadband Internet has the potential to result in a new set of applications of 3D environments Rafey, Gibbs, Hoch, Le Van Gong and Wang (2001) describe work at the Sony Research Laboratories in the US towards the development of interactive 3D environments modelled on live sporting events. For example, they describe a prototype that allows the user to experience a car race from within a virtual car with the ability to interactively access a range of data about the car's current performance.

This section has discussed applications of 3D environments which use models of real places and objects. The following section discusses applications which use visual models of abstract or non-visual data.

2.2.3.2 Data Visualisation and Abstract Environments

According to Vince (1995), "scientific visualisation is a well-defined domain of computer graphics, where various types of data are interpreted using images" (p. 332). It involves the graphical display of 2D, 3D and multidimensional data sets. In some cases, the data has a natural spatial representation and the non-spatial characteristics of the object or space are represented as additional attributes of the display, such as additional components of the physical model or colour or lighting attributes. An example of this is a virtual wind tunnel, which allows for exploration of the characteristics of high-speed objects by visualising the complex airflow behaviour (Bryson, 1996). Another is the visualisation of underwater electric fields in order to understand the complex way that fish detect the properties of objects in their environments (Vince, 1995). A third is the visualisation of relativistic effects, such as in the systems described by Hsiung and Dunn (1989).

In some cases the data is non-spatial, and the display is essentially a form of a 3D graph, with colour, lighting or texture used to represent additional data attributes or a fourth or fifth dimension to the data. Dickenson and Jern (1995) describe a desktop 3D system, allowing for the interactive visualisation of both discrete and continuous data sets. The system allows for the exploration of the physical properties of an object, such as the stress intensity in a mechanical part, as well as for the display of 3D graphs of non-spatial data sets. Interactive tools within the system include the ability to dynamically modify the aspects of the data that contribute to the visualised model, and the ability to highlight aspects of the visualisation by modifying the lighting characteristics, along with annotation tools.

An alternative to the use of a 3D environment to visualise a data set is the provision of a 3D interface as a way of accessing data. An example of this is a 3D Geographical Information System (GIS) such as that developed by Coors and Jung (1998), which allows for the modelling of the terrain of an environment and for the ability to interactively access geographical information about objects and locations within the environment. Another is the Environmental Visualisation Information System (EVIS), an example of which includes a 3D model of the Abercrombie Caves in Australia as an interface to geological and archaeological information about the caves (Moore & Curry, 1998).

'Information visualisation' is a more recent field of research, which uses ideas from scientific visualisation in presenting visual models of non-scientific data and information, such as business information. For example, Grantham (1993) describes a system that models organisational data flow. Another example is the system described by Feijs and De Jong (1998), which facilitates software design by providing a 3D visualisation of the classes, objects and relationships within the system architecture.

Another application of abstract 3D environments is the use of a 3D metaphorical representation as an alternative interface to information on a desktop computer. For example, Card, Robertson and York (1996) describe the 'Web Book' and the 'Web Forager', which provide a 3D model of books embedded within a hierarchical 3D workspace as a way of storing and retrieving documents. This has been extended by Robertson et al. (2001) to create a 3D interface for Microsoft Windows as an alternative to the traditional 2D desktop metaphor. A similar interface for the X-Windows environment for Unix has been developed by Leach, Al-Qaimari, Grieve, Jinks and McKay (1997).

Wann and Mon-Williams (1996) argue that there is a danger in making the assumption that a realistic environment will automatically provide a more efficient interface to data than a traditional desktop interface. They give the example of a virtual supermarket, where the user has to walk along virtual aisles to locate products. They say "why would anyone want to locomote up and down virtual aisles, vainly searching for the virtual spaghetti hoops, before standing in a virtual queue, and avoiding eye contact with the other virtual people" (p. 845). Miles and Howes (1999) argue, however, that virtual shopping environments can have utility as long as navigational aids such as landmarks and maps are provided and realistic navigation techniques are supplemented by standard desktop computer techniques such as hyperlinking.

In some applications it is appropriate to combine real and abstract components, such as an environment modelled on a real environment but annotated with abstract objects, 3D icons or explanatory text. For example Brown, Cobb and Eastgate (1995) describe a 3D learning environment developed as part of their Learning in Virtual Environments (LIVE) program, designed to allow children with severe language problems to learn the symbolic icons within the 'Makaton' vocabulary along with corresponding sign language gestures. Learners can move around a virtual environment and as they encounter objects within the environment the corresponding Makaton symbols and sign language gestures are shown.

2.2.3.3 User-editable Environments

User-editable environments are those that allow the user to create or explicitly modify objects and structures. This is a step beyond the dynamic environments discussed above, in which the user's actions result in changes to the position or visual appearance of objects. User-editable environments can allow the user to create their own environments from scratch.

The main such application, according to Vince (1995), is Computer Aided Design (CAD). CAD tools that use virtual environment technologies allow for the accurate specification of the dimensions, appearance and behaviour of components and for the visualisation of these components and the machines that they make up in their final form. For example, he describes a study carried out by Rolls-Royce in the UK, which explored the feasibility of using a VR system developed by the Advanced Robotics Research Laboratory to allow visualisation of engine designs to avoid the need to develop non-functional replicas of designs before commencing production. Other examples include submarine design, architectural design and industrial design.

Architectural design is an application of virtual environment technologies which is generally accepted to have significant potential. Schmitt (1993) lists three specific architectural applications: 'virtual past', allowing for the modelling and exploration of historical buildings; 'virtual analysis', allowing for various aspects of a design to be checked for consistency and feasibility of construction; and 'virtual design', which has the potential to substantially change the psychological process of design by allowing for immediate visualisation of designs as they are produced. Moloney (2001) notes that in practice immediate visualisation of designs can be difficult to achieve because of the time it takes to produce a virtual design. She goes on to describe how, through the use of computer game engines, students at Auckland School of Architecture are able to rapidly produce 3D visualisations of their designs.

Bowman, Wineman, Hodges and Allison (1998) note that one of the problems with the use of virtual environments as support for design is that typically the design cannot be modified from within the virtual environment but instead has to be edited in separate CAD tools. They describe an immersive system for designing animal habitats that allows for design and exploration from within the same immersive environment.

This section has discussed applications of 3D environments where the user develops or modifies the environment model. The following section discusses applications of 3D environments where simulated actions are used to control a remote vehicle or machine.

2.2.3.4 Tele-operation

Research into tele-operation and tele-robotics has provided stimulation for virtual environment research (Ellis, 1991). The process of controlling a robot or vehicle at another location is very similar to the process of controlling a vehicle or robot in a virtual environment. The interface for remote control of a vehicle or robot may consist of a 3D simulation showing the controls along with either a video projection or a 3D simulation showing the vehicle or robot's viewpoint. The technologies involved in generating the view and in providing a user interface for remote control are very similar to those used in virtual environments. Additionally, control of a virtual robot or vehicle in a virtual environment is a common way of rehearsing for tele-operation.

Vince (1995) describes the Telepresence-controlled Remotely Operated Vehicle (TROV), an un-manned mini submarine used to explore the seabed 240 metres below the surface. The control interface is a virtual environment modelled using seabed digital terrain data. However, unlike normal virtual environments, the controls provided to move around in the virtual environment also move the submarine around. Additionally, the submarine's own sensors provide input back into the system so that the virtual image is supplemented by images based on real data. The 'JASON' project (Ballard, 1992) involved a similar unmanned submarine, which could be controlled by students at various museum sites across the US and Canada.

This section and the preceding three sections have discussed single-user applications of 3D environments. The following section concludes the discussion of applications of 3D environments by discussing multi-user collaborative applications.

2.2.3.5 Communication

As the use of the Internet has become widespread many stand-alone applications of the computer have evolved into multi-user applications with the Internet acting as a medium for communication and cooperation between users. Applications of 3D environments have particularly benefited from this, with the advent of Collaborative Virtual Environments (CVEs). The Active Worlds platform, for example, allows for the development of CVEs explored using a desktop computer (Active Worlds, 2003; Bruce, 2001). Riva (1999) states that multi-user virtual environments are at "the leading edge of a general evolution of present communication interfaces" and that the "disappearance of mediation" is one of their important distinguishing features (p. 95). At a more complex level are immersive environments that allow multiple users to share a virtual workspace (Dias, Galli, Almeida, Belo & Rebordao, 1997).

Saar (1999) describes potential applications of CVEs in military, entertainment and commercial domains. Broll and Prinz (1999) describe applications of CVEs for distributed workplaces, while Fellner and Hopp (1999) describe a distributed presentation system. Multi-player online games are another application of CVEs.

The examples presented in this and the preceding sections illustrate the breadth of possible applications of 3D technologies. Many of these applications can be readily adapted for educational purposes. Additionally, there are a number of approaches to the use of 3D environments that are unique to educational applications. Examples illustrating the wide range of potential educational applications of 3D environments are presented in Section 2.4

2.3 Learning Theory

Having discussed developments in 3D technologies and their applications, this section discusses developments in learning theory leading into a discussion of the consequences of various learning theories for computer assisted learning resources and particularly 3D learning environments.

Recent changes in teaching and learning practices have had their roots in two broad theoretical developments. The first development, in the field of psychology, was a rejection of the 'behaviourist' view in favour of the 'cognitive' view of learning. A behaviourist view of learning emphasises teaching strategies that involve repetitive conditioning of learner responses. A cognitive view, on the other hand, places importance on the learner's cognitive activity and the mental models they form (Leahey & Harris, 1993; Schultz & Schultz, 1992).

The second development, which is more of a philosophical shift than a new movement in psychology, was the gradual rejection of 'objectivism', which is the assumption, held by many cognitivists, that there is an objectively correct knowledge representation. The alternative view, termed 'constructivism', is that within a domain of knowledge there may be a number of individually constructed knowledge representations that are equally valid. The focus of teaching then becomes one of guiding the learner as they build on and modify their existing mental models, that is, a focus on knowledge construction rather than knowledge transmission (McInerney & McInerney, 1994; Slavin, 1994).

There are three broad principles that together define the constructivist view of learning. The fundamental principle, attributed to Kant and later adopted by Dewey, is that each person forms their own representation of knowledge, building on their individual experiences, and consequently that there is no single 'correct' representation of knowledge (Von Glaserfeld, 1984). The second principle, normally attributed to Piaget, is that people learn through active exploration, and that learning occurs when the learner's exploration uncovers an inconsistency between their current knowledge representation and their experience (McInerney & McInerney; 1994; Slavin, 1994). The third principle, normally attributed to Vygotsky, is that learning occurs within a social context, and that interaction between learners, their peers, and teachers is a necessary part of the learning process (Vygotsky, 1978).

Although there is general agreement on the basic tenets of constructivism, the consequences for teaching and learning are not as clear. It is generally agreed that learning involves building on prior experiences, which differ from learner to learner. Consequently, each learner should have a say in what they are to learn, different learning styles must be catered for and information must be presented within a context to give learners the opportunity to relate the information to prior experience. It is also generally agreed that the process of learning is an active one, so the emphasis should be on learner activity rather than teacher instruction.

However, from here there is significant disagreement about the details of how to implement these broad principles. An extreme interpretation of constructivism would suggest that learners should be placed within the environment they are learning about so that they can construct their own mental model, with only limited support provided by a teacher or facilitator. A more moderate interpretation would be that formal instruction is still appropriate, but that learners should then engage in thought oriented activities to allow them to apply and generalise the information and concepts provided in order to construct their own model of the knowledge (Perkins, 1991). Adding a third dimension is the social constructivist view that knowledge construction occurs best within an environment that allows collaboration between learners, their peers, experts in the field and teachers (Phillips, 1995).

These different interpretations of constructivism have been labelled by Moshman (1982) as *endogenous*, *exogenous* and *dialectical*, as follows:

- Endogenous constructivism emphasises the individual nature of each learner's knowledge construction process, and suggests that the role of the teacher should be to act as a facilitator in providing experiences which are likely to result in challenges to learners' existing models.

- Exogenous constructivism is the view that formal instruction, in conjunction with exercises requiring learners to be cognitively active, can help learners to form knowledge representations which they can later apply to realistic tasks.

- Dialectical constructivism is the view that learning occurs through realistic experience, but that learners require 'scaffolding' provided by teachers or experts as well as collaboration with peers.

This study examines the potential of 3D learning environments based on the premise of a constructivist view of learning. Rather than adopting one of Moshman's interpretations of constructivism, the study works from the assumption that each can be appropriate in particular learning situations. That is, the degree of explicit instruction and the degree of social interaction that are necessary or appropriate will depend on the learning domain, the specific intended learning outcomes, and the individual characteristics of the learner.

2.4 Constructivism, Computer Assisted Learning and 3D Environments

Having looked at the origins and the various interpretations of constructivism, this section identifies types of Computer Assisted Learning (CAL) resources consistent with a constructivist view of learning. In doing so, Moshman's three interpretations of constructivist theory provide a useful framework. In each case the discussion will begin with traditional (that is, not necessarily 3D) CAL techniques. An analysis of the consequences for CAL of each of Moshman's interpretations of constructivism has been carried out as part of earlier work by the researcher (Dalgarno, 1996; 2001) and this analysis has been drawn upon here.

The degree to which each of the CAL techniques can be implemented or extended using 3D techniques is then discussed. Additionally, techniques unique to 3D and consistent with each interpretation are identified. The degree to which 3D technologies have the potential to provide for unique learning advantages over non-3D techniques is analysed. In particular, the assumptions about cognition and learning using a 3D environment that are implicit in any statement about the potential value of such environments are identified. These untested assumptions have the potential to form the basis of the questions addressed by this research.

It is recognised by the researcher that few educators would describe themselves as solely following one of Moshman's interpretations of constructivism. The interpretations have been used because they provide a convenient way to classify constructivist CAL resources. It is also recognised that few CAL resources fit into only one of the categories identified, but rather draw on aspects of a number of the categories. This categorisation of resources provides a convenient starting point for identifying the possibilities for 3D learning environments allowing an exploration of the assumptions about learning implicit within each.

In order to set a context for the discussion of CAL resources consistent with Moshman's interpretations of constructivism, it is appropriate to first look at the nature of traditional CAL resources based on non-constructivist views of teaching and learning.

2.4.1 Non-constructivist approaches

Traditional CAL resources consist primarily of tutorials, many of which are essentially computer based forms of Programmed Instruction (PI), drawing heavily on the behaviourist views of Skinner. These tutorials typically contain sequences of content broken into sections, with end-of-section questions to determine whether the learner requires remedial content or is ready to go on to the next section. They also include drill and practice materials, consistent with the behavioural psychology emphasis on producing automatic responses by repeated reinforcement (Rieber, 1994).

An alternative is the Intelligent Tutoring Systems (ITS) approach. These systems maintain models of an expert's knowledge and models of the learner's current knowledge and use Artificial Intelligence (AI) techniques to dynamically generate a sequence of instruction to suit the needs of the learner (Orey & Nelson, 1993). Such systems are consistent with the cognitivist view that the instruction should depend on the learner's current cognitive state, but are based on an implicit objectivist assumption that there is a single correct representation of a given body of knowledge (Jonassen, 1992a).

2.4.2 Endogenous constructivist approaches

Endogenous constructivism emphasises the importance of learner-directed discovery of knowledge. Constructivist CAL materials that draw on this view include hypertext and hypermedia environments allowing learner-controlled browsing of content, and simulations and microworlds, which allow active exploration within a virtual environment.

2.4.2.1 Hypermedia and information spaces

The term hypertext was first coined by Ted Nelson in the 1960s, but the concepts are normally traced to Vannevar Bush in 1945 (Park & Hannafin, 1993). Hypertext consists of chunks of textual information (nodes) with groups of words acting as automatic links to other chunks (McKnight, Dillon & Richardson, 1991). Hypermedia is a more general term, indicating that the nodes can be composed of a variety of media and that screen objects such as icons, 'hot areas' within pictures and graphical buttons can act as links in addition to words within text. As well as becoming popular for use in instructional systems, hypermedia has also found widespread application as a way of organising and accessing large information databases, and the Hypertext Markup Language (HTML) is the information delivery standard for the World Wide Web.

Because hypermedia information databases typically allow browsing under complete learner control, with learners following a sequence of links that makes sense to them, it is suggested that they facilitate the formation of individual knowledge representations (Rieber, 1994). This freedom to browse through the content is consistent with the constructivist principle that learners should be given the opportunity to discover knowledge through their own active exploration.

Hypertext has also been advocated as a mechanism for applying cognitive flexibility theory, a theory that focuses on advanced knowledge acquisition in ill-structured or complex domains (Spiro, Feltovich, Jacobson & Coulson, 1991). The use of hypertext links allows the learner to choose from a range of relevant examples of the theme or concept being illustrated. It also allows for a particular area of the content to be examined a number of times, from different perspectives.

A number of studies have found that learners can have difficulty navigating hypermedia environments, with the problems characterised by the "lost in hyperspace" phenomenon (McKnight, Dillen & Richardson, 1991) where learners lose track of how they arrived at a node and have no clear model of the overall environment structure. The provision of an interface that allows easy navigation through the information, while maintaining a sense for the overall structure of the resources and the connections between ideas, is problematic. It is possible that a 3D model of the information would provide for a clearer understanding and that consequently a 3D interface would provide for easier navigation. The use of a navigation metaphor has been found to be effective in many applications (for example the desktop metaphor used ubiquitously on personal computers), and the extension of such metaphors to 3D may have potential benefits. For example Robertson et al. (2000) describe the use of a 3D interface for task management on a PC.

3D environments have been specifically advocated as an interface for navigating through complex information spaces (Card et al., 1996). For example the information space may be able to be represented as a 3D model with the x, y and z axes representing attributes of the nodes and the connections between nodes representing relationships between concepts. If learners can form their own 3D cognitive model of the information space as a result of exploring such an environment, it is likely that the efficiency of exploration and the degree to which the learner develops their conceptual understanding will be enhanced.

2.4.2.2 Simulations and microworlds

There is no accepted definition of simulations and microworlds that allows for a clear distinction between the two. Typically a simulation is defined as a model of a real-world environment, usually with the facility for the user to interact with the environment (Thurman, 1993). A microworld can be defined as a model of a concept space, which may be a very simplified version of a real-world environment, or it may be a completely abstract environment. Normally, a user can create some sort of constructions within the microworld which will behave in a way consistent with the concepts being modelled (Papert, 1993; Rieber, 1992).

Simulations and microworlds are popular with constructivists for two reasons. Firstly, simulations (and some microworlds) provide a realistic context in which learners can explore and experiment, with these explorations allowing the learner to construct their own mental model of the environment. Secondly, the interactivity inherent in microworlds (and usually in simulations) allows learners to see immediate results as they create models or try out their theories about the concepts modelled (Rieber, 1992).

Simulations have been used as part of CAL materials for at least three decades. One of the more well known examples is 'Sim City' (Wright, 1989). Simulated 3D environments modelled on real places and objects have the potential to provide a greatly enhanced sense of realism and a greater psychological sense of immersion than non-3D environments. The fidelity can in some cases be so great that such environments can provide an alternative to visiting the real place, especially if there are practical barriers to visiting the real place. For example Alberti, Marini and Trapani (1998) describe a 3D environment modelled on a historic theatre in Italy. Another example is the exploration of microscopic environments, such as molecular structures (see for example Tsernoglou, Petsko, McQueen & Hermans, 1977, cited in Wann & Mon-Williams, 1996).

If the ability to move freely around the environment and view it from any position leads to a more complete cognitive model of the real place and the objects within it then such environments will have learning advantages over alternatives which use photographic or video material or panoramic photographic techniques such as those provided by Apple's QuickTime VR.

The most important potential benefits of simulations, particularly from an endogenous constructivist perspective, are through the learner interacting with objects within the environment. Any knowledge domains in which the learner is expected to develop an understanding of entities exhibiting dynamic behaviours may be suited to simulations with this greater level of interactivity. For example, in the discipline of physics, students are expected to understand how objects will respond to forces. By exploring an environment that allows for specific forces to be applied to objects and for the resultant object behaviours to be observed and measured, learners may improve their conceptual understanding. 3D technologies are well suited to such physical simulations because they allow for the modelling of the full physical behaviour of objects rather than restricting the motion and behaviour to two dimensions. Learning benefits over 2D simulations will occur if the use of a 3D environment like this leads to a 3D conceptual model of the physical concepts rather than a simplified 2D conceptual model.

As well as facilitating the development of a conceptual understanding of the dynamic behaviour of entities within an environment, simulations can also allow the learner to practice skills. The use of simulated environments for practicing skills can be particularly appropriate when the tasks to be learned are expensive or dangerous to undertake in the real world. For example, 3D environments have been used to train nuclear power plant workers in Japan (Akiyoshi, Miwa & Nishida, 1996 cited in Winn & Jackson, 1999), to train astronauts in how to repair a space telescope (Psotka, 1995; Moore, 1995) and to train forestry machine operators (Lapointe & Robert, 2000). However, simulations may be of value for any tasks that cannot be conveniently carried out by learners as often as they need to. An implicit assumption here is that skill training in a 3D environment will lead to greater transfer to the real world than an equivalent 2D simulation and than viewing videos or photographs showing the skills being practiced.

In some knowledge domains the concepts to be learned are abstract and do not correspond directly to material objects. The term "microworld" is often used to describe simulations of abstract environments designed for concept formation (Rieber, 1992). The term was first coined by Papert (1993) who described the 'Logo' microworld for exploring and constructing within a geometrical concept space. Other popular examples include 'The Incredible Machine' (1992), a mechanical problem-solving environment, and 'The Geometer's Sketchpad' (1995), a geometric exploration environment.

In a similar way, 3D environments can also represent abstract concepts. Hedberg and Alexander (1994) discuss the potential for such environments to represent real or metaphorical objects, attributes and conceptual relationships and suggest that the three-dimensionality of the virtual environment may allow the learner to incorporate these ideas into a three-dimensional cognitive model. Winn and Jackson (1999) concur, suggesting that virtual environments are "most useful when they embody concepts and principles that are not normally accessible to the senses" (p. 7). They use the term 'reification' to describe the representation of phenomena that have no natural form. For example, they describe an environment that allows learners to control greenhouse gas emissions and to view models that metaphorically represent the effects of global climate change. Another example they describe is a Japanese language tutor that uses a 3D model of blocks which speak their position in space in Japanese. Kaufmann, Schmalstieg and Wagner (2000) describe a 3D environment for developing a learner's understanding of geometry. 3D environments have the potential to provide unique advantages over 2D microworlds, if the formation by the learner of a 3D mental model of the concepts will improve their understanding.

Ruzic (1999) also notes the potential for the use of metaphorical entities within virtual environments, suggesting that such environments incorporate two types of objects, "tangible (sensory) objects called sensory transducers, and intangible, cognitive objects called cognitive transducers" (p. 189). Sanchez, Berreiro and Maojo (2000) describe a model for developing educational virtual environments which has the use of metaphorical models as a central component. They use the example of a 3D hierarchical model representing zoological taxonomies. They state that their aim is "to design and develop virtual worlds that provide visualisation of cognition", describing visualisation of cognition as "the externalisation of mental representations embodied in artificial environments" (p. 359). Salzman et al. (1999) suggest that virtual environments designed in this way can help learners to comprehend abstract information because of their "biologically innate ability to make sense of physical space and perceptual phenomena" (p. 4). They describe three immersive environments that are part of 'Project Science Space' and which provide abstract spatial representations allowing learners to explore Newtonian mechanics, electrostatic forces and molecular bonding. In a similar way the simulated radioactivity laboratory described by Crosier, Cobb and Wilson (2000) allows learners to carry out tasks and measure the results at the laboratory level and then to zoom in and visualise what is happening at the atomic level.

One of the potential learning benefits of simulations and microworlds is that they can be intrinsically motivating due to the high degree of engagement as the learner attempts to achieve individual goals within the environment. According to Csikszentmihalyi (1990) some activities can be so engaging that our mental focus is shifted away from our surroundings and from the day-to-day stresses in our lives, allowing us to focus entirely on the task. He uses the term 'flow' to describe the learner's experience in these situations. The high degree of fidelity and the natural interface of 3D environments may increase the likelihood that the learner will experience this feeling of flow as they become psychologically immersed within the environment.

2.4.3 Exogenous constructivist approaches

The exogenous view of constructivism recognises the value of direct instruction, but not the teacher-centred single sequence of instruction of behaviourists. Direct instruction is seen as important in helping the learner to form their own conceptual model of the ideas to be learned, supported by activities that allow them to test and further tailor their knowledge representation. According to the exogenous view, learners should have some control over the sequence and selection of content, should have the opportunity to regularly articulate their knowledge representation and, after instruction, should have the opportunity to apply their knowledge to realistic tasks. Constructivist CAL materials that draw on the exogenous view include tutorials that incorporate learner control over sequence, or conversely, hypermedia browsing environments that include context-sensitive pedagogical guidance. The use of 'cognitive tools', to assist with knowledge construction and articulation during instruction, including concept mapping tools and hypertext editing tools, is consistent with exogenous constructivism. Practice modules, for example quizzes and problem solving exercises, that allow the learner to obtain feedback on their own construction of knowledge, are also consistent with this view.

2.4.3.1 Hypermedia with instructional support

By providing more explicit instructional support within a hypermedia environment, such an environment can be used either as a tutorial or as a discovery learning resource. This approach is quite different from the tutorial systems based on Skinner's programmed instruction because, although a natural instructional sequence may be provided, the learner is encouraged to choose alternative sequences, or to use the materials as a discovery learning resource if they are so inclined. Consequently such systems are consistent with constructivist theories. These resources may also have within them practice exercises as well as annotation tools that allow learners to articulate their knowledge constructions. For example, 'Investigating Lake Illuka' (Harper et al., 1995) is an environmental education resource providing a hypermedia interface along with annotation tools and suggested exercises. Although designed as a discovery learning environment, its structure also allows it to be used as a learner-controlled tutorial.

A 3D equivalent would be a 3D environment that simulates part of the knowledge domain, but unlike an environment consistent with an endogenous interpretation, it would be supported by conventional learning resources. That is, as the learner explores and carries out tasks within the virtual environment they would have access to conventional instructional materials which may include text, graphics, audio and video. For example Antonietti, Imperio, Rasi and Sacco (2001) describe a learning environment for teaching the use of a lathe, which integrates a 3D model of a lathe with conventional hypermedia resources.

Sweller, van Merrienboer, and Paas (1998) discuss the importance of reducing the cognitive load in presenting instructional information, by minimising the demands on working memory. One effect discussed is termed the 'split attention effect', which occurs when the learner has to refer to two or more distinct information representations, such as a picture and a separate caption, resulting in an increased cognitive load. Sweller et al.'s research suggests that if the various sources of information can instead be integrated the demands on working memory can be reduced and consequently the cognitive load is reduced. The integration of graphical and textual information, possibly supported by audio, within a 3D environment is consistent with these ideas.

It can also be argued that there will be better transfer if the learning is carried out within an environment modelled on the context in which the knowledge is expected to be applied. Specifically, because a 3D environment can provide a level of visual realism and interactivity consistent with the real-world, ideas learned within the environment should be more readily recalled and applied within the corresponding real-world environment. This is a logical corollary to the idea that knowledge can be internally anchored to experience. This idea is supported by research carried out by Baddeley (1993) suggesting that facts learned by divers under water are better recalled while diving than facts learnt on land. Ruzic (1999) emphasises the situated nature of learning in virtual environments, and consequently the potential for transfer to similar real environments, suggesting that "the advantages of VR-based teleteaching are individualised, interactive and realistic learning that makes virtual reality a tool for apprenticeship training, providing a unique opportunity for situated learning" (p. 188). McLellan (1996) also notes the potential for 3D environments to situate learning, drawing on Brown, Collins and Duguid's theory of situated cognition (1989).

2.4.3.2 Cognitive tools

All three views of constructivism emphasise the importance of individual knowledge construction. A consequence of this is the use of metacognitive strategies, that is, strategies employed by the learner to improve their comprehension, retention and individual construction of knowledge. Explicitly teaching these strategies to students is particularly consistent with exogenous constructivist principles. It has been proposed that the use of computer based cognitive tools can be of assistance with these strategies. According to Jonassen, such tools "amplify thinking and facilitate knowledge construction" (1992a, p. 4), while Wild and Kirkpatrick state that these tools can "provide the means by which learners can construct, manipulate and evaluate representations of knowledge" (1996, p. 414). These tools include text and hypertext editing tools, modelling tools and concept mapping tools.

The node-link structure of hypermedia environments has been compared with the way information is stored in the brain (Lohr, Ross & Morrison, 1995). Consequently, it has been argued that an effective way for learners to articulate their knowledge representation is to construct their own hypermedia databases (Jonassen, 1992b).

Concept mapping (also called semantic networking), whereby the learner draws a diagram indicating the concepts that make up an area of knowledge and the ways in which these concepts relate to each other, has long been advocated as an effective metacognitive strategy (Fisher, 1992; Gaines & Shaw, 1995). A number of computer assisted concept mapping tools have been developed, including *SemNet* (Fisher, 1992) and *Inspiration* (Inspiration Software, 1999).

The use of modelling tools that allow the learner to develop their own simulation of a particular aspect of the world can require the learner to develop a very deep understanding of the concepts involved. *Stella* (1996) is a modelling tool that provides a graphical environment allowing the learner to specify the quantities to be modelled and their relationship, and will then carry out the simulation, producing charts showing the changes in quantities over time.

There is scope for the development of 3D versions of cognitive tools. If the concepts being explored or articulated (whether concrete or abstract) are more clearly understood with a 3D mental model, or if the data to be visualised has three components, then 3D concept mapping or 3D graphing tools may be more appropriate than their 2D alternatives. Alternatively, there is scope for the use of tools allowing the learner to construct their own 3D environment as a way of articulating their spatial model of the concepts within the learning domain.

2.4.3.3 Practice modules

If direct instruction is to be used, an important element of the instructional process is the provision of opportunities for the learner to put their knowledge into practice and receive feedback on their knowledge constructions. This might occur through the learner articulating their knowledge representation in a written form or in the form of a hypertext database, and receiving feedback from a tutor or facilitator. In some knowledge domains this could occur through the learner carrying out activities within a

2D or 3D simulated environment or a microworld. For example, the 3D environment could be embedded within a tutorial resource, in which the learner is expected to work their way through conventional instructional materials and then periodically carry out activities within the virtual environment, before continuing with the next section of the materials. Alternatively, a set of instructional materials may include a number of smaller 3D environments or even discrete 3D models of objects, which are made available to the learner to explore or manipulate when appropriate as they work their way through the resources.

In some cases, the use of simple practice exercises with feedback is quite appropriate. These might consist of multiple choice, single word or numeric answer quizzes, or the graphical matching or grouping of words and symbols. There is scope for the use of a 3D environment as an interface to these exercises, either as a way of providing a more interesting or motivating user interface, or to interactively test a learner's spatial model of the concepts within the learning domain.

2.4.4 Dialectical constructivist approaches

The dialectical interpretation of constructivism emphasises the undertaking of authentic activities by the learner with support, or 'scaffolding', provided by peers, experts or teachers. In some cases software tools can also fulfil a role in providing this scaffolding. Groups of learners working together and developing their understanding of concepts through a social learning process is also important. The use of computer supported collaborative learning (CSCL) environments to allow learners to communicate and, ideally, work together on tasks is consistent with this interpretation.

2.4.4.1 Computer supported collaborative learning

Technologies used for Computer Supported Collaborative Learning (CSCL) can be divided into three groups: those that are general purpose Computer Mediated Communication (CMC) tools, those that are designed for Computer Supported Cooperative Work (CSCW) and lastly those that have features specifically for group learning (O'Malley, 1995).

CMC technologies can be classified according to the type of communication that they allow, that is, whether they allow one-to-one or group communication and whether they allow synchronous (parties communicating at the same time) or asynchronous (parties communicating with a time delay) communication (Bonk, Medury & Reynolds, 1994). Technologies that are helpful with asynchronous communication include Email for one-to-one and mailing lists, news groups and Web-based bulletin boards for group communication. Technologies that are helpful with synchronous communication include 'chat' and computer conferencing programs such as Internet Relay Chat (IRC), ICQ or MSN Messenger. Dalgarno and Atkinson (1999) describe the use of such tools to facilitate group learning tasks.

CSCW tools, commonly known as 'groupware', typically include CMC tools along with shared workspaces for collaborative work, scheduling tools and workflow organisers (Grudin, 1990). Although designed primarily for use within the workplace, groupware tools have been found to be useful in a learning context for group projects (Collings, Richards-Smith & Walker, 1995).

Systems designed specifically for collaborative learning typically include a CMC component as well as tools for group learning tasks. These may include tools for group writing, tools to facilitate discussions (such as allowing role-play within the discussion), tools for shared annotation of hypermedia spaces or tools for shared problem solving (Bonk et al., 1994; Harasim, Hiltz, Teles & Turoff, 1995; Scardamalia & Bereiter, 1996).

Multi-user 3D environments, also termed Collaborative Virtual Environments (CVEs), allow geographically dispersed users to explore an environment concurrently, with each represented by an 'avatar' visible to other users, and with tools allowing text-based or audio communication. Such environments have potential as CSCL tools for a number of reasons. Firstly, communication within a simulated environment relevant to the ideas being discussed can provide a greater 'sense of place' than other text-based alternatives such as Multi User Domains (MUDs) and consequently a greater closeness within the group and richer communication. If role-play strategies are used, it is likely that learners will more easily 'lose themselves' as they adopt their role due to the great fidelity of the environment. Dede (1995) discusses the possibility of combining the capabilities of virtual environments with the capabilities of CMC tools to allow collaborative learning within a distributed virtual world. The Cybertown online community provides a multi-user 3D environment, with each participant represented by a unique avatar within the environment (Cybertown, 2004). The environment is explored over the Internet using a Virtual Reality Modelling Language (VRML) browser and allows for text and audio communication between participants.

Most importantly, the distributed 3D environment can allow learners to undertake tasks together rather than just communicate. For example, Brna (1999) describes a study using a desktop 3D environment called 'Bowls World', in which two learners, each with their own view of the environment, collaborate to control the distance a ball rolls after being released at the top of a ramp by manipulating parameters such as gravity and friction. Additionally, distributed 3D environments can allow for a teacher or domain expert to provide support to the learner as they undertake tasks. The fact that these tasks are carried out in a 3D environment modelled on the environment in which the concepts will be applied has the potential to result in greater transfer to the real world due to memory cues.

2.4.4.2 Task support

An important element of constructivist theory is the idea that learners should be given the opportunity to carry out realistic tasks, with assistance or scaffolding provided to enable them to complete the larger task without needing to learn all of the sub-tasks involved. Ideally, as a by-product, the learner will learn how to complete the sub-tasks so that eventually they will be able to carry out the larger task unassisted. The provision of scaffolding as the learner attempts to carry out authentic tasks is consistent with Vygotsky's emphasis on learners undertaking activities just beyond their capabilities, in what he terms their 'Zone of Proximal Development' (Vygotsky, 1978).

Scaffolding can be provided by the computer through support software. At a simple level this may just be a system-based help facility activated by the learner, possibly sensitive to the context of the task being undertaken. Sometimes in 3D environments there is a tendency for designers to not provide sufficient scaffolding in an attempt to provide a realistic experience. Whitelock, Romano, Jelfs and Brna (2000) describe a study using a QuickTime VR environment called 'Oak Wood', in which students became frustrated because they were unable to find specimens such as an adder and a deer. Whitelock et al. note that "our subjects did not want to search in the same way they would in real life" but "wanted to use the 'magic of the computer' to assist their discovery of specimens" (p. 284). One way of providing scaffolding within a virtual environment is to allow the learner to have greater navigational control than they would have in the real world as well as control over system parameters such as the speed at which time passes. Romano and Brna (1998) describe a collaborative 3D environment for fire-fighter training, which provides a number of what they term, 'super-powers', including the ability to switch to the point of view of another user within the environment as well as the ability to manipulate the speed of the simulation.

Scaffolding may in some cases take the form of an intelligent agent with a visual representation within the environment, acting as a guide to the learner. 3D environments provide the opportunity for a greater sense of realism in the use of such agents and a closer integration with the task at hand. This may lead to more effective task support because of reduced cognitive load in switching between attending to the agent and attending to the task. In some cases the agent, rather than providing direct task support, fills the role of a person that the learners are likely to encounter and have to respond to when applying their knowledge in the real world. For example, Stevens (1989) describes an environment using interactive video to teach team-based code inspection to software engineers, with the learner able to choose which team role they wish to practice and with agents filling the roles of the other team members.

Another type of scaffolding is the provision of support tools to help the learner undertake tasks, such as calculators, graphing tools or language translators. In some cases the tools may be developed specifically for this purpose, such as the lesson planning tool described by Wild and Kirkpatrick (1996). Alternatively, general purpose software, such as a language translator, a spell checker, a thesaurus, or a spreadsheet program, can fill a similar role. In some learning situations there may be scope for specifically 3D support tools such as a 3D concept-mapping tool or a 3D graphing tool. If used with a 3D environment, these, whether 2D or 3D, could either be shown alongside the 3D environment or embedded realistically within it. For example Dede, Salzman, Loftin and Ash (1997) describe the redesign of 'Newton World', an immersive environment for learning Newtonian physics, which includes an embedded 'scoreboard' showing numerical and graphical representations of mass, velocity, momentum and elasticity of objects within the environment.

2.4.5 Summary and analysis

The previous three sections have discussed applications of Computer Assisted Learning resources and 3D learning environments consistent with each of Moshman's three interpretations of constructivism. In each case the degree to which 3D environments have the potential to provide learning advantages over non-3D CAL resources hinges on certain assumptions about the use of 3D virtual environments and spatial cognition. Table 2.1 provides a summary of the applications of 3D learning environments identified and the implicit assumptions within each. This table has been derived by the researcher from the literature review and associated analysis presented above.

<table>
<tr><td colspan="3" align="center">**Table 2.1**
Applications of 3D learning environments and implicit assumptions</td></tr>
<tr><td colspan="3">**Endogenous Constructivist Applications**</td></tr>
<tr><td>**Application**</td><td>**Explanation**</td><td>**Key Assumptions**</td></tr>
<tr>
<td>**3D simulations**</td>
<td>Simulation of hard to visit places

Simulation of microscopic environments

Simulation of physical environments containing entities with dynamic behaviours

Visual modelling of abstract concepts in 3D

Simulations of dangerous or expensive environments for skill practice</td>
<td>Free view control within a 3D environment will lead to a 3D spatial cognitive model of the simulated place, and thus a more complete cognitive model than one formed through alternative resources.

Manipulating objects within a 3D environment will lead to a 3D spatial cognitive model of the behaviour of the objects.

Practicing spatial skills within a 3D environment will be more effective than non-3D simulations because the learner will develop a 3D model of the tools, the context and the processes to be undertaken.

Using a 3D environment will result in greater transfer to the real world than non-3D simulations due to the greater fidelity and sense of presence.

Using a 3D environment is more likely to be intrinsically motivating than non-3D simulations due to the greater fidelity and sense of presence.</td>
</tr>
<tr>
<td>**3D information spaces**</td>
<td>3D interface to complex information structures</td>
<td>The learner will form a 3D spatial model matching the environment model and this will lead to more efficient navigation through the information.</td>
</tr>
</table>

Table 2.1 (continued)
Applications of 3D Learning Environments and Implicit Assumptions

Exogenous Constructivist Applications

Application	Explanation	Key Assumptions
3D environments with instructional support	3D environments supported by conventional learning resources or tutorial resources situated within a 3D environment	Using resources within a 3D environment modelled on the environment in which the concepts will be applied will result in greater transfer to the real world due to memory cues. Integration of instructional resources within a 3D environment will result in reduced cognitive load.
Cognitive tools	3D cognitive tools	Allowing learners to model their understanding using a 3D environment will lead to stronger 3D spatial cognitive models.
Practice modules	3D models or small 3D environments embedded within instructional resources	Exploring and/or experimenting within a 3D environment will lead to a corresponding 3D spatial cognitive model.

Dialectical Constructivist Applications

Application	Explanation	Key Assumptions
3D environments with embedded Computer Supported Collaborative Learning (CSCL) Tools	3D environments providing a 'sense of place' as part of computer mediated communication Distributed 3D environments allowing learners to collaborate on tasks at a distance	Communicating within a 3D environment modelled on the environment in which the concepts will be applied will result in greater transfer to the real world due to memory cues. Role-plays carried out within a 3D environment will be more effective due to the greater fidelity.
Task support	Distributed 3D environments allowing teachers or experts to provide support as learners undertake tasks Intelligent agents visible within the 3D environment providing context sensitive pedagogical guidance Tools to provide support or scaffolding as the learner undertakes tasks in a 3D environment	Carrying out tasks within a 3D environment modelled on the environment in which the concepts will be applied will result in greater transfer to the real world due to memory cues. Task support agents within a 3D environment can be more closely integrated with the task and thus there is less cognitive load in switching between attending to the agent and attending to the task. 3D support tools which implicitly model spatial concepts will lead to stronger 3D spatial cognitive models.

Looking at the implicit assumptions within the various applications of 3D learning environments as summarised in Table 2.1, there are two assumptions that recur a number of times. One assumption is that the fidelity provided by a 3D environment will lead to greater transfer. Although video and photographic resources normally provide a greater degree of visual realism than a 3D environment, the fact that realistic tasks and communication can be carried out within a 3D environment, along with the fact that objects within the environment can be programmed with realistic behaviours, means that the overall fidelity can be greater. The assumption that this higher fidelity will lead to greater transfer is built on some subsidiary assumptions, firstly that the greater fidelity will lead to a greater sense of presence and secondly that this greater sense of presence will lead to greater engagement and greater transfer (Psotka, 1995). The assumption that there will be greater transfer to the real environment as a result of this greater fidelity appears intuitively to be valid, however empirical research is needed to provide confirmation.

A second assumption, and one that is implicit within many of the applications of 3D learning environments identified above, is that the use of a 3D environment is more effective in supporting the learner in forming a 3D spatial cognitive model than alternative learning resources. It is the exploration of this second assumption that forms the major focus of this study. The exploration of the assumption that 3D environments can lead to greater transfer has been the focus of other research (see for example McLellan, 1996), and is outside of the scope of this study.

A number of studies have found that learners can develop spatial knowledge through exploring a virtual environment (see for example Arthur, Hancock & Chrysler, 1997; Witmer et al., 1996). However, studies comparing exploration of a 3D environment with alternatives, such as viewing static images of the same environment, have been inconclusive (see for example Christou & Bulhoff, 1999; Peruch, Vercher & Gauthier, 1995). It is well established that the form of presentation of information affects the way that it is cognitively encoded (Baddeley, 1993; Salomon, 1994), however it is clear that there is a need for research that investigates the cognitive encoding resulting from the exploration of a 3D environment.

Additionally, the particular aspects of 3D environments that are important in this process is also in need of investigation. For example, if it can be shown that 3D environments are an effective resource for developing the learner's 3D cognitive model, the reason may be because of the fidelity of the representation, the dynamic display of viewpoint changes or the learner-controlled interaction that is possible within the environment. Identification of the aspects of 3D environments that contribute to learning is important for designers of such environments, who want to put their efforts into the aspects of their learning resources that are most important for learning.

Before exploring the degree to which learners develop spatial cognitive models as a result of exploring a 3D learning environment it is appropriate to discuss spatial perception and cognition. The next section provides an overview of current understanding of these areas.

2.5 Spatial Perception and Cognition

Many activities in our day-to-day life depend on our ability to recognise the three-dimensionality of the environment around us. The segments of information that we use to determine the three-dimensionality of objects within our environment are termed depth cues (Vince, 1995). Vince (1995) identifies four types of depth cues: visual cues, somatic cues (touch), aural cues, and vestibular cues (using our inner ear mechanism which senses the direction of gravity, rotation, and acceleration). Given that the key distinguishing characteristics of desktop 3D environments are visual, only visual cues will be discussed here.

Cutting and Vishton (1995), in an attempt to isolate the most important cues involved in the visual perception of layout (depth perception), identify three groups of cues. The first group, primary cues, includes 'accommodation', 'vergence' and 'binocular disparity'. The second group, secondary cues or 'pictorial cues', includes 'occlusion', 'relative size and density', 'height in the visual field' and 'aerial perspective'. The third group, 'motion cues', includes 'motion parallax' and 'motion perspective'. Ellis (1993) distinguishes between cues involved in the perception of a virtual image, including accommodative vergence and 'stereoscopic' cues, and cues involved in the construction of a virtual space, including 'perspective', 'shading', 'occlusion' and 'texture gradients'. He also identifies cues involved in the virtualisation of the environment, which includes motion parallax. Combining those cues that are equivalent it can be seen that these authors identify a total of 13 cues. Table 2.2 lists and explains these cues as well as identifying which are available within desktop 3D environments.

Table 2.2 Visual depth cues		
Cue	Explanation	Availability in desktop 3D
accommodation	The adjustment to the optic lens required to bring the object into focus	no
vergence	The convergence or divergence of the eyes required to produce an apparently single image	no
binocular disparity	The difference between the image as viewed by the two eyes	no
occlusion	The hiding of parts of an object by other objects	yes
relative size	The proportion of the view taken up by an object	yes
relative density	How close together objects appear	yes
height in visual field	The up-down position within the visual field	yes
aerial perspective	The degree of atmospheric colour distortion (normally making distant objects appear more blue)	yes
perspective	The convergence of parallel lines going away from the viewer	yes
shading	The differences in apparent colour of surfaces depending on their angle from the light source	yes
texture gradients	The density of object textures (objects further away will have more dense textures)	yes
motion parallax	The change in occlusion of objects as the view position changes (especially moving left-right)	yes
motion perspective	Changes in object size and density as the view position changes (especially moving nearer-further)	yes

The important thing to note in Table 2.2 is that of the thirteen visual depth cues identified only three are not available in desktop 3D environments. In order to judge how similar depth perception in a desktop 3D environments is to real-world depth perception it is important to determine the relative importance of the various depth cues. Cutting and Vishton (1995) compare the theoretical effectiveness of each of the visual depth cues for objects at various distances from the viewer. They find that accommodation and vergence are of negligible use for objects greater than one metre from the viewer and that binocular disparity becomes of negligible use for objects more than about ten metres from the viewer. On the other hand occlusion, relative size, and relative density remain important regardless of how far away the object is. Additionally, they find that height in the visual field and motion perspective are more important than convergence, accommodation and binocular disparity for all objects more than a metre away. The most important result of this analysis for this study is that the depth cues not available in desktop 3D environments, namely accommodation, vergence and binocular disparity, are very important only for objects very close to the viewer. Consequently, for objects more than a few metres away from the viewer within the virtual environment we should expect desktop 3D environments to provide a similar sense of three-dimensionality to viewing the same object in the real world, if other parameters such as field of view, texture resolution and the accuracy of the 3D model are comparable.

In discussing spatial cognitive models it is important to include a discussion of the way that we understand and encode knowledge about the objects and locations in the space and their relationships beyond just the structure and appearance of the space and objects.

Kitchin (1994), differentiates between knowledge of the spatial structure of an environment, which he terms 'spatial cognition', and other knowledge about the environment, which he terms 'environmental cognition'. Hart and Moore (1973) define spatial cognition as "the knowledge or internal cognitive representation of the structure, entities and relations of space" (p. 248). On the other hand, Moore and Golledge (1976) define environmental cognition as "the study of the subjective information, images, impressions and beliefs that people have about the environment". Additionally, according to Kitchin (1994), environmental cognition encompasses the meaning and significance that an individual places on aspects of the environment, that is, the view that our cognitive models "are not just a set of spatial mental structures denoting relative position, they contain attributive values and meanings" (p. 2).

This study is concerned with spatial knowledge within the scope of Hart and Moore's (1973) definition of spatial cognition. Knowledge of the associated non-spatial attributes of the environment, which Kitchen (1994) and Moore and Golledge (1976) refer to as environmental cognition, is outside the scope of this study. From here on, the term 'spatial knowledge' is used to refer to knowledge within the scope of Hart and Moore's (1973) definition.

It is proposed by this researcher that an effective way to understand spatial knowledge is to think of it as a set of entities with static and dynamic properties. Three distinct entities can be identified within our environment, each with properties to be understood. These are: the 'space' itself, containing immovable structures and landmarks; 'objects' within the space, which move or change state under certain conditions; and the 'person' perceiving the space, whose actions cause changes within the environment. The space and the objects each have static properties that we need to encode, which consist of their appearance from various viewpoints and possibly also their 3D structures (see discussion below relating to view-dependent versus view-independent representations). The dynamic properties encapsulate the way that the objects in the environment behave under certain conditions. They are characterised by relationships between the person, the space and the objects, including the affordances for interaction provided by each. Figure 2.1 illustrates this model of our environment.

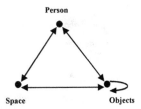

Figure 2.1
This researcher's model of spatial knowledge

The nature of the dynamic properties of our environment is informed by the discipline of ecological psychology (McLellan, 1996; Kitchin, 1994), from which the term affordances originates (Greeno, 1994). The interaction with objects is often termed object manipulation. The skills involved are termed by McLellan (1996) 'spatial procedural skills'. Interaction with the environment is often termed navigation and consequently McLellan (1996) terms the skills involved 'spatial navigational skills'.

Studies of the way that we encode static properties of the environment are particularly important in the context of this study because the learning potential of 3D virtual environments depends to a large degree on our ability to develop a related 3D spatial cognitive model. Such studies tend to focus either on our cognitive models of space, or of discrete objects. However, there are important similarities in the issues addressed and the conclusions reached. One of the fundamental questions is whether spatial knowledge is encoded in a view-dependent or view-independent way. As discussed below this has been the focus of many studies of spatial cognition and object recognition.

After studies exploring the spatial knowledge acquired from maps and from navigation, Thorndyke and Hayes-Roth (1982) proposed that we primarily rely on two distinct types of spatial knowledge: procedural descriptions of routes, and survey knowledge (topological representations of the environment). They also discuss the role of a third type of knowledge, knowledge of landmarks. Darken and Sibert (1996), summarising this and later work (for example, Thorndyke and Golden, 1983), state that spatial knowledge of an environment (by which they mean the larger space around us not the structure of the objects within the space) can be described in terms of three hierarchical levels of information, as follows:

> 1. **Landmark knowledge** is information about the visual details of specific locations in the environment. It is memory for notable perceptual features, such as a unique building.
>
> 2. **Procedural knowledge** (also known as route knowledge) is information about the sequence of actions required to follow a particular route. Procedural knowledge is built by connecting isolated bits of landmark knowledge into larger, more complex structures.
>
> 3. **Survey knowledge** is configural or topological information. Object locations and interobject distances are encoded in terms of a geocentric, fixed frame of reference. A geocentric frame of reference is a global, map-like view, whereas an egocentric frame of reference is a first-person, ground-view relative to the observer.
> (p. 50-51)

Witmer et al. (1996) discuss the way that we acquire these levels of knowledge. They suggest that the simplest knowledge of spaces is the noticing of and remembering of landmarks, followed by route knowledge, including route distances, orientation cues and ordering of landmarks. At the highest level is 'Gestalt' or configuration knowledge, about which they note the following: "configuration knowledge can accumulate incrementally as a result of repeated direct experience with an environment, or it can be learned from a map" (p. 415). Patrick et al. (2000) agree, and citing Thorndyke and Hayes-Roth (1982), suggest that

> cognitive maps for real-world environments are more accurate when they are formed by viewing a paper map of the environment than from cursory navigation through the environment. However, repeated navigation in the environment results in a cognitive map that is as accurate as if it was learned from a paper map. (p. 478)

However, it is worth noting that the results of a study by Ruddle, Payne and Jones (1997) suggest that effective navigation through an environment by participants learning an environment through studying of maps is dependent on the existence of recognisable landmarks with orientation cues.

Richardson, Montello and Hegarty (1999) explain Ruddle et al.'s findings in terms of the 'alignment effect'. This effect was demonstrated by Levine, Marchon and Hanley (1984) in a study exploring the difference in navigation performance for participants provided with aligned and misaligned 'you-are-here' maps. Levine et al. (1984) summarise the alignment effect as follows: "when an individual learns an environment from a map and is then tested in the environment, he or she is typically very accurate when aligned with the original orientation of the map and shows poor performance when contra-aligned" (p. 742). However, it is important to note that a study by Rossano, Warren and Kenan (1995) found that there are strong individual differences in the alignment effect, with some people able to ignore it completely.

The degree to which and the circumstances in which people exhibit this alignment effect contribute to the debate about whether we form a view-dependent or a view-independent model of the space around us. Christou and Bulthoff (1999) describe a view-independent representation (also termed an allocentric representation) as one where the space is encoded "according to view-independent features or components ... involving abstraction in order to reduce dependence on image-specific detail" (p. 996). On the other hand a view-dependent representation (also termed an egocentric representation) uses "an image-based representation in which the spatial detail is represented only implicitly" (p. 996) and space is encoded "with respect to the observer's body reference frame, as determined by experience." (p. 996).

Hunt and Waller (1999) point out that it is possible to exhibit view-independent behaviour even if we have a view-dependent representation, by computing new views from our remembered views. They note that the cognitive processing required to compute a view-independent representation at the time that we experience a view is termed 'early computation', whereas the processing required to compute new views when required is termed 'late computation'. They note that we would expect slower responses to questions requiring us to generate a new view if late computation is used.

A number of studies have been undertaken to determine whether we use a view-dependent or a view-independent representation, but the findings are inconclusive. For example, Christou and Bulthoff (1999) note that studies showing that after viewing a scene from a number of directions people are able to recognise novel views, would tend to indicate a view-independent representation. However, they also note that "results from an increasing number of spatial layout studies suggest that although view generalization occurs to a limited extent around familiar directions, performance is reduced with increasing displacement of viewing perspective from the familiar directions" (p. 997). This suggests a view-dependent representation.

Christou and Bulthoff (1999) discuss the difference between static (or stationary) views of an environment and dynamic views of an environment, with smooth transitions between viewpoints. They also discuss the difference between dynamic views controlled by the viewer's own motion and dynamic views not controlled by the user. They list a number of studies which suggest that the "dynamic nature of visual perception could influence not only the detection of invariant information but also memory for spatial detail" (p. 997).

Gillner and Mallot (1998) discuss similarities in the cognitive representation of space and of objects and in particular the similar debate about view independence. They note that "the view-based approach to navigation is closely related to view-based mechanisms for direction-invariant object recognition" (p. 448). Studies into the cognitive representation of objects by Bulthoff, Edelman and Tarr (1995) suggest that object representations are viewpoint-dependent. Wallis and Bulthoff (1999), reviewing evidence from a large number of studies, suggest that objects are encoded using a linked combination of features. They propose that each feature is encoded as a series of two-dimensional views and is reused in the representation of multiple objects. Wallis (2002) suggests that our mechanism for collating the multiple images of each object (and possibly also the individual features of those objects), is to use temporal information, on the assumption that images viewed very closely in time are likely to be views of the same object, either in different positions if the object is moving, or from different angles if it is rotating. Kourtzi and Nakayama (2002) studied perception and cognitive encoding of moving and static objects, concluding that different mechanisms are used for each.

Despite the fact that the issue of view-dependence is important both to studies exploring the cognitive encoding of space and studies exploring object recognition, there appears to be little cross citation between these studies. Additionally, object recognition studies are often carried out artificially with potential cues from the wider environment hidden. Christou, Tjan and Bulthoff (1999) on the other hand, explored object recognition within a familiar environment and found that "object identification can be aided by knowledge of where we are in space and in which direction we are looking" (p. 1).

Although the findings about view-independence in both space and object studies are inconclusive, it seems clear that whatever representation we use is more complex than simply a 3D geometrical representation. It seems more likely that we encode the space around us and the objects within it using a complex network of two-dimensional views rather than a cohesive three-dimensional cognitive model, and that when we execute behaviours consistent with a three-dimensional representation, we are in fact relying on our ability to process recalled two-dimensional views in a complex way.

This is important because as well as being counter-intuitive, it contradicts the assumptions of a number of researchers exploring the learning benefits of 3D environments. For example, Hedberg and Alexander (1994) suggest that "as ideas are represented in a three-dimensional world, three-dimensional thinking can be enhanced, and the mental transformation of information from two to three-dimensions can be facilitated" (p. 216). Similarly Moore (1995), in describing Osberg's (1997) Puzzle

World, suggests that "the central hypothesis was that by teaching the students to think in 3D, using visualisation techniques their spatial cognition would be enhanced" (p. 5).

This is not quite as discouraging as it first seems, however. Even if we don't actually form a three-dimensional cognitive model through exploration of a 3D environment, we may develop a larger database of views and stronger mechanisms for retrieving and processing these views than through other means. Consequently, we may be better able to understand and negotiate the corresponding real-world environment as a result. If the 3D environment is a metaphorical representation of abstract ideas, it may be that by developing an integrated database of two-dimensional views of a three-dimensional model of the concepts, we are better able to make sense of the concepts than through other instructional approaches.

2.6 Spatial Learning in Real and Virtual Environments

Having discussed the nature of spatial cognition we can now explore the effectiveness of 3D environments for developing spatial knowledge. A number of studies have compared spatial knowledge acquisition in virtual environments with spatial knowledge acquisition in similar real environments.

A study by Arthur et al. (1997) found that there was no significant difference between real-world exploration and virtual environment exploration for drawing a map of objects and estimating inter-object distances within a single-room environment. A study by Richardson et al. (1999) found that there was no significant difference between the performance of a real navigation group and a desktop virtual navigation group on a relative route estimation task or on a relative straight-line distance estimation task.

Ruddle et al. (1997) discuss a number of studies indicating that subjects exploring a virtual environment (VE) are able to develop both route knowledge (eg. ability to navigate) and survey knowledge (eg. ability to draw a map). However, they also discuss studies comparing spatial knowledge developed in a virtual environment with spatial knowledge developed in the real world and note that these studies "suggest that either spatial knowledge is developed more quickly in the real world than in an equivalent VE or the ultimate accuracy of spatial knowledge developed in a VE is lower than that developed in the real world." (p. 144).

In their own study they found that virtual environment navigation participants made less accurate direction estimates than real-world navigation estimates but the differences were not large. They also found that virtual environment navigation participants had less accurate Euclidean and route distance correlations (relative distance estimates) than real-world navigation participants, but the difference was not large. However, absolute distance estimates for virtual environment navigation participants varied widely and on average were nearly twice as inaccurate as real-world navigation participants. The poor performance of virtual environment participants in judging distances was consistent with the findings of Henry and Furness (1993) and Witmer and Kline (1998). In both of these studies, virtual environment participants consistently underestimated distances. Richardson et al. (1999), note that there is general agreement that VE participants have difficulty estimating distances and sizes accurately, and specifically suggest that "preliminary evidence suggests that distance and the size of environment is often underestimated in VEs" (p. 742). However, Ruddle et al. (1997) note that their VE navigation participants "varied widely in accuracy and showed no consistent tendency to either under or overestimate the VE-Euclidean or VE-route distances" (p. 150).

A study by Christou and Bulthoff (1999) found that navigation within a desktop virtual environment allowed participants to form cognitive models sufficient to allow them to identify novel views and topographical maps. In a study of the ability of participants to navigate through a maze blind-folded after learning the environment in the real maze, through an immersive virtual maze and through a desktop virtual maze, Waller, Hunt and Knapp (1998) found that real-world participants performed significantly better than immersive and desktop VE participants in time taken to navigate through the maze. Witmer et al. (1996) in a study comparing route-finding performance and configuration knowledge after rehearsal in a real building, a virtual building and using static images, found that a virtual environment "can be almost as effective as real-world environments in training participants to follow a designated route" (p. 425).

Wilson, Foreman and Tlauka (1997), in a study comparing the spatial knowledge acquired from navigation in a real building versus a virtual building found that for ground floor pointing tasks there was no significant difference between the real group and the virtual group, but that both performed significantly better than the control group, who had no navigational experience. However, for pointing to items on the first floor, the virtual environment group performed significantly worse than the real group and not significantly better than the control group. The environment contained a stairwell with no directional cues, and it was concluded that virtual environment participants became disoriented after climbing the virtual stairs.

These studies provide strong support for the idea that people are able to develop spatial knowledge representations as a result of exploration of a virtual environment. They suggest that, aside from the absolute dimensions of the environment, these spatial representations are in many cases as accurate or nearly as accurate as representations formed as a result of exploring a real environment. Waller et al. (1998) concur, and propose that "researchers now no longer need to question whether VEs can be effective in training spatial knowledge. Today's more pressing questions involve examining the variables that mediate the training effects of VEs" (p. 127).

2.7 Distinguishing Characteristics of 3D Learning Environments

Having ascertained that using a 3D learning environment can lead to spatial learning we now need to identify the aspects or characteristics of 3D environments that are important in this process. First, however, we need to explore in more detail the characteristics of 3D environments that distinguish them from other types of learning resources.

It could be argued that 3D environments have a unique set of characteristics from a pedagogical point of view. Hedberg and Alexander (1994) suggest that their most important defining feature is the "transparent interface with which the user directly controls the objects in the context of the virtual world" (p. 215). In identifying the features of virtual environments that make them distinct from interactive multimedia, they highlight three aspects of virtual environments that contribute to this transparency and through which such environments have "the potential to offer a superior learning experience" (p. 218), increased 'immersion', increased 'fidelity', and a higher level of 'active learner participation'.

Whitelock et al. (1996) propose a theoretical framework in order to explore the relationship between virtual environments and conceptual learning. Their framework, which extends the work of Zeltzer, includes the identification of three properties or dimensions of educational 3D virtual environments, 'representational fidelity', 'immediacy of control' and 'presence'. Zeltzer's framework, which focuses on virtual environments in general, not specifically educational environments, identifies three dimensions: 'autonomy', 'interaction' and 'presence' (Zeltzer, 1992). Zeltzer's autonomy describes the degree to which objects in the environment have their own autonomous behaviours. Whitelock et al.'s representational fidelity is broader than this because it also encompasses the degree to which these behaviours are realistic, the degree to which they are familiar to the learner, as well as the degree of realism of the technological delivery. On the other hand, Whitelock et al.'s immediacy of control is more specific than Zeltzer's interaction, because it focuses particularly on the degree to which the interface allows immediate or unmediated interaction.

There is a degree of agreement between Hedberg and Alexander's ideas and Whitelock et al.'s model. Fidelity appears as a factor in both, immersion and presence are similar ideas, and Whitelock et al.'s immediacy of control equates very closely to Hedberg and Alexander's active learner participation.

The degree of realism, or fidelity, and the mechanisms for learner control also figure in the model proposed by Thurman and Mattoon (1994). Their model contains three dimensions: 'verity', which is the degree of realism on a scale from physical to abstract; 'integration', which is the degree of human integration into the environment ranging from batch processing to total inclusion, and 'interface', which ranges from natural to artificial. McLellan (1996) emphasises the importance of immersion, suggesting that "the sense of presence or immersion is a critical feature distinguishing virtual reality from other types of computer applications" (p. 457).

It is the view of this researcher that the sense of presence or immersion in a 3D environment occurs as a consequence of the fidelity of representation and the high degree of interaction or user control, rather than being a unique attribute of the environment. The dependency of immersion on other aspects of the environment is noted by Hedberg and Alexander (1994) when they suggest that "the interaction of representational fidelity with sensory, conceptual and motivational immersion needs to be examined to determine the complexity of sensory input necessary to establish the learning outcome" (p. 217).

The two most important visual factors in the fidelity of a 3D environment are the degree of realism provided by the rendered 3D images, and the degree of realism provided by temporal changes to these images. The display of objects using realistic perspective and occlusion, and realistic texture and lighting calculations allows for a degree of realism that can approach photographic quality if the 3D model is defined with sufficient detail. However, even when the images do not approach photographic quality, with sufficient frame rates (15 frames per second is normally considered the minimum), the image changes that reflect the viewer's motion or the motion of objects, can appear smooth enough to provide a very high degree of realism. Another aspect of the fidelity of the representation is the degree to which objects behave in realistic ways or in ways consistent with the ideas being modelled.

The two aspects of learner control, or learner activity, that are unique to 3D environments are the ability to change the view position or direction, giving the impression of smooth movement through the environment, and the ability to pick up, examine and manipulate objects within the virtual environment. Additionally, in 3D environments that involve objects moving autonomously, simulating real-world or abstract properties, the learner can be given control over the parameters of the simulation or the speed at which the simulation proceeds.

Taking the view that immersion is a consequence of other factors, rather then being a unique characteristic, and summarising the factors that contribute to fidelity and learner control, Table 2.3 lists the characteristics of 3D learning environments that distinguish such environments from other interactive learning resources.

Table 2.3
Distinguishing characteristics of 3D learning environments

Category	Characteristic
Fidelity	Realistic display, including 3D perspective, lighting and occlusion
	Smooth update of views showing viewer motion or panning
	Smooth display of object motion
	Consistency of object behaviour
Learner activity	Control of view position and direction
	Object manipulation
	Control of object model and simulation parameters

2.8 Researchable Issues

From the earlier discussion, it is clear that perception of a 3D environment is comparable to real-world perception. Although we might not necessarily form a 3D cognitive model, we are able to exhibit a degree of 3D understanding through complex processing of recalled 2D views, and exploration of a 3D environment can lead to such a 3D understanding. Consequently, we can be confident that 3D environments have potential in learning situations where a spatial cognitive representation is desirable. To proceed from here, however, we need more specific information about the aspects of 3D environments that are important in spatial knowledge development and the learning tasks that are appropriate in this process. This provides the focus question for this research:

> **What are the distinguishing characteristics of 3D learning environments; does each characteristic contribute to spatial learning; and does the design of the learning task contribute to spatial learning in such environments?**

A set of distinguishing characteristics has been identified through the literature and presented in Table 2.3. Addressing the contribution of each characteristic to spatial learning requires the following more specific questions to be answered.

> **Does the degree of realism of the display in a 3D learning environment contribute to spatial learning?**

Does smooth display of view changes in a 3D learning environment contribute to spatial learning?

Does smooth display of object motion in a 3D learning environment contribute to spatial learning?

Does consistent modelling of object behaviour in a 3D learning environment contribute to spatial learning?

Does user control over view position and direction in a 3D learning environment contribute to spatial learning?

Does object manipulation in a 3D learning environment contribute to spatial learning?

Does user control of object model and simulation parameters in a 3D learning environment contribute to spatial learning?

It is likely, however, that merely providing an environment with a high degree of fidelity and user control, modelled on a real-world system or a set of abstract concepts, will not necessarily facilitate the development of conceptual understanding. It would seem likely that an appropriate set of learning tasks would need to be designed, with appropriate task support, to ensure that the activities that the learners undertake as they explore the environment do in fact require them to develop such an understanding. This leads to the following additional question that needs to be addressed:

How does the design of the learning task within a 3D environment affect the spatial learning that occurs?

Once these questions are addressed educational designers and developers considering the use of a 3D learning environment will have a firm basis for their decision. For example, in some applications a designer may need to decide whether to use a 3D environment or a video. The degree to which user control over view and object manipulation are important for learning will be an important factor in the decision. Another alternative might be the use of a Web site containing static images. The degree to which the perception of smooth view changes and the perception of object motion are important will be factors in this decision. In summary, then, once more is known about the aspects of such environments that are important for learning, there will be a much greater likelihood that the resources developed will do more than simply impress the learner with technological 'niftiness' or visual realism, but will actually facilitate learning.

Addressing all of the questions identified in this section was considered to be beyond the scope of a doctorate. Consequently, a subset of these questions was chosen for investigation in this study. In particular, the contributions to spatial learning of the degree of realism, modelling of object behaviour and user control over simulation parameters were not addressed in this study. This left the following as the questions addressed in the study:

Question 1. Does smooth display of view changes in a 3D learning environment contribute to spatial learning?

Question 2. Does smooth display of object motion in a 3D learning environment contribute to spatial learning?

Question 3. Does user control over view position and direction in a 3D learning environment contribute to spatial learning?

Question 4. Does object manipulation in a 3D learning environment contribute to spatial learning?

Question 5. How does the design of the learning task within a 3D environment affect the spatial learning that occurs?

2.9 Related Work

A number of researchers have commented on the lack of systematic research into the learning potential of 3D environments and have proposed research agendas to address this. McLellan (1996) notes that "as yet, very little research on virtual realities as a tool for learning has been carried out" (p. 25). Whitelock et al. (1996) concur, noting that "there is little principled empirical work that has been carried out on the effectiveness of Virtual Reality Environments for educational purposes" (p. 1). Boman (1993, cited in McLellan, 1996) recommends a number of avenues for research into learning in virtual environments. These include the following: "conduct experimental studies to establish the effectiveness of VE simulations in facilitating learning at the cognitive process level"; "develop criteria for specifying the characteristics of tasks that would benefit from virtual-environment training for media selection"; and "conduct summative evaluation of system performance, usability and utility, and of training outcomes" (p. 10).

Ferrington and Lage (1992) list a series of questions relating to 3D learning environments that remain unanswered. These include: "how is learning in virtual reality different than that of a traditional educational environment?" and "what do we know about multi-sensory learning that will have application and be of value in determining the effectiveness of this technology?" (p. 18). Winn (1997) provides the strongest support for the need for empirical research such as that proposed in the research agenda above:

> *If VR is to improve student comprehension and performance relative to other technologies, it will do so because of its unique characteristics not through the characteristics it shares with other technologies. ... Part of our task is therefore to identify unique attributes of VR that might improve understanding and performance. These attributes can then be manipulated as independent variables in experimental studies of VR. (p. 2).*

Although a number of researchers have attempted to identify the characteristics that distinguish 3D environments from other types of learning resources, there has not been a systematic attempt to look at the relationship between these characteristics and learning. Sanchez et al. (2000) comment that:

> *Almost all the efforts carried out in this field have focused on implementing special-purpose systems or limited-scope prototypes. The theoretical questions related to the design of models, methodologies and evaluation have hardly ever been addressed and studied in depth. (p. 346)*

Denise Whitelock at the Open University and Paul Brna at University of Leeds have proposed a theoretical framework for 3D learning environments, including a three-dimensional 'cube' describing the attributes of such environments along with hypothesised connections between these attributes and conceptual learning (Whitelock et al., 1996). In later work (see for example Brna, 1999; Whitelock et al., 2000) they have explored aspects of these hypotheses. However, their work has consisted of open-ended exploratory studies, and consequently their results have been inconclusive.

Specifically they have not undertaken studies controlling the various attributes and they have not attempted to measure their participants' conceptual learning.

The most comprehensive empirical studies to date have been those carried out by Marilyn Salzman, Chris Dede and their colleagues at George Mason University (see for example, Salzman et al., 1999). They propose a detailed model of virtual learning environments, including relationships between the features of the environment, the concepts to be learned, the learner characteristics, the interaction experience, the learning experience and the learning process, ultimately leading to learning outcomes. Through evaluation of a series of immersive virtual environments developed as part of their 'Project Science Space' they have investigated aspects of this model. These environments, 'Newton World', 'Maxwell World' and 'Pauling World', model concepts in Newtonian mechanics, electrostatic charges and quantum mechanics respectively.

Like those of Whitelock and Brna, Salzman and Dede's research goals were also quite open-ended and exploratory. However, their approach was to some extent similar to the approach taken in this study, in that they developed authentic learning environments designed to achieve specific learning outcomes and then carried out evaluations using these environments as instruments to explore specific aspects of the learning process. Their studies did not, however, explore spatial learning specifically and thus do not shed light on the research questions addressed by this study.

Two studies have been carried out that specifically address aspects of the questions addressed here. The first of these studies, carried out by Peruch et al. (1995) explored the ability of participants to recall the shortest path to locations within a desktop 3D environment after viewing static images, viewing an animated tour and after exploring the environment under their own control. They found that participants who explored under their own control exhibited significantly greater spatial learning, but that there was no significant difference between those who viewed static images and those who viewed an animated tour.

The second of these studies, carried out by Christou and Bulthoff (1999), explored the ability of participants to recognise novel views and topographical maps of a 3D space after viewing static images, after viewing animated tours, and after undertaking viewer-controlled movement through a desktop 3D environment. They found that exposure to dynamic views, whether viewer-controlled or not, provided significantly increased ability to recognise novel views when compared with exposure to static views. However, there was no significant difference between the viewer-controlled and passive conditions. The no significant difference result for the comparison of active and passive observers is at odds with the findings of Peruch et al. (1995) as is the finding of a difference between static and animated views. Christou and Bulthoff surmise that the user interface provided to their viewer-controlled motion participants may have added additional cognitive load during exploration. They suggest that it was possible that "the use of the Space Ball (which, for some subjects, proved somewhat cumbersome to control) distracted the active explorers during the learning stages" (p. 1005). They note that the Peruch et al. study used a joystick, which may be simpler to use and thus impose less cognitive load on the learner.

These studies illustrate an important point of contention relating to the degree to which learner control over view position and direction is important for spatial learning. Clearly, there is a need for further studies in order to determine whether Christou and Bulthoff's explanation for the conflicting results is correct. Durlach et al. (2000) have also identified the need for further research exploring the effect of active versus passive movement through a 3D environment. Additionally, the usability problems relating to the use of the Space Ball illustrate the importance of refining the user interface provided to the learners to ensure that the cognitive load is minimised.

Arthur et al. (1997) carried out a study comparing spatial learning from exploration of a virtual environment, a real environment and a static view of the real environment. They tested their participants on their ability to draw a map of the environment and estimate relative inter-object distances. The environment was a room full of furniture, and all furniture could be viewed from the location of the static view. They found that the maps drawn by the single fixed view group were significantly more accurate than either the real-world exploration or virtual environment exploration groups, which were not significantly different. They note, however, that in retrospect their findings are not surprising since participants were asked to map the environment from the same orientation as the single fixed view group viewed the environment, and it was possible that participants in the other groups may never have viewed the environment from this position. This study illustrates one of the potential difficulties with this type of research, which is the problem of ensuring that the test used does not favour one group of participants over the others. It provides a compelling argument for the use of multiple tests of spatial learning, to improve the validity of any conclusions reached. This issue is discussed further in Chapter 3.

A study by Witmer et al. (1996) compared route-finding ability in a real environment after route-rehearsal in the real environment and in a virtual environment (using a head-mounted display) and using static images with route descriptions. They found that real building rehearsal participants and virtual environment rehearsal participants made significantly fewer wrong turns and took significantly less time to traverse the building than static image rehearsal participants. These results are consistent with those of Christou and Bulthoff (1999) but not with those of Peruch et al. (1995) and Arthur et al. (1997). The explanation given by Arthur et al. for their unexpected results seems plausible, however there is no obvious explanation for the contrary findings of Peruch et al. (1995). It seems clear that there is a need for further research exploring the importance of smooth view changes within 3D environments for spatial learning.

This section has provided a brief review of research addressing similar questions to those of this study. The review illustrates that the importance for spatial learning of smooth view changes and of user control are highly contentious issues within the literature. The lack of conclusive findings and the apparent contradictions between the findings to date provide clear encouragement for this study.

2.10 Summary

This chapter has introduced 3D environment technologies and has discussed recent developments in learning theory. Potential applications of 3D learning environments have been described and the pedagogical assumptions implicit within each have been identified. Of these the assumption that the use of a 3D environment can help facilitate the formation of a spatial cognitive model has been identified as particularly important. The testing of aspects of this assumption is the central focus of this thesis.

The characteristics of 3D learning environments that differentiate them from other types of learning resources have been identified and this has led to a series of specific research questions that need to be addressed. These questions ask about the degree to which each of these characteristics is important for spatial learning. The importance for spatial learning of smooth view changes and of user control have been identified as being of particular interest within this study. Additionally, the importance of learning task design has been identified as an additional focus. It has been argued that these questions are important to designers considering the use of 3D learning environments and needing to weigh up the potential benefits of such environments when compared with alternatives such as videos, animations, or static Web pages.

Research that addresses aspects of these questions has been reviewed, and it has been shown that the results to date are inconclusive. The apparently contradictory findings in the research literature, together with the importance of the identified questions for educational designers, clearly demonstrates the need for this study.

Chapter 3 explains the methodological basis for this study as well as describing in detail the methods used in each of the three investigations that make up the study. The design and development of the 3D environment used as a research instrument within the study, a 3D virtual chemistry laboratory, is also described.

Chapter 3. Methodology and Research Design

3.1 Introduction

The research carried out in this study addressed the broad focus question identified in Chapter 2:

> **What are the distinguishing characteristics of 3D learning environments; does each characteristic contribute to spatial learning; and does the design of the learning task contribute to spatial learning in such environments?**

Addressing this question will allow educational designers and developers to make sound decisions about the appropriate use or design of 3D learning environments.

This chapter describes the methodology used in the study. It begins with a discussion of the theoretical background to the methods chosen. Next an overview of the research design is presented, followed by a more detailed discussion of the main aspects of the research design, including the design of the virtual environment used as a research instrument. Lastly, the technological development of this environment is discussed.

3.2 Methodology Background

3.2.1 Theoretical assumptions

There are three broad methodological positions that educational researchers tend to take as a starting point for choosing appropriate methods. These are positivism (or more recently post-positivism), interpretivism, and critical theory (Mertens, 1997).

Positivism has as its underlying assumption that there is some absolute knowledge about human behaviour, or the way that people learn, to be discovered and that if the research is done correctly subjectivism can be removed from the study. Post-positivism is a more moderate position, which accepts that there is always a degree of subjectivism caused by judgements made by the researcher, the selection of participants, the design of the learning materials or learning conditions and so on, but that if the research is done correctly these factors can be minimised and conclusions can be made about the behaviour of the population, which can be expressed in terms of their statistical probability of correctness. Post-positivist research tends to involve the application of 'scientific method' to human studies. For example, it is common to first randomly group participants and then apply different treatments to participants in each group. The behaviour or learning performance of the individuals in each group is then measured in a quantitative way and statistical methods are used to identify differences in the performance or behaviour across the groups and to determine if these differences are 'significant' enough to allow generalisation to the population as a whole (Williamson, Burstein & McKemmish, 2002).

Interpretivism has an implicit social constructivist view of knowledge within it, that is, an assumption that there is no absolute knowledge, but instead all knowledge is socially constructed. A consequence of this position is that rather than making generalisable conclusions about the way all people behave or learn it is more appropriate to select participants who typify certain groups and explore the way that these individuals think and act. The focus then is why individuals behave or learn in a particular way rather than how the population as a whole behaves or learns. Interpretivist research tends to involve interviews, questionnaires or observation of behaviour, with qualitative analysis used to draw conclusions from the data (Williamson et al., 2002).

Critical theory draws heavily on Marxist theories and attempts to address power imbalances in research by allowing the participants to drive the research. Methods used in critical theory research tend to be similar to those used in interpretivist research, with the main difference being the degree to which the researcher participates in the observed activity. Interpretivist research does allow for participant observation, but critical theorists would normally have the researcher as an equal peer with the participants (Mertens, 1997).

The view taken in this study is that the three positions are not necessarily mutually exclusive. In particular, it is the view of the researcher that even though human knowledge is socially constructed and human behaviour is individual, depending very much on each individual's knowledge construction, there are enough similarities in people's behaviour and the way people learn to look for generalisations about the way the majority of the population behave and learn. That is, although there are many areas of research in which it is most useful to try to explain the behaviour of individuals rather than make generalisations about the behaviour of a group, there are situations where, even though individual differences in behaviour exist, it is useful to know about the behaviour of the majority of the population.

Often a combination is appropriate, with quantitative techniques used to draw broad conclusions about the way the majority of the population behave or learn, and then qualitative techniques used to identify sub-groups within the population that behave differently and to analyse why individuals from the different sub-groups behave in different ways. Importantly, it is the view of this researcher that having a constructivist view of learning does not necessarily preclude the use of post-positivist, quantitative research methods.

Creswell (1994) notes that qualitative rather than quantitative techniques are appropriate where "little information exists on the topic" and "the variables are largely unknown" (p. 10). This is not the case in this study. The theoretical analysis undertaken in Chapter 2 has identified characteristics of 3D learning environments, and by having participants use environments including or excluding these characteristics, they can be manipulated as independent variables. There is substantial literature on spatial learning and the types of tests that can be used to measure it. Many of the studies into spatial learning in real and virtual environments discussed in Chapter 2 have used such tests. Participants' scores on such tests after exploring 3D environments are suitable as dependent variables.

3.2.2 Methods in educational media research

A common approach to research in educational media is to set up a quantitative study whereby groups of participants are exposed to learning experiences using different media designed to facilitate learning of the same concepts, with post-tests carried out to determine whether there are differences in learning performance using these different media. This approach has been the subject of criticism from a number of researchers, most notably Clark (1983; 1994). These criticisms are outlined in the following paragraphs, followed by counter-arguments.

Clark (1983) uses evidence from a meta-analysis of educational media research to argue that there is no connection between media and learning. He argues that on balance the numerous studies that have been undertaken suggest that there is no significant difference between different learning media. He also argues that many studies that report a difference have in fact confounded the media with the teaching method. That is, they have compared the teaching of a concept using a particular type of media and a particular instructional design with an alternative design with a different type of media. He argues that the results indicate that it is the difference in instructional design that is the main factor in the difference rather than the media.

Clark (1983) does, however, acknowledge that by focussing on certain attributes of media in conjunction with certain instructional design techniques using media, consistent learning effects can be found. Examples include Salomon's (1979) studies of video instruction that identified techniques such as zooming as specific media attributes and which found significant learning benefits for such techniques. Clark argues against the term 'media attributes' because the individual techniques are really aspects of an instructional design that could be implemented using a range of media. This researcher concurs and thus the term 'instructional media techniques' has been coined for use in the following discussion.

Clark (1983) argues that although the results of studies such as those carried out by Salomon suggest that certain instructional media techniques are 'sufficient' for learning to occur, they are not a 'necessary' condition. His line of argument here is that for any given learning outcome, it is possible to achieve the outcome using more than one such technique. He argues that findings where instructional media techniques are 'sufficient' for learning are of interest to educational designers, but do not contribute to educational theory.

This last point is important for this study, because the specific characteristics of 3D environments that are the focus of the study can also be considered to be instructional media techniques. Consequently, Clark's conclusion that there is no value to be gained from research into connections between such techniques and learning is of concern. However, the dismissal of research that finds sufficient but not necessary conditions for learning is quite contentious, as argued by Kozma (1994).

Kozma (1994) argues that when scientists want to eliminate some undesirable event, such as a disease, they need to find the necessary conditions leading to this event. If they can eliminate such necessary conditions they can eliminate the disease. On the other hand, when scientists are interested in making some desirable event occur, such as the achievement of a particular learning outcome, they need only find sufficient conditions that will allow the event to occur. If they can then produce these sufficient conditions they can ensure that the event occurs.

Kozma (1994) also argues that because of the complexity of the learning situations that occur in the real-world (as distinct from in controlled laboratory experiments) the concept of a 'sufficient' condition has to be viewed in terms of probability. That is, it is unlikely that a certain learning design or media attribute will ever be found to be sufficient for the achievement of a particular learning outcome for all learners. Differences in learners' aptitudes, motivations and prior experience ensure that there will always be differences in the learning outcomes obtained from any learning experience. Consequently, if a particular media attribute can be found to result in statistically significant learning improvements then that provides a strong argument for its use by educators.

The goal of the researcher then becomes to demonstrate that in certain circumstances, for certain learners, certain learning outcomes are achieved using a particular learning design and type of media more or less effectively than using an alternative and to explore why this is the case. The clear documentation of this educational situation will then allow educators to make a judgement about whether similar resources will be appropriate in their own learning situation.

For example, Salzman et al. (1999) describe some of the outcomes of their evaluation of a set of immersive 3D environments as follows: "3-D immersive representations can be motivating and can support learning beyond 2-D non-immersive representations" (p. 39). The important word here is 'can'. The educator reading their results takes away the idea that such resources can be effective and thus their use may be warranted in some circumstances. At no stage is there any suggestion that such environments 'will' be effective for any specific outcomes, because their effectiveness will always depend on the particular learning design and the characteristics of the individual learners.

Clark's (1983) argument that aspects of media cannot be viewed in isolation from the educational design within which they are applied is very valid. This, along with the fact that the learning experiences required to achieve particular learning outcomes will vary for different learners in different learning situations, led Kozma (1994) to conclude that we should move from the question "do media influence learning?" (p. 18) to "in what ways can we use the capabilities of media to influence learning for particular students, tasks and situations?" (p. 18). Certainly, a finding that a certain instructional media technique has significant learning benefits for a particular outcome in a particular learning situation should not be taken by an educator to mean that they can be sure that this particular technique will achieve different learning outcomes in a different learning situation. Rather, educators will tend to look for studies that demonstrate the successful application of instructional media techniques for the achievement of learning outcomes similar to the ones they desire and in learning situations that are similar to their own. If certain techniques can be found to be advantageous in one situation then there is hope that they can be found to be advantageous in another.

Many of the studies Clark cites in his meta-analysis focus on the passive use of media by learners, that is, the application of the media to the learner rather than the active use of the media by the learner. To some extent this reflects the time in which Clark was writing, and in particular the prevailing educational theories at the time as well as the computer technologies available. Where he refers to studies of Computer Assisted Learning resources, they are primarily those based on a lock-step Programmed Instruction design. Jonassen, Campbell and Davidson (1994) argue that Clark's "concern with the role of media attributes and methods for purveying information or conveying knowledge is inappropriate" (p. 31). Instead, the debate should focus on "the role of media in supporting not controlling the learning process" (p. 31) and "concerns about media from this perspective are best conceived in terms of the affordances that media provide to the human perceiver and processor" (p. 32).

This argument is very pertinent to this study because characteristics of 3D environments such as the ability to control the viewpoint or to manipulate objects are interactive characteristics. The visual information presented by a video or 3D animation is essentially the same as that provided by an interactive 3D environment, but it is the connection between the learner's actions and the information provided that has the potential to result in a different learning experience. Thus, the concept of the environment 'affording' certain learning activities, which can then result in the desired learning outcomes rather than the environment 'conveying knowledge' is much more appropriate.

Reeves (1995) has been critical of the large number of quantitative studies within the educational technology discipline, claiming that many such studies explore the use of a particular technology outside of the intended context. He proposes instead that research should be carried out in a natural setting, using participants who have a reason to achieve the intended learning outcomes.

Salomon (1991) uses the terms 'analytic' and 'systemic' to refer to two different types of research: research in an artificial setting that attempts to control the variables, and research which is undertaken in an authentic context. He notes that analytic research has an underlying assumption that "discrete elements of complex educational phenomena can be isolated for study" (p. 10). On the other hand, systemic research has an underlying assumption that "elements are interdependent, inseparable, and even define each other in a transactional manner" and "thus requires the study of patterns not single variables" (p. 10). He argues that rather than one approach being superior to the other, the two approaches can be used in a complementary fashion.

Ross and Morison (1989) differentiate between 'developmental' research, which "is oriented toward improving technology as in instructional tool", and 'basic' research, which is "oriented towards furthering our understanding of how these applications affect learning and motivation" (p. 20). Basic research, which normally uses experimental methods, attempts to maintain high internal validity by controlling variables and eliminating extraneous factors. Developmental research, however, which is normally carried out in an authentic context, can often have greater external validity, because the results can more readily be related to real-life applications. They argue that there is a need for both types of research. They state that:

> highly controlled studies ... serve to operationally define and validate new constructs
> [and] establish methodologies for their investigation. Once that foundation is
> established, determining the replicability of findings in more applied contexts seems
> essential from the perspective of instructional technology goals. (p. 26)

Although there have now been more than 10 years of research into 3D learning environments, much of this research has been very open ended, exploring broad aspects of usability and potential effectiveness. In this study variables representing characteristics of 3D learning environments have been defined and the effect of these characteristics on spatial learning has been investigated. This research fits into Ross and

Morrison's (1989) category of 'basic' research and Salomon's (1991) category of 'analytic' research. As suggested by Salomon (1991) and by Ross and Morrison (1989), there is also scope for follow-up work of a more systemic nature, exploring for example the value of the virtual laboratory as a tool for familiarising students with the real laboratory. Such research is beyond the scope of this study.

In addition to his criticisms about the lack of a realistic context, Reeves' (1995) also argues that many quantitative studies in educational technology use unsound experimental methods. He uses the term 'pseudoscience' to describe the methods used in these studies, and defines this term by listing a number of characteristics. He labels examples of research as pseudoscience if they exhibit two or more of the listed characteristics. Table 3.1, adapted from Reeves (1995) lists the characteristics of pseudoscience, along with this researcher's arguments for why this study does not exhibit each characteristic. The table indicates that only one of Reeves' characteristics of pseudoscience is exhibited by this study, and only in one of the two investigations. Specifically, in the first major investigation, it could be argued that there were 'inconsequential outcome measures', because the participants were information technology students without an obvious motivation to learn about the chemistry laboratory. The reason why it was necessary to use information technology students as participants in the first major investigation are explained in Section 3.3.3.

Table 3.1

Characteristics of pseudoscience, from Reeves (1995), along with arguments for why this study does not exhibit each

Psuedoscience characteristic	Explanation	Argument for why this research does not exhibit this characteristic
Specification error	Vague definitions of the primary independent variables (eg. learner control versus program control)	The identified characteristics of 3D learning environments are clear and unambiguous and environments with or without each characteristic have been produced.
Lack of linkage to robust theory	Little more than nominal attention to the underlying learning and instructional theories that are relevant to the investigation	A cohesive theoretical position was developed and presented in Chapter 2 and the research questions have been drawn from this theoretical analysis.
Inadequate literature review	Cursory literature review focussed on the results of closely related studies with little or no consideration of alternative findings	A thorough literature review of research into educational media and 3D learning environments was presented in Chapter 2.
Inadequate treatment implementation	Infrequent (usually single) treatment implementation often averaging less than 30 minutes	The implementation is described in Section 3.3. Two major investigations have been used, each including multiple spatial tests.
Measurement flaws	Precise measurement of easy-to-measure variables (eg. time); no effort to establish the reliability and validity of measures of other variables	The test instruments used for measuring spatial learning have been designed after a thorough review of literature describing similar such studies in the psychology, human-computer interaction and education disciplines.
Inconsequential outcome measures	A lack of intentionality in the learning context, usually represented by outcome measures that have little or no relevance for the subjects in the study	This criticism could apply to the first major investigation, where IT students were used as participants. However, the pilot investigation and the second major investigation used chemistry students with a clear interest in the intended learning outcomes.
Inadequate sample sizes	Small samples of convenience, eg. the ubiquitous undergraduate teacher education or psychology majors	Samples sizes in each investigation were a compromise between the ideal and the manageable. However, they were large enough to allow statistically significant differences, as evidenced by other studies in the literature.
Inappropriate statistical analysis	Use of obscure statistical procedures in an effort to tease statistically significant findings out of the data	Statistical techniques used have been informed by extended advice from statistical consultants and supervisors and are similar to those used by numerous studies in the literature.
Meaningless discussion of results	Rambling, often incoherent, rationale for failing to find statistically significant findings	A clear hypothesis for the lack of statistical significance from the first major investigation was formed and the second major investigation was structured to allow this hypothesis to be tested.

3.2.3 Methods in 3D environments and learning research

Research studies involving the use of 3D environments by participants can be divided into two types. Firstly, there are studies which aim to find out about the way people develop spatial knowledge in general, with 3D environments used purely as a research tool. Secondly, there are studies that aim to find out about learning through the use of 3D environments as well as about the effectiveness of 3D user interface technologies. Many studies about spatial learning in general that use a 3D environment as a research tool also contribute to knowledge about 3D environments.

In both cases the methods used have tended to include random allocation of subjects to groups, completion of some task within a virtual environment, with either the task or the environment differing across groups, and completion of a test to gauge spatial learning. This tends to be followed by statistical analysis of the test results in order to determine whether there is a significant difference in the performance across groups, allowing conclusions to be made about whether differences in the virtual environment or in the tasks carried out by each group were a factor in performance.

For example, a study by Christou and Bulthoff (1999), which focussed on the degree to which cognitive spatial models are view-dependent, involved participants viewing static images, viewing dynamic animated tours, and undertaking viewer-controlled movement in a desktop virtual environment, before being tested on their ability to distinguish between correct and incorrect environment views and correct and incorrect topographical maps. A study by Arthur et al. (1997), which compared spatial learning from exploring a virtual environment with that from exploring a real environment and a static view of the real environment, required learners to draw a map and estimate relative inter-object distances after exploration. In each of the investigations carried out in this study an approach has been used which is similar to the studies by Christou and Bulthoff and by Arthur et al.

The aspects of the research design for such studies can be categorised into: virtual environment design; selection and grouping of participants; learning task design; spatial learning test design; and data analysis. The issues considered and the specific decisions made about each aspect are discussed in Sections 3.3.2 to 3.3.7 of this chapter.

3.3 Research Design

3.3.1 Overview

The study investigated the importance for spatial learning of identified characteristics of 3D learning environments, along with the importance of learning task design in such environments. The following specific research questions were identified in Chapter 2:

Question 1. Does smooth display of view changes in a 3D learning environment contribute to spatial learning?

Question 2. Does smooth display of object motion in a 3D learning environment contribute to spatial learning?

Question 3. Does user control over view position and direction in a 3D learning environment contribute to spatial learning?

Question 4. Does object manipulation in a 3D learning environment contribute to spatial learning?

Question 5. How does the design of the learning task within a 3D environment affect the spatial learning that occurs?

The study used a post-positivist approach, with quantitative data gathering and analysis techniques used to compare the spatial learning of participants who used various versions of a virtual environment. The 3D environment used as a research instrument was modelled on an undergraduate chemistry laboratory. This environment is termed the 'virtual laboratory'. The study consisted of a series of investigations of spatial learning as a result of using this environment, compared with the spatial learning from using alternative versions of the environment with certain features removed or disabled. For example, in the second investigation one group used the full virtual environment, another used a version that provided an animated tour but did not allow for user controlled view changes or for object manipulation, and a third used a version that provided only static rather than animated view changes.

The study began with a pilot investigation designed to explore the design of the virtual laboratory and the appropriateness of various learning tasks and spatial test instruments. The pilot investigation was designed as a comparison of the level of laboratory familiarity as evidenced by performance on written tests, of a group of volunteer undergraduate chemistry students who explored the virtual laboratory, with that of a group who received a verbal introduction to the laboratory. The decision to undertake a pilot investigation prior to the first major investigation is consistent with the approach taken by Salzman et al. (1999). To ensure that their attempts to study learning in 3D environments weren't adversely affected by user interface design problems Salzman et al. carried out an initial study focusing primarily on the effectiveness of the user interface before attempting to measure the learning benefits of the resource. They explain this as follows:

> In our first evaluation, we focused on the interaction experience; however, outcomes
> shed light on other issues relating to the learning experience, learning process and
> outcomes, as well as the potential trade-off between designing for interaction vs.
> designing for learning. (p. 18)

After completion of the pilot investigation, two major investigations were carried out, hereafter referred to as Investigation 1 and Investigation 2. Each involved the use of versions of the virtual laboratory by groups of participants followed by tests of their spatial knowledge.

Investigation 1 addressed research questions 3 and 4, relating to user control over view and object manipulation. The performance on written spatial tests of a group of volunteer undergraduate information technology (IT) students who explored the virtual environment (the 'User-control group') was compared with that of a group who used a version of the virtual laboratory which provided an animated tour rather than user controlled movement and object manipulation (the 'Dynamic Views' group). A third group who were given a tour of the real laboratory (the 'Real Laboratory group') was used in order to provide a measure of the effectiveness for spatial learning of the virtual environment compared with a real environment. Although this was not necessary to address the research questions, it was considered desirable in order to be confident that the design of the virtual environment was adequate. Other studies have shown that spatial learning from virtual environment exploration can be close to that from exploration of a similar real environment (Arthur et al., 1997; Richardson et al., 1999).

Investigation 2 addressed all of the research questions, that is, questions 1, 2, 3, 4 and 5. The performance of a group of undergraduate chemistry students who explored the virtual laboratory (the 'User-control group') was compared with that of a group who explored a version of the virtual laboratory providing an animated tour (the 'Dynamic Views group') and with a third group who used a version of the virtual laboratory providing a static tour, that is, a tour without animated view changes (the 'Static Views group').

In this second investigation more extensive object manipulation capability was provided, including the ability to connect items of apparatus together as though setting up an experiment. This addressed one of the limitations of the first major investigation, in which only limited object manipulation was possible. Additionally, User-control participants undertook a more authentic task, that of collecting and setting up the apparatus for an experiment and then putting the items away in their correct storage location. A comparison of the relative performance of the User-control and Dynamic Views participants across the two investigations was intended to shed light on question 5, which relates to learning task design. Practical tests in the real laboratory were also carried out in addition to written spatial tests, and participants also completed a questionnaire.

Table 3.2 shows an overview of the timing, purpose and methods used in each investigation. Further discussion about the design of the environment, the selection and grouping of participants, the learning tasks and tests, is contained in Sections 3.3.2 to 3.3.5. The details about the methods used in each investigation are also summarised in Chapters 4, 5 and 6, which describe the three investigations and the results obtained from each.

Table 3.2
Research summary

Date and task	Purpose	Explanation
February 2002 Pilot investigation	To evaluate the design of the virtual laboratory To evaluate the training process, the learning tasks and the written tests prior to Investigation 1	Ten undergraduate chemistry students were divided into two groups. One group carried out tasks in the virtual laboratory and the other were given a verbal introduction within the laboratory itself. All participants completed a written test on their spatial learning. A few days later the groups were reversed and were then given the same test again. While the 10 participants used the virtual laboratory, they were observed and encouraged to 'think-aloud' and point out problems and possible improvements. A further week later, after completing their first chemistry laboratory practical session, participants undertook a structured interview.
May 2002 Investigation 1	To address questions 3 and 4, which focus on user control over view and object manipulation	Thirty four undergraduate IT students were divided into three groups. One group carried out a task in the real laboratory. A second group carried out a similar task in the virtual laboratory. A third group viewed a series of animated displays generated from the virtual laboratory showing a similar sequence to the task undertaken by the second group. Participants undertook a written test on their spatial learning.
February/ March 2003 Investigation 2	To address questions 1, 2, 3, 4 and 5, which focus on smooth display of view changes, smooth display of object motion, user control over view, object manipulation and learning task design	Ninety two first year undergraduate chemistry students were divided into three groups. One group carried out a task in the virtual laboratory. A second group viewed a series of animated displays generated from the virtual laboratory showing a similar sequence to the first group. A third group viewed a series of still images corresponding to the displays viewed by the second group but without animated transitions between views. Participants undertook a written test on their spatial learning and a week later undertook tasks within the real laboratory. Participants also completed a questionnaire.

3.3.2 Design of the Environments

This section describes the design of the environments used in the study. It begins with a discussion of the broad requirements and initial design decisions. The delivery platform, and the design of the 3D model and the user interface are discussed in subsequent sections.

3.3.2.1 Background and requirements

A virtual environment was required that was of sufficient complexity so that learning of its spatial structure would be non-trivial. In order to explore the importance of smooth view changes and of learner control over view, the environment required an interface and rendering software allowing for both user controlled and system controlled movement through the environment and for both smooth (animated) view changes and for static (non-animated) view changes. Additionally, in order to explore the importance of object manipulation and smooth changes in object position, the environment required an interface allowing the learner to pickup or move objects in some way. Importantly, it was necessary for the environment to allow each of these features to be disabled, so that spatial learning in an environment with each characteristic present or absent could be explored. This last requirement led to the decision to develop a 3D environment specifically for this study rather than using an existing 3D environment.

In order to address the concerns raised by Reeves (1995), it was desirable for the participants to undertake their tasks in an authentic learning context so that they would have a personal reason for developing spatial knowledge of the environment. Consequently, it was seen as desirable for the environment developed to serve the learning needs of a cohort of students in the context of their course of study. The fact that such an environment could potentially continue to be of benefit to students after the conclusion of the research was seen as an additional benefit of this approach. After discussions with colleagues lecturing in chemistry at Charles Sturt University (CSU), it was decided to develop a model of the CSU Wagga Wagga campus undergraduate chemistry teaching laboratory. Chemistry lecturers indicated an interest in using such a virtual environment with their students, and in contributing to the design of the environment.

Chemistry lecturers indicated that many students were quite anxious about their first laboratory sessions and a virtual environment that allowed the students to become familiar with the laboratory and its apparatus had the potential to help alleviate this. The potential for learners to more quickly become productive in their use of the laboratory was seen as an additional benefit. These requirements were seen as consistent with the objectives of this study. The laboratory layout and the structure of the apparatus were seen as being sufficiently complex to make them suitable as the subject of spatial learning tests. Consequently, it was determined that having participants explore versions of an environment modelled on the laboratory, and then testing them on their knowledge of the structure of the laboratory and its apparatus, would allow the research questions about the importance of the various characteristics of 3D environments for spatial learning to be effectively investigated.

3.3.2.2 Delivery Platform

Having made the decision to develop an environment modelled on a chemistry laboratory, the next decision to make was whether to use a desktop or an immersive environment. As discussed in Section 2.2.2, there are a number of usability problems with the use of immersive environments and it is not clear that they have any advantages over desktop environments for spatial learning. Consequently the decision was made to use a desktop rather than an immersive environment. Due to the availability of Microsoft Windows based computer laboratories at Charles Sturt University and convenient access to a Windows based development platform for the researcher, the Windows platform was chosen.

3.3.2.3 Structures and Objects Modelled

The environment included a detailed model of the chemistry laboratory itself along with a preparation room and an equipment room at either end of the laboratory, and a walkway leading to the laboratory entrance. The exteriors of nearby buildings were also modelled, as well as the landscape and some of the trees outside the building. Inside the laboratory all of the main items of furniture and equipment were modelled, along with 30 items of apparatus. When modelling 3D environments, realism can be enhanced through the use of detailed textures on walls, floors and furniture. However, such textures tend to have a high negative impact on rendering performance and thus frame rates. The choice of textures to use was a compromise between realism and performance. In some cases items of equipment were modelled with little detail, but with photographic textures applied. In other cases, flat colour was used on surfaces rather than texture, to improve performance. The use of texture on floor surfaces can assist motion control because it allows the visual changes in the position of the floor to contribute to the overall optic flow, which provides an important cue to the speed of movement (Ware, 1995; Hunt & Waller, 1999). Consequently, a photographic texture was used for the interior floor surface. Appendix A lists the structures and objects included in the 3D model. Figure 3.1, Figure 3.2 and Figure 3.3 show three different views of the virtual laboratory.

Figure 3.1
The virtual laboratory from outside
(version used in Investigation 1)

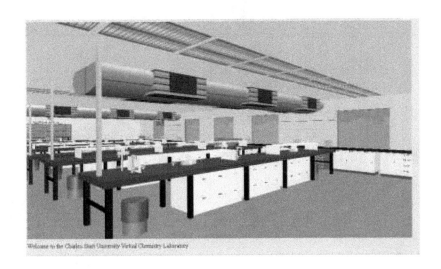

Welcome to the Charles Sturt University Virtual Chemistry Laboratory

Figure 3.2
Looking across the virtual laboratory
(version used in Investigation 1)

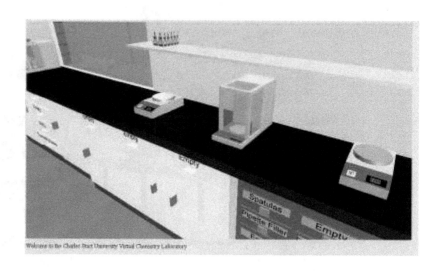

Figure 3.3
Cupboards, drawers and apparatus in the virtual laboratory
(version used in Investigation 1)

3.3.2.4 User Interface

Many 3D environment studies report unexpected difficulty by participants in using the 3D environment. For example, in attempting to explain the lack of a significant difference between the spatial learning of active and passive observers of a desktop 3D environment, Christou and Bulthoff (1999) surmise that "it may have been the case here that the use of the Space Ball (which, for some subjects, proved somewhat cumbersome to control) distracted the active explorers during the learning stages" (p. 1005).

Consequently, the design of the interface for navigation and motion control in the environment and for manipulating objects within the environment is very important. Some of the important interface issues to consider include:

- Visual display parameters such as size of computer monitor, viewing distance, field of view angle and frame rate;

- The use of a first-person view of the environment versus a third-person or 'birds-eye' view;

- Motion and view control mechanisms;

- Object manipulation mechanisms; and

- The provision of navigation cues.

These issues are discussed in the following sections.

3.3.2.5 Visual Display Parameters

The virtual environment runs embedded within the Internet Explorer web browser, however, Internet Explorer was configured to run full-screen, so that none of the tool bars, window borders or menus were visible. That is, only the virtual environment itself was visible.

In the pilot investigation, a menu bar to the left of the 3D environment was provided, which allowed for information about the laboratory (for example safety procedures) and items of apparatus (for example usage procedures) to be selected, along with the ability to move directly to certain positions within the laboratory and to locate specific items of apparatus. A text area below the 3D environment was also provided, and this was used to display information about the laboratory and items of apparatus in response either to menu selections or to selection of items of apparatus within the environment. Options were provided to switch between the three movement modes, 'Walk', 'Pan' and 'Jump'. An option was also provided, allowing for the menu and text frames to be hidden, allowing for a greater part of the screen to be devoted to displaying the 3D environment.

Figure 3.4 and Figure 3.5 show the screen layout of the pilot investigation version of the virtual laboratory. Figure 3.4 shows the normal layout and Figure 3.5 shows the layout after the option to hide the menu and text frame has been chosen.

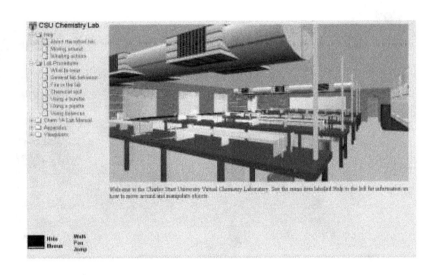

Figure 3.4
Screen layout of the pilot investigation version of the virtual laboratory with menus shown

Figure 3.5
Screen layout of the pilot investigation version of the virtual laboratory with menus hidden

In the two major investigations, the left hand menu bar was not provided and the text area was reduced in size. The text area was only used to display the names of items of apparatus, after selection with the mouse, in these versions. The decision to remove the more detailed information was made because it was surmised that providing additional information beyond that required for spatial learning purposes would distract participants. The versions of the virtual laboratory used by the Dynamic Views and Static Views groups did not allow for selection of items of apparatus with the mouse. However, when the tour took the participant to a position where a particular item of apparatus was displayed, the name of the item was displayed in the text area.

Figure 3.6 shows the screen layout of the Investigation 1 User-control version of the virtual laboratory and Figure 3.7 shows the layout of the corresponding Investigation 2 version. The purpose of the hand icon in the Investigation 2 version is discussed below.

Figure 3.6
Screen layout of the Investigation 1 user-control version of the virtual laboratory

Figure 3.7
Screen layout of the Investigation 2 user-control version of the virtual laboratory

In desktop virtual environments, the field of view provided by the virtual environment doesn't necessarily match the effective field of view of the display, especially if there is no control over the distance that the user sits from the monitor. The field of view provided by the display is the angle between the eye and the edges of the monitor. For rectangular monitors, the horizontal and vertical fields of view will be slightly different. The field of view of the virtual environment is a configurable rendering parameter. Ideally this should match the effective field of view defined by the monitor and the user's seating position. If the effective field of view is smaller than the virtual environment field of view, objects appear smaller or further away than intended or vice versa. This is an important issue if absolute distance estimates are required.

An additional problem is that as the user adjusts their seating position relative to the monitor, they also adjust their effective field of view. For example in attempting to explain the large variance in spatial learning exhibited by participants who used a desktop environment, Patrick et al. (2000) noted that the "participant's seated position when viewing the monitor was not artificially fixed, and it is possible that small movements forward or backward from the display might have altered their field of view, causing differences in their interpretation of the spatial relationships between landmarks in the experimental environment" (p. 484).

In this study, absolute distance estimates were not used in any of the tests and consequently this was less of an issue. The field of view used was the default VRML field of view of 45 degrees and the viewing distance was not controlled but is typically between 50cm and 60cm, which, for a 15 inch monitor (viewing area 30cm by 23cm) is an effective field of view of between 22 and 26 degrees (calculated using vertical monitor size, since in VRML the field of view angle defines the minimum of the horizontal and vertical field of view angles).

The target frame rate for the environment was 12 to 15 frames per second, which is considered to be the minimum that will create the illusion of motion (Chapman & Chapman, 2000). This illusion of motion was considered important for the User-control and Dynamic Views versions of the environment in order to differentiate them from the Static Views version and thus to explore the importance of smooth display of view changes for spatial learning. The actual frame rate within the virtual laboratory varied depending on the complexity of the geometry currently visible. High frame rates occurred when positioned outside the laboratory, looking away from the laboratory, and much lower frame rates occurred when inside the laboratory, looking at complex items of apparatus or laboratory structure. Table 3.3 shows the frame rates achieved from various viewpoints in the version of the virtual laboratory used in each of the two major investigations. The frame rate for animated view changes in the version used by the Dynamic Views groups in Investigations 1 and 2 was the same as for the User-control versions.

Table 3.3 Frame rates achieved by the version of the virtual laboratory used in each major investigation			
	Outside the laboratory looking towards it	Looking from the equipment room doorway across the inside of the laboratory	Looking into the preparation room from the doorway
Investigation 1 version	5 frames per second	6.5 frames per second	11 frames per second
Investigation 2 version	8 frames per second	6.5 frames per second	10 frames per second

3.3.2.6 First Person or Third Person View

The use of third-person and first-person views of the environment are both common within computer games. A third-person view is normally provided in action-adventure games such as the 'Tomb Raider' series (Eidos Interactive, 2004), where complex actions such as ducking, climbing, swimming or object manipulations such as opening cupboards, turning wheels or lighting flares can best be illustrated by viewing one's visual representation (avatar) from a distance. A first-person view is normally provided in shooting games such as the 'Quake series' (Id Software, 2004) and 'Unreal Tournament' (Epic Games, 2004), where a greater sense of realism and suspense can be obtained from a first-person view. Either a first-person or a third-person view could have been chosen for this study. The main reason for choosing a first-person view was that there is potential for the appearance of the avatar to affect the participants' motivation and performance. In earlier research carried out by the researcher, some participants reported that the appearance of their avatar was a factor in their motivation to carry out tasks in a virtual environment (Dalgarno and Scott, 2000). It would be difficult to choose an avatar that had the same psychological connotations for all participants.

3.3.2.7 Motion Control Interface

The Blaxxun Contact VRML browser, which was the chosen rendering environment (see Section 3.4), provides a keyboard movement interface using the arrow keys for forward and backward movement and for turning left or right, in the default movement mode ('Walk' mode). It also provided a mouse-driven movement interface, where clicking and dragging the mouse within the environment allowed for movement in a particular direction, with the length of the drag dictating the speed. This mouse interface, pioneered in the *WebSpace* VRML browser (Mohageg et al., 1996) was found to be more difficult to use than the arrow key interface within the earlier studies carried out by the researcher (Dalgarno and Scott, 2000). Zhai, Kandogan, Smith and Selker (1999) also found that users had difficulty with this type of mouse interface. Consequently, although the mouse interface was not disabled, the keyboard interface was emphasised in participant training and in command summaries developed for participants.

Blaxxun Contact provides a number of options through a menu accessible by right-clicking within the environment. Many of these options were considered to be potentially confusing for new users and consequently this menu was disabled in Investigations 1 and 2. Where functionality available through this menu was required it was instead provided through options always visible within a frame next to the virtual environment or through keyboard operations (such as by holding down the shift key). In this way a simplified interface was provided that needed less training to use than the full Blaxxun Contact interface.

Blaxxun Contact provides a series of movement modes in addition to the default 'Walk' mode. These modes, called 'Slide', 'Examine', 'Pan', 'Fly' and 'Jump' each change the operation of the arrow keys and mouse drags in a particular way. For example, Pan mode allows the participant to look left, right, up and down without moving, and Jump mode allows the participant to click on an object to move very close to it. Blaxxun Contact allows the mode to be changed by pressing a key combination or by choosing an item from the right-click menu. In the pilot investigation, participants were encouraged to use the Walk, Pan and Jump movement modes and visible options alongside the environment were provided for changing between these modes.

There is potential for problems to occur with participants becoming confused about what mode they are in. The mouse icon includes a letter to indicate the current mode, but this was not obvious to participants. The participants in the pilot investigation were able to understand the three movement modes and used them effectively. However, in earlier research carried out by the researcher, problems with recognising or remembering the current mode were encountered by some participants (Dalgarno and Scott, 2000). Similar problems were found by participants in a study by Zhai et al. (1999). Additionally, modal interfaces for motion control have been found to be inefficient because of the requirement to frequently switch between modes (Mackinlay, Card and Robertson, 1990). Consequently, a modeless interface was used in subsequent investigations. In the versions used in Investigations 1 and 2, User-control participants could look (or pan) around by holding down the shift key as they pressed the arrow keys. This provided a similar function to the Pan mode used in the pilot, but without potential confusion about the currently selected mode.

Some participants in the pilot investigation encountered a problem with the Jump facility when, after moving up close to objects, they were unable to easily get back to their previous position. Consequently, no facility for moving up close to an object was provided in Investigation 1. In Investigation 2, it was necessary to provide such an option, because participants needed to be able to look at objects up close, such as the burette and the pipette filler, in order to manipulate their levers and knobs. Consequently, participants of the User-control group were provided with a facility to move close to an object by holding down the F3 key while clicking on the object. They could then return to their previous position by pressing the Home key. Mackinlay et al. (1990), who pioneered the 'Point of Interest' interface for moving towards a selected object, recognised the potential problems of accidentally selecting the wrong object. They proposed that a visual cue be provided to indicate which object is being selected. The ability to undo the movement was in this study considered to be equally effective.

As discussed above, in the version used in the pilot investigation, in addition to the keyboard motion control mechanism, a menu frame was provided next to the environment area, providing the ability to jump to a position within the laboratory or to the position of a selected item of apparatus.

In the pilot investigation some participants had difficulty viewing the inside of drawers, because it was necessary to first move to the drawer, then open the drawer by clicking on it and then change to Pan mode to look into the drawer. The use of the shift key in conjunction with the arrow keys for looking up and down, as implemented in Investigation 1, was intended to address this to some extent. Additionally, to make this easier, in Investigations 1 and 2, when a cupboard or drawer was clicked on, as well as the cupboard or drawer being opened, the participant was moved to a position in front of the cupboard or drawer with a view direction allowing them to see its contents.

As discussed, the versions of the virtual environment used by the Dynamic Views and Static Views groups in Investigations 1 and 2 did not allow free motion control. Instead 'Next View' and 'Previous View' options were provided (see Figure 3.8). The initial view of the environment was outside the laboratory and each time a participant clicked on the Next View option they moved to a new location on a tour of the laboratory. The name of the part of the laboratory they were shown was displayed in the text area. Sometimes when they clicked on Next View they were taken to an item of apparatus and the name of that item was displayed in the text area. In some cases a drawer or cupboard was first opened. As discussed below, certain objects were also picked up, rotated and, in Investigation 2, carried and connected together, simulating the object manipulations performed by the User-control group. In the case of the Dynamic Views group changes in view position were animated, whereas the version used by the Static Views group showed only a series of still images from different positions and orientations.

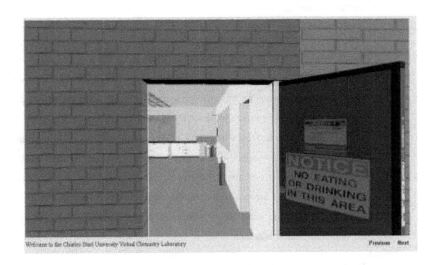

Figure 3.8
Screen layout of the Investigation 1 Dynamic Views and Static Views versions of the virtual laboratory

3.3.2.8 Object manipulation mechanisms

Interaction with cupboards, drawers and doors was relatively straightforward. All cupboards, drawers and doors within the virtual laboratory were programmed so that when the user clicked on them they would open and when clicked again they would close. Interaction mechanisms for examining and working with apparatus were more complex to design.

Providing an easy to use interface within a desktop 3D environment, allowing for object manipulation with six degrees of freedom (movement in the x-y, x-z and y-z planes and rotation around the x, y and z axes) is problematic (see Hand, 1997 for a discussion). One of the main reasons for this problem is the fact that the standard mouse provides only two degrees of freedom. Some CAD environments address this problem by providing a modal interface, where the user can switch the function of the mouse between translation in a specific plane (eg. x-y, x-z, or y-z) and rotation around a specific axis. As discussed above, earlier research carried out by the researcher found that modal interfaces for motion control were difficult to use for many users (Dalgarno & Scott, 2000). It was expected that similar difficulties would be encountered for modal object manipulation interfaces.

For the purposes of the pilot investigation, it was not seen as necessary to provide for full object manipulation capability. Instead, the ability to drag objects around within a single plane (for example the surface of a desk) was provided, along with the ability to 'pick up' an object and place it in an area to the bottom left of the screen, by double-clicking on it. Once picked up, an object could be carried to a new location and 'dropped' by again double-clicking on it. Figure 3.9 shows a screen dump showing an object that has been picked up. Additionally the menu frame included options to move certain items of apparatus to a specific location.

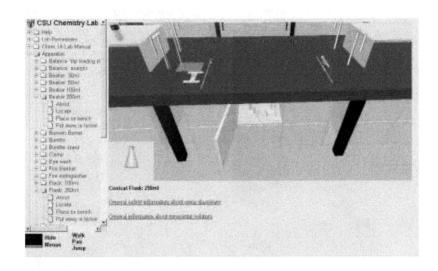

Figure 3.9
Screen layout of the pilot investigation version of the virtual laboratory after
picking up a conical flask

Problems were encountered with the interface for dragging objects, with some users dragging objects into adjacent cupboards and not being able to get them back. Consequently, in Investigation 1, the ability to drag objects around was not provided. A mechanism for picking up objects was provided for User-control participants, with such objects placed in a suspended position in the middle of the screen. Objects that had been picked up could then be rotated by dragging them with the mouse, or alternatively by clicking on them. After one click the object rotated left-right and after another click the object rotated up-down. In this Investigation 1 version, objects could not be placed elsewhere in the laboratory. Figure 3.10 shows the appearance of an object that has been picked up.

Figure 3.10
Screen layout of the Investigation 1 version of the virtual laboratory after picking
up a Bunsen burner

In Investigation 2, in which participants in the User-control group carried out a more authentic task within the environment, it was necessary to provide an interface that allowed for the assembly of items of apparatus. Initially an interface modelled on that described by Chen, Mountford and Sellen (1988) was developed. With this interface, when an object was clicked on, a transparent sphere was shown around it, and this sphere could then be dragged left-right, top-bottom or around in a circle to provide for three degrees of rotation. Usability tests suggested that with some training this interface could be mastered. However, it was determined that the apparatus connection tasks would have taken too long if participants had to rotate each item to the correct orientation and thus this interface was not used. Instead, an interface was developed that allowed for objects to be dragged on top of other items of apparatus and for these items of apparatus to then be automatically 'snapped' together. Initial usability tests revealed that in order to ensure that an object could always be dragged on top of any other visible object, the drag plane had to vary depending on the position of the viewer. The interface developed ensured that objects were always dragged in a plane perpendicular to the view direction. Objects could be 'snapped together' by dragging and releasing one object either behind or in front of the other object. A highlight colour was used to indicate when an object was in a position where it could be dropped. Figure 3.11 shows a series of screen captures illustrating the connecting together of items of apparatus.

Figure 3.11
The process of connecting objects together using the Investigation 2 user control
version of the virtual laboratory (mouse pointer simulated as black arrow)
The participant drags the object (left), the target object is highlighted when the
object can be dropped (right), and when released the object snaps to its connected
position (bottom)

Once the apparatus was assembled, participants of the User-control group in Investigation 2 were required to carry out steps equivalent to the steps they would carry out if they were to measure liquid between a series of vessels. Part of this task required them to operate a burette tap and a lever and dial on a pipette filler. The burette tap is illustrated in Figure 3.12 and the parts of the pipette filler are illustrated in Figure 3.13.

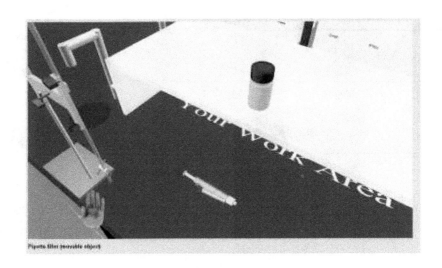

Pipette filler (moveable object)

Figure 3.12
The pipette filler lever and dial

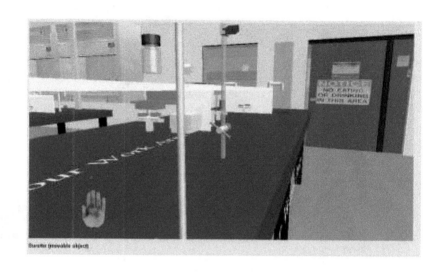

Figure 3.13
The burette tap

Objects could also be dragged and dropped on top of a hand icon. Such items were then able to be carried around the laboratory and placed in one of a series of preset positions. Figure 3.14 shows an object being carried in the hand. This interface was inspired by the 'inventories' used by many role-playing and adventure games, which allow for objects to be collected and carried, with such objects displayed in an area usually at the bottom of the screen (see Rollings and Adams, 2003 for a discussion). On the advice of chemistry lecturers who wanted to discourage students from carrying more than one item at a time in the real laboratory, the interface was designed in such a way that users were restricted to carrying one item at a time.

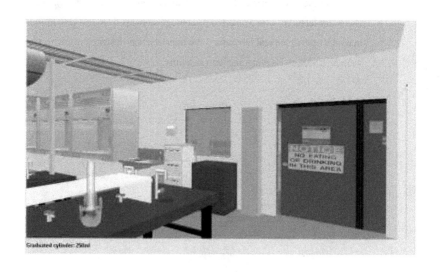

Figure 3.14
A held object in the Investigation 2 version of the virtual laboratory

In addition to not allowing motion control, the version of the virtual laboratory used by the Dynamic Views and Static Views groups did not allow user controlled object manipulation. Instead, at certain points on the recorded tour, objects were automatically picked up and rotated and in the case of Investigation 2, carried, placed elsewhere in the laboratory, and connected together. The version used by the Dynamic Views groups showed animated movement and rotation of objects, whereas the version used by the Static Views group showed only a series of static views of the objects in different positions and at different orientations.

3.3.2.9 Navigation Cues

Important issues in the design of virtual environments are the choice of navigation cues and navigational support tools. Ruddle et al. (1997) note that "empirical evidence suggests that users frequently have problems navigating VEs when supplementary aids (eg. maps, artificial landmarks, etc) are not provided" (p. 143). Darken and Sibert (1996) propose a set of principles for designing the structure of a virtual environment, which they term 'organisational principles', along with a set of principles for the design of a virtual map, which they suggest should always be provided in the environment. Their proposed organisational principles are as follows: divide the large world into distinct small parts; organise the small parts under a simple principle, such as using a grid; and provide frequent directional cues, such as directional landmarks or a virtual compass.

It is important to note that Darken and Sibert state that their proposed principles are primarily aimed at large virtual worlds, that is, worlds "that cannot be viewed from a single vantage point and consequently require extensive movement to navigate" (p. 50). Because the virtual laboratory is a relatively simple environment, it was not considered necessary to sub-divide the environment into smaller spaces or to provide maps or artificial landmarks. However, it is worth noting that one participant in the pilot study suggested that the provision of a small two-dimensional map within the environment, with an indication of the user's current position, would have aided navigation. This type of a map has also been proposed by Ruddle et al. (1997).

3.3.3 Selection and Grouping of Participants

The selection of participants and the allocation of participants to groups can have an important effect on the validity of the results obtained. Some of the issues to be considered are the following:

- Volunteer participation versus compulsory participation as part of a learner's study;

- Selection of participants with an interest in achieving the intended learning outcomes versus those without such an interest;

- Number of participants;

- Controlling for individual differences such as gender, age or prior experience; and

- Testing and controlling for individual aptitudes such as spatial ability or vision.

Volunteer participation appears on the surface to be the most ethical. However, as discussed in Section 3.2.2 (and see for example Reeves, 1995), if the learners have no reason to learn the concepts being measured then it could be argued that the learning situation is so artificial that the results will not transfer to a more realistic learning situation. Thus, choosing participants who are studying a related subject, ideally with participation as an integrated part of a learner's study, can be more appropriate. Many studies reported in the literature used participants who volunteered in order to obtain credit points towards a degree. Requiring undergraduate students to participate in a certain number of research projects, or to provide credit points for doing so, is common practice in the psychology discipline. The rationale is that they would benefit from exposure to the research methods used in the project. Clearly the issue of the lack of authenticity in the learning situation remains in this case.

In the pilot investigation, 10 volunteer chemistry students were used as participants. These students were recruited during orientation week, that is, the week before the commencement of their first semester of tertiary study. Since participants were tested on their spatial knowledge of the virtual laboratory, which was modelled on the real laboratory, it was important that participants had not been in the real laboratory prior to their involvement in the study. The pilot investigation was carried out in February 2002, prior to the first chemistry class and consequently none of the students had ever been in the chemistry laboratory. The students had an interest in learning about the chemistry laboratory, as they would shortly commence their practical work in the corresponding real laboratory. Because the pilot investigation involved intensive observations of the participants using the virtual laboratory as well as interviews with each participant, it was considered appropriate to use a small number of participants. Because there was no attempt to obtain statistically significant data from this investigation, the small number of participants was not considered a problem.

Investigation 1 was carried out in May of 2002 and consequently it was not possible to use chemistry students as participants. At CSU Wagga Wagga, introductory chemistry subjects run only in the first teaching session, and laboratory sessions normally begin in the first, second or third week of session. Consequently, given the importance of participants having no prior knowledge of the laboratory, if chemistry students were to be used, the investigation would have had to be delayed for over six months. Thus, in Investigation 1, IT students were used rather than chemistry students. The students volunteered to participate. None of the students had ever been in the chemistry laboratory. Thirty four participants volunteered. This number was considered sufficient to obtain statistically significant results. Fewer participants had been used in a number of other published studies, which either explored the use of 3D environments or explored spatial learning using a 3D environment as a research instrument (see, for example Henry and Furness, 1993; Witmer and Kline, 1998) and in each case statistically significant results were obtained.

Investigation 2 was carried out in February 2003, at the beginning of the first semester of study and so once again it was feasible to use chemistry students. It was desirable in this investigation to use a larger number of participants than in Investigation 1. The tests in Investigation 1 found no significant difference between the spatial learning of the User-control and Dynamic Views groups, and although there were reasons hypothesised for this, limitations in the sample size could not be ruled out as a contributing factor. Discussions with the lecturer of one of the introductory chemistry subjects at CSU led to the decision to make the use of the virtual laboratory a formal part of the laboratory orientation process for all students in the subject. In all, 92 students participated in this investigation, although only 80 participants' results were used. Eleven students' results were not used because they had been in the laboratory prior to the investigation and one additional student withdrew due to discomfort.

The evidence for gender differences in learning performance using virtual environments is inconclusive. Hunt and Waller (1999) discuss a number of studies which found male superiority in spatial tasks, including a study by Arthur et al. (1997) of "retention of information after examining a scene" (p. 44), a study by Matthews (1987) of "exploring an area" (p. 44) and studies by Anooshian and Young (1981) and Lawton, Charleston and Zieles (1996) of "traversing a pre-specified route" (p. 44). In general, Arthur et al. suggest that "women tend to use strategies appropriate to tracking and piloting, while men use strategies appropriate for navigation" (p. 44). Gillner and Mallot (1998) on the other hand, noted in their study that "subjects differed strongly in terms of the number of errors made when searching a goal as well as in the quality of their distance estimates" but that "no clustering in different groups can be obtained from our data" and in particular "no significant gender differences were found." (p. 458). Waller et al. (1998) found gender differences in their study, and conclude that the common practice of controlling for gender in 3D environment studies is necessary.

In the pilot investigation, the participants were recruited from students enrolled in a pharmacy degree, a course which attracts more females than males. Consequently, there were 8 female and 2 male participants. The two males were allocated to separate groups to ensure an even gender distribution between the groups. In Investigation 1, students were undergraduate IT students, a course in which there are substantially more males than females. Consequently there were 20 male and 14 female participants. Six males and five females were allocated to the Dynamic Views group, seven males and five females were allocated to the User-control group, and seven males and four females were allocated to the Real Laboratory group. The slightly uneven allocation was due to the fact that some volunteer students failed to attend their allocated session, and so did not participate.

In Investigation 2, for which participation was a formal part of the students' course, there were 92 participants, although as discussed above, there were only 80 participants, 31 females and 49 males, whose results were used. The participants were randomly allocated to three groups. However, because some students did not attend their allocated session, the number of students in each group differed slightly. There were 10 females and 14 males in the User-control group, 9 females and 17 males in the Dynamic Views group and 12 females and 18 males in the Static Views group.

Earlier research carried out by the researcher found a tendency for younger participants to be much more comfortable than older participants in using a 3D environment (Dalgarno and Scott, 2000). In this study the participants were all undergraduate university students, and thus were within a relatively narrow age range. The age range of participants in the pilot investigation was 17 to 28. Participants were not asked their age in Investigation 1. In Investigation 2 the age range was 18 to 39. In Investigation 2 the age of participants was only gathered after they had explored the virtual environment and consequently could not be used for grouping purposes. Gathering this data was intended to allow for a check that the ages of participants were balanced across the groups.

A number of researchers have tested their participants' spatial ability prior to the use of a virtual environment, allowing them to either exclude participants with exceptionally high or low ability, or to ensure an even distribution of spatial skill across groups. For example, Patrick et al. (2000) carried out a pre-test of spatial abilities, Educational Testing Service Surface Development Test, VZ3, an "instrument to measure ability for mental manipulation of 2-dimensional objects into 3 dimensions" (p. 480) and excluded from their study the data from participants scoring more than one standard deviation from the mean in either direction in their results. Nineteen out of 69 participants were excluded for this reason. It is also interesting to note that the "pretest score was found to be a significant predictor of posttest score for all 69 participants" (p. 483). This last finding is at odds with Richardson et al. (1999), who suggest that conventional psychometric measures of mental spatial manipulation measure something quite different to the skills of geographic direction awareness, landmark memory or route knowledge within a real environment, and further that "there is currently no psychometric spatial abilities test that is a good predictor of environmental spatial ability" (p. 743).

Waller et al. (1998) administered the Guilford Zimmerman standardized test of spatial orientation ability at the beginning of their study. They also required that participants could navigate through a test virtual environment in under a set time before they were allowed to proceed. They note that four of their subjects were unable to do so and were thus randomly re-assigned to one of their three non-virtual conditions. They found that the test was 'moderately predictive' of a participant's overall performance on a test of spatial knowledge after learning of a virtual maze, but not of blindfolded navigation performance.

In each of the investigations carried out in this study, sufficient time was required to be able to train participants in the use of a virtual environment, carry out the learning tasks in the virtual laboratory and complete a written spatial test. All of this took up to two hours to complete. Because of this, it was decided not to also include a spatial abilities test. To complete such a test prior to commencing the use of the virtual environment may have resulted in the participants becoming fatigued due to the extended period of their involvement. To complete such a test at an earlier or later time was also considered a problem. In the pilot investigation and Investigation 1, where volunteer participants were used, it was considered likely that if they were required to come for an additional session insufficient participants would have volunteered. In Investigation 2, where participation was carried out as a formal part of the students' chemistry study, there was no scope in the timetable to allow for an additional session where they could complete a spatial skills test.

An alternative to administering a spatial skills test is to ask participants to rate their own spatial ability. For example, Kozlowski and Bryant (1977) found that the answer to the question, "how good is your sense of direction" (p. 591) is a strong predictor of performance on a range of spatial tasks. Based on this finding, Witmer et al. (1996) used a similar question to gauge participants' spatial ability prior to their own study. This approach was used in Investigation 1, with participants asked to indicate the degree to which they agreed or disagreed with the statement, 'you have a good sense of direction', by placing a stroke on a line with very strongly agree at one end and very strongly disagree at the other end. Participants were also asked to indicate the extent to which they agreed with the statement, 'when you use a street directory or a map you normally turn it around to match the direction you are going'. The Pearson correlation between the Investigation 1 responses to the two spatial ability questions indicated that they did not correlate significantly ($p=0.182$). This suggests that they were testing different aspects of spatial ability or that one or both were not testing spatial ability at all. The responses also did not correlate highly with the results on any of the spatial test items (see the results section of Chapter 5 for further discussion). As a result of this, in Investigation 2, an alternative statement, 'you are good at finding your way around unfamiliar places', was used.

Because these questions were answered by the participants at the time that they completed their written tests, that is, after virtual environment exploration, these questions were not used for grouping purposes. Rather, the data was gathered to allow for a check of whether spatial skill was evenly distributed across the groups in each investigation.

As well as excluding participants with very high or very low spatial skills, some researchers have also excluded participants with substantial experience with 3D software, such as CAD systems or computer games (see for example Patrick et al., 2000). Patrick et al. also excluded participants without 20/20 vision (either naturally or while wearing glasses or contact lenses). In this study such participants were not excluded.

However, as discussed above, it was necessary to exclude participants with prior exposure to the chemistry laboratory. In addition to prior exposure to the CSU chemistry laboratory having the potential to confound the results, extensive prior exposure to laboratory work in other chemistry laboratories could have been an advantage. Consequently, an additional two questions asking the highest level of chemistry studied and the year in which this study occurred were administered at the time of the spatial test in each investigation. Because these questions were completed after exploration of the virtual laboratory, they could not be used for grouping purposes. Rather, the data was gathered to allow for later analysis and in particular to allow a check that chemistry experience was balanced across groups in each investigation.

3.3.4 Learning Task Design

It is generally accepted that the effectiveness of educational media cannot be judged independently of the instructional design used, and particularly the learning tasks carried out (Clark, 1983; Kozma, 1994). Some of the issues to consider in designing learning tasks for spatial learning in 3D environments are:

- The use of open ended exploration versus structured tasks;

- The need for learning task equivalency across groups, so that tasks performed by one group don't provide them with a view of the environment that advantages them on the test items;

- Control of time spent in the environment and control of distance travelled within the environment, across groups;

- The methods of training participants to use the virtual environment interface; and

- Having participants undertake tasks individually or as a group in a computer laboratory.

These issues are discussed in turn in the following sections.

3.3.4.1 Exploration versus structured tasks

An important decision to make in designing 3D environment studies is the degree of structure to impose on the participants as they explore the environment. For example, learners could be advised to follow a particular route through the environment or could be allowed to navigate freely. Another possibility is to provide them with a task to carry out such as locating certain landmarks or objects within the environment.

In Investigation 1, User-control participants were encouraged to freely explore the laboratory. They were asked to learn the layout of the laboratory, locate as many items of apparatus as they could, and to learn the structure of each item. They were asked to indicate which items of apparatus they located by ticking a list provided and to make any additional notes that they thought would help them to remember the layout of the laboratory and its apparatus.

Participants in the Dynamic Views group were also asked to learn the layout of the laboratory, locate as many items of apparatus as they could, and to learn the structure of each item. They were also provided with a list of apparatus. As discussed in Section 3.3.2.7, the version of the virtual laboratory that they used had no motion control capability except for buttons labelled 'Next View' and 'Previous View'. These buttons allowed the user to move to successive positions along the pre-recorded tour, which took them around the laboratory and showed them all items of apparatus. This tour included 210 positions within the laboratory and apparatus display steps. That is, the participant was required to click the Next View button 210 times to complete the tour.

Analysis of the results of the spatial learning tests in Investigation 1 indicated that there was a need to refine the learning task. In Investigation 2, participants in the User-control group undertook a more specific task, which involved collecting a series of items of apparatus, assembling the items as though preparing to undertake an experiment and then putting the items away again.

Participants were given a printed worksheet (see Appendix M) listing a series of tasks to complete in the virtual laboratory. The first task was to locate 11 items of apparatus and carry these items to a bench in the lab. While doing so participants were also asked to familiarise themselves with 10 specific laboratory features and furniture. Participants were also verbally asked to tick on a list each item of apparatus, laboratory feature and item of furniture once located. If all items were not found after 20 minutes, participants were told where to find the remaining items. If all items were not collected after 30 minutes, a version of the environment with all items collected and placed on the desk was loaded.

The second task was to connect the items together following a series of specific instructions provided on a worksheet, which simulated the process they would follow if they were to undertake an experiment. Their third task was to disassemble the apparatus, again following a series of specific instructions, and their last task was to put the items of apparatus away again. It was surmised that successful completion of this series of tasks would have required participants to learn the layout of the laboratory and the structure of the apparatus.

Participants of the Dynamic Views and Static Views groups in Investigation 2 instead viewed a series of images equivalent to what they would have seen had they undertaken this task, again with the pace controlled through 'Next View' and 'Previous View' options. This included 429 positions within the laboratory and apparatus display steps. That is, the participants were required to click the Next View button 429 times to see the complete series of views. As discussed in Section 3.3.2.7, the difference between the versions used by these groups was that the Dynamic Views participants were shown animated transitions between views, whereas the Static Views participants were shown only a series of static images. They were given a similar worksheet to the User-control participants so that they had a similar sense for the overall task (see Appendix N). Participants were also asked to tick each item of apparatus, laboratory location and item of furniture once located.

3.3.4.2 Potential group bias due to differing views

Another important issue to consider is the question of whether the learning tasks carried out by participants of one group might expose them to views of the environment that advantaged them on certain test items. For example, Gabrielli, Rogers and Scaife (2000) found that one test item indicated that active exploration was more effective than passive exploration and that there was no significant difference between survey and route exploration. However, another item indicated that there was no significant difference between active and passive exploration and that survey exploration was more effective than route exploration. They explained these results in terms of matches between the test tasks and the exploration conditions.

This type of problem is particularly likely to occur when controlling the view of the environment provided during exploration (for example, the way that it is controlled in the Dynamic Views and Static Views groups), and then using a specific view during testing (for example the use of tests requiring the recognition of certain views or the drawing of views from a particular view position). For example, a study by Arthur et al. (1997) found that participants who viewed an environment from a single fixed viewpoint performed better on a map-drawing task than participants who explored the environment and participants who explored a 3D model of the same environment. They suggested that this finding was due to the fact that the single fixed viewpoint was from a position similar to the viewpoint for a topological map, and this view of the environment may not have been experienced by either of the other two groups.

One approach to eliminating differing views of the environment as a factor in comparing the performance of active and passive participants was that taken by Christou and Bulthoff (1999). They paired passive viewers with active viewers, with each passive viewer seeing a movie of an active viewer's observations. This approach ensures that passive viewers do not see a more efficient or complete view of the environment than active viewers.

This problem is likely to be very important for large virtual environments, in which participants might not ever see all of the environment, or in which participants might frequently become lost or at least be unsure of where they are within the environment. The virtual laboratory is a relatively simple environment, and thus it was surmised that participants would see all of the environment in a relatively short time and would not become lost. Consequently, in Investigations 1 and 2, no attempt was made to ensure that the Dynamic Views and Static Views participants saw the same views of the environment as the User-control participants. Instead specific learning tasks were provided to guide the participants on their exploration. Pilot studies indicated that in each case the tasks that the User-control participants were to carry out would ensure that they would view the laboratory from many different positions in many different directions and that consequently there would be a sufficient degree of equivalence of exposure.

3.3.4.3 Controlling time versus controlling distance

The issue of controlling time across the different learning conditions is one that can be approached in various ways. One approach, if comparing real navigation with virtual environment navigation for spatial learning, is to allow the real and virtual navigation groups to travel the same distance even if the virtual environment group travels faster or slower. Alternatively, Richardson et al. (1999) ensured that each participant spent the same time learning an environment from a map or navigating through a real or virtual environment, but slowed the speed of movement through the virtual environment to be equal to normal walking speed.

In Investigations 1 and 2 all groups were exposed to the virtual laboratory (or in the case of the Real Laboratory group, the laboratory itself) for the same time. In Investigation 1 the allocated time was 40 minutes and in Investigation 2, for which the task carried out was more detailed, the allocated time was 60 minutes. Participants in the Dynamic Views and Static Views groups completed their tour in well under the allocated time in each case and were encouraged to go through the tour again in order to ensure that they were engaged within the environment for the same time as the User-control group. Given that participants could view the main part of the laboratory by looking around from a single position, the relative speed of movement through the environment was not considered to be a factor in how much of the laboratory they saw, and so speed of movement through the virtual laboratory was not controlled.

3.3.4.4 Training in use of the interface

Another issue to consider is the type of training in the use of the 3D interface provided. If the study includes a comparison, for example, of a group using a 3D environment and a group exploring a corresponding real environment or some alternative computer-based resource, there is normally a need for the 3D environment group to spend additional time learning the interface. If this training is carried out in the virtual environment, this will result in unequal exposure to the environment, confounding the results. The usual approach is to develop a training environment with the same user interface as the main environment but with a different and normally simpler layout (see for example Ruddle et al., 1999; Richardson et al., 1999).

In this study an existing 3D environment based on a model of the National Gallery of Ireland (McAtamney, 2000) was tailored in each investigation to have the same user interface as the virtual laboratory used in that investigation. Additionally, a version that matched the Dynamic Views interface was developed. In Investigation 1, the Dynamic Views group and the User-control group began with 10 minutes of training using this environment. However, it was found that participants of the Dynamic Views group had no difficulty mastering the interface. Consequently, in Investigation 2 User-control participants undertook 10 minutes of training but no training was provided for the Dynamic Views or Static Views groups.

3.3.4.5 Individual versus group participation

Another issue to consider was whether to put participants through the virtual environment individually or together as a group. Many published studies involved participants working individually (see for example Witmer et al., 1996; Riecke, van Veen & Bulthoff, 2002). The likely reason for this is that specialised hardware was used and only one set-up was available. This is likely to be the case even for desktop environment studies, which until recently required an expensive graphics workstation. Only recently have standard desktop computers had the graphics capability to allow 3D environments to be used effectively. For this study a laboratory of computers with sufficient graphics capability was available and consequently, the learning was undertaken using individual machines for each participant in a computer laboratory, with multiple participants undertaking their exploration simultaneously. In the pilot investigation, each group of five participants undertook their exploration together. In Investigation 1, there were two session times for each group, with numbers in each session varying from three to eight. In Investigation 2, there were two session times and participants in the three groups undertook their learning simultaneously in separate computer laboratories. The number of participants in each computer laboratory during each session varied from 10 to 15.

3.3.5 Spatial Test Design

This section describes the tests used to measure spatial learning in each investigation. The final written test instruments can be found in Appendix J and Appendix O. The tests assessed two aspects of participants' spatial knowledge, knowledge of the overall environment and knowledge of the apparatus. Tests of spatial knowledge of an environment can be classified according to Thorndyke's categories of spatial knowledge discussed in Section 2.5, that is, tests of landmark knowledge, tests of route knowledge and tests of configurational knowledge (see for example Thorndyke and Hayes-Roth, 1982). Tests of spatial knowledge of objects include tests of recognition of objects by name and tests requiring recall of object structure.

Landmark and route knowledge are particularly important for larger environments, where the ability to find a path from one location to another without getting lost is of prime importance. The chemistry laboratory consists of one main room as well as a walkway, an equipment room and a preparation room (see Figure 3.15 for a map of the laboratory). Learners are unlikely to become lost, and recall of routes is not necessary. The spatial learning within the virtual laboratory that is most important is the location of items of furniture such as desks, shelves, storage cupboards and sinks, along with the location of items of apparatus. This is configurational knowledge. Knowledge of the name and structure of apparatus is also important. The following sections discuss methods for testing configuration spatial knowledge of an environment, and methods for testing spatial knowledge of objects.

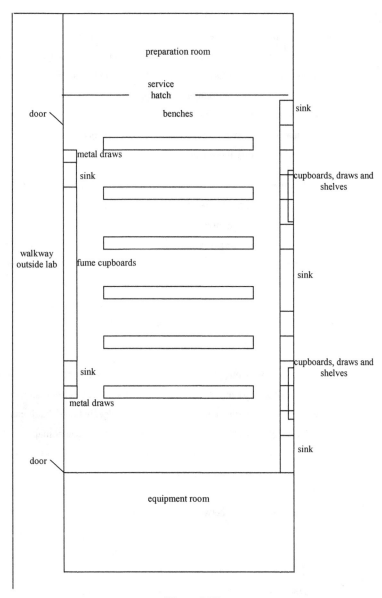

Figure 3.15
Topological map of the virtual laboratory

3.3.5.1 Testing spatial knowledge of an environment

There are a number of approaches to measuring configuration knowledge. The most common are map drawing, estimation of the distance from one position to another, and estimation of the direction from one location to another. Other approaches include requiring the participant to find their way between locations in either the virtual environment or a real environment, with measurements of distance travelled, time taken or the number of errors as measures of spatial knowledge. Another approach is to provide a series of drawn maps, some containing errors and some correct, and ask participants to identify the correct ones.

Given that there were a number of aspects of spatial knowledge to be measured (for example layout of furniture, position of apparatus and structure of apparatus) it was necessary to include a number of spatial test items in each investigation. Additionally, given the number of alternative approaches available for measuring configurational knowledge and the fact that the literature does not suggest that any one approach is better than the others, it was decided to use more than one approach for testing each aspect. As a result, in Investigation 1, seven spatial test items were used (labelled Part A to Part G) and in Investigation 2, five spatial test items were used (labelled Part B to Part F). These are described in the following paragraphs.

The ability to draw a map is a common way to test the degree to which a person has formed a configurational model of the space. Witmer et al. (1996) advocate the use of a sketch map for measuring configurational knowledge, but note that it can be difficult to score the learner's map. Techniques for scoring of participants' maps are discussed in Section 3.3.7. Hunt and Waller (1999) note that "a good map is always evidence of a good [cognitive] representation, but a bad map may simply be a sign of a poor artist" (p. 8). They suggest the following alternatives to map drawing: choosing between a correct and an incorrect map, or between correct and incorrect views of an environment; filling in blank areas of a map; and construction of a map from blocks or shapes cut out of paper. Wilson et al. (1997) used the approach of requiring participants to fill in blank areas of a map. Specifically, they required participants to draw a map of a building given a piece of paper showing a map with one room already drawn.

In Investigation 1, Part C of the test required participants to draw a sketch of the laboratory showing all fixed furniture, doors and windows, given a plan of the laboratory with the external walkway and the two interior walls shown. Part D was similar, also requiring participants to draw a sketch of the laboratory, but this time given a list of specific items of furniture, doors and windows to include. In this item, if there were multiples of a particular item of furniture this number was listed next to its name. Eleven items were listed, and counting multiple occurrences, 43 items were required on the map. Colour photos were also provided of each item, to ensure that recall of the names of items was not an issue. Pearson's Correlation Coefficients indicated that scores on these two items were highly correlated. Because of this and in order to accommodate some additional test items, in Investigation 2 only the second of these items was used (labelled Part D on the Investigation 2 test). The item was modified slightly in Investigation 2, with 9 items of furniture listed and a total of 41 items including multiple occurrences.

Patrick et al. (2000) tested participants' spatial knowledge by asking them to place ten 3cm by 3cm foam squares on a 1m square piece of paper, with each square labelled with a landmark from within the virtual environment. This tested participants' knowledge of the location of objects or landmarks without requiring them to be able to recall their size or shape. An alternative approach is for participants to indicate the location of landmarks by making a written mark on a topological map. For example, Ruddle et al. (1997), in replicating a famous study by Thorndyke and Hayes-Roth (1982), required participants to indicate the position of named landmarks on a piece of paper which showed the position of other named locations. An approach similar to this was used for testing participants' knowledge of the location of apparatus in Part F of the test in each investigation. Participants were asked to indicate with a cross and a number the location of each item on a topological plan of the laboratory. The plan provided to participants contained all doors, windows, benches and storage compartments. Colour photos of each item of apparatus were provided, to ensure that recall of the names of items was not a factor. In Investigation 1, 10 items were required to be positioned. Participants were asked to indicate multiple positions if an item of apparatus could be found in more than one location, but the number of occurrences was not given to them. Three of the items could be found in two locations, and thus 13 positions were to be identified. In

Investigation 2, 11 items were required to be positioned, none of which appeared in more than one location.

A common spatial learning test is one that assesses the ability of the participant to identify the distance or the direction from one location to another. However, a number of studies have indicated that ability to estimate the absolute distance between positions in an environment after virtual environment exploration is very difficult. Richardson et al. (1999) note the potential problems of using absolute distance estimates, noting that such estimates can have very high variances. In their study the average total route distance estimate was 457 feet, but the highest was 3000 feet. They suggest that relative distance estimates can be more suitable. They use correlations between objective distances and estimated distances as a measure of relative distance performance. Hunt and Waller (1999) also note the problems involved in using absolute distance estimation as a measure of spatial knowledge, stating that "distance estimates are psychophysical functions of actual distance, and are not equivalent to actual distances even when a person looking at [*sic*] the distance to be estimated" (p. 9). For the purposes of this study, recall of absolute size or distance is not of major importance. The ability to position locations on a map requires recall of relative distance and this was considered to be adequate.

A number of techniques are available for measuring recall of the direction from one location to another. Wilson et al. (1997) used a mechanical pointing device to test participants' ability to point to non-visible locations within the environment, as well as a similar virtual pointing device in the virtual environment. Richardson et al. (1999) also used a mechanical device. They describe their method as follows:

> *Direction estimates were made with a rigid circular dial with a wire pointer. The dial measured 25cm in diameter. A single radius line, visible on top of the dial, was used to orient the dial to the participant, and direction estimates were read off the bottom of the dial, which was marked in single degree increments. (p. 743)*

Witmer et al. (1996) measured participants' configuration knowledge by requiring them to estimate the distance and direction from three locations to four goal sites and to draw a line from a dot on a piece of paper to the point they believed to be the location of the goal site. They term this technique the 'projective convergence technique'. Measurements derived from these estimates include consistency (using the perimeter of the triangle formed by linking the endpoints drawn from each citing location to a specific goal), accuracy (distance from geometric centre of the triangle to the goal), average distance error (using lengths of vectors), and average miss distance (using estimated target positions). Hunt and Waller (1999) discuss a technique for measuring configurational knowledge, similar to the projective convergence technique, which they term 'mental triangulation'. The idea is that if the person has an accurate spatial model, the points at the end of three estimation vectors should coincide.

In Investigations 1 and 2, Part E of the test drew on ideas from both of these approaches. Rather than positioning participants within the environment and requiring them to point in the direction of a named location, participants were shown a series of six photographs taken from positions within the laboratory and were asked to indicate the position and direction of the camera on a topological plan of the laboratory, with the external walkway and interior walls shown. Participants indicated the position and direction of the camera by ruling a line from the camera position to the wall in the direction of the camera.

In Investigation 1, Part G of the test required participants to recall the location of 10 items of apparatus by annotating one of a series of 10 colour photos of the laboratory, making up a 360-degree panorama (see Figure 3.16). The panorama was provided in colour on a computer and they recorded the position of each item by annotating a printed black and white copy of the panoramic photos. Participants were also given a colour photo of each item. Some students found it difficult to understand the requirements of this question (for example they just indicated which photograph contained the item of apparatus rather than the position of the item within the photo). Because of this and because of constraints in the time available for testing, this item was not used in Investigation 2.

Figure 3.16
Images making up a panorama provided in test Part G in Investigation 1

An alternative to written tests for measuring spatial knowledge is to require participants to undertake tasks either in a virtual or a real environment. For example, Waller et al. (1998) recorded their participants' behaviour in attempting to navigate through the real environment blindfolded as their main method of measuring spatial knowledge. Specifically, they measured the time taken and the number of times the participants bumped into walls.

In Investigation 2, participants undertook two test tasks within the real laboratory one week after completing the virtual laboratory task. The tasks were carried out individually. The first task was to locate 10 items of apparatus. Each item name was read out and participants were required to walk to the location within the laboratory where they could find the item. If after 30 seconds they had not located the item they moved on to the next item. The total time was recorded, along with the specific items located and the total number of items located. The items participants were required to find were the same items they were required to locate in the virtual laboratory, except that a reagent bottle was not included.

The second task required participants to carry out a series of operations using a set of apparatus. Specifically, they were required to burette some water into a flask and pipette some water from the flask into a beaker. The operation of a burette tap and a pipette filler was part of the apparatus manipulation task performed in the virtual environment, although the measuring and pouring of water were not simulated. The operation required to be carried out was read out verbally and participants were instructed to ask for help if necessary. For each operation a critical step was identified and observation notes were made indicating whether this critical step was carried out immediately, after delay, after experimenting, after verbal assistance or never. Participants were not given a time limit for the tasks and the time taken was not recorded. However, all participants were able to complete the task with or without assistance in less than 5 minutes.

3.3.5.2 Testing spatial knowledge of objects

A great deal of research involving object recognition in 3D environments has been carried out with a focus on determining whether we hold view-dependent or view-independent cognitive representations of objects (see Bulthoff et al., 1995 for a review).

A typical approach (for example Tarr & Pinker, 1989) is to expose participants to a virtual object from certain viewpoints and to then test them on their recognition of this object, for example by indicating which of a series of object views (both seen views and novel views) match and do not match the original object. The time taken to identify the correct object is normally measured, as it is an indication of the degree of processing required. If a view-invariant representation is held the recognition time should be similar for all novel views, whereas if a view-dependent representation is held, the time will vary depending on the closeness of the view to those views already seen.

In this study there are two aspects of object recognition that are important. The first is simply the ability to identify items of apparatus by name having been exposed to the item and its name in the virtual environment. The second is the ability to differentiate between the item of apparatus and an alternative item with a similar but not identical structure.

In Investigation 1, Part A of the test required participants to identify 10 items of apparatus from colour photos, given a list of 29 apparatus names. Part B of the test was designed to test more precisely the accuracy of participants' spatial cognitive models of the items of apparatus. In this item, participants were required to identify the correct model of 8 items of apparatus given colour images of four alternative models each shown from three different views (see Figure 3.17).

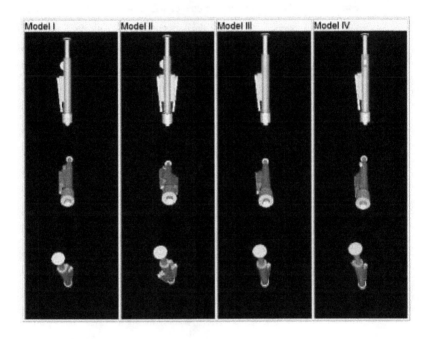

Figure 3.17
Example question from test Part B in Investigation 1

In Investigation 2, Part B of the test required both identification of items of apparatus and recognition of correct apparatus structure. This item contained 10 questions each requiring participants, given pictures of two models of an item of apparatus (one correctly modelled and the other modelled with at least one incorrect feature) to name the item of apparatus and identify the correct model. The pipette filler and the burette were used for six of these questions, with three pairs of models of each. Students carried out a task using a pipette and a burette, and each had a number of features that could be modified in an incorrect model. The remaining four questions used models of different items of apparatus, specifically a conical flask, a pipette, a reagent bottle and a beaker. See Figure 3.18 for an example of this type of question.

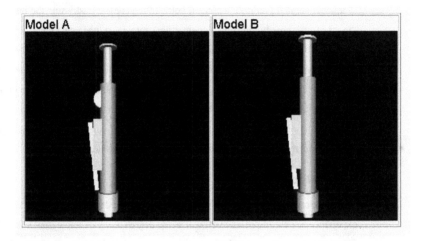

Figure 3.18
Example question from test Part B in Investigation 2

As discussed in Section 2.5, an additional aspect of spatial knowledge, apart from the structure of the space and the objects within the space, is the relationships between the objects, the space and people. In Investigation 2, participants undertook a task requiring them to assemble and use items of apparatus. Recall of the procedure for this task is essentially recall of aspects of the relationship between objects, the space, and the participants themselves. Part C of the test required participants to list the steps required to transfer some liquid from a reagent bottle into a conical flask using the burette and to then measure some liquid from a conical flask into a test tube using the pipette. They were asked to include all of the steps required to assemble the apparatus as well as the detailed steps in operating the burette and the pipette filler. This task was identical to the apparatus manipulation task performed by the User-control group in the virtual laboratory and demonstrated to the Dynamic Views and Static Views groups as part of their pre-recorded laboratory tour. Participants were provided with a colour diagram showing the apparatus assembled for the task, with each item labelled.

3.3.6 Additional Data

In 3D environment research it is common to assess the degree to which participants experience a sense of presence as well as the degree to which unpleasant side-effects are experienced. There are standard questionnaires available for both. For example, after their participants carried out tasks in a virtual environment, Witmer et al. (1996), administered a 'Simulator Sickness Questionnaire' (see Kennedy, Lane, Berbaum and Lilienthal, 1993) and Witmer and Singer's 'Presence Questionnaire' (see Witmer and Singer, 1998).

As discussed earlier, simulator sickness is much more prevalent in immersive environments. In the pilot investigation, none of the participants experienced negative symptoms and all indicated on their questionnaire that they enjoyed the experience. Consequently, rather than using a simulator sickness questionnaire in the major investigations, it was made clear on the participants' consent forms that they were free to withdraw at any stage if discomfort occurred. One participant in Investigation 2 experienced discomfort and withdrew after about five minutes of virtual environment usage. One participant in Investigation 1 seemed to experience discomfort, but chose not to withdraw. However, because he was unable to complete the learning task adequately, his test data was not used.

Although not required to address the research questions, participants of the User-control and Dynamic Views groups in Investigation 1 were asked three questions designed to gauge the degree to which they felt present within the virtual environment. These questions were taken from the presence questionnaire developed by Witmer and Singer (1998). Each question asked them to indicate the degree to which they agreed or disagreed with a statement, by making a mark along a line, with one end labelled very strongly agree and the other end labelled very strongly disagree. In Question 4 the statement was, 'you felt involved in the virtual environment experience'. In Question 5 the statement was, 'you felt a compelling sense of moving around inside the virtual environment'. In Question 6 the statement was, 'you were involved in the task to the extent that you lost track of time'. In Investigation 2, in which the greater time required to complete the learning task led to the need to reduce the length of the written test, the first two of these questions were used but not the last.

3.3.7 Data Analysis

Before statistical analysis techniques can be chosen, the participants' spatial tests have to be marked or checked in such a way as to provide data suitable for analysis. For some test items this is relatively straightforward, such as tests requiring the correct identification of items of apparatus. For others, such as test items requiring direction estimates or map drawing tests, this is not straightforward.

One approach to assessing the accuracy of distance or direction estimates is to measure the error in the estimate (see for example Ruddle et al., 1997). In the case of direction estimates, using the size of the error as a measure of the degree of correctness has an implicit assumption that, for example, a participant who is 90 degrees away from the correct angle is more correct than one who is 180 degrees away from being correct. This was considered not to be the case and consequently a scoring system was used where a direction estimate was marked as being correct or incorrect depending on whether it was closer than a particular threshold to the correct value. The specific thresholds used in each case are discussed in the results sections of Chapters 5 and 6.

Some researchers have used complex analysis techniques to compare the degree of correctness of maps. For example Patrick et al. (2000) tested participants spatial knowledge by asking them to place ten 3cm by 3cm foam squares on a 1m square piece of paper, with each square labelled with a landmark from within the virtual environment. The positions of the squares and their relative distances were then analysed. Specifically, the following analysis was undertaken:

> For each landmark pair $(_{10}C_2 = 45)$, we oriented and scaled the entire reported map until the pair matched its analog in the virtual environment. Distance error (in meters) was then calculated for the remaining eight transformed landmarks. The cumulative placement score (360 distance measurements per participant) evenly weights every landmark relationship. (p. 482-483)

It is the view of this researcher that such complex techniques have the potential to produce meaningless data, that is, data that has no intuitive meaning and thus the reader is expected to make a great leap of faith in trying to make sense of any conclusions reached. Consequently, a scoring system where each item placed on the map was marked as either correct or incorrect was used here. In each case a set of rules were defined for determining how close an item had to be to the correct size and position to be marked as correct. The specific rules used for marking the maps in each test item are discussed in the results sections of Chapters 5 and 6.

Once the method of scoring the various test items has been determined, appropriate statistical analysis techniques can be chosen. Often the first thing to be done is to examine the data manually. For example, if the scores on a test item are very high across all groups, it may indicate that 'ceiling effects' have occurred. For example, a study by Gabrielli et al. (2000), found no significant difference between the four groups, but the authors noted that this may have been because the task was found to be relatively easy for all groups. Similarly, Ruddle et al. (1997) in discussing a study by Henry (1992), note that:

> there were no significant differences between the three groups in terms of participants' directional accuracy when pointing to unseen locations. However, this lack of an effect of display mode may be explained by the simplicity of the building (seven rooms), which allowed participants to obtain near perfect spatial knowledge. (p. 144)

Another technique that is commonly used prior to group comparisons is Pearson's Correlation Coefficient. This can be used to determine if two variables are highly correlated, which may indicate that they are testing the same thing, in which case it may be appropriate to use only one of the items. For example, Waller et al. (1998) used the number of times participants bumped into a wall and the time taken as separate measures of ability to navigate a maze blindfolded. After finding that they were highly correlated they used time taken only, for subsequent analysis.

Once these initial exploratory techniques have been applied, there are three main data analysis techniques that are commonly used to compare performance across groups. Where the performances of two groups of participants are being compared, such as males and females, T-tests are normally used. Where three or more groups of participants are being compared, an analysis of variance (ANOVA) is used. Where this analysis of variance indicates that there is a significant difference between two or more of the groups, a post hoc test, such as Tukey's Honestly Significant Difference (HSD) test allows the performance of each pair of participant groups to be compared (Kerlinger and Lee, 2000).

If there are two or more independent variables, for example learning condition (such as virtual environment and real environment) and gender, a factorial analysis of variance is normally carried out. This allows 'main effects', that is, effects of one or other of the independent variables, as well as interactions between the variables to be identified (for example males may do better in a real environment, but females in a virtual environment). For example Kozak, Hancock, Arthur and Chrysler (1993) tested participants on an object manipulation task 30 times, using 6 blocks of 5 tests. Their participants were grouped into three groups, one who undertook no training, one who undertook training in a virtual environment and one who undertook real-world training. They analysed their data using a two way factorial ANOVA, with group and trial block as the factors.

All of the comparison tests discussed above provide a probability 'p' that any difference between the means is due to chance. It is normally accepted that a p value of less than 0.05 (ie. 5%) represents a statistically significant difference (Cramer, 1998). This convention is followed in this thesis. Where a p value of between 0.05 and 0.1 is found, the difference between the means is reported in this thesis as 'significant at the 90% level'.

It is important to ensure that the data satisfies the assumptions implicit within each of these techniques. For example, the T-test and the analyses of variance tests assume that the data is normally distributed and that the variance of each group of values is equal. A test like the Kolmogorov-Smirnov statistic can be used to check that the values of certain variables are normally distributed. The Levene test will check for equality of variance. Additionally, T-tests and analysis of variance tests can only be used with data where the values represent a quantity, for example they cannot be used for ranked data. Data that does not satisfy these tests has to be analysed instead using nonparametric statistical methods. For example Belingard and Peruch (2000) used the Kolmogorov-Smirnov test and found that their participants' rotation and distance estimate errors were not normally distributed, and consequently the non-parametric Kruskal-Wallis test was used instead of ANOVA tests.

3.3.8 Ethics Approval

Ethics approval was obtained from the Charles Sturt University Ethics in Human Research Committee (protocol number 00/011 dated 19th May 2000) for the pilot investigation and Investigation 1, as part of a Charles Sturt University Small Research Grant. The Information Statement and Consent Form provided to participants for the pilot investigation can be found in Appendix G. The Information Statement and Consent Form for Investigation 1 can be found in Appendix K. Ethics approval for Investigation 2 was obtained from the University Of Wollongong/Illawarra Area Health Service Human Research Ethics Committee (ethics number HE 02/422 dated 28th November 2002). The Information Statement and Consent Form for Investigation 2 can be found in Appendix R.

The key ethical issues identified were:

- The potential for ergonomic problems in the use of the virtual environments;

- The potential for participants to find the use of the virtual environment and the completion of the written spatial tests difficult, leading to a feeling of stress;

- The potential for participants in Investigation 2 to feel obliged to participate due to the fact that participation occurred during timetabled class time.

The voluntary nature of participation was stressed to participants both verbally and in the written information statements and consent forms. Additionally, participants were informed that they were free to withdraw from the study at any time.

3.3.9 Quality of Study

3.3.9.1 Reliability

The crucial aspects of the study which had the potential to affect the reliability of the results were the learning task procedure and the design of the test instruments. The learning tasks were administered in a consistent way, with scripted verbal instructions and common written instructions and with strict control over time. Assistance during the tasks was provided to ensure that participants were able to use the interface. The spatial test items included on the test instruments were based on tests performed frequently by other researchers. Tests such as map drawing, positioning of objects on maps and identification of the direction of views are well established as being reliable ways to test spatial knowledge.

3.3.9.2 Validity

As discussed in Section 3.2.2, educational media research often requires a trade-off between internal and external validity. To ensure internal validity independent variables need to be tightly controlled to ensure that only the variables of interest can have an effect on the dependent variables. However, tightly controlling all variables can result in learning conditions that are so different to the learning conditions likely to be experienced by students, that the results obtained may have limited external validity.

As discussed in Section 3.2.2, Ross and Morison (1989) argue that there is a need for both 'basic' research, which attempts to maintain high internal validity by controlling variables and eliminating extraneous factors, and 'developmental' research, which is carried out in an authentic context and will typically have greater external validity.

This study is closer to Ross and Morison's conception of basic research, in that care has been taken to control the independent variables as much as possible. However, the use of chemistry students, undertaking learning tasks within their class time, with intended learning outcomes appropriate to them at that stage of their studies, should allow for a degree of external validity for the results obtained from Investigation 2.

3.3.9.3 Limitations of the Study

The number of participants in Investigation 1 was relatively small, which had the potential to limit the statistical power of the analysis. Specifically, a small sample has the potential to increase the possibility of Type II errors, whereby performance differences between groups are picked up as being non-significant, when in fact a larger sample may have shown them to be significant (Kerlinger and Lee, 2000).

The use of undergraduate information technology and chemistry students as participants is a potential limitation because such students are not likely to be representative of the wider population. Specifically, one would expect such students to have a relatively narrow age range and to have particular aptitudes and abilities that are not representative of the population. A consequence of the use of such participants is that the findings may not be able to be generalised to other student groups.

The lack of a pre-test for spatial ability and thus the lack of control for spatial ability across the groups is another potential limitation. The random allocation of participants to groups was expected to address this to some extent. Additionally, the use of questions designed to gauge participants' perceptions of their own spatial ability was expected to provide an indication of whether spatial ability was in fact evenly spread across groups.

Finally, it is important to emphasise the complexity of the process of learning in 3D environments in terms of the human-computer interactions and the cognitive processing involved and the range of participant abilities and prior experiences that could be contributing factors. This complexity requires that the study to some extent must be seen as exploratory and the analysis of results must be undertaken in a way that allows for the emergence of additional unexpected factors.

3.4 Development of the Environments

This section discusses the development of the virtual environments, including the rationale for the choice of technologies, the overall development process and timetable, and the specific approaches used to develop aspects of the 3D model and the user interface.

3.4.1 Development Requirements and Constraints

As discussed in Section 3.3.2.1, a 3D environment was required that:

- was of sufficient complexity so that learning of its spatial structure would be non-trivial;

- provided sufficient frame rate to create the illusion of smooth movement through the environment and smooth object movement;

- provided an interface allowing the learner to pickup or move objects in some way; and

- allowed for tailoring of the user-interface and in particular the ability to provide an animated tour rather than user control over viewpoint and a static tour, without animated view changes.

The requirement to be able to tailor the user interface meant that an existing environment such as a computer game could not be used and consequently the decision was made to develop an environment based on the CSU Wagga Wagga campus undergraduate chemistry teaching laboratory.

As discussed in Section 3.3.2.2, due to usability issues and the availability of laboratory hardware, it was decided to develop a desktop environment, which would run on the Microsoft Windows platform. The target platform for the initial investigation was a Pentium 3 running at 800 MHz with 256M RAM.

Grant money was obtained to purchase hardware and software and to pay for technical assistance. This researcher undertook the overall design, as well as positioning the models of the furniture and apparatus within the virtual laboratory, and programming the user interface. Paid technical assistants, under the guidance of this researcher, carried out the 3D modelling of the laboratory building, the furniture and the apparatus.

3.4.2 Overview of 3D Technologies

The section provides an overview of 3D environment technologies to assist the reader to understand the technical material in the following sections.

The following are the main technical characteristics of a 3D environment:

- The environment is defined in terms of three-dimensional geometry;

- The user normally has some control over their view position and direction, that is, an interface is provided allowing the user to move through and look around the environment;

- The view of the environment is rendered dynamically using mathematical calculations based on the current view position and direction;

- Objects within the environment can be programmed to respond to actions of the user and events generated by other objects or to move autonomously;

- The view of the environment can be either a 'first-person' view, or alternatively a 'third-person' or 'birds-eye' view, in which case a representation of the user (termed an 'avatar') will be visible;

- Environments can be stand-alone supporting a single-user or alternatively can be networked allowing multiple-users to be present and to see each other's avatar, to communicate or to work together on a task; and

- Environments can be explored using standard desktop computer hardware ('desktop 3D environments') or can be explored using specialised hardware, such as a head-mounted display ('immersive 3D environments) or alternatively can be explored using a 3D projection system ('semi-immersive 3D environments).

As discussed in Chapter 2, this study uses a stand-alone, single-user desktop 3D environment, and this overview of technologies focuses on these environments.

A 3D environment is made up of 3D objects. Each object is defined in terms of its geometry in 3D space, specifically the x, y and z coordinates of the points that make up each surface. For example, a file containing a 3D model of a rectangular room might include the x, y and z coordinates of two corners of the room.

When 2D images such as scanned photographs are stored electronically, the colour of each pixel within the image is stored explicitly. With 3D images, the colour of a particular point on a surface will vary depending on the angle between the view position, the surface and the light sources. Consequently, instead of the colour of each pixel being stored, the material properties of each surface are stored and the actual colour of each point along the surface is calculated dynamically.

Light sources within the environment are defined in terms of the quantity of red, green and blue light emitted and whether the light is emitted in all directions or within a certain angular radius. The material properties of surfaces are specified in terms of the percentage of red, green and blue light they reflect. The degree to which the surface is transparent can also be specified. Surfaces can also have images mapped to them, which allows, for example, for wall and floor textures to be used and for photographic images to be 'hung' on the walls.

The process of displaying a view of the environment is called 'rendering'. This involves complex mathematical operations using matrices and vectors. These operations include the following:

- Projecting the 3D objects onto a 2D plane, taking into account the position of the viewer, their view direction and their field of view angle;

- Rendering each object in turn, ensuring that near objects are rendered last; and

- Calculating the red, green and blue values of each pixel, depending on the lighting and material properties, using a shading algorithm.

Clearly, there is a great deal of processing required and this processing has to be performed for each frame. In animated movies, the frames are not required to be rendered in 'real-time'. For example, one minute of footage might take 12 hours to render. For virtual environments, in which the position of the user may be constantly changing, the frames have to be rendered in real-time at a frame rate of at least 10 to 15 frames per second to give the impression of smooth movement.

The calculation of the colour of each pixel (the shading) is the most computationally expensive part of the process. There are a number of shading algorithms available and the algorithm chosen is normally a trade-off between realism and rendering performance. The most common algorithms are: flat shading, which is quick but not highly realistic due to the fact that each surface will be shaded with the same colour intensity across the entire surface; Gouraud shading, which allows for graduated shading across surfaces and is supported by most desktop computer graphics hardware; and ray tracing, which is highly realistic but is so performance intensive that it cannot be used for real-time rendering.

Other factors in the design of the environment that affect the rendering performance are the number of light sources within the environment, the number of textures and the image resolution of each texture. There are also a number of advanced rendering features, which each can improve realism, but can also slow performance. These include: depth cuing, which can ensure that nearer objects are always rendered on top; anti-aliasing, which ensures that diagonal lines do not appear jagged; and multi-texturing, which allows for multiple textures to be superimposed on the one surface.

In practice it is impossible to get real-time performance in a 3D environment if the Central Processing Unit (CPU) of the computer does the rendering calculations. This is because, even if the CPU is very fast, the time required to transfer each of the images from the CPU to the display hardware becomes the limiting performance factor. Consequently, a graphics display card that has 'hardware 3D acceleration' is required. Such graphics cards now come as standard on all new personal computers. In fact the cards that are provided as standard on new computers include hardware acceleration which outperforms specialised graphics workstations of five years ago that cost at the time more than $A20,000.

When hardware acceleration is used, the CPU sends a description of the 3D objects, the textures and the light sources to the card, along with the current view position, and the card renders the frames to the screen. The more expensive cards also support some of the advanced rendering features listed above.

To develop a 3D environment, the first task required is to develop the 3D geometry and this is normally done using a 3D modelling tool, such as '3D Studio Max' (Discreet

Software, 2004) or 'Maya' (Alias, 2004). Once this is done, a user interface for controlling motion and manipulating objects is required and any simulated object behaviours need to be programmed. There are a number of approaches available for programming this interactivity and simulated behaviour. Some of these are as follows:

- Programming using an Application Programming Interface (API) such as 'OpenGL' (Neider, Davis and Woo, 1993) or 'DirectX' (Microsoft, 2004);

- Using one of the many computer game 'engines' as the rendering software, and defining the environment using the proprietary file format defined for the specific engine (see GarageGames, 2004 for a review); and

- Using the ISO standard Virtual Reality Modelling Language (VRML) along with a VRML browser as the rendering software;

Writing program code directly, using an API, is the most difficult and time-consuming approach, but can allow the greatest performance. Because the user interface has to be programmed essentially from scratch, this approach allows the most control over the user interface. The programming language normally used for graphics API programming is C++, and the skills tend to be highly specialised and thus it can be difficult or expensive to employ programmers.

Using a game engine is normally much easier than programming the environment directly. Typically the user interface for motion control is provided with the engine, along with built-in capability for common game features, such as shooting of bullets, explosions and so on. The performance of game engines tends to be very good, because this can be essential for a game to sell. There are 'level editors' available for most game engines, which are modelling tools with some capability for specifying interactivity and behaviours. If all that is required is an interface for moving around an environment, then there may be no programming required. Basic object behaviours can be implemented using small amounts of code in a scripting language. More advanced object behaviours, or tailoring of the motion control or object manipulation interface, typically requires more complex programming (Reinhart, 1999; Simpson, 2002).

The Virtual Reality Modelling Language (VRML) provides a platform independent file format for specifying the geometry, lighting and material properties of a 3D environment, as well as a scripting interface for specifying object behaviours (Carson, Puk & Carey, 1999; Carey & Bell, 1997). The first version of the VRML standard was specified in 1995, with the current version, version 2.0 ratified as an International Standards Organisation (ISO) standard in 1997 (Bell, Parisi & Pesce, 1995; Web3D Consortium, 1997). A VRML browser is required as a rendering platform and this browser provides the motion control interface and facilitates the rendering of views via the graphics hardware. Scripting of object behaviours and enhancements to the user interface are normally carried out using the Java or JavaScript programming languages.

The VRML standard allows for distributed online environments, that is, environments delivered from a web server and hyperlinked to environments on other servers. Consequently, the VRML browser normally runs within a web browser, as either a plug-in or an ActiveX control. The most common VRML browsers available are Blaxxun Contact, recent versions of which are called BS Contact (Blaxxun Technologies, 2004; Bitmanagement, 2004) and Parallel Graphics Cortona (Parallel Graphics, 2004). Both of these browsers provide enhanced APIs in addition to their support for the standard VRML scripting mechanisms. These enhancements can allow for more control over the user interface and simpler programming of object behaviours.

The VRML standards body, the Web 3D Consortium, is currently working on a new standard to replace VRML, called X3D. However, the VRML browsers currently available are more mature and more robust products than the emerging X3D browsers.

In addition to the approaches listed above there are a number of development tools and rendering systems available, which are either less commonly used or have only recently become available. One of these is 'Active Worlds', which is a multi-user online 3D environment, that allows individual subscribers to tailor and build within their allocated space in the environment. Another is 'Shockwave 3D', which is a rendering environment installed as a plug-in or ActiveX control within a web browser, and renders 3D environments created using Macromedia Director.

3.4.3 Technologies Chosen

It was decided to develop the virtual laboratory using VRML. Although not necessary for this study, the ability to use the virtual laboratory online was likely to be of benefit to chemistry students. Additionally, the use of a platform such as VRML rather than programming the laboratory directly using OpenGL or DirectX was likely to be less time consuming. Aside from the potential for online delivery, VRML was chosen ahead of game engines because the VRML browsers are freely available, whereas it is normally necessary to purchase a copy of the game for each user machine in order to use a system built on top of a game engine.

It was originally intended to develop the laboratory using standard VRML alone, and in particular the VRML 2 (also called VRML97) standard. However, once development commenced it became desirable to use proprietary capabilities provided by the VRML browsers which were not available in the standard, and consequently it was seen as necessary to target a specific browser platform. The Blaxxun Contact VRML browser was chosen as the target platform. Blaxxun Contact provides an interface for external scripting using JavaScript, allowing, for example, a scripted tour controlled by JavaScript code running within the web browser to be implemented. The capability that allowed participants to pick up, carry and put down objects, and to connect objects together was also programmed using APIs provided by Blaxxun Contact. Microsoft Internet Explorer was chosen as the target platform for the JavaScript scripts running within the web browser. In the discussions below, Microsoft's proprietary name 'Jscript' is used to refer to these scripts to differentiate them from the JavaScript code running within Blaxxun Contact.

The version of the virtual laboratory used in the pilot investigation included a set of pull-down menus in a frame to the left of the virtual environment. A shareware menu system called Morten's Tree-Menu (Wang, 2003) was used to develop these menus. Morten's Tree-Menu is a set of JavaScript scripts which provide a menu system based on a definition contained in configuration files. Although this menu system was not used in the version used in Investigations 1 and 2, it is intended to be used again in future versions of the virtual laboratory to be used by chemistry students.

3.4.4 Design and Development Process and Timetable

The design of the virtual laboratory was informed by an ongoing process of formative evaluation. Specifically, in addition to the formal pilot investigation, smaller pilot tests were conducted leading up to each investigation. In each case the tasks to be performed by the participants in that investigation were piloted and in some cases the pilot testers also completed the items in the test instrument. Very early versions of the virtual laboratory were also tested by the chemistry lecturers, by user interface design lecturers and by delegates at the 2001 ASCILITE conference who attended a workshop led by the researcher on 3D learning environments.

Table 3.4 shows the design and development timetable, including the key differences from one version to the next, and the phases of formative evaluation undertaken.

Table 3.4
Development timetable

Date	Development Phase	Explanation
January 2000 to January 2002	Initial virtual laboratory development	Initial development of the virtual laboratory included models of the landscape, buildings and apparatus and a user interface allowing for movement and very basic object manipulation.
January 2000 to December 2001	Informal usability tests	Chemistry lecturers, lecturers in User Interface Design and delegates at the 2001 ASCILITE used the virtual laboratory and provided advice on the interface.
January 2002	Pilot investigation	Ten first-year undergraduate chemistry students were observed using the virtual laboratory, completed a spatial learning test and undertook a structured interview.
February 2002 to May 2002	Development towards Investigation 1	The user interface for controlling movement and viewing apparatus was refined, addressing usability issues identified in the pilot investigation.
May 2002	Usability testing and pilot of tasks leading up to Investigation 1	Three IT students undertook tasks in either a version of the virtual laboratory or in the real laboratory and then were tested on their spatial learning. Each student pilot tested the environment, tasks and tests for one of the 3 groups used in Investigation 1. This led to a number of refinements to the user interface and to the test instrument.
May 2002 to February 2003	Further development	The user interface was enhanced to allow for carrying of apparatus and for connecting of apparatus together by dragging and dropping.
February 2003	Usability testing leading up to Investigation 2	Two academic staff undertook tasks in the new version of the virtual environment, leading to a number of refinements to the interface.
February 2003	Pilot of tasks leading up to Investigation 2	Three IT students undertook tasks in a version of the virtual laboratory. Each student pilot tested the environment, tasks and tests for one of the 3 groups used in Investigation 2. This led to minor refinements to the task description and test instrument.

3.4.5 Components of the environments

The underlying components of the virtual laboratory are as follows:

- Hypertext Markup Language (HTML) pages defining the frame layout used to embed the virtual laboratory within the Internet Explorer web browser;

- JScript code within these HTML pages allowing the menu frame to be hidden or shown;

- JScript code for Morton's Tree-Menu, along with associated configuration files;

- JScript code for sending messages into the Blaxxun Contact VRML browser to control the tour, including code for moving the viewpoint and code for picking up and connecting objects together;

- HTML files for each of the apparatus text descriptions (in the case of the pilot versions) or apparatus names (in Investigations 1 and 2);

- Cascading Stylesheet (CSS) files defining the text formatting used in the main HTML files as well as the apparatus name and description files;

- VRML files containing the laboratory structure and lighting characteristics as well as the structure of each item of apparatus;

- JPEG and PNG files containing textures used within the VRML models; and

- VRML files containing JavaScript code for the user interface enhancements, each programmed as reusable prototypes.

All versions of the virtual laboratory, including source code, have been provided on a CD-ROM attached to this thesis so that interested readers can install and use the virtual laboratory and explore its components. The CD-ROM contains a file **readme.html**, which includes a list of the contents of the CD-ROM along with installation instructions. The contents of the readme.html file have also been included in Appendix S.

The key issues involved in the design and development of the 3D model, the 3D user interface and the HTML container are discussed in the following paragraphs.

3.4.6 3D Model Development

The 3D models of the landscape and buildings were developed by firstly taking a series of measurements of the buildings and surrounding landscape using a tape measure and a Global Positioning System (GPS) device. This data was then entered into a text editor to create the initial VRML files. Measurements were then taken of all of the furniture in the laboratory and this data was entered into text files in a similar way. The items of apparatus were modelled using various 3D modelling tools, primarily 'Lightwave', and then converted to VRML. The 'Cosmo Worlds' VRML editor was also used. The items of furniture and apparatus were placed in the laboratory initially using a text editor, but later using 'Parallel Graphics VRMLPad' VRML editor.

Generally, when developing a 3D environment, there is a compromise between visual realism and frame rate. For example, the use of photographic textures for all surfaces within an environment will tend to increase the degree of realism, but can have a significant negative effect on frame rates. The actual frame rate within a virtual environment will also vary depending on the complexity of the geometry currently visible. In the virtual laboratory, high frame rates tended to occur when positioned outside the laboratory, looking away from the laboratory, and much lower frame rates occurred when inside the laboratory, looking at complex items of apparatus or laboratory structure. The version used in Investigation 2 suffered an overhead in the frame rate due to the processing required to implement the extra interactive capabilities, but the hardware platform used was more powerful. Table 3.3 showed the frame rates achieved from various viewpoints within the virtual laboratory in the versions of the virtual laboratory used in Investigations 1 and 2.

3.4.7 User Interface Development

The Blaxxun Contact VRML browser provides two user interface mechanisms for free motion control, a keyboard mechanism and a mouse-driven mechanism. In the default movement mode, 'Walk' mode, the keyboard mechanism allows for movement forward and backwards, and for turning left and right using the four arrow keys. In Walk mode, the mouse-driven mechanism allows for movement in any direction by clicking and dragging the mouse to define the direction, with the speed of the movement determined by the length of the vector. As discussed in Section 3.3.2.7, various movement modes are supported, which can be changed either by choosing an item from a right-click menu or by pressing a function key combination. These modes are Slide, Examine, Pan, Fly and Jump. Blaxxun Contact also provides for the ability to move to a predefined viewpoint within the environment by choosing from a right-click menu. The right-click menu was disabled in Investigations 1 and 2, as it contained options that were considered too complex for new users.

Enhancements to Blaxxun Contact's standard motion control interface were as follows:

- Buttons for changing between Walk, Pan and Jump modes were provided in a frame beside the virtual environment, implemented using JScript code within Internet Explorer passing messages to JavaScript code running within Blaxxun Contact (version used in the pilot investigation);

- Menu options allowing the participant to jump to a position within the laboratory, or to the location of an item of apparatus, were implemented using JScript code within Internet Explorer passing messages to JavaScript code running within Blaxxun Contact (version used in the pilot investigation);

- The ability to look around without moving, by holding down the shift key while using the arrow keys, was programmed using JavaScript code running within Blaxxun Contact (versions used in Investigations 1 and 2); and

- The ability to move up close to an object to inspect it by using the F3 key, and the ability to undo this operation using the Home key, was programmed using JavaScript code running within Blaxxun Contact (version used in Investigation 2).

The VRML standard provides for basic object manipulation. By defining in VRML various mouse sensors and routing the events generated by these sensors to objects within the environment, objects can be specified as able to be rotated using the mouse. Objects can also be specified to be able to be dragged within a particular plane or to move in an animated path when clicked upon. These features were made use of in the following ways:

- Cupboards, drawers and doors were created so that when the user clicked on them they would open and when they were clicked again they would shut; and

- Certain objects in the pilot investigation were created so that they could be dragged around on a surface.

Beyond these basic object manipulation capabilities, VRML requires programming. The following enhancements to the basic capabilities were programmed for the version used in the pilot investigation:

- The ability to double-click on an object to carry the object and then double-click again to place it in a new location, was programmed using JavaScript code running within Blaxxun Contact; and

- Menu options allowing the participant to move items of apparatus from one location to another within the laboratory, were implemented using JScript code within Internet Explorer passing messages to JavaScript code running within Blaxxun Contact.

The following enhancements to the basic object manipulation capabilities were developed for the version used in Investigation 1, each programmed using JavaScript code running within Blaxxun Contact:

- The ability to 'pickup' an object by double-clicking on it so that it was moved to a suspended position in the middle of the screen and to 'put down' the object by double-clicking again;

- The ability to rotate an object that is in the picked up state by clicking with the mouse to rotate around the y axis and clicking again to rotate around the x axis; and

- The ability to script the same actions so that they could be simulated as part of a virtual tour taken by the Dynamic Views group.

The following enhancements to the basic object manipulation capabilities were developed for the version used in Investigation 2, each programmed using JavaScript code running within Blaxxun Contact:

- The ability to drag certain objects within a plane perpendicular to a line from the viewer to the object (once dropped the object returned to its original position, unless dropped on a predefined target object);

- The ability to carry an object by dragging and dropping it on top of a hand icon;

- The ability to place an object in a target location by dragging it from its held position on top of the hand icon and dropping it on the specified location;

- The ability to connect objects together by dragging an object and dropping it on an object which has been predefined as being suitable for connections to this object;

- The ability to turn a burette tap (see Figure 3.13);

- The ability to control a pipette filler, by turning a dial to raise or lower the plunger and by pressing a lever to lower the plunger (see Figure 3.13); and

- The ability to script these actions so that they could be simulated as part of a virtual tour taken by the Dynamic Views or Static Views groups.

The Next View and Previous View options provided to Dynamic Views and Static Views participants in Investigations 1 and 2 were implemented using JScript code running within Internet Explorer sending messages to JavaScript code running within Blaxxun Contact.

Blaxxun Contact also provided automatic collision detection, as well as automatic gravity which ensured that while in 'Walk' mode the participant followed the surface of the ground.

The VRMLPad VRML editor was used for entering and editing the VRML JavaScript code. A standard text editor was used for creating the JScript files.

VRML provides a mechanism for creating reusable geometry or reusable behaviours by creating a prototype node. These prototypes can then be used from within any other VRML file. This prototyping mechanism was used extensively in the development of the laboratory, for example to create cupboards and drawers which could be opened, and to develop the interactive burette and pipette filler. In addition, a movingObject prototype was developed, defining objects that could be picked up, and an interactiveObject prototype was developed defining objects that could be picked up, carried and connected together. Appendix T lists the VRML prototypes developed and their source code file names. The source code for each version of the virtual laboratory has been provided on the CD-ROM included with this thesis.

3.4.8 Creation of the HTML files and the menu

A standard text editor was used for creating the main HTML files, which defined the frame layout, along with the JScript code which allowed for changes to the frame layout (for example, in the pilot version the menu frame could be hidden or shown). The HTML files listing the names of the apparatus and in the pilot version listing apparatus descriptions were created by entering the data into a text file using a text editor and then generating the HTML files using VBScript scripts. The configuration files defining the Morton's Tree-Menu menus used in the pilot version were created using a text editor, with some parts also generated using VBScript scripts.

3.5 Summary

This chapter has outlined the research methods used in the study to address the research questions identified in Chapter 2. The study consisted of participants, who were undergraduate chemistry or information technology students, undertaking tasks in one of a number of versions of a virtual environment and then being tested on their spatial knowledge, using written and practical tests. The versions of the virtual environment each included or excluded certain characteristics, specifically animated view changes, user control over view, object animation, and object manipulation. Quantitative data analysis techniques were used to compare the spatial learning of participants who used each version of the virtual environment, in order to determine the contribution of each characteristic to spatial learning. This chapter has also described the design and development of the 3D environments, which were modelled on the Charles Sturt University undergraduate chemistry laboratory.

The study included three phases of investigation. The first phase, a pilot investigation explored the usability of the virtual laboratory environment and the effectiveness of the training process, learning tasks and test instruments to be used in later investigations. The pilot investigation is discussed in Chapter 4. The first major investigation, Investigation 1, focussed on the importance of user control over view, and object manipulation, for spatial learning. Investigation 1 is discussed in Chapter 5. The second major investigation, Investigation 2, focussed on the importance of smooth view changes, smooth display of object motion, user control over view, object manipulation and learning task design, for spatial learning. Investigation 2 is discussed in Chapter 6.

Chapter 4. Pilot Investigation

4.1 Introduction

This chapter describes a pilot investigation, which evaluated the design of the virtual laboratory along with aspects of the research methods to be used in subsequent investigations. The overall design of the pilot and a summary of the methods used are presented in Section 4.2. The results are presented in Section 4.3 and the consequences for the remainder of the study are discussed in Section 4.4.

The specific aims of the pilot evaluation were as follows:

- To explore the way participants used the virtual laboratory and aspects of its design that might impact on its effectiveness as a research instrument;

- To test the appropriateness of the process used to train participants in the use of the virtual environment;

- To test the feasibility of the learning tasks for possible use in subsequent investigations;

- To evaluate possible test items for use in subsequent investigations; and

- To gather initial data on the effectiveness of the virtual laboratory for learning based on test results and participant comments.

4.2 Method

4.2.1 Overview

The pilot investigation was designed as a comparison of the use of the virtual laboratory with a verbal introduction delivered in the real laboratory along with reading of a printed laboratory manual. Participants, who were volunteer undergraduate chemistry students, were divided into two groups (Group 1 and Group 2), who undertook their learning using either the virtual laboratory or the verbal introduction and the laboratory manual. They then completed a written test on their familiarity with the laboratory. A few days later, the learning conditions were reversed, that is, Group 1 read the laboratory manual and attended a verbal introduction to the laboratory and Group 2 used the virtual laboratory. After this, participants again completed the written test. All participants were observed as they used the virtual laboratory and were encouraged to comment on its design and usability. A week after the reversal of the learning conditions, participants were observed as they undertook their first laboratory session as part of their chemistry course. Each participant was subsequently interviewed. Table 4.1 shows a summary and timetable for the investigation.

The pilot investigation was designed with a broad focus with the intention that the results would contribute to the refinement of the research questions prior to the major investigations. In particular, the pilot investigation explored recall of information about the laboratory and apparatus as well as spatial learning. Consequently, the version of the virtual laboratory used in the pilot included written information about the laboratory, including safety procedures and procedures for the use of apparatus, and recall of this information was included in the test instrument.

It was not intended that statistically significant results would be obtained. The small sample precluded this. Additionally, it was recognised that a comparison of active learning using the virtual laboratory with relatively passive learning through a verbal introduction and reading of the laboratory manual would not allow clear conclusions about the value of the virtual environment due to the very different learning approaches. However, it was expected that a comparison of the test results would give an initial indication of the learning that occurred through exploring the virtual laboratory compared with more traditional means. Additionally, observation of the learners using the virtual laboratory and follow-up interviews were expected to give an initial indication of the effectiveness of the virtual laboratory as a research instrument.

Table 4.1
Pilot investigation summary and timetable

Date	Task
15th February 2002	Participants in Group 1 undertook the virtual laboratory learning condition and the written test
19th February 2002	Participants in Groups 1 and 2 undertook the real laboratory learning condition and the written test
21st February 2002	Participants in Group 2 undertook the virtual laboratory learning condition and the written test
26th February 2002	All participants were observed during their first laboratory session as part of their chemistry course
28th February 2002	All participants were interviewed

4.2.2 Participants

The participants were volunteers from first year students enrolled in a pharmacy degree, and in the subject Chemistry 1A at Charles Sturt University (CSU). There were two groups of five participants, each containing four females and one male. The ages ranged from 17 to 28 years. None of the participants had been in the laboratory prior to the investigation.

4.2.3 Virtual Laboratory

The virtual laboratory was explored through Internet Explorer 5.5 and the Blaxxun Contact VRML browser version 5.104, using a PC with a 15 inch screen and a standard keyboard and mouse, running Windows 2000. The PCs had basic hardware acceleration, allowing a frame rate of between 5 and 15 frames per second (depending on the part of the virtual environment visible at the time). Internet Explorer was configured to run full-screen, so that none of the Internet Explorer options, or the Windows taskbar were visible. The learning was undertaken in a computer laboratory, with all five participants in a group working concurrently, each on their own computer.

The virtual laboratory included the following laboratory locations, apparatus and equipment:

- the service hatch;
- the fume cupboard;
- exits and evacuation assembly points;
- drawers containing Bunsens, gauze and tripods;
- lockers containing glassware.
- lab coat, safety glasses, footwear;
- safety shower/eye wash;
- fire blanket and extinguisher;
- waste bins and glass bins;
- laboratory balances (top loading balance, analytic balance);
- volumetric glassware (graduated cylinder, pipette, burette); and
- flasks and beakers.

Figure 4.1 shows the screen layout of the pilot investigation version of the virtual laboratory. The features of this version are described in Section 3.3.2.

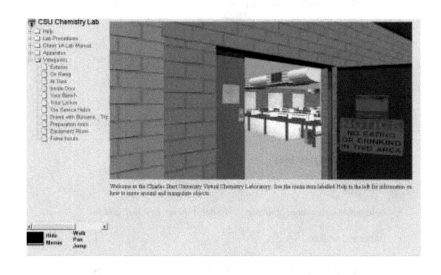

Figure 4.1
Screen layout of the pilot investigation version of the virtual laboratory

4.2.4 Training Procedure

Prior to using the virtual laboratory, participants in each group spent 20 minutes learning to use a 3D environment. They did this using a 3D environment modelled on the National Gallery of Ireland, but with a very similar interface to the virtual laboratory. A brief explanation about 3D environments was provided, and the navigation and object manipulation functions were demonstrated. Participants were given a handout containing navigation and object manipulation instructions and practice tasks (see Appendix B). After completion of this training participants had a 5 minute break.

4.2.5 Learning tasks and procedure: virtual laboratory condition

Participants spent 60 minutes exploring the virtual laboratory, guided by a worksheet containing a list of tasks (see Appendix C). The worksheet included short sections to fill in for some tasks, and learners were also asked to tick each task as they completed it. Tasks included:

- Entering the laboratory (after putting on lab coat and glasses);

- Moving around and looking around the laboratory;

- Selecting items of apparatus and reading about them;

- Carrying apparatus from storage locations to the bench; and

- Reading about procedures to follow in the laboratory, including links to move to specific viewpoints, and options showing the assembly of apparatus.

While using the virtual laboratory, participants were observed by the researcher along with a colleague with expertise in user interface design and evaluation. Participants were encouraged to 'think-aloud' as they undertook the tasks and specifically to comment on the design of the virtual laboratory, problems they encountered in using it and any possible improvements.

Thirty minutes after completing the virtual laboratory tasks, learners undertook a written test in the actual laboratory (see Section 0).

4.2.6 Learning tasks and procedure: real laboratory condition

Participants in Group 2 were given an extract from their laboratory manual to read within 24 hours prior to coming to the laboratory. The extract included the introductory section of the laboratory manual along with the discussion section of the first experiment. They were asked to spend about 30 minutes reading this extract and were given a worksheet to complete during this time (see Appendix D). This worksheet required participants to:

- Record their start time and finish time for the reading;

- Write one line of information on each of the laboratory safety issues (eg. clothing, behaviour, emergencies); and

- Write one line of information about each of a list of apparatus.

Participants listened to a 30 minute verbal introduction to the laboratory, carried out by an experienced chemistry lecturer, in the laboratory.

The verbal introduction and laboratory manual extract included references to the same series of furniture, apparatus, equipment and laboratory locations as those included in the virtual laboratory (see Section 4.2.5).

Forty-five minutes after listening to this introduction, learners undertook the written test described in the following section.

4.2.7 Test Tasks and Procedure

The written test was designed to assess the degree to which participants achieved the following learning outcomes:

- Name apparatus and sections of the laboratory;

- Identify apparatus and sections of the laboratory given their name;

- Locate apparatus and sections of the laboratory;

- Describe the functions of apparatus and equipment;

- Explain rules about general laboratory behaviour, including things to do and things not to do;

- Describe the procedures to follow in the event of various accident scenarios;

- Describe the correct procedures for safe and effective use of various types of balances to determine the mass of liquids and solids;

- Describe the correct procedures for safe and effective use of graduated cylinders, pipettes and burettes; and

- Determine when to use graduated cylinders, pipettes and burettes to measure volumes of liquids.

The written test (see Appendix E) required participants to:

- Answer eight multiple choice questions about laboratory behaviour, safety procedures and use of apparatus;

- Name five items of apparatus placed on a desk;

- Indicate the position of seven named locations within the laboratory, and the locations of six named items of apparatus or equipment, on a laboratory map showing the walls and doorways;

- Draw a labelled diagram to show apparatus components involved in the use of a burette and a pipette and the correct procedure for using this apparatus; and

- List the steps to be followed in the event of a fire or a chemical spill.

4.2.8 Observation During Laboratory Session

After the reversal of the learning conditions (seven days after Group 1 completed the reading and the verbal introduction and five days after Group 2 completed their virtual laboratory tasks), all participants were observed as they undertook their first laboratory practical session. As well as the 10 participants involved in the investigation, around 40 other chemistry students undertook the same practical session. The focus of this observation was the degree to which the virtual laboratory prepared participants for their laboratory tasks and the identification of additional knowledge or skills required for these tasks.

4.2.9 Interview

Two days after the laboratory practical session, all 10 participants were interviewed.

The interviews were undertaken by the researcher and were structured, using a written questionnaire completed by the researcher in view of the participant. Additional comments of participants were also noted. The questionnaire (see Appendix F), included the following types of questions:

- Questions about the participant, including date of birth and highest level of chemistry studied;

- Questions about the effectiveness of various aspects of the virtual laboratory, the laboratory manual and the verbal introduction, structured as statements requiring the participant to indicate the degree to which they agreed or disagreed, using a 7 point Likert scale from very strongly agree to very strongly disagree;

- Open-ended questions asking the participant to elaborate on their answers to the questions above;

- A question asking the participant to discuss things that they thought they needed to learn but did not learn from either the virtual laboratory, the laboratory manual or the verbal introduction;

- Specific questions listing changes to the virtual laboratory identified earlier by the participants or the observers while they used the virtual laboratory, and asking for the learners to indicate their degree of agreement or disagreement, using a 7 point Likert scale; and

- Open ended questions about things that the participant found particularly effective about the virtual laboratory and possible improvements they could suggest.

4.3 Results

This section presents the results obtained from the written test (Section 4.3.1), observations of participants using the virtual laboratory (Section 4.3.2), observations of participants while undertaking their first laboratory practical (Section 4.3.3) and interviews with participants (Section 4.3.4). The consequences of these results for the remainder of the study are discussed in Section 4.4.

4.3.1 Written test results

The results obtained by participants on each section of the written test are discussed in the following paragraphs. In each case descriptive statistics only (totals and means) have been presented. The small sample size meant that it was inappropriate to test for statistically significant differences.

4.3.1.1 Recall of information about laboratory clothing and procedures

Questions 1 to 8 were multiple-choice questions about appropriate protective clothing and laboratory procedures. Table 4.2 shows the results.

Table 4.2 Number of participants correctly answering each multiple choice question (out of five participants in each group)				
Question	Group 1 after virtual laboratory tasks	Group 2 after reading and verbal introduction	Group 1 after both	Group 2 after both
1. Footwear	5	5	5	5
2. Clothing	5	3	4	4
3. Eye protection	5	5	5	5
4. Undertaking experiments	5	5	5	5
5. Balances procedure	5	5	5	5
6. When to use burette	4	4	5	5
7. When to use pipette	4	4	4	5
8. When to use graduated cylinder	5	4	4	5

Given that most participants answered almost all questions correctly, there is little that can be concluded from these results. Only Question 2 showed large differences between the scores of the two groups after their first condition. However, this can be explained by the fact that the lecturer provided information in the verbal introduction that contradicted the information in the laboratory manual and the virtual laboratory (she said that students had to wear a white lab coat while the information accessible from within the virtual laboratory suggested that students could wear any similar covering).

4.3.1.2 Identification of apparatus

Questions 9 to 13 required participants to name five items of apparatus placed on the desk in front of them. A half mark was awarded to one participant on question 12 because their answer was partially correct. Table 4.3 shows the results.

Question	Group 1 after virtual laboratory tasks	Group 2 after reading and talk	Group 1 after both	Group 2 after both
9. Beaker	5	5	5	5
10. Pipette	4	4	5	5
11. Burette	4	5	5	5
12. Flask	4.5	4	4.5	5
13. Graduated cylinder	5	5	5	5

Table 4.3
Number of participants correctly able to identify each item of apparatus (out of five participants in each group)

Again most participants answered all questions correctly and the differences between the performance of the two groups on each question were either small or zero. Participants' responses to questions in the interviews suggested that most could already identify all apparatus, so nothing can be concluded about object identification.

4.3.1.3 Positioning of named locations

Questions 15 to 20 required participants to indicate on a laboratory map the location of various landmarks within the laboratory. Participants were marked correct if they marked the position of each landmark within 5 metres of the correct location. Table 4.4 shows the results.

Table 4.4
Number of participants correctly able to indicate the position of locations within the laboratory
(out of five participants in each group)

Question	Group 1 after virtual laboratory tasks	Group 2 after reading and talk	Group 1 after both	Group 2 after both
15. Fume cupboard	5	5	5	5
16. Service hatch	5	4	5	5
17. Nearest sink	4	5	5	5
18. Nearest exit	5	5	4	5
19. Equipment room	3	1	4	3
20. Preparation room	3	2	5	4

Most participants answered questions 15, 16, 17 and 18 correctly and the differences between the performances of the two groups on these questions is small or zero. It should be noted that all of the locations were visible from the participants' positions where they did the test. Thus, even if they could not recall the location of a position, they would have been able to find it if they could identify it by sight.

Results on questions 19 and 20 indicate that many participants confused the equipment room and the preparation room. Little emphasis was placed on this in the verbal introduction, as undergraduates do not normally enter either room. Similarly, although participants were asked to enter each room in the virtual laboratory, there were no other tasks requiring students to use these rooms. Both groups improved their results on these questions after task reversal, perhaps indicating that having been tested on this they then took particular note of it during the second learning condition.

4.3.1.4 Positioning of apparatus and equipment

Questions 21 to 26 required participants to indicate on a laboratory map the location of various items of apparatus and equipment. Participants were marked correct if they marked the position of each item of apparatus or equipment within 2.5 metres of the correct location. A half a mark was awarded if they marked a position within 5 metres of the correct location. Table 4.5 shows the results.

Table 4.5
Number of participants correctly able to indicate the position of items of
apparatus and equipment within the laboratory
(out of five participants in each group)

Question	Group 1 after virtual laboratory tasks	Group 2 after reading and talk	Group 1 after both	Group 2 after both
21. Bunsen burner	5	4	5	3.5
22. 100ml beaker	4	2	5	5
23. Top-loading balance	5	3	5	5
24. Tripod stand	4	3	5	3.5
25. Nearest glass bin	3.5	5	5	5
26. Nearest waste bin	5	1.5	4	4.5

The results on these questions suggest that participants in Group 1, who had explored the virtual laboratory, performed better than participants in Group 2, who had read the laboratory manual extract and listened to a verbal introduction, on questions requiring them to indicate the location of apparatus within the laboratory. Although the various storage locations were pointed out to students in Group 2 they had not actually opened cupboards and drawers and removed objects. Thus, the fact that Group 1 participants had manipulated objects to a greater extent than Group 2 participants is the most likely reason for this result. Results for the two groups after task reversal were similar, which suggests that the different scores were not the result of differences in aptitude or prior learning.

4.3.1.5 Description of procedures

Questions 27 to 30 required participants to describe the procedures for using a burette and a pipette and the procedures to follow in the event of a chemical spill or a fire. In each case a percentage score was allocated depending on the number of steps correctly described. Half marks were awarded for steps described partially correctly. Table 4.6 shows the results.

Question	Table 4.6 Average group scores on procedural description questions			
	Group 1 after virtual laboratory tasks	Group 2 after reading and talk	Group 1 after both	Group 2 after both
27. Using a burette	62%	58%	56%	66%
28. Using a pipette	49%	54%	50%	69%
29. Fire	60%	41%	60%	48%
30. Chemical spill	63%	49%	64%	66%

The results on the procedural description questions show very little difference between Group 1 and Group 2 participants. The scores in the questions are lower than the scores on other questions. This can partly be explained by the fact that questions requiring explanations are more difficult. However, it also suggests that neither learning condition was highly effective for the outcomes tested by these questions. It should be noted that the virtual laboratory did not contain demonstrations of any of these procedures, nor the opportunity to practice the procedures. Rather, it contained written descriptions of procedures, with some links to allow viewing of apparatus or moving to relevant locations in the laboratory. There is potential therefore for improved results for virtual laboratory participants if demonstrations and practice of task procedures are made available.

4.3.2 Observations during virtual laboratory tasks

Participants were observed as they used the virtual laboratory and were encouraged to comment on problems encountered as well as possible improvements. The tables in this section list the observations noted as the participants used the virtual laboratory along with participant comments, and the implications of each, in terms of possible changes to the virtual laboratory. The actual changes made as a result of the pilot study are discussed in Section 4.4. Table 4.7 lists observed problems with the task design, Table 4.8 lists observed problems with the use of the menu and the display of information, Table 4.9 lists observed problems with motion and view control, Table 4.10 lists problems with object manipulation, Table 4.11 lists observations of participants using the environment in unexpected ways and Table 4.12 lists observed limitations of the 3D models.

Table 4.7	
Observed problems with the task design	
Observations	**Implications (possible changes)**
It was originally intended to give students 30 minutes in the training environment to learn to use the virtual environment interface, however students appeared to be confident after about 10 minutes and were becoming bored by 20 minutes.	Allocate less time to training.
Students did not use the sheet of interface instructions provided as they explored the training environment.	Show students where to find help within the environment instead of providing printed instructions.
The time spent on each section varied but it was difficult to record times for each student.	Get students to write down on the task sheet the time they commenced each task as well as ticking it when completed.

Table 4.8	
Observed problems with the menu and information display	
Observations	**Implications (possible changes)**
Messages shown in the text area in response to an action remain there, and as a result are sometimes read much later when they are no longer relevant.	Consider a more conventional alert mechanism, which requires the user to click an ok button.
Following a link in the 'using a Burette' page, which points to the pipette page leads to an error.	Fix this link
Because the environment was viewed full-screen with the Windows task bar hidden, links at the bottom of the text area were difficult to select, because moving the mouse there made the task bar visible.	Place some additional space at the bottom of each text page if it contains a link at the bottom.
Some students commented that the menus were cumbersome to use because the fact that the sub-menus stayed open meant that too much scrolling was required to locate the particular menu required.	Consider changing the menus so that only one branch is expanded at a time.

Table 4.9

Observed motion and view control problems

Observations	Implications (possible changes)
The arrow keys as a method of navigation worked initially but after clicking in another frame, no longer worked.	Fix the arrow keys so that they can always be used for movement
Some students had difficulty moving around the desks, and particularly had problems when they collided with a desk that was out of their view.	Provide a 'see myself' option to help avoid getting stuck behind desks Make users automatically slide along or around objects if they run into them
Some students suggested that they needed an option allowing them to go back to a previous viewpoint, for example if they chose a viewpoint in error.	Implement a back to previous position, or perhaps a general undo option.

Table 4.10
Observed object manipulation problems

Observations	Implications (possible changes)
Double-clicking on an object to drop it was not initially intuitive. Students tried to drag objects from the 'held objects' area to the environment	Allow dragging of objects from the held objects area as an alternative to double-clicking.
Objects could become lost by either dropping them in an out of sight location, or dragging them through surfaces.	Restrict where an object can be dropped to positions within a certain range. Restrict where an object can be dragged, so that objects can't be dragged through surfaces. Change the locate option so that it locates the current object position rather than the original position or provide a menu option to return an object to its original location in case it becomes lost.
Students tried to drop objects in places where they couldn't be dropped and were frustrated at the lack of feedback on where an object could be dropped.	Provide a list of choices of where objects can be dropped when the user tries to drop an object. Consider allowing the user to double-click a location to drop an object at that location. Consider also allowing the user to drag an object from the held area to a particular location (as discussed above). Provide more menu options to place objects in specific locations (eg. on bench).
Getting objects out of the top metal drawer was difficult, as it required a combination of walking and panning.	Provide viewpoints for accessing each drawer, so that moving and panning isn't required, possibly activated when drawer is opened.
The position of objects in the metal drawers continued to be relative to the position of the drawer even after taking them out of the drawer, and consequently the objects moved when the drawer was slid open or shut.	When an object is removed from the drawer, remove its positional relationship to the drawer.
Objects that were placed on the desk, then dragged, then picked up and then placed back in the locker, were positioned in the locker at a shifted location because of the drag.	When an object is picked up and dropped or moved using a menu item, reset the drag translation before placing the object.
Picking up the tripod from the drawer was difficult because it is quite thin and clicking just to the left or right of it results in the drawer being shut.	Create an invisible box around the tripod so that it can be selected more easily.
When dropping an object on the desk it will go in the locker if the locker is visible too.	Correct dropping algorithm to choose the nearest visible location rather than the first visible location found.

Table 4.11
Observations of unexpected usage

Observations	Implications (possible changes)
At least five out of the ten students discovered and used the additional navigation options available by right-clicking or double-clicking within the environment. They used this as a faster way of changing the movement mode or jumping to a specific viewpoint. Some found this menu disconcerting, especially if they activated it by double-clicking on an object which they hoped to pick up.	Include information about this option in the online help. Investigate ways of disabling the double-click menu and keeping only the right-click menu.
One student working with the menus hidden didn't realise that information about objects was available.	Consider showing the menus automatically if the user clicks on an object.
A number of students used the arrow keys to scroll the text areas.	In fixing the problem with navigation using the arrow keys don't prevent the use of the arrow keys for scrolling of the text area.
The yellow 'tool tips' provided automatically when the mouse was over some objects, such as the balances, was considered informative.	Investigate ways of providing these tool tips over all objects.
Students tried to click on virtually every item within the laboratory to find out information about it.	Make a greater number of items in the laboratory clickable, with information about them available. Also make sure that if one fire extinguisher (for example) is clickable, all are.
Students tried to pick up or drag objects that were not movable.	Provide a message if user tries to drag or pick up an object that cannot be moved.
Students expected to find glassware in all lockers.	Make only the student's locker openable, with a message if they try to open another locker, or alternatively populate all lockers, but only at the point that the cupboard is opened (to avoid performance problems).
Students expected the various machines in the laboratory, such as the electronic balances, to actually work.	Consider adding information letting the student know whether or not a piece of equipment is useable as part of the information provided when the item is selected.

Table 4.12
Observed limitations of the 3D model

Observations	Implications (possible changes)
One student became disoriented in the laboratory and suggested that a map be provided.	Provide a transparent overlay map showing the user's current position within the laboratory
The clock at the end of the laboratory is upside down.	Flip the clock.
Movement in the training environment seemed more realistic, perhaps because of the textured floor.	Use a texture for the floor in the virtual laboratory, matching the textured lino in the real laboratory.
Ceiling colour in the virtual laboratory is not realistic and was considered distasteful by one student.	Match ceiling colour better to real laboratory.
One student suggested that the equipment room and the preparation room need more equipment and objects to provide better cues for orientation.	Add more objects to these rooms.

4.3.3 Observations during laboratory session

Because there were around 40 other students undertaking their practical at the same time as the 10 students involved in this investigation, it was not possible to gather specific data on the performance of the students involved in the investigation. Instead, general observations about the skills required for this practical session were made. Table 4.13 lists the observations and the possible changes to the virtual laboratory as a consequence.

Table 4.13	
Observations during laboratory session	
Observation	**Implications (possible changes)**
There are a number of important items of furniture missing from the virtual laboratory, including the brown drawers containing pipettes, the sinks, and one of the entrance doors.	Add missing brown drawers, sinks, and missing door.
The use of the burette and the pipette includes a number of steps, which are not very clear in the laboratory manual or in the text in the virtual laboratory.	Provide an animated demonstration of the procedures for using a burette and a pipette. Provide options allowing you to use a burette and a pipette in a similar way to how you would use them in the real laboratory, including pouring and measuring of liquid.
Lecturers and laboratory staff emphasise correct clothing, footwear and eyewear very strongly. Additionally, certain items such as calculators, completed pre-lab exercises, writing implements and the laboratory manual are required for every practical.	Consider starting the user in a virtual bedroom and requiring them to collect everything they need before the practical (labcoat, glasses, footwear, calculator, laboratory manual, pre-lab exercises)
The laboratory contains numerous posters and notices, some of which would be helpful for orientation and some of which would provide useful information in the virtual laboratory.	Include the following posters in the virtual laboratory: - Fire extinguisher signs - Laboratory rules poster - No smoking sign - Periodic table posters (possibly with links to information about each element) - Exit signs - Board containing examples of glassware with labels.
Laboratory staff like to point out a burn mark on the ceiling as an example of what can happen in some experiments and thus the need for correct eyewear to be warn.	Include this burn mark in the virtual laboratory, with link to information about how it got there and the implications.

4.3.4 Interview results

Participants were each interviewed individually at the conclusion of the investigation. The interviews were structured, that is, specific questions were asked of each participant. Some of the questions consisted of statements, and the participant was asked to indicate the degree to which they agreed or disagreed with each, with their responses recorded using a Likert scale. Other questions were more open-ended and a summary of the participants' responses was written down.

Table 4.14 shows the answers to the first 10 questions, which, aside from the first question, ask for the participants' general impressions of the virtual laboratory.

Table 4.14
Summary of structured interview responses to questions about participants' general impressions of the virtual laboratory

Question	Avge	Number of responses (n=10)						
		7. very strongly agree	6. strongly agree	5. agree	4. neutral	3. disagree	2. strongly disagree	1. very strongly disagree
1. You enjoy playing computer games.	4.6	1	1	4	2	1	1	0
2. You enjoyed using the virtual lab.	5.5	1	3	6	0	0	0	0
3. Overall the virtual lab helped you to become familiar with the real lab.	5.5	0	7	2	0	1	0	0
4. The use of the virtual lab alone was sufficient to prepare you for your first laboratory experiment.	4.6	2	0	2	4	2	0	0
5a. The virtual lab was more helpful for familiarising you with the lab than the lab manual.	5.5	2	4	1	3	0	0	0
5b. The virtual lab was more helpful for familiarising you with the lab than the verbal introduction in the first practical session.	5.1	1	2	4	3	0	0	0
6. The virtual lab is an accurate representation of the real lab.	5.3	1	2	6	1	0	0	0
7. The information accessible from within the virtual lab is accurate and consistent with the information provided in the lab manual.	5.7	2	4	3	1	0	0	0
8. The information accessible from within the virtual lab is accurate and consistent with the information provided by your lecturers.	5.6	1	4	5	0	0	0	0
9. The virtual lab is easy to use.	5.6	0	6	4	0	0	0	0
10. The training exercise using the national gallery of Ireland environment was sufficient to allow you to use the virtual lab easily.	5.9	1	7	2	0	0	0	0

All participants enjoyed using the virtual laboratory even though only six stated that they enjoyed playing computer games. The participants on the whole seemed to be enthusiastic and conscientious learners (which may in fact be why they volunteered to participate in the study). A possible explanation for the fact that some participants enjoyed using the laboratory but not playing computer games is that these participants could see a purpose to the use of the virtual laboratory but not to playing games. It is possible also that the fact that the researcher undertook the interview created a positive bias in participants' responses.

Nine participants stated that the virtual laboratory helped them to become familiar with the real laboratory. The student who did not was from Group 2, and thus had already spent time in the laboratory by the time he used the virtual laboratory. He stated in his comments that he was already familiar with the laboratory and thus could not become familiar again. Most students did not think that the virtual laboratory alone was sufficient for preparing them for their first experiment but seven students thought that the virtual laboratory was more helpful than the laboratory manual or the verbal introduction.

There was a strong consensus that the virtual laboratory was an accurate representation and that the information accessible from within it was consistent with the information provided by the lecturers and in the laboratory manual. There was also a strong consensus that the virtual laboratory was easy to use and that the training exercise was sufficient.

Table 4.15 shows the answers to questions 11 to 23 that asked for the participants' impressions of specific aspects of the virtual laboratory.

Table 4.15
Summary of structured interview responses to questions about participants'
impressions of specific aspects of the virtual laboratory

Question	Average	Number of responses (n=10)						
		7. very strongly agree	6. strongly agree	5. agree	4. neutral	3. disagree	2. strongly disagree	1. very strongly disagree
11. The virtual lab helped you to become familiar with the layout of the lab building.	6	3	4	3	0	0	0	0
12. The virtual lab helped you to be able to identify items of apparatus.	5.2	1	3	3	3	0	0	0
13. The virtual lab helped you to be able to locate items within the lab.	5.8	2	4	4	0	0	0	0
14. The virtual lab helped you to become familiar with the procedure for using a burette.	4.6	0	0	7	2	1	0	0
15. The virtual lab helped you to become familiar with the procedure for using a pipette.	4.7	0	2	4	3	1	0	0
16. The virtual lab helped you to become familiar with the procedure for using a laboratory balance.	4.6	0	0	7	2	1	0	0
17. The virtual lab helped you to become familiar with safety procedures in the lab.	5.9	2	5	3	0	0	0	0
18. You are more likely to remember procedures if you read about them while carrying out related tasks in the virtual lab than if you read about them in the lab manual away from the lab.	6.3	4	5	1	0	0	0	0

Table 4.15 (cont)
**Summary of structured interview responses to questions about participants'
impressions of specific aspects of the virtual laboratory**

Question	Average	Number of responses (n=10)						
		7. very strongly agree	6. strongly agree	5. agree	4. neutral	3. disagree	2. strongly disagree	1. very strongly disagree
19. In its current form, you would recommend that new students use the virtual lab prior to their first laboratory experiment.	6	3	4	3	0	0	0	0
20. In its current form, you would use the virtual lab prior to laboratory sessions to practice setting up the apparatus.	5.1	1	3	3	2	1	0	0
21. If the mechanisms for manipulating apparatus were improved and if all required apparatus were available in the virtual lab, you would use it prior to laboratory sessions to practice setting up the apparatus.	5.9	3	3	4	0	0	0	0
22. If the virtual lab allowed you to carry out virtual experiments, you would use it prior to laboratory sessions to practice the experiments.	6.3	4	5	1	0	0	0	0
23. You would prefer to prepare for laboratory sessions using a virtual lab than reading the lab manual	6.2	5	3	1	1	0	0	0

Questions 12, 14, 15 and 16 asked about the participant's view of the effectiveness of the virtual laboratory for familiarising them with various apparatus and the procedures for using them. The participants who did not agree that the laboratory was effective for this purpose stated that they were already familiar with these apparatus and thus could not be made familiar again.

All participants agreed that the virtual laboratory helped them to become familiar with the layout of the laboratory, the location of apparatus and laboratory safety procedures.

There was strong agreement that procedures learnt by reading about them in the virtual laboratory would be more likely to be remembered than procedures learnt through reading the laboratory manual.

Participants agreed that they would recommend the use of the virtual laboratory to new students prior to their first laboratory session. Similarly, all participants agreed that they would use the virtual laboratory prior to laboratory sessions if the mechanisms for manipulating apparatus were improved and the required apparatus were available, or if virtual experiments were possible. Nine of the ten participants indicated that they would prefer to prepare for their laboratory sessions using the virtual laboratory than using the laboratory manual. One commented that using the computer makes a change from the norm.

Question 24 asked participants to comment on aspects of the virtual laboratory that they found useful in familiarising them with the real laboratory. Comments included the following:

- "I was immediately aware of the layout of the lab straight away".
- "The layout of the lab including benches and equipment and a basic idea of how to use apparatus".
- "Knowing where all equipment is, especially what is in lockers and what is on [the] side [benches]".
- "Safety procedures were clearer in the virtual laboratory".
- "I tend to pay more attention when reading than listening".
- "The information in the virtual laboratory was more memorable because I was doing tasks at the same time as reading; visualising at the same time".

Two students commented that they felt more confident in their first practical session because of their exploration of the virtual laboratory and particularly more confident than other students who had not participated in the investigation and thus had not used the virtual laboratory. However, one student commented that their laboratory partner, who had not used the virtual laboratory, had no trouble finding their way around.

These comments are very encouraging for the use of virtual environments for learning in general and for this study in particular.

Question 25 asked participants what information or skills they needed to help with their first laboratory experiment that were not provided in the virtual laboratory. Information and skills identified included the following:

- Identification and location of apparatus in the brown drawers;

- Demonstrations of experiment procedures;

- Actual practice with experiment procedures, specifically setting up apparatus;

- Detailed information about use of pipette and filler;

- Methods of filling up burettes, including how to avoid air bubbles;

- More accurate models and information about how to use balances;

- Practice with calculations; and

- Simulations of emergency situation, allowing practice of procedures like using safety shower.

Question 26 asked participants to comment on learning from their use of the virtual laboratory that was not assessed in the test. All students found this difficult to answer. One student suggested that a useful test question could have been to identify a series of named items of apparatus from a display showing a large number of apparatus including unknown items. Another suggested that they learnt about the contents of their lockers, but were not tested on this knowledge.

Questions 27 to 34 asked participants to indicate which of a series of apparatus they would have already been able to identify prior to coming to CSU. Table 4.16 shows the results.

Table 4.16
Summary of structured interview responses to questions about apparatus already able to be identified by the participant prior to the study

Apparatus	Number already familiar (n=10)	Number not already familiar (n=10)
Burette	8	2
Pipette	8	2
Beaker	10	0
Conical Flask	10	0
Graduated Cylinder	8	2
Bunsen Burner	10	0
Analytic Balance	2	8
Top Loading Balance	7	3

Clearly, the vast majority of participants were already familiar with all apparatus except for the analytic balance. A consequence of this is that the results of test questions requiring participants to identify these items of apparatus are of limited use.

Questions 35, 36 and 37 required participants to indicate which procedures for using apparatus they were already familiar with. Table 4.17 shows their responses.

Table 4.17
Summary of structured interview responses to questions about apparatus procedures already familiar to the participant prior to the study

Procedure	Number already familiar (n=10)	Number not already familiar (n=10)
Procedure for using a burette	7	3
Procedure for using a pipette	8	2
Procedure for using some type of electronic balance	10	0

Again, the majority of participants indicated that they were already familiar with all procedures, which means that the results of test questions about apparatus procedures may be of limited use.

Questions 38 to 53 required participants to indicate the degree to which they agreed with statements about the usefulness of various aspects of the virtual laboratory and whether various aspects were clear and worked as expected. Table 4.18 shows the responses to each question.

Table 4.18

Summary of structured interview responses to questions about the usefulness and ease of use of aspects of the virtual laboratory

Question	Avge	Number of responses (n=10)						
		7. very strongly agree	6. strongly agree	5. agree	4. neutral	3. disagree	2. strongly disagree	1. very strongly disagree
38. The menus at the left of the screen were useful.	6	2	6	2	0	0	0	0
39. The use of the menus at the left of the screen was clear and worked as expected.	5.8	1	6	3	0	0	0	0
40. The three movement modes (walk, pan and jump) were useful.	5.8	1	6	3	0	0	0	0
41. The use of the three movement modes was clear and worked as expected.	5.3	0	3	7	0	0	0	0
42. The ability to click on objects to find out information about them was a useful feature.	6.2	3	6	1	0	0	0	0
43. The ability to drag objects around was a useful feature.	5.9	1	7	2	0	0	0	0
44. The mechanism for dragging objects around was clear and worked as expected.	4.1	1	0	2	4	2	1	0
45. The ability to pickup objects and carry them to a new location was a useful feature.	6	1	8	1	0	0	0	0
46. The mechanism for picking up and carrying objects was clear and worked as expected.	5.4	1	5	3	0	0	1	0
47. The ability to move some objects to a specific location by choosing an option in the menus was a useful feature.	5.8	3	4	1	2	0	0	0

Table 4.18 (cont)

Summary of structured interview responses to questions about the usefulness and ease of use of aspects of the virtual laboratory

Question	Avge	Number of responses (n=10)						
		7. very strongly agree	6. strongly agree	5. agree	4. neutral	3. disagree	2. strongly disagree	1. very strongly disagree
48. The options provided by right-clicking or double-clicking in the environment window were useful.	5.4	1	6	0	2	1	0	0
49. Using the arrow keys to move around (when they worked) was easier than using the mouse.	5.9	5	3	0	0	2	0	0
50. Using the mouse to move around was easier than the arrow keys (when the arrow keys worked).	2.3	0	0	2	0	1	3	4
51. The ability to hide the menus and expand the size of the virtual lab on the screen was a useful feature.	5.9	2	6	1	1	0	0	0
52. The ability to locate items of apparatus using the options in the menu was a useful feature.	6	2	6	2	0	0	0	0
53. The options in the help menu were useful.	4.4	0	1	2	7	0	0	0

There was general agreement that most of the features listed were useful. The only one that there was any disagreement with was the option provided by right-clicking or double-clicking in the environment window and only one participant disagreed.

Two participants stated that they disagreed that the mechanism for dragging objects around was clear and worked as expected. This is not surprising, given that problems with losing objects after dragging them through walls were observed.

Eight participants preferred to use the keyboard for movement over the mouse, which was consistent with earlier research carried out by the researcher (Dalgarno and Scott, 2000). This suggested that addressing the problems observed with the arrows ceasing to work for movement after clicking within the menu frame was necessary.

Seven participants indicated that they did not notice the help menu options. This may suggest that they did not have sufficient problems using the environment to need to look for help.

Questions 54 to 69 asked students to indicate the degree to which they agreed or disagreed with a series of possible changes to the virtual laboratory. The list of changes arose from observations and student comments while using the virtual laboratory. Table 4.19 shows the responses.

Table 4.19
Summary of structured interview responses to questions about proposed changes to the virtual laboratory

Question	Average	Number of responses (n=10)						
		7. very strongly agree	6. strongly agree	5. agree	4. neutral	3. disagree	2. strongly disagree	1. very strongly disagree
54. Adding missing furniture, such as brown drawers and sinks, as well as missing door	6.2	3	6	1	0	0	0	0
55. Making a greater number of items in the lab clickable, with information about them available	6.3	3	7	0	0	0	0	0
56. Fixing the arrow keys so that they can always be used for movement	6.5	5	5	0	0	0	0	0
57. Restricting where an object can be dragged, so that objects can't be dragged through surfaces	6.4	4	6	0	0	0	0	0
58. Providing a list of choices of where objects can be dropped if you try to drop an object	5.8	1	6	3	0	0	0	0
59. Changing the locate option so that it locates the current object position rather than the original position	6.4	4	6	0	0	0	0	0
60. Providing a menu option to return an object to its original location in case it becomes lost	6.4	4	6	0	0	0	0	0
61. Providing a "see myself" option to help avoid getting stuck behind desks	6	1	8	1	0	0	0	0
62. Making you automatically slide along or around objects if you run into them	5.9	3	5	1	0	1	0	0
63. Providing viewpoints for accessing each drawer, so that moving and panning isn't required	6	2	6	2	0	0	0	0

Table 4.19 (cont)
Summary of structured interview responses to questions about proposed changes to the virtual laboratory

Question	Average	Number of responses (n=10)						
		7. very strongly agree	6. strongly agree	5. agree	4. neutral	3. disagree	2. strongly disagree	1. very strongly disagree
64. Providing more menu options to place objects in specific locations (eg. on desk)	5.8	0	8	2	0	0	0	0
65. Providing a transparent overlay map showing your current position within the lab	5.6	3	4	1	0	2	0	0
66. Providing an animated demonstration of the procedures for using apparatus (eg. burette)	6.3	3	7	0	0	0	0	0
67. Providing options allowing you to use items of apparatus in a similar way to how you would use them in the real laboratory (eg. burette)	6.4	5	4	1	0	0	0	0
68. Providing options allowing you to simulate experiments including chemical reactions	6.5	5	5	0	0	0	0	0
69. Starting you in a virtual bedroom and requiring you to collect everything you need before the prac (labcoat, glasses, footwear, calculator, lab manual, pre-lab exercises)	5.7	2	4	3	1	0	0	0

There was general agreement to all proposed changes. The only proposed changes that attracted any disagreement were the proposal to make the user automatically slide along objects collided with (one participant disagreed) and providing a transparent overlay map showing the laboratory and the user's current position (two participants disagreed). One participant suggested that automatically sliding along surfaces collided with might be disconcerting if the participant wanted to move close to the desk to do something. One participant suggested that because the virtual laboratory is not a very complex space there is no need to provide a map. Another suggested that the map would be ok if there was an option to hide/show it. Another suggested that a current direction indicator would be helpful.

The strongest agreement was for the idea of fixing the arrows so that they can be used for movement all of the time and for the idea of providing options allowing the simulation of virtual experiments. Other proposed changes with very strong agreement were restricting the dragging of objects so that they can't be dragged through surfaces, fixing the locate object option so that it finds the object no matter where it is, providing a menu option to return an object to its original position and allowing apparatus to be used in the same way they are used in the real laboratory.

Question 70 asked participants to comment on additional features of the virtual laboratory that they thought would improve it as a resource for familiarising students with the real laboratory. The following are some suggestions:

- Provide more objects of apparatus or equipment so that the virtual laboratory is as cluttered as the real laboratory;

- Allow dropping of objects on the floor in the virtual laboratory and procedures for cleaning up;

- Provide a "back" option to go to previous text screen (necessary because full-screen mode removes the browser back button);

- Allow student to use the locker in the virtual laboratory that corresponds to their allocated locker in the real laboratory;

- Include demonstrations of experiments for each practical session; and

- Allow participants to carry out experiments.

Question 71 asked participants to list any additional inconsistencies between the virtual laboratory and the real laboratory that they noticed. The following additional inconsistencies were identified:

- The inside of the virtual laboratory is raw brick, but the actual laboratory is painted on the inside;

- The real laboratory is more brightly lit;

- The real laboratory contains a lot more apparatus and equipment and more objects on shelves;

- There are bag racks under the fume cupboards in the real laboratory;

- The vacuum and gas taps are missing from the virtual laboratory;

- The ceiling and many of the surfaces in the virtual laboratory are a yellow or green colour rather than a white or cream colour;

- The door that is usually used to enter the real laboratory doesn't exist in the virtual laboratory, and consequently some students felt disoriented when entering the real laboratory; and

- There are large square blue objects of furniture in the virtual laboratory that are not in the real laboratory.

Question 72 asked participants to list any additional inconsistencies between the information contained in the virtual laboratory and the information provided in the laboratory manual or the information provided by their lecturers. The following additional inconsistencies were identified:

- The laboratory manual contains more detail about some aspects of using the apparatus and it was suggested that links into the laboratory manual from within the virtual laboratory would be helpful;

- The lecturer suggested that a white lab coat is required, whereas the information in the virtual laboratory said that an alternative type of covering was ok;

- The lecturer's demonstration contained more detail about the use of the eye wash/safety shower; and

- The laboratory manual explained how to use a bulb with a pipette, whereas the virtual laboratory contained a pipette filler (similar to the one used in the real laboratory).

Question 73 asked participants to comment on any additional aspects of using the virtual laboratory that they found were unclear or didn't work as expected. The following additional problems were identified:

- It was possible to accidentally go outside the laboratory through the window near the eye-droppers;

- It was not clear whether or not an object was interactive (could be clicked on, dragged, or picked up);

- The pan movement mode was confusing at first;

- The jump movement mode sometimes moved too close to an object and this was a problem because there was no "back" or "undo" option; and

- The menu, once expanded, contained too many options, making it very time consuming to scroll and find the sought after option.

Question 74 asked participants to comment on any additional improvements to the design of the virtual laboratory that would make its use clearer and easier. The following improvements were suggested:

- Additional movement modes, such as examine mode, should be explicitly supported;

- Virtual demonstrators should be included;

- Include a search option for locating apparatus; and

- The options for moving objects to specific locations should be provided as links within the informative text rather than in the menus, because the use of the menus was cumbersome, due to the scrolling required.

Question 75 asked participants to comment on any improvements to the training exercise using the National Gallery of Ireland environment that would have helped them to be able to use the virtual laboratory. The following improvements were suggested:

- More objects to explore and manipulate should be provided with more alternatives for places to put them down after picking them up;

- There should be more to do in general;

- Objects should not be able to be lost;

- Opening doors should be included;

- More obstacles to walk around should be included; and

- Information about each painting should be included (to keep the user's interest as they explore).

4.4 Discussion

The original aims of the pilot investigation were to explore the virtual laboratory design, the training process, the learning tasks, the test items and the overall effectiveness of the virtual laboratory for learning. The conclusions that can be drawn from the pilot in each of these areas are discussed in the following sections.

4.4.1 Virtual laboratory design

Comments of the participants during the interviews indicated that they were very enthusiastic about the use of the virtual laboratory. All participants agreed that the virtual laboratory helped them to become familiar with the layout of the laboratory, the location of apparatus and laboratory safety procedures. There was also strong agreement that procedures learnt by reading about them in the virtual laboratory would be more likely to be remembered than procedures learnt through reading the laboratory manual. Participants agreed that they would recommend the use of the virtual laboratory to new students prior to their first laboratory session. Similarly, all participants agreed that they would use the virtual laboratory prior to laboratory sessions if the mechanisms for manipulating apparatus were improved and the required apparatus were available, or if virtual experiments were possible. These comments provided encouragement to the researcher in the use of the virtual laboratory as a research instrument and in the value of the research generally.

Through observations of participants using the virtual laboratory, along with comments made by the participants as they used it and during the interviews, a large number of design issues were identified. The various problems identified were presented in Section 4.3.2 along with possible changes initially identified. The changes actually made to the virtual laboratory as a result of the pilot investigation are presented in the following paragraphs.

The following changes were made to the 3D models within the virtual laboratory for Investigation 1 as a result of findings from the pilot:

- An invisible box was created around the tripods so that they could be more easily selected, dragged or picked up;

- A greater number of objects were made clickable so that the name of the item would be displayed when clicked;

- The word 'empty' was placed on all lockers except the one containing glassware, on which was placed the words 'general glassware';

- The upside-down clock was placed the correct way up;

- A texture was added to the floor, the colour of the ceiling was changed, the interior walls were changed from brick to white and the lighting inside the laboratory was increased;

- Two sets of 24 brown drawers containing miscellaneous items of apparatus were added;

- Five sets of sinks with taps and eyewashes were added;

- Gas taps and power points were added to each bench;

- A missing entrance door to the laboratory was added; and

- Some large blue items of furniture initially intended as placeholders to be replaced by sinks were removed.

The following changes to the motion control interface for Investigation 1 were made as a result of findings from the pilot:

- The Pan and Jump movement modes were removed and instead the ability to pan by holding down the shift key while using the arrow keys was introduced;

- The problem that caused the arrow keys to stop responding was resolved;

- When a drawer or cupboard was opened by clicking with the mouse, the viewpoint was moved to a position and direction which allowed the user to view the contents of the drawer or cupboard; and

- The right-click menu was disabled along with its activation by double-clicking.

In Investigation 1, the options for carrying objects around the laboratory and dragging them across surfaces were removed. Instead, objects could be picked up and rotated, then returned to their original position. Moving objects to other positions in the laboratory was not considered necessary to allow participants to develop their knowledge of the spatial structure of objects. In Investigation 2, in which participants undertook an authentic apparatus manipulation task, these options were once again implemented. A number of the object manipulation problems identified in the pilot were addressed in this version. The following are the changes made to the object manipulation interface used in Investigation 2 as a result of findings from the pilot:

- A hand icon was used to more clearly show that an object was currently being held or carried;

- Rather than double-clicking to release held objects, objects could be dragged from the hand to a highlighted target position, which was considered more intuitive, provided more control over where an object was to be released and prevented objects accidentally being released to locations out of sight; and

- The problem in which objects that had been removed from drawers moved when the drawer was opened or closed was fixed.

In addition to the changes listed above, a number of changes were made to the virtual laboratory so that it would better meet the requirements of Investigation 1. The major change was the removal of the left-hand pull-down menu, along with the text information about the laboratory, equipment and apparatus. The text information was removed in order to focus the participants' attention specifically on spatial aspects of the laboratory. The navigation options were not provided in Investigation 1 because it was seen as desirable for the User-control group to locate the items of apparatus through free exploration without the aid of this menu.

There were a number of changes suggested by participants, or identified as possible solutions to problems, which were not implemented. These are presented in Table 4.20 along with the rationale for not implementing each possible change.

Table 4.20
Identified changes not implemented

Possible change	Reason for not implementing
Provide a 'see myself' option to help avoid getting stuck behind desks. Make users automatically slide along or around objects if they run into them.	The problem of users getting stuck behind desks was instead addressed by removing collision detection for an area at the ends of the desks, so that in effect the user could pass through these parts of the desk. Testing indicated that passing through this part of the desk was not noticeable and did not affect the sense of realism.
Implement a back to previous position, or perhaps a general undo option.	This problem was mainly a problem with the 'jump' movement mode, which was not provided in the version used in Investigation 1. In Investigation 2, where a 'jump' option was provided through the use of the F3 key in conjunction with the mouse, a back to previous position option was provided using the Home key.
Restrict where an object can be dragged, so that objects can't be dragged through surfaces.	In Investigation 2, where dragging of objects was provided, objects could be dragged through surfaces, but unless dropped in a target location, they returned to their original position when released. This prevented objects being released in positions out of sight and becoming lost.
Provide yellow 'tool-tips' when mouse is placed over all objects.	This was not possible. The tool-tips are automatically shown by Blaxxun Contact over objects that are hyperlinks to information but not objects linked to a script. Thus the tool-tips could not be provided for interactive objects (objects able to be dragged or carried).
Provide a message if the user tries to drag or pickup an object that cannot be moved.	This was not done, but the problem of identifying movable objects was addressed in Investigation 2 by the words 'movable object' being displayed next to the object name in the text area after the object had been clicked on.
Provide a transparent overlay map showing the user's current position in the laboratory.	This was not considered necessary by most participants in the pilot as the virtual laboratory is a relatively simple environment.

4.4.2 Training Process

The training process, which involved the use of another 3D environment, modelled on the National Gallery of Ireland, supported by a task worksheet, was very effective. However, the time allocated to training (30 minutes) was clearly too great, with all participants demonstrating competent use of the interface in under 10 minutes and showing signs of boredom by about 20 minutes. Consequently in Investigations 1 and 2, only 10 minutes was allocated for training.

Participants suggested including more objects and more information in the training environment. This may have been because they were required to spend longer using it than was necessary to learn the interface, and consequently they may have requested a more complex environment to make it more interesting. With the training time reduced in Investigations 1 and 2, it was not seen as necessary to add more objects or information to the training environment.

None of the participants used the user interface instructions provided within the training task worksheet. This may have been because they found the interface sufficiently easy to use that they did not need to read further information. Nevertheless, the user interface instructions were changed for subsequent investigations (see Appendix H and Appendix L). The instructions were simplified and made less wordy, to make it easier to quickly refer to them when needed.

4.4.3 Learning Tasks

The tasks that participants carried out using the virtual laboratory were to: read and summarise information about appropriate laboratory clothing; visit a series of positions within the virtual laboratory; locate each of a series of items of apparatus; read and summarise a series of safety procedure descriptions; and explore, manipulate and make notes on the usage procedures for a series of items of apparatus. These tasks seemed to be quite effective in familiarising participants with the laboratory.

However, there were a number of changes to the tasks for Investigation 1, in order to better meet the requirements of this investigation. With the removal of the text descriptions from the environment for Investigation 1, the tasks of reading and summarising textual information were not appropriate. Additionally, because Investigation 1 compared spatial learning from undertaking a virtual tour with spatial learning from free exploration, it was considered appropriate to remove the initial sequential list of locations to visit. Instead User-control participants in Investigation 1 were just asked to find a series of laboratory landmarks, items of equipment and items of apparatus and to explore and manipulate each item of apparatus. Some of the apparatus manipulation tasks trialed in the pilot were reintroduced in Investigation 2, which involved the more authentic task of locating, collecting and assembling the apparatus for an experiment.

4.4.4 Test Items

The test results indicated that many of the questions were too easy for the participants. For test items requiring the identification of apparatus, this was due to the participants' prior knowledge. For test items requiring recall of the location of items of equipment and apparatus, this was due to the fact that the test was undertaken in the actual laboratory and too much visual information was available to them at the time that they undertook the test. For test items requiring recall of factual information about clothing and safety procedures, the information was straight-forward and easily remembered. Only the test items requiring recall of step-by-step procedures for carrying out tasks using apparatus were sufficiently difficult to provide a spread of results.

Clearly, if tests requiring identification of apparatus were to be used in the major investigations, additional items of apparatus unfamiliar to participants would be required or participants with less prior chemistry knowledge would have to be used. Using non-chemistry students was initially considered undesirable because the lack of a genuine interest in the content could impact on the external validity of the results. In fact, it became necessary to use non-chemistry students in Investigation 1, in any case, because the investigation occurred midway through the year and all chemistry students had had too much experience in the laboratory by that time. In Investigation 2, chemistry students were used, but these students were drawn from a course in which most students had not completed chemistry at senior high school level. Additionally, in Investigations 1 and 2, knowledge of the details of apparatus structure was also tested in addition to identification of apparatus. It was surmised that tests requiring recall of configurational knowledge of items of apparatus viewed in the virtual laboratory would be sufficiently difficult, even for participants with prior familiarity with similar items of apparatus.

The tests were undertaken in the actual laboratory on the basis that this was the context in which learning from either the laboratory manual or the virtual laboratory was to be applied. It was surmised that learning undertaken within a virtual environment would be better applied within the corresponding real environment than learning undertaken in another context (such as reading undertaken in the participant's home). However, a consequence of this was that test items requiring the participant to indicate places within the laboratory were too easy. It was concluded that it would be necessary to carry out the tests in an alternative location to make the test items sufficiently difficult that ceiling effects would be avoided.

Results on the tests carried out after task reversal were similar for the two groups. This may suggest that the two groups were similar in aptitude and possibly prior learning. However, it is more likely to be due to ceiling effects, with most test items being too easy. It may be very difficult to develop tests that are sufficiently difficult that participants completing the test for a second time, after two learning conditions directed towards the test, do not obtain near perfect performance. An alternative may have been to use a pre-test rather than task reversal, so that actual learning as a result of each condition could have been determined. However, if the same test was to be used for a pre-test and a post-test it may have encouraged participants to focus specifically on the concepts covered in the test during their learning tasks. On the other hand if different tests were to be used, it may have been difficult to ensure equivalency. Given the problems associated with both the use of a pre-test and a design involving task-reversal, it was decided to do neither in the major investigations. It was surmised that as long as the sample sizes were sufficient and participants were randomly assigned to groups, it could be assumed that aptitude and prior knowledge would be evenly distributed between the groups.

4.4.5 Effectiveness of the virtual laboratory for learning

Because of limitations in the test instruments, specifically the fact that most questions were too easy and ceiling effects occurred, it is difficult to draw any conclusions about the effectiveness of the virtual laboratory for learning as compared to the alternative approach of a verbal introduction and reading of the laboratory manual. However, the observations of the students using the environment and the students' comments in the interviews suggest that the virtual laboratory is an effective learning resource. The information obtained during the pilot provided encouragement for the researcher in proceeding with the study. The researcher was able to prepare for the next investigation confident that after the changes to the virtual laboratory design, the test instrument and the learning tasks were made, the research questions about the effect of the identified characteristics of 3D learning environments on spatial learning would be able to be addressed.

4.5 Conclusion

This chapter has described a pilot investigation designed to explore the usability of the virtual laboratory and to evaluate the training process, the learning tasks and the test instruments prior to the major investigations. As a result of this pilot a number of changes to the virtual laboratory were made and the planned learning tasks, training processes and test items also evolved. Chapter 5 describes the first major investigation, Investigation 1, which explored the contribution of user control over view and object manipulation to spatial learning.

Chapter 5. Investigation 1

5.1 Introduction

Investigation 1, the first major investigation in this study, was undertaken in May 2002, three months after the completion of the pilot investigation. It focussed on the importance of two characteristics of 3D learning environments, user control over view and user controlled object manipulation for spatial learning. In order to explore the importance of these characteristics, two versions of the virtual laboratory were developed, one allowing full user control and a second providing similar animated visual images, but providing a tour of the virtual laboratory with control only over the length of the pause between viewing each animated step. Participants in one group, the 'User-control group' explored the version of the virtual laboratory, providing full user control and participants of a second group, the 'Dynamic Views group', viewed the animated tour. Participants were then tested on their spatial learning.

As discussed in Chapter 2, an investigation of the characteristics of 3D environments that are important for spatial knowledge formation is essential in order to establish whether such environments can provide advantages over traditional interactive multimedia resources for conceptual learning. In particular, the characteristics of user control over view and of object manipulation distinguish 3D environments from video and animation, and consequently, an exploration of whether these characteristics contribute to spatial learning is particularly important.

5.2 Questions Addressed by This Investigation

This investigation addressed the third and fourth research questions, which were:

- Question 3. Does user control over view position and direction in a 3D learning environment contribute to spatial learning?

- Question 4. Does object manipulation in a 3D learning environment contribute to spatial learning?

5.3 Method

5.3.1 Overview

Participants were divided into three groups: a User-control group who explored the
virtual laboratory with full control over view and a degree of object manipulation
capability, a Dynamic Views group who viewed a series of animated images making up
a tour of the virtual laboratory, and a Real Laboratory group who explored the real
laboratory. Participants of each group were then tested on their spatial learning. Table
5.1 shows the time allocated to each task for each of the three groups of participants.

A comparison of the performance of the User-control group and the Dynamic Views
group was expected to address the research questions relating to the importance of user
control over view and object manipulation. The performance of the Real Laboratory
group was intended to allow an assessment of the overall effectiveness of the virtual
laboratory for spatial learning. This was seen as necessary because if spatial learning
from the virtual laboratory was not comparable to learning from the real laboratory, it
could be argued that the virtual laboratory was not effective enough for the results to be
of interest to educators.

Table 5.1
Allocated time for each task in Investigation 1

	Dynamic Views group	User-control group	Real laboratory group
Training environment	10min	10min	N/A
Virtual environment or real laboratory exploration	40min	40min	40min
Rest	5min	5min	5min
Test	45min	45min	45min
Total	1hour 40min	1h 40min	1hour 30min

5.3.2 Participants

The participants were undergraduate Information Technology (IT) students. Twenty-one
males and 15 females were initially recruited and were allocated evenly into three

groups, each containing 7 males and 5 females. However, because two participants failed to attend their allocated session, the number of participants and the ratio of males to females in each group differed. Additionally, one male member of the User-control group struggled with the navigation interface and suffered noticeable stress. Because of his difficulty moving around the laboratory he was able to locate only 11 of the 29 items of apparatus in the given time, and consequently his data was excluded from the analysis. The exclusion of participants' data due to discomfort or being unable to complete the learning condition adequately is relatively common for research involving immersive environments (see for example Ruddle et al., 1999; Witmer et al., 1996) although less common for desktop environments. All other members of the User-control group were able to move around the virtual laboratory without noticeable difficulty, leaving a total of 33 participants, 6 males and 5 females in the User-control group, 6 males and 5 females in the Dynamic Views group and 7 males and 4 females in the Real Laboratory group. Table 5.2 summarises the allocation of participants into groups.

Table 5.2 Participants in Investigation 1			
	Dynamic Views Group	**User-control Group**	**Real Laboratory Group**
Males	6	6	7
Females	5	5	4
Total	11	11	11

5.3.3 Virtual Laboratory

The virtual laboratory was explored through Internet Explorer 5.5 and the Blaxxun Contact VRML browser version 5.104, using a PC with a 15 inch screen and a standard keyboard and mouse, running Windows 2000. The PCs had basic hardware acceleration, allowing a frame rate of between 5 and 15 frames per second (depending on the part of the virtual environment visible at the time). Internet Explorer was configured to run full-screen, so that none of the Internet Explorer options, or the Windows taskbar were visible. The learning was undertaken in a computer laboratory, with up to eight participants working concurrently, each on their own computer.

The version of the virtual laboratory used by the User-control group contained a text area and a virtual environment area. Participants were able to move through the environment using the arrow keys and were able to look up down, left or right by holding down the Shift key while using the arrows keys. If they clicked on a cupboard door or a drawer, it opened and their viewpoint was adjusted so that they could see into it. It would then shut when they clicked on it again. The environment contained cues to help locate items of apparatus, such as labels on cupboards and drawers. If they clicked on an item of apparatus the name of the item was displayed in the text area. If they double-clicked on an item of apparatus the item would move up close so that it could be inspected. If the object was clicked while being inspected, it would automatically rotate left-right and if clicked again it would rotate up-down. They could then put the item back down by double-clicking on it again. See Figure 5.1for a screen shot showing this version of the virtual laboratory.

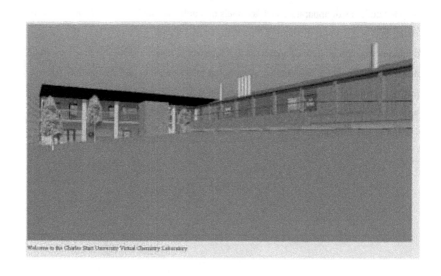

Figure 5.1
Screen layout of the Investigation 1 user-control version of the virtual laboratory

The Dynamic Views group were provided with a similar virtual environment, containing a text area, and a virtual environment area, along with Next View and Previous View options. These two options were their only way to move through the environment. They began outside the laboratory and each time they clicked on the Next View option they moved to a new location on a tour of the laboratory. The name of the location or the part of the laboratory they were shown was displayed in the text area. Sometimes when they clicked on Next View they were taken to an item of apparatus and the name of that item was displayed in the text area. In some cases a drawer or cupboard was first opened. The subsequent time they clicked on Next View, the item was moved up close for inspection and after subsequent clicks on Next View it was rotated around so that they could view it from all sides, before returning to its position. See Figure 5.2 for a screen shot showing the controls provided to the Dynamic Views group. The tour included 210 positions within the laboratory and apparatus display steps. That is, the participant was required to click the Next View button 210 times to complete the tour. The frame rate for animated view changes within the version used by the Dynamic Views group was identical to the frame rate for corresponding movements in the version used by the User-control group.

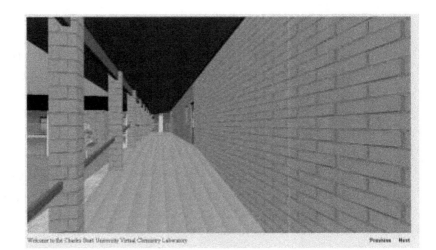

Figure 5.2
Screen layout of the Investigation 1 Dynamic Views version of the virtual laboratory

5.3.4 Training Procedure

Participants in the User-control and Dynamic Views groups began with 10 minutes of guided exploration of a 3D environment, modelled on an art gallery, with screen layout and navigation options the same as in the corresponding virtual environment used by that group. User-control participants were provided with a one-page sheet of instructions (see Appendix H). Participants used the sheet of instructions as a reference as they undertook their tasks in the virtual laboratory.

5.3.5 Learning Tasks and Procedure

After the training phase, participants in the User-control and Dynamic Views groups explored their allocated version of the virtual laboratory for a period of 40 minutes. They were asked to learn the layout of the laboratory, locate as many items of apparatus as they could, and to learn the structure of each item. They were asked to record which items of apparatus they found by ticking a list provided and to make any additional notes that they thought would help them to remember the layout of the laboratory and its apparatus. It was made clear that they would have to hand these notes in before commencing the test.

Participants in the Real Laboratory group were, as a group, taken on a tour of the real laboratory, which matched the tour undertaken by the Dynamic Views group. They were taken in turn to each laboratory location and to the location of each item of apparatus. Locations in the laboratory were pointed out to them and verbally named as were items of apparatus. Participants were asked to pick up and examine each item of apparatus, or for larger items participants were asked to view them from a variety of angles. Once the tour was complete they were encouraged to explore the laboratory further for the remainder of the allocated 40 minutes.

Table 5.3 shows the items of apparatus and smaller equipment that were accessible to User-control participants and were included in the tour. Table 5.4 shows the laboratory furniture and landmarks that were accessible to User-control participants and included in the tour.

Table 5.3
Items of apparatus and small equipment
included in Investigation 1 versions of the virtual
laboratory

Analytic Balance	Crucible (Evaporating Dishes)	Volumetric Pipette
Atomic Absorption Spectrometer	Dropper Bottles with Sodium and Nitrate Solutions	Pipette Filler
Beaker	Eye Wash	Reagent Bottle
Bunsen Burner	Fire Blanket	Safety Glasses
Burette	Fire Extinguisher	Test Tube
Burette Stand	Funnel	Tongs
Clamp	Gauze	Top Loading Balance
Clay Triangle	Glass Bin	Waste Bin
Conductivity Meter	Graduated Cylinder	
Conical Flask	Pasteur Pipette	

Table 5.4
Items of furniture and landmarks included in Investigation
1 versions of the virtual laboratory (number of
occurrences bracketed)

Lab Benches (6)	Service hatch
Metal drawers (2)	Whiteboard
Fume cupboard	Shelves at side
Brown drawers (2)	Benches in equipment room
Cream cupboards (8)	Benches in preparation room
Sinks (5)	

5.3.6 Test Tasks and Procedure

Participants undertook a test on completion of the learning phase of the investigation. The test was delivered on paper but with supporting materials on computer (viewed through the Internet Explorer Web browser) to allow for the use of full colour images.

Participants recorded their responses on paper. The test began with background questions about prior study of chemistry, perceived spatial ability and the degree to which a sense of presence was experienced. The remainder of the test was in seven parts (labelled A to G) and each part was completed and submitted before commencing the next part. Participants in a particular session completed each part of the test at the same time so that there was no chance that a participant used an image on another participant's screen to help them to answer a question. The complete test is provided in Appendix J.

The background questions about spatial ability required participants to indicate the degree to which they agreed or disagreed with two statements, by placing a mark on a line, with one end of the line labelled 'very strongly agree' and the other end labelled 'very strongly disagree'. The statements were, 'you have a good sense of direction' and, 'when you use a street directory or a map you normally turn it around to match the direction you are going'. See Section 3.3.3 for a more detailed discussion of these questions.

The background questions about sense of presence required participants to indicate their degree of agreement or disagreement with three statements. The statements were, 'you felt involved in the virtual laboratory experience', 'you felt a compelling sense of moving around inside the virtual environment', and 'you were involved in the task to the extent that you lost track of time'. The first two of these questions were not provided to Real Laboratory participants. See Section 3.3.6 for a more detailed discussion of these questions.

The requirements of parts A to G of the test were as follows.

Part A required participants to identify 10 items of apparatus from colour photos, given a list of 29 apparatus names. Participants were also required to indicate for each item whether they would have already been able to identify it prior to their participation in the study. The maximum time allowed for this item was seven minutes.

Part B required participants to identify the correct model of eight items of apparatus given colour images of four alternative models each shown from three different views (see Figure 3.17). This tested more precisely the accuracy of participants' spatial cognitive model of the items of apparatus. The maximum time allowed for this item was seven minutes.

Part C required participants to draw a labelled plan of the laboratory showing furniture, doors and windows, given an outline of the laboratory with the walkway indicated to show the orientation. This tested recall of the items of furniture in the laboratory and their layout. The maximum time allowed for this item was seven minutes.

Part D required participants to draw another plan of the laboratory, given an outline of the laboratory, but this time also given a list of 11 items of furniture to include and a colour photo of each. Where an item appeared in more than one location in the laboratory, the number of occurrences was indicated. The total number of items including multiple occurrences was 43. This tested the participants' spatial cognitive models of the relative positions of the laboratory furniture without also requiring them to remember what was actually there. The maximum time allowed for this item was seven minutes.

Part E required participants to indicate on an outline of the laboratory, the position and direction of the camera, given photos taken from six positions within the laboratory. They were required to indicate the camera position and direction by drawing a line from the camera position to the opposite wall on the printed laboratory outline. This tested the ability of participants to use their spatial model to orient them within the laboratory. The maximum time allowed for this item was six minutes.

Part F required participants to indicate on a plan of the laboratory the location where each of a list of 10 items of apparatus would normally be found, given a colour photo of each item. The printed plan of the laboratory included labelled furniture and landmarks. This tested recall of apparatus locations in relation to a topological laboratory representation. The maximum time allowed for this item was five minutes.

Part G required participants to indicate the location where each of a list of 10 items of apparatus would normally be found, given a colour photo of each item, by annotating printed black and white laboratory photos. The laboratory photos were taken from the one position in the laboratory, by successively rotating the camera, and together made up a 360 degree panorama. The photos were also provided in colour on computer. This tested transfer of recollection of apparatus locations to the real laboratory. The maximum time allowed for this item was five minutes.

5.4 Results

The results obtained in the investigation are presented in this section. Firstly the results of an initial analysis to determine whether there were interactions between any of the three independent variables, group, gender and prior experience are discussed. An analysis of test performance by gender and prior experience is presented next. Although these gender and prior experience results are not central to the study they are presented first because an uneven distribution of gender and prior experience between the groups has the potential to limit the conclusions that can be drawn from the group comparisons if gender or prior experience were a factor in performance. A comparison of the performance of the groups on each part of the written test are then presented, beginning with the part of the test that measured ability to identify apparatus. Finally, the results of the background questions on spatial ability and sense of presence are discussed.

5.4.1 Initial analysis

A factorial Analysis of Variance (ANOVA) was undertaken with group, gender and prior chemistry experience as factors and each of the background questions and test items as dependent variables. The statistical software used adjusted values for the sums of squares to account for the unbalanced design. The results of this analysis indicated that there were no significant interactions between group and gender, group and chemistry experience or gender and chemistry experience and no significant three-way interactions. Consequently, main effects of group, gender and chemistry experience were explored using single factor ANOVAs. These results are discussed in the following sections.

5.4.2 Gender

This section discusses male versus female performance on the various parts of the spatial knowledge test.

Table 5.5 shows a comparison of male and female responses on each part of the spatial knowledge test. In general females performed better than males, although the only part of the test for which there was a significant difference between male and female performance was Part C, which required participants to draw a map of the laboratory, where females (mean of 28 items correctly located) performed better than males (mean of 20 items). Given that the Real Laboratory group contained fewer females than the other two groups (four out of eleven compared to five out of eleven), statistical comparisons of the performance of the Real Laboratory group with the other two groups may not be appropriate on Part C of the test. This is not considered a major problem, however, because it is a comparison of the performance of the Dynamic Views and User-control groups that was intended to address the research questions that were the focus of this investigation.

Test Part		Male	Female
Part A. Identification of apparatus (Total number of items of apparatus identified)	n	19	14
	mean	7.47	8.43
	SD	2.95	2.62
	T Test	p= 0.343 (not significant)	
Part A. Identification of apparatus (Percentage of items of apparatus identified that were new to this participant)	n	19	14
	mean	68%	84%
	SD	35%	27%
	T Test	p= 0.166 (not significant)	
Part B. Recollection of apparatus structure (Number of correct models identified)	n	19	14
	mean	4.95	4.07
	SD	1.61	1.77
	T Test	p=0.150 (not significant)	
Part C. Laboratory plan (Number of correctly positioned items of furniture and landmarks on plan)	n	19	14
	mean	19.84	27.57
	SD	9.50	11.14
	T Test	**p=0.046 (significant)**	
Part D. Laboratory plan with given list of items to include (Number of correctly positioned items of furniture and landmarks on plan)	n	19	14
	mean	27.32	27.21
	SD	7.40	9.22
	T Test	p=0.973 (not significant)	
Part E. Positioning of views (Number of views correctly identified)	n	19	14
	mean	2.79	3.21
	SD	1.65	1.53
	T Test	p= 0.457 (not significant)	
Part F. Location of apparatus on map (Number of items correctly located)	n	19	14
	mean	6.97	8.39
	SD	2.99	2.61
	T Test	p= 0.166 (not significant)	

Table 5.5
Performance on spatial learning test by gender

Table 5.5 (cont.) Performance on spatial learning test by gender		Male	Female
Part G. Location of apparatus on panoramic photographs (Number of items placed within the correct set of cupboards or drawers)	n	17*	14
	mean	4.18	4.86
	SD	2.04	2.07
	T Test	p=0.366 (not significant)	
Part G. Location of apparatus on panoramic photographs (Number of items correctly placed in the exact drawer or cupboard)	n	17*	14
	mean	2.06	2.71
	SD	1.82	1.59
	T Test	p=0.300 (not significant)	

* Two participants did not complete Part G correctly and their results were discarded.

5.4.3 Prior Study of Chemistry

Participants were asked to indicate the highest level of chemistry study completed (high school Year 11, high school Year 12, high school Year 10, tertiary or other) prior to this investigation and the year in which this study was undertaken. Based on this data, participants' data was grouped into the following chemistry experience levels for analysis purposes:

- Recent highly relevant experience: those who had studied Year 11, Year 12 or tertiary chemistry in the past 5 years;

- Any other relevant experience: those who were not in the first category, but who had studied any chemistry in the past 10 years; and

- No relevant experience: those who had not studied any chemistry in the past 10 years (it was assumed that chemistry studied prior to 10 years ago would have involved the use of quite different laboratory equipment and would have been very poorly recalled by participants).

There were seven participants with the highest level of experience, eighteen with the second and eight with no relevant experience. Table 5.6 shows the number of participants with each level of experience in each of the three groups within the investigation. Because the information about the level of chemistry experience was gathered after exploration at the time that participants completed their spatial learning test, it was not possible to use this information for grouping purposes. Consequently, the distribution of experience across the three groups was not equal, and so the degree to which chemistry experience affects performance on the spatial tests is an important issue.

Table 5.6 Chemistry experience levels within each group			
	Recent highly relevant experience (year 11, year 12 or tertiary chemistry within last 5 years)	Other relevant experience (any chemistry experience within last 10 years)	No relevant experience (no chemistry experience during last 10 years)
Dynamic Views	3	4	4
User-control	2	6	3
Real laboratory	2	8	1

An ANOVA was used to compare the results on each part of the test of participants with each level of experience. Table 5.7 shows a summary of the results and analysis.

Table 5.7

Performance on spatial learning test by prior chemistry experience

Test Part		Recent highly relevant experience	Any relevant experience	No relevant experience
Part A. Recognition of apparatus (Total number of items of apparatus identified)	n	7	18	8
	mean	9.43	7.78	6.75
	SD	1.51	3.04	2.82
	ANOVA	p=0.182 (not significant)		
Part A. Recognition of apparatus (Percentage of items of apparatus identified that were new to this participant)	n	7	18	8
	mean	92%	72%	65%
	SD	22%	37%	28%
	ANOVA	p=0.251 (not significant)		
Part B. Recollection of apparatus structure (Number of correct models identified out of 8)	n	7	18	8
	mean	4.71	4.56	4.50
	SD	1.38	1.76	2.07
	ANOVA	p=0.970 (not significant)		
Part C. Laboratory plan (Number of correctly positioned items of furniture and landmarks on plan)	n	7	18	8
	mean	24.29	23.78	20.63
	SD	8.36	8.77	16.59
	ANOVA	p=0.761 (not significant)		
Part D. Laboratory plan with given list of items to include (Number of correctly positioned items of furniture and landmarks on plan)	n	7	18	8
	mean	27.29	28.33	24.88
	SD	6.10	7.10	11.62
	ANOVA	p=0.617 (not significant)		
Part E. Positioning of views (Number of views correctly identified)	n	7	18	8
	mean	3.29	3.17	2.25
	SD	1.38	1.58	1.75
	ANOVA	p=0.345 (not significant)		

Table 5.7 (continued)
Performance on spatial learning test by prior chemistry experience

Test Part		Recent highly relevant experience	Any relevant experience	No relevant experience
Part F. Location of apparatus on map (Number of items correctly located)	n	7	18	8
	mean	7.36	8.19	6.38
	SD	2.81	2.13	4.19
	ANOVA	p=0.334 (not significant)		
Part G. Location of apparatus on panoramic photographs (Number of items placed within the correct set of cupboards or drawers)	n	6	18	7
	mean	5.33	4.78	3.00
	SD	1.63	1.90	2.24
	ANOVA	p=0.074 (significant at 90% level)		
	Post-Hoc Tukey's HSD Tests	Recent highly relevant experience v any other relevant experience p=0.816 (not significant)		
			Any other relevant experience v no relevant experience p=0.115 (not significant)	
		Recent highly relevant experience v no experience p=0.094 (significant at 90% level)		
Part G. Location of apparatus on panoramic photographs (Number of items correctly placed in the exact drawer or cupboard)	n	6	18	7
	mean	2.83	2.39	1.86
	SD	1.47	1.61	2.27
	ANOVA	p=0.606 (not significant)		

The parts of the test where it was considered most likely that participants with more experience in a chemistry laboratory would perform better were Parts A and B, which required recognition of apparatus and recall of apparatus structure. It was also considered possible that participants who were more familiar with the items of apparatus may have been better able to recall the location of the items, because their existing knowledge of the apparatus may have given them better 'mental hooks' to place the information on. If this was the case, participants with greater experience in a chemistry laboratory would have performed better also in Part F of the test, which required participants to recall the location of apparatus.

In Part A of the test, participants with recent highly relevant chemistry experience performed better than participants with any other relevant experience, who performed better than participants with no relevant chemistry experience, in the total number of items of apparatus identified as well as the number of unfamiliar items identified. However, an ANOVA indicated that none of these differences were significant. Performance on Part B of the test, which required participants to recall the correct structure of items of apparatus, was similar for the three chemistry experience groups. These results are somewhat surprising. They may indicate that the items of apparatus used in this particular laboratory are sufficiently different from the items of apparatus used in other laboratories that prior experience did not help the participants a great deal.

In Part F of the test, which required participants to indicate the location of items of apparatus within the laboratory, by annotating a map of the laboratory, participants with the second level of experience performed best, followed by those with the highest level of experience, followed by those with no experience, however, the differences were not significant. Part G of the test, which required participants to indicate the location of items of apparatus within the laboratory by annotating one of a set of photographs taken from within the laboratory, was marked two ways. Firstly, a score was recorded for the number of items positioned in the correct set of drawers or cupboards. Secondly, a score was recorded for the number of items placed, not just in the correct set of drawers or cupboards, but within the correct drawer or cupboard. In both cases, participants with the highest level of chemistry experience performed best, followed by those with the next level, followed by those with no relevant experience. For the number of items placed in the correct cupboard or drawer, an ANOVA indicated that the differences were not significant. For the number of items placed in the correct set of cupboards or drawers, an ANOVA indicated that some of the differences may have been significant ($p=0.074$). Post-Hoc analysis was performed using Tukey's Honestly Significant Difference (HSD) test. This indicated that none of the differences between the groups were significant at the 95% level.

Page 252

As expected, there was no significant difference between the scores of participants with the different levels of chemistry experience on Parts C and D of the test, which required the participant to draw a map of the laboratory or on Part E of the test, which required participants to identify the position and direction of views of the laboratory. These parts of the test required recall of the structure of this particular laboratory and it was considered unlikely that prior chemistry experience would be a factor in performance.

The lack of a significant difference between the performance of participants with each level of experience, suggests that the differing number of participants in each group with each level of experience need not be considered a problem.

5.4.4 Identification of Apparatus

Part A of the test required participants to identify 10 items of apparatus from colour photos. Participants were given 29 apparatus names, which included the 10 items shown. Each participant's score was recorded as the number of items correctly identified. A summary of these results and the corresponding analysis are shown in Table 5.8. Participants were also asked to indicate which items of apparatus they would have already been able to identify before this investigation. Using this, a second score was calculated, the percentage of unfamiliar items able to be identified, that is, their score as a percentage excluding those items which were both correctly identified and marked as already familiar. Table 5.9 shows a summary of these results and the corresponding analysis.

Table 5.8
Performance on Part A of the test, requiring identification of apparatus
Score is number of items correctly identified

	Dynamic Views group	User-control group	Real Laboratory group
n	11	11	11
mean	8.64	6.91	8.09
SD	2.54	2.98	2.88
ANOVA	p=0.350 (not significant)		

	Dynamic Views group	User-control group	Real Laboratory group
Table 5.9 **Performance on Part A of the test, requiring identification of apparatus** **Score is percentage of unfamiliar items able to be identified**			
n	11	11	11
mean	78%	66%	79%
SD	36%	31%	32%
ANOVA	p=0.584 (not significant)		

Using the total number of items identified, Dynamic Views participants scored the highest, followed by Real Laboratory participants and then User-control participants. However, an ANOVA indicated that none of these differences were significant. Using the percentage of unfamiliar items identified, the Dynamic Views and Real Laboratory group performances were similar (means of 78% and 79% respectively) and each was slightly better than the User-control group (mean of 66%), but again an ANOVA indicated that none of the differences were significant. If user control over view or object manipulation contributes to spatial learning, then it would have been expected that User-control participants would perform better than Dynamic Views participants. However, identification of apparatus from photographs does not require knowledge of the spatial structure of the items and consequently the ability to manipulate the items of apparatus or the viewpoints to control the angle from which the items were viewed may not be important.

The high standard deviations (31% to 36%) suggest that participants varied widely in the degree to which they were able to learn about the apparatus using the learning activities they undertook. This may be due to wide differences in spatial ability. The large standard deviation, or variance, is important, because large variance in the data generally makes it more difficult to find significant differences. Put another way, it means that with the moderate sample size used in this investigation, significant differences that might be found in a larger sample may not be found.

It is worth noting that the photographs of the items of apparatus were taken using the same items of apparatus as the Real Laboratory group explored. Although the 3D models explored by the Dynamic Views and User-control groups were intended to match as closely as possible the real items of apparatus, in most cases there were differences, with the real items containing more detail. Consequently, one might have expected the Real Laboratory group to perform better on this test. The fact that the virtual laboratory groups performed as well as the Real Laboratory group is encouraging for the use of a virtual environment as a resource to help learners to identify apparatus.

5.4.5 Recollection of Apparatus Structure

Part B of the test required participants to identify the correct model of 10 items of apparatus given colour images of four alternative models each shown from three different views (see Figure 3.17). Table 5.10 shows a summary of these results and the corresponding analysis.

	Dynamic Views group	User-control group	Real Laboratory group
Table 5.10 Performance on Part B of the test, requiring recognition of apparatus structure			
n	11	11	11
mean	4.64	4.64	4.45
SD	1.91	1.29	2.02
ANOVA	p=0.962 (not significant)		

The means were quite low, indicating that students had difficulty recalling the details of apparatus structure. The Dynamic Views group and User-control group both averaged 4.64 items out of a possible 8 and the Real Laboratory group averaged 4.45. An ANOVA indicated that there was no significant difference between the performances of the three groups (p = 0.962).

It was originally intended that the User-control group would be able to freely rotate the items using a comfortable interface and would thus have a better chance of recalling the various structural aspects of the items. However, problems with the interface meant that it was difficult to control the rotation of the items and consequently an alternative mechanism where participants could view scripted rotations of the item, firstly horizontally and then vertically, by successively clicking, was provided. Consequently the view of the items was very similar for the Dynamic Views and User-control groups and so the closeness of the results is not surprising.

The images used in this test were produced using the same 3D model as used in the virtual laboratory with minor structural modification in the case of the incorrect models. Although the 3D models were intended to match as closely as possible the real items of apparatus, there were differences, with the real items containing more detail. Consequently, the Real Laboratory group were at a slight disadvantage in this part of the test. This could explain why they did not perform better, despite the fact that learners were able to hold and explore the items, giving them more control over the views seen and additionally allowing them to use tactile information.

5.4.6 Recall of Laboratory Layout

Part C of the test required participants to draw a labelled plan of the laboratory showing furniture, doors and windows, given an outline of the laboratory with the walkway indicated to show the orientation. In scoring participants' plans, a mark was given for each correct item. Items were scored as correct if they were:

- placed with their centre within 2m of the correct location;
- sized between 50% and 200% of the correct size in each direction;
- sized within 2m of the correct size in each direction;
- placed in the correct room; and
- at the correct orientation.

There were 67 possible items to include on the plan so the maximum possible score was 67. Table 5.11 summarises the results and analysis for this test item.

Table 5.11
Performance on Part C of the test, requiring drawing of a map containing laboratory furniture, doors and windows

	Dynamic Views group	User-control group	Real Laboratory group
n	11	11	11
mean	20.27	20.91	28.18
SD	14.57	8.09	7.18
ANOVA	p=0.162 (not significant)		

Real Laboratory participants were able to identify the most items (mean of 28), followed by User-control participants (mean of 21) and then followed by Dynamic Views participants (mean of 20). An ANOVA comparing the group means suggested that none of the differences were significant.

Part D of the test required participants to draw another plan of the laboratory, given an outline of the laboratory, but this time participants were only required to place a given list of 20 items of furniture on their plan. A colour photo of each item of furniture was provided. Where an item of furniture appeared in the laboratory multiple times this was indicated and consequently there were 43 items to include. Table 5.12 shows a summary of the results and data analysis for this item.

Table 5.12
Performance on Part D of the test, requiring drawing of a map given a list of laboratory furniture, doors and windows to include

	Dynamic Views group	User-control group	Real Laboratory group
n	11	11	11
mean	23.00	28.00	30.82
SD	10.59	5.97	5.17
ANOVA	p= 0.067(significant at 90% level)		
Post-Hoc Tukey's HSD Tests	Dynamic Views v User-control p=0.288 (not significant)		
		User-control v Real Laboratory p= 0.665 (not significant)	
	Dynamic Views v Real Laboratory p= 0.057 (significant at 90% level)		

Again Real Laboratory participants were able to correctly locate the most items (mean of 31), which was better than User-control participants (mean of 28), which was better than Dynamic Views participants (mean of 23). An ANOVA suggested that there may be a significant difference (p=0.067) and so Post Hoc Tukey's HSD tests were carried out to compare each pair of groups. These tests suggested that only the difference between the Dynamic Views and Real Laboratory groups may have been significant (p=0.057, which is significant at the 90% level but not at the 95% level).

It would be reasonable to expect that the Real Laboratory participants with a wider field of view and natural navigation and view control would be able to recall and correctly locate more parts of the laboratory. If user control over view contributed to spatial learning in a virtual environment, it would be expected that User-control participants would develop a more complete spatial cognitive model and consequently be able to recall and correctly locate more items than the Dynamic Views group. The fact that the two virtual laboratory groups did not differ suggests that user control over view does not contribute to spatial learning. Alternative reasons for this result are discussed in the discussion section of this chapter.

5.4.7 Positioning of Views

Part E of the test required participants to indicate on an outline of the laboratory, the position, direction and field of view of the camera, given photos taken from 8 positions within the laboratory, by drawing a line from the camera position to the opposite wall. The number of correct views was recorded, where views were marked correct if they were within 4 metres of the correct location in the north-south direction and within 2.5 metres of the correct location in the east-west direction and within 30 degrees of the correct direction. The 4 metre by 2.5 metre tolerance for correct answers was chosen so that the tolerance in the north-south and east-west directions were equal relative to the dimensions of the room. The dimensions of the main part of the laboratory are 17.9 metres by 11.6 meters, so the tolerance for correct answers was 22% in each direction. Table 5.13 shows a summary of the results and data analysis for this item.

Table 5.13 Performance on Part E of the test, requiring indication of position and direction of given views of the laboratory			
	Dynamic Views group	**User-control group**	**Real Laboratory group**
n	11	11	11
mean	1.82	3.36	3.73
SD	1.33	1.43	1.42
ANOVA	p=0.007 (significant)		
Post-Hoc Tukey's HSD Tests	Dynamic Views v User-control p=0.037 (significant)		
		User-control v Real Laboratory p= 0.815 (not significant)	
	Dynamic Views v Real Laboratory p= 0.009 (significant)		

An ANOVA comparing group performances suggested that there may have been a significant difference between the performance of the groups (p=0.007). The Real Laboratory group performed best (mean of 3.73 correct views), followed by the User-control group (mean of 3.36) and then the Dynamic Views group (mean of 1.82). A Post-Hoc Tukey's HSD test indicated that the difference between the Real Laboratory group and the Dynamic Views group was significant (p=0.009), as was the difference between the User-control and Dynamic Views group (p=0.037).

Performance on this part of the test was as expected. The Real Laboratory group had an advantage on this part of the test, because the real laboratory contained some additional detail not found in the virtual laboratory, and thus the photos may have contained additional cues to help the Real Laboratory group to determine the position and direction of the camera. Even aside from this, it was expected that the Real Laboratory group would perform better because of their wider field of view and easier mechanism for looking around the laboratory. It was expected that the User-control group would perform better than the Dynamic Views group because of the ability of participants to look around the laboratory under their own control, leading to a greater range of views and also better recall because of the active learning process.

5.4.8 Location of Apparatus

Part F of the test required participants to indicate the location where each of a list of 10 items of apparatus would normally be found, given a plan of the laboratory, including labelled furniture, and given a colour photo of each item. The number of correctly placed items was recorded. Where an item appeared in more than one location, the number of correct locations identified was recorded. The maximum possible score was 13 (3 of the 10 items appeared in 2 locations). If the participant's plan showed an item in the adjacent storage location to the correct location they were given half a mark. For items not found in a cupboard or drawer (such as the fire extinguishers) or found in a large storage location (such as the laboratory benches) they were marked as correct if within 2m of the correct location as long as they were placed in the correct room. If an item was placed between 2m and 3m from the correct location and in the correct room, half a mark was awarded. Table 5.14 shows a summary of the results and analysis for this item.

	Dynamic Views group	User-control group	Real Laboratory group
Table 5.14 Performance on Part F of the test, requiring indication of location of items of apparatus on laboratory plan			
n	11	11	11
mean	6.95	6.73	9.05
SD	3.08	3.37	1.47
ANOVA	p=0.114 (not significant)		

Participants of the Real Laboratory group performed best (mean of 9.05 items) followed by the Dynamic Views group (mean of 6.95 items) and then the User-control group (mean of 6.73 items). An ANOVA suggested that none of the differences were significant.

The better performance of the Real Laboratory participants was expected because of their wider field of view and easier opportunities for looking around the room. However, it was expected that the User-control group would perform better than the Dynamic Views group because it was assumed that they would have been more cognitively active in searching for items of apparatus than the Dynamic Views group who moved through a sequence of views, being shown the location of items without any control.

Part G of the test required participants to indicate the location where each of a list of 10 items of apparatus would normally be found, given 10 colour photos taken from the one position in the laboratory, making up a 360 degree panorama and given a colour photo of each item of apparatus, by annotating printed black and white copies of the laboratory photos. Two separate scores were recorded for each participant. Firstly, the number of items placed in the correct set of cupboards or drawers was recorded, and secondly the number of items placed in the correct cupboard or drawer was recorded. Two participants in the User-control group misinterpreted the task, and only indicated which photograph contained each item of apparatus. The data from these participants was excluded from the analysis. Table 5.15 shows a summary of the results and data analysis for this item.

Table 5.15
Performance on Part G of the test, requiring location of apparatus within laboratory photographs

Correct set of cupboards or set of drawers		Dynamic Views group	User-control group	Real Laboratory group
	n	11	9	11
	mean	3.73	4.22	5.45
	SD	2.33	1.56	1.86
	ANOVA	p=0.126 (not significant)		
Correct cupboard or drawer		Dynamic Views group	User-control group	Real laboratory group
	n	11	9	11
	mean	2.45	2.22	2.36
	SD	2.11	1.48	1.63
	ANOVA	p=0.959 (not significant)		

For placement of items in the correct set of cupboards or drawers, the Real Laboratory participants performed best (mean of 5.45 items), followed by the User-control participants (mean of 4.22 items), and then the Dynamic Views participants (mean of 3.73). An ANOVA indicated that none of the differences were significant. Once again the better performance of the Real Laboratory group was as expected, as was the superior performance of the User-control group over the Dynamic Views group, however, once again it was expected that the differences would be significant.

For placement of items in the correct drawer or cupboard, performance was poor for all groups and there was no significant difference between the groups (Real Laboratory group mean was 2.36, User-control group mean was 2.22 and Dynamic Views group mean was 2.45).

5.4.9 Spatial ability

Participants were asked two questions designed to gauge their spatial ability. The first, Background Question 2, asked them to indicate the degree to which they agreed or disagreed with the statement, 'you have a good sense of direction'. Kozlowski and

Bryant (1977) found that the answer to the question, "how good is your sense of direction" is a strong predictor of performance on a range of spatial tasks (p. 591). Participants' answers were recorded as a number from 0 (very strongly disagree) to 100 (very strongly agree). Table 5.16 shows an analysis of responses to this question by group. The Dynamic Views group (mean of 73) rated themselves higher on average than the Real Laboratory group (mean of 62) who rated themselves higher than the User-control group (mean of 57). An ANOVA showed that none of these differences were significant (p=0.225).

In the second spatial ability question, participants were asked to indicate the extent to which they agreed with the statement, 'When you use a street directory or a map you normally turn it around to match the direction you are going'. In this case a score close to 0 (very strongly disagree) should indicate good spatial ability and a score close to 100 (very strongly agree) should mean poor spatial ability. The means for the User-control, Dynamic Views and Real Laboratory groups were 63, 58 and 70 respectively, but again none of the differences were significant (in an ANOVA p=0.744).

These results indicate that, if we can assume that self reported spatial ability correlates with actual spatial ability, then spatial ability is distributed evenly across the groups, and thus should not contribute to performance differences across groups.

Table 5.16
Responses to questions requiring self-report of spatial ability by group

Background Question		Dynamic Views group	User-control group	Real Laboratory group
2. Degree of agreement with statement, "You have a good sense of direction"	n	11	11	11
	mean	73.00	57.36	61.91
	SD	18.10	22.45	23.00
	ANOVA	p= 0.225 (not significant)		
3. Degree of agreement with statement, "When you use a street directory or a map you normally turn it around to match the direction you are going"	n	11	11	11
	mean	63.73	57.82	69.64
	SD	35.74	35.27	36.52
	ANOVA	p= 0.744 (not significant)		

Table 5.17 shows a comparison of male and female responses to the background questions on sense of direction. The T-test results indicate that there was no difference between male and female responses.

Table 5.17
Responses to questions requiring self-report of spatial ability by gender

Background Question		Male	Female
2. Degree of agreement with statement, "You have a good sense of direction"	n	19	14
	mean	64.11	64.07
	SD	20.55	23.90
	T Test	p=0.997 (not significant)	
3. Degree of agreement with statement, "When you use a street directory or a map you normally turn it around to match the direction you are going"	n	19	14
	mean	63.63	63.86
	SD	33.16	38.76
	T Test	p=0.986 (not significant)	

Pearson's correlation coefficient was calculated between responses to the two spatial ability questions. The correlation coefficient was -0.280 which was not significant (p=0.115). A significant negative correlation would have been expected, that is, one would expect that participants rating their sense of direction as good would also indicate that they did not need to orient a map to the direction they were facing. The lack of a significant correlation between responses to the two spatial ability questions suggests that they may have been measuring different aspects of participants' perceptions of their spatial ability.

Pearson's correlation coefficients were also calculated between each of these spatial ability questions and performance on the various test items, and these are shown in Table 5.18. Background Question 2 correlated with performance only in Part A of the test, which measured identification of apparatus (for total items identified p=0.010 and for percentage of items identified of those new to the participant p=0.061). Background Question 3 correlated negatively with performance on Part D of the test, which measured recall of laboratory structure (p=0.026) and part G of the test, which measured recall of the location of apparatus (p=0.027).

Table 5.18
Pearson's Correlations (PC) between questions on spatial ability and performance on spatial tests

Test Part		Correlation with Question 2	Correlation with Question 3
Part A. Recognition of apparatus (Total number of items of apparatus identified)	Pearson Correlation	0.444	-0.261
	Significance	p=0.010 (significant)	p=0.142 (not significant)
Part A. Recognition of apparatus (Percentage of items of apparatus identified that were new to this participant)	Pearson Correlation	0.329	-0.234
	Significance	p=0.061 (significant at the 90% level)	p=0.191 (not significant)
Part B. Recollection of apparatus structure (Number of correct models identified out of 8)	Pearson Correlation	0.040	-0.087
	Significance	p=0.826 (not significant)	p=0.631 (not significant)
Part C. Laboratory plan (Number of correctly positioned items of furniture and landmarks on plan)	Pearson Correlation	0.193	-0.238
	Significance	p=0.281 (not significant)	p=0.183 (not significant)
Part D. Laboratory plan with given list of items to include (Number of correctly positioned items of furniture and landmarks on plan)	Pearson Correlation	0.237	-0.387
	Significance	p=0.183 (not significant)	p=0.026 (significant)
Part E. Positioning of views (Number of views correctly identified)	Pearson Correlation	-0.141	-0.124
	Significance	p=0.433 (not significant)	p=0.492 (not significant)
Part F. Location of apparatus on map(Number of items correctly located)	Pearson Correlation	0.205	-0.276
	Significance	p=0.253 (not significant)	p=0.120 (not significant)

Table 5.18 (cont.)
Pearson's Correlation (PC) between background questions on spatial ability and performance on spatial tests

Test Part		Correlation with Question 2	Correlation with Question 3
Part G. Location of apparatus on panoramic photographs(Number of items placed within the correct set of cupboards or drawers)	Pearson Correlation	0.029	-0.282
	Significance	p=0.877 (not significant)	p=0.124 (not significant)
Part G. Location of apparatus on panoramic photographs(Number of items correctly placed in the exact drawer or cupboard)	Pearson Correlation	0.261	-0.397
	Significance	p=0.156 (not significant)	p=0.027 (significant)

If the two questions were effective in measuring participants' spatial ability, and if spatial ability was a factor in test performance, a significant positive correlation between Question 2 and all test scores and a significant negative correlation between Question 3 and all test scores would be expected. (It was assumed that high scores on Question 3 indicated low self reported spatial ability). Instead, Question 2 correlated significantly positively with one test item out of seven, and Question 3 correlated significantly negatively with two test items. This lack of correlation with most test items, could indicate one of three things. It could indicate that self reported spatial ability does not in fact correlate with actual spatial ability. It could indicate that the types of spatial ability measured are different to the abilities needed for spatial learning in a 3D environment. Alternatively, it could indicate that spatial ability was not a significant factor in performance in most parts of the test. If this was the case, it would be at odds with other reported studies. For example, Patrick et al. (2000) found that performance on a pre-test of spatial ability, using a standard instrument, was a significant predictor of participants' post-test scores on spatial learning from a virtual environment. Waller et al. (1998) administered a standard test of spatial orientation ability at the beginning of their study and found that the test was 'moderately predictive' of a participant's overall performance on a test of spatial knowledge after learning of a virtual maze. Richardson et al. (1999) argue that the skills required to learn the structure of a virtual environment are quite different to those tested by spatial ability tests. It may be that the questions used to gauge participants' views about their own spatial ability were also asking about skills that are different to those required in a virtual environment. This is discussed further in Chapter 7.

5.4.10 Presence

Participants were asked three questions designed to gauge the degree to which they felt present within the virtual environment. These questions were taken from the presence questionnaire developed by Witmer and Singer (1998). Each question asked them to indicate the degree to which they agreed or disagreed with a statement. In Background Question 4 the statement was, 'you felt involved in the virtual environment experience'. In Background Question 5 the statement was, 'you felt a compelling sense of moving around inside the virtual environment'. In Background Question 6 the statement was, 'you were involved in the task to the extent that you lost track of time'. Participants in the Real Laboratory group were not asked to answer Background Questions 4 and 5. Table 5.19 shows a summary of the responses and the corresponding analysis.

For Background Question 4, which asked about participants' feeling of involvement in the experience, User-control participants averaged greater agreement than Dynamic Views participants (a mean of 77 compared with a mean of 70), but a T-test indicated that there was no significant difference (p=0.206). For Background Question 5, which asked about the degree to which participants felt a sense of moving around inside the environment, User-control participants again averaged a greater degree of agreement than Dynamic Views participants (a mean of 78 compared to a mean of 66). A T-test indicated that the difference was significant only at the 90% level (p=0.075). For Background Question 6, which was answered by all three groups, and which asked about the degree to which participants were involved to the extent that they lost track of time, User-control participants (mean of 76) indicated greater agreement than Real Laboratory participants (mean of 63) who indicated greater agreement than Dynamic Views participants (mean of 44). An ANOVA indicated that there were significant differences between the groups, and Post-Hoc Tukey's HSD tests indicated that the difference between the User-control and Dynamic Views groups were significant (p=0.014) but that the other differences were not significant.

These results suggest that having control over their navigation, rather than following a pre-defined tour resulted in the User-control participants experiencing a greater sense of presence.

Table 5.19 Responses to questions on sense of presence by group				
Background Question		**Dynamic Views group**	**User-control group**	**Real Laboratory group**
4. Degree of agreement with statement, "You felt involved in the virtual environment experience"	**n**	11	11	NA
	mean	69.73	77.00	
	SD	11.16	14.62	
	T-test	p= 0.206 (not significant)		
5. Degree of agreement with statement, "You felt a compelling sense of moving around inside the virtual environment"	**n**	11	11	NA
	mean	66.27	78.09	
	SD	10.51	18.05	
	T-test	**p= 0.075 (significant at the 90% level)**		
6. Degree of agreement with statement, "You were involved in the task to the extent that you lost track of time"	**n**	11	11	11
	mean	44.09	75.91	62.73
	SD	27.11	22.07	24.67
	ANOVA	**p=0.018 (significant)**		
	Post-Hoc Tukey's HSD Tests	Dynamic Views v User-control **p=0.014 (significant)**		
		User-control v Real Laboratory p=0.433 (not significant)		
		Dynamic Views v Real Laboratory p=0.197 (not significant)		

Table 5.20 shows a comparison of male and female responses to the background questions on degree to which a sense of presence was experienced. The results indicate that male participants experienced a stronger sense of presence than female participants. The differences between the means are substantial on all three questions, although,

possibly due to the high variance in the data, a T-test showed a statistically significant difference only on Background Question 4, which asked about the degree to which the participant felt involved in the virtual environment experience.

Table 5.20 Responses to questions on sense of presence by gender			
Background Question		**Male**	**Female**
4. Degree of agreement with statement, "You felt involved in the virtual environment experience"	n	12	10
	mean	78.67	67.00
	SD	12.03	12.21
	T Test	**p=0.036 (significant)**	
5. Degree of agreement with statement, "You felt a compelling sense of moving around inside the virtual environment"	n	12	10
	mean	76.33	67.20
	SD	15.04	15.59
	T Test	p= 0.178 (not significant)	
6. Degree of agreement with statement, "You were involved in the task to the extent that you lost track of time"	n	19	14
	mean	65.21	55.07
	SD	23.13	32.20
	T Test	p= 0.300 (not significant)	

Pearson's correlation coefficients were calculated to compare the responses to questions about sense of presence with performance on the test items. Table 5.21 shows a summary. There were no significant correlations between responses to Background Questions 4, 5 and 6 and test performance. This is interesting because it is generally accepted that a greater sense of presence leads to greater learning (Winn, 2002). These results suggest that this may not in fact always be the case.

Table 5.21
Pearson's Correlations (PC) between sense of presence and performance on spatial tests

Test Part		Correlation with question 4	Correlation with question 5	Correlation with question 6
Part A. Recognition of apparatus (Total number of items of apparatus identified)	**Pearson Correlation**	-0.369	-0.320	-0.021
	Significance	p=0.091 (significant at 90% level)	p=0.146 (not significant)	p=0.908 (not significant)
Part A. Recognition of apparatus (Percentage of items of apparatus identified that were new to this participant)	**Pearson Correlation**	-0.288	-0.272	-0.027
	Significance	p=0.194 (not significant)	p=0.220 (not significant)	p=0.883 (not significant)
Part B. Recollection of apparatus structure (Number of correct models identified out of 8)	**Pearson Correlation**	-0.052	-0.051	-0.014
	Significance	p=0.817 (not significant)	p=0.822 (not significant)	p=0.941 (not significant)
Part C. Laboratory plan (Number of correctly positioned items of furniture and landmarks on plan)	**Pearson Correlation**	-0.180	-0.228	-0.080
	Significance	p=0.423 (not significant)	p=0.308 (not significant)	p=0.658 (not significant)
Part D. Laboratory plan with given list of items to include (Number of correctly positioned items of furniture and landmarks on plan)	**Pearson Correlation**	-0.144	-0.039	-0.032
	Significance	p=0.521 (not significant)	p=0.865 (not significant)	p=0.859 (not significant)
Part E. Positioning of views (Number of views correctly identified)	**Pearson Correlation**	-0.073	0.087	0.266
	Significance	p=0.747 (not significant)	p=0.700 (not significant)	p=0.134 (not significant)

Table 5.21 (cont.) Pearson Correlation (PC) between background questions on presence and performance on spatial tests		Correlation with question 4	Correlation with question 5	Correlation with question 6
Test Part		**Correlation with question 4**	**Correlation with question 5**	**Correlation with question 6**
Part F. Location of apparatus on map(Number of items correctly located)	**Pearson Correlation**	-0.334	-0.333	-0.220
	Significance	p=0.129 (not significant)	p=0.130 (not significant)	p=0.219 (not significant)
Part G. Location of apparatus on panoramic photographs(Number of items placed within the correct set of cupboards or drawers)	**Pearson Correlation**	-0.100	-0.099	0.047
	Significance	p=0.674 (not significant)	p=0.677 (not significant)	p=0.802 (not significant)
Part G. Location of apparatus on panoramic photographs(Number of items correctly placed in the exact drawer or cupboard)	**Pearson Correlation**	-0.262	-0.137	-0.123
	Significance	p=0.264 (not significant)	p=0.564 (not significant)	p=0.510 (not significant)

5.5 Summary and Discussion

5.5.1 Summary of results on each test item

The following is a summary of the findings on each of the test items within this investigation:

- There was no significant difference between the three groups on the test item requiring identification of apparatus.

- There was no significant difference between the three groups on the test item requiring recollection of apparatus structure.

- There was no significant difference between the three groups on the test item requiring participants to draw a topological plan of the laboratory, without being given a list of items of furniture to include. On the item requiring participants to draw a plan of the laboratory given a list of furniture to include, Real Laboratory participants performed better than Dynamic Views participants (significant at the 90% level) but none of the other differences were significant.

- On the test item requiring participants to indicate the position of given views of the laboratory, Real Laboratory participants and User-control participants both performed significantly better than Dynamic Views participants. There was no significant difference between Real Laboratory and User-control participants on this item.

- There was no significant difference between the three groups on the test item requiring participants to indicate the location of items of apparatus on a plan of the laboratory.

- There was no significant difference between the three groups on the test item requiring participants to indicate the location of items of apparatus on a set of photographs making up a 360-degree panorama.

5.5.2 Discussion of findings in relation to the research questions addressed by this investigation

5.5.2.1 Question 3. Does user control over view position and direction in a 3D learning environment contribute to spatial learning?

If user control over view contributed to spatial learning it would be expected that User-control participants would have performed better than Dynamic Views participants on the parts of the test focussing on the structure of the laboratory and the location of apparatus.

There was no significant difference between the performance of User-control and Dynamic Views participants on the test parts requiring participants to draw a plan of the laboratory or on the test parts requiring recall of apparatus location. User-control participants performed significantly better than Dynamic Views participants only on Part E of the test, which required participants to indicate the position and direction of given views.

The superior performance of User-control participants over Dynamic Views participants on view recognition is consistent with what one might intuitively think to be the case. One would expect User-control participants to be more attentive to their views of the laboratory because being so would have been necessary in order to effectively control their motion. The result suggests that user control over view does contribute to spatial learning.

However, one would also intuitively expect that User-control participants would have better recall of the location of furniture and apparatus within the laboratory, due to their greater attentiveness as they moved around the laboratory searching for the items listed on their worksheet. That is, if user control over view contributes to spatial learning, one would expect that this control along with the ability to locate and freely explore items of apparatus would have led to a more accurate and more complete spatial cognitive model of the laboratory and its furniture and the location of apparatus. The performance of User-control participants was better than Dynamic Views participants on the test items requiring the drawing of a map of the items of furniture and major equipment in the laboratory, but the difference was not significant. On the part of the test requiring positioning of apparatus on a topological plan of the laboratory, Dynamic Views participants performed marginally (but not significantly) better than User-control participants. On the part of the test requiring participants to indicate the position on a photograph where specific items of apparatus could be found, User-control participants performed marginally worse than Dynamic Views participants where the test was scored using correct set of drawers or cupboards and marginally better than Dynamic Views participants when the test was scored using exact cupboard or drawer. These results suggest that user control over view does not in fact contribute to spatial learning. However, there are a number of alternative explanations for these results.

In attempting to explain a similar finding, Christou & Bulthoff (1999) suggested that the user interface provided for moving around and manipulating items of apparatus may have imposed an additional cognitive load on the users. In their study they used a space-ball, which is a six-degree of freedom mouse, held above the desk, and unfamiliar to all participants. Peruch et al. (1995) carried out a study comparing the performance of an active and a passive group on a spatial learning task and found that the active participation group performed better on spatial knowledge tests than the passive group. Their study used a joystick, which was likely to be easier to use than a space ball, supporting Christou & Bulthoff's explanation.

The motion control interface used in this investigation was very simple, with movement constrained to ground level and with the use of the arrow keys and the shift key to specify movement or changes in view direction. Its development was informed by comparative studies of desktop 3D motion control (Dalgarno & Scott, 2000) and had been successively simplified as a result of two pilot studies. Observations during this investigation suggested that, apart from a single participant who encountered significant difficulty and was excluded from the investigation, all participants found the interface easy to learn and comfortable to use. Additionally, the earlier comparative studies found that an arrow key motion control interface is as easy or easier to use than a joystick interface (Dalgarno & Scott, 2000).

Consequently, it would seem that additional cognitive load was not the reason that the performance of the User-control group was not significantly better than the Dynamic Views group, on recall of laboratory structure and the location of apparatus. Another explanation may be that the sample size was too small to allow for significant differences to reveal themselves. This possible explanation is explored to an extent in Investigation 2, which uses a larger sample size.

An alternative explanation may be that the tasks that the User-control participants carried out did not require that they developed a spatial cognitive model that included the position of items of furniture, equipment and apparatus. It could be argued that because the User-control task could be completed without paying specific attention to the location of furniture, equipment and apparatus, having control over their movement provided no learning advantage.

Waller et al. (1998) emphasise the role of the navigation task undertaken and the navigator's motivation in the type of spatial knowledge formed. They comment that "developing a surveyor's representation requires a conscious effort...which implies that people are motivated to learn it and the environment allows them to do so" (p. 130). The finding of Lindberg and Garling (1983) that the acquisition of a cognitive model of an environment requires effortful cognitive processing, supports Waller et al.'s assertion that the navigation task undertaken will have an effect on spatial learning. Waller et al. (1998) comment that "just as in a real-world environment, people can learn procedures for moving from point to point in a VE...however, if a task requires no more than this, a surveyor's representation may not develop" (p. 130).

It could be hypothesised that had the User-control participants carried out a task that was more closely aligned to the development of a spatial cognitive model of the laboratory, they may have performed better on the test. Such a task, for example, could have been one that required them to locate items of apparatus, carry them to their bench, and return the items to their correct cupboard or drawer. Performing such a task would have required the participants to pay particular attention to the location of apparatus and furniture and would not have been able to be completed without recalling from where items of apparatus were obtained. It could be hypothesised, then, that performing a task like this under user control would have led to the development of a superior spatial cognitive model to that obtained by viewing an equivalent series of animated views. This hypothesis was explored in Investigation 2, which used a task for User-control participants more closely aligned to aspects of the spatial learning assessed in the test.

If it could be shown that the reason User-control participants did not perform better than Dynamic Views participants on most test items was that their task did not require them to develop a spatial cognitive model, then it would be an important finding because it would mean that developers of 3D learning environments would need to take particular care in the design of the learning tasks to be undertaken.

5.5.2.2 Question 4. Does object manipulation in a 3D learning environment contribute to spatial learning?

If object manipulation contributed to spatial learning it would be expected that User-control participants would have performed better than Dynamic Views participants on those parts of the test requiring recognition of apparatus and recall of apparatus structure.

There was no significant difference between the performance of User-control participants and Dynamic Views participants on identification of apparatus or recall of apparatus structure. One might expect that the ability to manipulate objects, and thus control the angle from which the items are viewed, along with the greater attention as a result of user control, would have allowed User-control participants to develop a more complete cognitive model of items of apparatus. The fact that this was not found to be the case suggests that object manipulation does not contribute to spatial learning.

However, as discussed above, there were problems with this interface, which meant that free rotation of objects was difficult and most User-control participants instead just used the option that rotated the object first about one axis and then about another, rather than attempting free rotation. The experience of doing this would have been very similar to the experience of the Dynamic Views group and consequently the results may not provide a clear indication of whether the ability to manipulate objects leads to a learning advantage.

Additionally, the task that User-control participants undertook, which included locating items of apparatus, did not require participants to explore the structure of the items. It may be that had User-control participants been required to complete some task with the items of apparatus, for example assembling them or operating buttons and levers, they would have been able to better identify items of apparatus and recall their structure. This was explored in Investigation 2, in which User-control participants undertook a task requiring them to assemble items of apparatus and also to turn dials and press buttons.

5.5.3 Other findings

The following is a summary of additional findings from this investigation, which do not relate directly to the research questions:

- There was no significant difference between the performance of the Real Laboratory group and the User-control group on any of the test items.

- Females performed significantly better than males on the test item requiring participants to draw a topological plan of the laboratory without being given a list of items of furniture to include. There was no difference between male and female performance on any of the other test items.

- Participants with recent highly relevant chemistry experience performed better than participants with no relevant experience only on the test item requiring the positioning of items of apparatus on panoramic photographs (significant only at the 90% level). There was no significant effect of prior chemistry experience on any other test items.

- The correlation between self reported spatial ability and test performance was significant only on the test items requiring recognition of apparatus, drawing of a laboratory plan and locating of apparatus on panoramic photographs. In each case performance only correlated with one of the two spatial ability questions (in the first case with the first spatial ability question and in the second and third cases with the second spatial ability question).

- Responses to two of the three questions designed to determine the degree to which participants experienced a sense of presence indicated that User-control participants experienced a greater sense of presence than Dynamic Views participants. There was no difference on the other presence question.

- Responses to one of the three presence questions indicated that males experienced a greater sense of presence than female participants. There was no difference between male and female responses on the other presence questions.

- There was no significant correlation between responses to presence questions and performance on the test items.

It was expected that participants of the Real Laboratory group would perform better on all parts of the spatial knowledge test than participants of the two virtual laboratory groups, due to the greater fidelity provided by the experience of exploring the real laboratory. In fact there was no significant difference between Real Laboratory participants and User-control participants on any of the test items. The Real Laboratory group performed significantly better than the Dynamic Views group on the test item requiring participants to draw a topological plan of the map and on the test item requiring participants to indicate the position of given views of the laboratory. The fact that in each case there was no difference between Real Laboratory and User-control participants indicates that user control (which was available to both Real Laboratory and User-control participants but not to Dynamic Views participants) was the important factor rather than the greater fidelity provided by the real laboratory. This provides a degree of encouragement for the use of 3D learning environments.

There was very high variance in scores on all test items in this investigation. It is possible that the moderate sample size in conjunction with this high variance meant that differences between groups would have had to be of quite a high magnitude in order to appear significant. It was expected that the larger sample size in Investigation 2 would improve the likelihood of identifying any differences between groups.

The high variance in performance on the tests may indicate that participants' individual skills differed widely. This is consistent with other studies, which provide evidence that people's ability to use a virtual environment and their spatial learning vary greatly, and that this is not predictable in simple terms of age, gender or prior computer experience. For example Gillner and Mallot (1996) noted in their study that "subjects differed strongly in terms of the number of errors made when searching a goal as well as in the quality of their distance estimates" but that "no clustering in different groups can be obtained from our data" (p. 458). In earlier work carried out by this researcher (Dalgarno & Scott, 2000) it was also found that ability to navigate through a virtual environment varied greatly amongst participants.

There is evidence that spatial ability varies widely in the population. An example of the consequences of this can be found in a study by Ruddle et al. (1997), where participants had to redraw a map that they had viewed from memory, to indicate that they had successfully remembered the layout. They note that "one participant was unable to redraw even the building outline after three attempts and was replaced in the experiment" (p. 147). In another part of the same study, where participants were required to choose navigation paths through a virtual building, they found that "participants varied considerably in their ability, with some still travelling more than twice the minimum distance during their final (ninth) session" (p. 154). Hunt and Waller (1999) cite Moeser (1988) and Thorndyke and Hayes-Roth (1982) in suggesting that there are "well-documented reports that people can spend years in a building without acquiring configurational knowledge of it" (p. 45).

This evidence for widely varying spatial skills amongst the population suggests that an even distribution of spatial ability across the groups is very important. The lack of a significant correlation between self reported spatial ability and test performance on all test items suggests that there may be limitations in the spatial ability questions used. This limitation was addressed to an extent in Investigation 2 by modifying the spatial skill question. Additionally, the larger sample size in Investigation 2 was expected to increase the chances of an even distribution of spatial ability across the groups.

5.6 Conclusion

This chapter has described the method and results from the first major investigation, which explored the contribution of user control over view and object manipulation to spatial learning. Chapter 6 describes the second major investigation, which explored all five research questions.

Chapter 6. Investigation 2

6.1 Introduction

Investigation 2, the second and final major investigation in this study, was undertaken in February/March 2003, nine months after the completion of Investigation 1. Investigation 1 explored the importance of user control over view and object manipulation for spatial learning, but for most test items found no significant difference between the spatial learning of participants who had control of their view and undertook object manipulation and those who did not. It was hypothesised that the reason for this lack of difference in spatial learning was that the tasks carried out by User-control participants did not require that they develop a spatial cognitive model and thus the fact that they were more active in their learning process did not lead to learning benefits. Like the first investigation, the second investigation included a User-control group and a Dynamic Views group. However, in this investigation User-control participants were provided with a task requiring them to locate items of apparatus, carry the items to a bench, assemble and use them and then return the items to their correct cupboard or drawer. As discussed in Section 5.5, it was hypothesised that learners would develop a better spatial cognitive model of the laboratory as a consequence of carrying out this task.

In addition to further exploring the importance of control over view and object manipulation for spatial learning, this investigation also explored the importance of smooth display of view changes and smooth display of object animation for spatial learning. To allow this, a third group of participants, called the 'Static Views' group, was included, in addition to the User-control and Dynamic Views groups. This group undertook a virtual tour of the laboratory, similar to the Dynamic Views group, but were shown only still images of each position along the tour rather than animated view changes. Additionally, rather than viewing the movement of objects, they instead viewed the objects from multiple directions without animated view changes.

In addition to a written test to gauge participants' spatial learning, a practical test requiring participants to locate a series of items of apparatus in the real laboratory and to carry out a series of operations using selected items of apparatus was also used.

Additionally, participants undertook a questionnaire on the ease of use and effectiveness of the virtual laboratory and their enjoyment of the experience.

The results of this investigation will help to determine the circumstances in which 3D learning environments are more effective than alternative resources. Specifically, findings from an investigation of the importance of user control over view and object manipulation will help designers to determine whether to use a 3D learning environment rather than an animation or video. Findings from an investigation of the importance of smooth view changes and object animation will help designers to determine whether to use a resource consisting of still photographic images rather than a 3D learning environment.

6.2 Questions Addressed by This Investigation

This investigation addressed each of the questions addressed in the study as a whole. These questions are:

- Question 1. Does smooth display of view changes in a 3D learning environment contribute to spatial learning?

- Question 2. Does smooth display of object motion in a 3D learning environment contribute to spatial learning?

- Question 3. Does user control over view position and direction in a 3D learning environment contribute to spatial learning?

- Question 4. Does object manipulation in a 3D learning environment contribute to spatial learning?

- Question 5. How does the design of the learning task within a 3D environment affect the spatial learning that occurs?

6.3 Method

6.3.1 Overview

In this investigation participants were divided into three groups, a User-control group, a Dynamic Views group and a Static Views group. Each participant explored a virtual environment and was tested on their spatial knowledge through a written test and through a practical test carried out one week later in the real laboratory. The User-control group explored a virtual environment with control over their position and view direction and the ability to pick up, carry and place objects. The Dynamic Views group viewed an animated tour of the laboratory with control only over the pace. The Static Views group viewed a similar tour but consisting of still images only. Table 6.1 shows the time allocated to each task for each of the three groups of participants.

	Table 6.1 Allocated time for each task in Investigation 2		
	Static Views group	**Dynamic Views group**	**User-control group**
Training environment			10 min
Virtual environment exploration	60 min	60 min	60 min
Rest	5 min	5 min	5 min
Test	40 min	40 min	40 min
Total session 1	1 hour 45 min	1 hour 45 min	1 hour 55 min
Real laboratory apparatus location test	5 min	5 min	5 min
Real laboratory apparatus usage test	5 min	5 min	5 min
Total session 2	10 min	10 min	10 min

A comparison of the performance of the User-control and Dynamic Views groups on the spatial learning and practical tests was intended to address the research questions relating to the importance of user control over view and object manipulation. A comparison of the relative difference between the performances of these groups within this investigation and within Investigation 1 was intended to address the research question relating to the effect of learning task design. A comparison of the performances of the Dynamic Views and Static Views groups on the spatial learning and practical tests was intended to address the research questions relating to the importance of smooth display of view changes and smooth display of object animation.

6.3.2 Participants

Participants were undergraduate university chemistry students. The investigation was carried out during class time in an introductory subject and all students were expected to participate. In all 92 students participated. Students were asked for their consent in order for their results to be used in the investigation and all except one student gave this consent (this student also suffered discomfort and withdrew from the study after five minutes of virtual environment exploration). The results from 11 students were excluded because these students had been in the laboratory prior to the investigation. This left 80 participants whose results were used. The participants were randomly allocated in advance to three groups. Nine participants who explored a version of the virtual laboratory and undertook the written tests did not attend for the second session of the investigation, where practical tests were carried out in the real laboratory. Additionally one female participant in the Dynamic Views group only undertook the apparatus location test in the real laboratory but not the apparatus usage test and did not complete the questionnaire. Another female participant in the Dynamic Views group did not complete the apparatus location test in the real laboratory but undertook the apparatus usage test and completed the questionnaire. This left 70 participants in each part of the practical test in the real laboratory and 70 who completed the questionnaire. Table 6.2 shows the number of male and female participants in each group, for each part of the investigation.

Table 6.2 Participants in Investigation 2		Static Views Group	Dynamic Views Group	User-control Group
Virtual laboratory exploration and written tests	Males	18	17	14
	Females	12	9	10
	Total	30	26	24
Apparatus location and usage tests in the real laboratory and questionnaire	Males	16	17	10
	Females	10	7	10
	Total	26	24	20

6.3.3 Virtual Laboratory

The virtual laboratory was explored through Internet Explorer 5.5 and the Blaxxun Contact VRML browser version 5.104, using a PC with a 17 inch screen and a standard keyboard and mouse, running Windows XP. The PCs had basic hardware acceleration, allowing a frame rate of between 5 and 15 frames per second (depending on the part of the virtual environment visible at the time). Internet Explorer was configured to run full-screen, so that none of the Internet Explorer options, or the Windows taskbar were visible. The learning was undertaken in a computer laboratory, with up to 16 students working concurrently, each on their own computer.

The version of the virtual laboratory used by the User-control group was similar to the environment used in the first investigation. The screen layout was very much the same, containing a virtual environment area and a small text area below. Once again participants were able to move through the environment by using the arrow keys and were able to look up, down, left or right by holding down the Shift key while using the arrow keys. Unlike the first investigation, they could also zoom in to look up close at an object by using the F3 key, and zoom back out again using the Home key. Once again if participants clicked on a cupboard door or a drawer, it opened and their viewpoint was adjusted so that they could see into it. It would then shut when they clicked on it again. Once again the environment contained cues to help locate items of apparatus, such as labels on cupboards and drawers. If they clicked on an item of apparatus the name of the item was displayed in the text area.

One limitation of Investigation 1 was that the version of the virtual laboratory used by the User-control group provided little object manipulation capability beyond that provided by the Dynamic Views version. To address this, the interface for exploring and manipulating objects was redeveloped for Investigation 2, with the addition of mechanisms allowing the user to pick up, carry and place objects and to connect items of apparatus together. A hand icon was added to the screen layout, which always appeared at the bottom left of the screen. Objects could be picked up and carried by first dragging and dropping them on this icon. While carried, the object remained on top of this hand. To place objects, the user dragged the object to the new location. Objects could only be placed in certain locations and the target location glowed yellow when the object was dragged over it, to indicate where an object could be placed. The same technique was used for connecting objects together, with a target object glowing yellow when another object was dragged over the top of it, if the two objects could be connected. Certain components of objects, such as levers, dials and plungers could be operated by dragging them with the mouse. Figure 6.1 shows a screen shot from the version of the virtual laboratory used by the User-control group in this investigation.

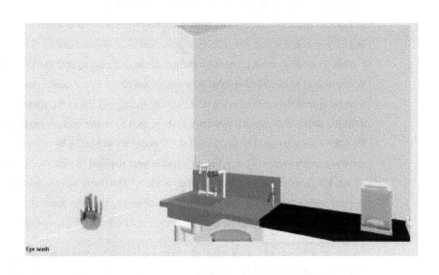

Figure 6.1
Screen layout of the Investigation 2 User-control version of the virtual laboratory

Once again the screen layout for the version used by the Dynamic Views group was identical to the version used by the User-control group, but with the addition of Next View and Previous View options to allow users to move through the environment. Again, users began outside the laboratory and each time they clicked on the Next View option they moved to a new location on a tour of the laboratory with the name of the location or the part of the laboratory they were shown displayed in the text area. Sometimes when users clicked on Next View they were taken to an item of apparatus and the name of that item was displayed in the text area. In some cases a drawer or cupboard was first opened. The subsequent time the user clicked on Next View, the item appeared to be picked up (that is, it was shown on top of the hand icon) and stayed with the user as they moved to the next location. In this way the virtual tour consisted of a similar series of animated movements to those seen by a user undertaking the tasks in the User-control group. The tour included 429 positions within the laboratory and apparatus display steps. That is, the participants were required to click the Next View button 428 times to see the complete series of views. The frame rate for animated view changes within the version used by the Dynamic Views group was again identical to the frame rate for corresponding movements in the version used by the User-control group.

The Static Views group saw a series of still images corresponding to positions along the guided tour. The screen layout was identical to the Dynamic Views group with Next View and Previous View options allowing them to move through the views. The number of images displayed was identical to the number of steps in the tour viewed by the dynamic tour group, that is, participants of the Static Views group also had to click Next View 428 times to complete their tour.

6.3.4 Training Procedure

Participants in the User-control group began with 10 minutes of guided exploration of a 3D environment, modelled on an art gallery, with screen layout and navigation options the same as in the virtual laboratory environment. Based on observations in Investigation 1, where participants were very quickly able to use the Dynamic Views version of the virtual laboratory, it was decided not to provide any training to participants of the Dynamic Views or Static Views groups. User-control participants were provided with a one-page sheet of instructions as well as a one-page list of suggested practice exercises (see Appendix L). Participants used the sheet of instructions as a reference as they undertook their tasks in the virtual laboratory.

6.3.5 Learning Tasks and Procedure

After the training, participants of the User-control group were given a printed worksheet (see Appendix M) listing a series of tasks to complete in the virtual laboratory. The first task was to locate a series of items of apparatus and carry these items to a bench in the laboratory. While doing so participants were also asked to familiarise themselves with specific laboratory features and furniture. Table 6.3 lists the apparatus, furniture and laboratory features listed on the worksheet. Participants were also asked verbally to tick each item of apparatus, laboratory location and item of furniture once located. If all items were not found after 20 minutes, participants were told where to find the remaining items. If all items were not collected after 30 minutes, a version of the environment with all items collected and placed on the desk was loaded.

Table 6.3
Apparatus and furniture listed on task worksheets

Apparatus	Laboratory features and furniture
Reagent bottle	The service hatch
250ml conical flask	The whiteboard
250ml beaker	6 lab benches
Burette	2 sets of metal drawers
Burette stand	5 fume cupboards
Clamp	2 sets of brown drawers
Burette funnel	8 cream cabinets (each containing cupboards and drawers)
Pipette	5 sinks
Pipette filler	5 doors
Test tube rack	7 windows
Test tube	

The second task was to connect the items together following a series of specific instructions provided on the worksheet, which simulated the process they would follow if they were to undertake an experiment. Table 6.4 lists the instructions provided on the worksheet for connecting the items of apparatus together. The third task was to disassemble the apparatus, again following a series of specific instructions and their last task was to put the items of apparatus away again.

Table 6.4 **Apparatus manipulation tasks**
Attach the clamp to the stand and the burette to the clamp.
Place the funnel in the burette and the conical flask at the base of the burette.
Drag the reagent bottle to the beaker to pretend that you are pouring liquid into it.
Place the reagent bottle back on the shelf.
Zoom in close to the burette tap using F3 and then turn the tap to pretend that you are making sure that it is shut (use Home to zoom out again).
Drag the beaker to the funnel to pretend that you are pouring liquid into the burette.
Place the beaker back on the bench.
Turn the tap on the burette to pretend that you are releasing liquid from the burette into the conical flask (you may need to zoom in close again using F3).
Place the conical flask back in its original position on the bench.
Connect the pipette filler to the pipette.
Place the pipette in the conical flask.
Zoom in close to the pipette filler using F3 and then press the **lever** to lower the plunger and then turn the **wheel** upwards to raise the plunger to pretend that you are extracting liquid from the conical flask to the pipette (use Home to zoom out again).
Place the test tube in the test tube rack.
Place the pipette in the test tube.
Press the **lever** on the pipette filler to pretend you are emptying liquid into the test tube (you may need to zoom in close again using F3).

Participants of the Dynamic Views and Static Views groups instead viewed a series of animated images equivalent to what they would have seen had they undertaken this task in the 3D environment. They were given a similar worksheet to the User-control participants so that they had a similar sense for the overall task (see Appendix N). Participants were also asked verbally to tick each item of apparatus, laboratory location and item of furniture once located. Participants were allowed a maximum of 60 minutes. Dynamic Views and Static Views participants were encouraged to view the animated images a second time if they completed it before the 60 minutes had elapsed, to ensure that the total exposure time of all participants was the same.

6.3.6 Written Test Tasks and Procedure

As with the first investigation, participants undertook a written test after exploring the virtual environment. Again, supporting materials were provided on computer (viewed through the Internet Explorer Web browser) to allow for the use of full colour images. Participants wrote their responses on paper. The test was divided into six parts, labelled A to F, with Part A containing background questions on prior experience with chemistry, spatial ability and the degree of immersion experienced. Each part was completed and submitted before commencing the next part. All participants did each part of the test at the same time. This was to prevent a participant from using an image from a later question on another participant's screen to help them to answer a question. The total time allowed for the test was 40 minutes. The test is included in Appendix O and the support Web site is included on the enclosed CD-ROM.

Part A of the test contained a series of questions to record the participants' prior chemistry experience, their perceived level of spatial skills and their perceived sense of presence. For the questions on spatial skills and presence, participants were asked to indicate the degree to which they agreed or disagreed with each of three statements by placing a mark on a line, with one end of the line labelled very strongly agree and the other end labelled very strongly disagree. The statements were as follows:

- You are good at finding your way around unfamiliar places;

- You felt involved in the virtual environment experience; and

- You felt a compelling sense of moving around inside the virtual environment.

The first statement was different to the questions designed to gauge participants' impressions of their own spatial ability in Investigation 1. As discussed in Section 5.4.9 there were doubts about the validity of these questions and the question used in this investigation was intended to more clearly reflect the type of spatial ability that would be relevant in navigating around a real or virtual environment. The other two statements were the same as statements used in the test in Investigation 1, to gauge the degree to which participants felt present in the virtual environment.

Part B of the test contained 10 questions. In each question, participants were provided with pictures of two models of an item of apparatus, with subtle structural differences.

They were asked to identify the item and to indicate which was the correct model, or to specify that neither was correct. Participants were also asked to indicate whether they would have already been able to name this item prior to their participation in the study. The pipette filler and the burette were used for six of these questions, with three pairs of models of each. Each of these items has a number of features that could be modified in an incorrect model. Additionally, participants of the User-control group manipulated the levers and dials on these items during their task, and consequently a comparison of the degree to which participants could recall their structure was expected to shed light on the contribution of object manipulation to spatial learning. The remaining 4 questions used models of a conical flask, a pipette, a reagent bottle and a beaker. Figure 3.18 shows an example of this type of question. The intention was that this would test the accuracy of participants' spatial cognitive models of the items of apparatus as well as their recall of the names of items. It replaced test items A and B from Investigation 1, which tested identification of apparatus and recall of apparatus structure separately. Participants were given a maximum time of eight minutes to complete this part.

Part C of the test required participants to list the steps required to transfer some liquid from a reagent bottle to a conical flask using the burette and then to measure some liquid from a conical flask to a test tube using the pipette. They were asked to include all of the steps required to assemble the apparatus as well as the detailed steps in operating the burette and the pipette filler. They were provided with a diagram showing the names of the items of apparatus and the diagram was also available in colour as part of the support Web site. Figure 6.2 shows the labelled diagram provided. This test item was a new item, not used in Investigation 1, which assessed learning as a result of the apparatus manipulation task carried out in this investigation. Participants were given a maximum time of eight minutes to complete this part.

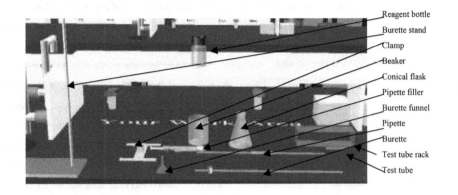

Reagent bottle
Burette stand
Clamp
Beaker
Conical flask
Pipette filler
Burette funnel
Pipette
Burette
Test tube rack
Test tube

Figure 6.2
Diagram of apparatus provided for test Part C in Investigation 2

Part D of the test required participants to draw a plan of the laboratory, given an outline of the laboratory, a list of nine laboratory features or items of furniture to include and a colour photo of each. The number of instances of each item in the laboratory was indicated, giving a total of 41 items for participants to include on their plan. The intention was that this would test the participants' spatial cognitive models of the relative positions of the laboratory furniture without also requiring them to remember what was actually there. The specific items listed differed slightly from those used in the first investigation. The items chosen were the same as those included in the list of laboratory features and furniture on the worksheets (see Table 6.3) except that the position of the service hatch was provided. Whereas in Investigation 1 a separate test item was included requiring participants to draw a plan of the laboratory without providing them with a list of items of furniture, this was not done in this investigation. A calculation of Pearson's correlation coefficient showed that results on the two items were very strongly correlated (PC = 0.729, p=0.000) indicating that they were testing the same thing and thus were not both required. Participants were given a maximum time of eight minutes to complete this part.

Part E of the test required participants to indicate on an outline of the laboratory, the position and direction of the camera, by ruling a line from the camera position to the centre of the camera view on the opposite wall, given photos taken from six positions within the laboratory. It was intended that this would test the ability of participants to use their spatial models to orient them within the laboratory. This item was identical to one used in Investigation 1. Participants were given a maximum time of seven minutes to complete this part.

Part F was similar to Part F in the first investigation, where participants were required to indicate the position on a plan of the laboratory where they could expect to find each of 11 items of apparatus. The items listed matched the list of apparatus on the worksheet, that is, those that the User-control participants collected and returned in the virtual laboratory. A different set of apparatus was used to that used in the first investigation. Participants were given access to a labelled diagram showing all items as part of the support Web site. Participants were given a maximum time of six minutes to complete this part. In Investigation 1 a second item was used that tested participants' recall of the location of apparatus. This item required participants to indicate the position of each item on a set of photographs making up a panorama. Because some participants found the requirements of this item confusing it was not used in Investigation 2.

6.3.7 Real Laboratory Test Tasks and Procedure

All participants undertook two test tasks within the real laboratory one week after completing the virtual laboratory task. The tasks were carried out individually. The first task was to locate 10 items of apparatus. Each item name was read out and participants were required to walk to the location within the laboratory where they could find the item. If after 30 seconds they had not located the item they moved on to the next item. The total time and the total number of items located were recorded. The items participants were required to find were the same items listed on their worksheet, except that the reagent bottle was not included.

The second task required participants to carry out a series of operations using a set of apparatus. Each operation was read out and participants were asked to try themselves first and then ask for help if necessary. For each operation a critical step was identified and observation notes were made indicating whether this critical step was carried out immediately, after delay, after experimenting, after verbal assistance or never. The operations carried out along with the identified critical steps are listed in Table 6.5. Participants were not given a time limit for the tasks and the time taken was not recorded. However, all participants were able to complete the task within about five minutes.

Table 6.5	
Apparatus manipulation test carried out in real laboratory	
Task	**Critical step**
Pipette some water into the burette using Pasteur pipette without letting any out into the conical flask.	Closed the burette tap first
Empty some water from the burette into the conical flask.	Opened the burette tap
Extract some water from the conical flask using the pipette.	Lowered plunger on pipette filler first
	Used dial to lower and/or raise plunger
Empty some of the water from the pipette into the test tube.	Used dial to lower plunger
Empty all of the remaining water from the pipette back into the beaker.	Used lever to empty all of the liquid

A sample of the observation form completed for each participant is included in Appendix P. The participant's gender was also recorded on this form.

6.3.8 Questionnaire

After completing the laboratory tasks participants completed a questionnaire on their perceptions of the ease of use and the value of the virtual laboratory as a tool for familiarising them with the laboratory as well as the degree to which they enjoyed the experience. The questionnaire was structured as a series of statements and in each case participants were asked to indicate the degree to which they agreed or disagreed, using a seven point scale from very strongly disagree to very strongly agree. Table 6.6 lists the statements included. Participants were also asked to suggest aspects of the virtual laboratory that could be improved. They were also asked for their date of birth so that their age could be calculated. The questionnaire has been included in Appendix Q.

Table 6.6
Statements included in questionnaire
1. You enjoy playing computer games.
2. You enjoyed using the virtual lab.
3. Overall the virtual lab helped you to become familiar with the real lab.
4. The virtual lab is an accurate representation of the real lab.
5. The virtual lab is easy to use.
6. The virtual lab helped you to become familiar with the layout of the lab building.
7. The virtual lab helped you to be able to identify items of apparatus.
8. The virtual lab helped you to be able to locate items within the lab.
9. The virtual lab helped you to become familiar with the procedure for using a burette.
10. The virtual lab helped you to become familiar with the procedure for using a pipette.
11. In its current form, you would recommend that new students use the virtual lab prior to their first laboratory experiment.
12. If the virtual lab allowed you to carry out virtual experiments, you would use it prior to laboratory sessions to practice the experiments.

6.4 Results

The results obtained in the investigation are presented in this section. Firstly the results of an initial analysis to determine whether there were interactions between any of the three independent variables, group, gender and prior experience are discussed. Analyses of test performance by gender and prior experience are presented next. As was the case in Investigation 1, these results are presented first because of the potential validity problems if gender or prior experience were a factor in performance, given the uneven distribution of gender and the potential uneven distribution of prior experience between the groups. A comparison of the performances of the groups on each part of the written test are then presented, followed by comparisons of the performances of the groups on the real laboratory tests. The results of the background questions on spatial ability and sense of presence are discussed next, followed by a discussion of the questionnaire results.

6.4.1 Initial Analysis

A factorial Analysis of Variance (ANOVA) was undertaken with group, gender and prior chemistry experience as factors and each of the background questions, written test items, real laboratory tasks and questionnaire items as dependent variables. The statistical software used adjusted values for the sums of squares to account for the unbalanced design. The interactions identified are shown in Table 6.7.

<table>
<tr><td colspan="2" align="center">Table 6.7
Interactions identified in Investigation 2</td></tr>
<tr><td>Dependent Variable</td><td>Interaction</td></tr>
<tr><td>Test Part B. Recollection of apparatus structure</td><td>Gender * Group * Chemistry Experience (p=0.014)</td></tr>
<tr><td>Questionnaire Question 6</td><td>Gender * Chemistry Experience (p=0.036)</td></tr>
</table>

For the two dependent variables where interactions were identified a factorial ANOVA was used to identify main effects of group, gender and chemistry experience. For all other dependent variables there were no significant interactions between group and gender, group and chemistry experience or gender and chemistry experience and no significant three-way interactions. Consequently, for the remaining items, main effects of group, gender and chemistry experience were explored using single factor ANOVAs.

6.4.2 Gender

This section compares the performances of males and females on each part of the written test and real laboratory test in order to determine whether the uneven distribution of males and females across groups is important.

Table 6.8 shows a comparison of male and female responses on each part of the written spatial knowledge test. The scoring of participants' tests is explained in Sections 6.4.4 to 6.4.8. As discussed in Section 6.4.1 there were significant interactions between gender, group and chemistry experience on the recollection of apparatus structure part of test Part B. Consequently, a factorial ANOVA was used to determine if there was a main effect of gender on this item. For all other items a T-test was used to determine if the difference between male and female performances was significant. The analysis indicated that there was no significant difference between male and female performances on any of the test items.

Test Part		Male	Female
Part B. Identification of apparatus (Percentage of items of apparatus identified)	n	49	31
	mean	83%	81%
	SD	22%	21%
	T Test	p= 0.664 (not significant)	
Part B. Identification of apparatus (Percentage of items of apparatus identified that were new to this participant)	n	49	31
	mean	62%	60%
	SD	37%	37%
	T Test	p= 0.889 (not significant)	
Part B. Recollection of apparatus structure (Percentage of correct models identified)	n	49	31
	mean	71%	69%
	SD	21%	21%
	ANOVA	p=0.957 (not significant)	
Part C. Assembling and using apparatus (Number of steps correctly described, maximum 14)	n	49	31
	mean	8.13	8.87
	SD	3.16	3.59
	T Test	p= 0.338 (not significant)	
Part C. Assembling and using apparatus (Number of key steps correctly described, maximum 4)	n	49	31
	mean	1.99	2.03
	SD	1.39	1.56
	T Test	p= 0.899 (not significant)	
Part D. Laboratory plan (Number of correctly positioned items of furniture and landmarks on plan, maximum 41)	n	49	31
	mean	20.57	24.71
	SD	11.09	10.43
	T Test	p=0.100 (not significant)	

Table 6.8
Performance on spatial learning test by gender

Test Part		Male	Female
Part E. Positioning of views (Number of views correctly identified, maximum 6)	n	49	31
	mean	2.90	2.90
	SD	1.56	1.33
	T Test	p= 0.988 (not significant)	
Part F. Location of apparatus on map (Number of items correctly located, maximum 11)	n	49	31
	mean	4.09	3.85
	SD	2.44	2.81
	T Test	p= 0.691 (not significant)	

Table 6.8 (cont.)
Performance on spatial learning test by gender

Table 6.9 shows a comparison of male and female performances on the parts of the real laboratory test involving working with apparatus. For each step a score was calculated indicating whether the critical step was carried out immediately (scoring 5), after a delay (4), after experimenting (3), after verbal assistance (2) or never (1). Because these scores are qualitative and non-linear, it was not appropriate to use a T-test. Instead the scores were ranked and Mann-Witney's U-test was used to compare the male and female ranks. The results of the U-tests indicate that there was no significant difference between male and female performances.

Table 6.9
Performance on real laboratory apparatus usage test by gender

Critical Step		Male	Female
1.Closed the burette tap first	n	43	27
	mean rank	35.8	35.0
	Mann-Whitney	p= 0.811 (not significant)	
2.Opened the burette tap	n	43	27
	mean rank	35.5	35.5
	Mann-Whitney	1.000 (not significant)	
3.Lowered plunger on pipette filler first	n	43	27
	mean rank	37.9	31.6
	Mann-Whitney	p=0.183 (not significant)	
4.Used dial to lower and/or raise plunger	n	43	27
	mean rank	37.5	32.4
	Mann-Whitney	p= 0.280 (not significant)	
5.Used dial to lower plunger	n	43	27
	mean rank	33.5	38.7
	Mann-Whitney	p= 0.179 (not significant)	
6.Used lever to empty all of the liquid	n	43	27
	mean rank	38.1	31.4
	Mann-Whitney	p=0.121 (not significant)	

Table 6.10 shows a comparison of male and female performances on the part of the real laboratory test requiring the location of items of apparatus. T-tests indicated that there was no significant difference between male and female performances on either item.

<table>
<tr><td colspan="5" align="center">Table 6.10
Performance on real laboratory apparatus location test by gender</td></tr>
<tr><td>Score</td><td></td><td></td><td>Male</td><td>Female</td></tr>
<tr><td rowspan="4">Number of items located (maximum 10)</td><td>n</td><td></td><td>43</td><td>27</td></tr>
<tr><td>mean</td><td></td><td>7.49</td><td>7.85</td></tr>
<tr><td>SD</td><td></td><td>1.55</td><td>1.49</td></tr>
<tr><td>T Test</td><td colspan="3" align="center">p= 0.335 (not significant)</td></tr>
<tr><td rowspan="4">Total time taken (seconds)</td><td>n</td><td></td><td>43</td><td>27</td></tr>
<tr><td>mean</td><td></td><td>169.37</td><td>156.85</td></tr>
<tr><td>SD</td><td></td><td>44.09</td><td>44.63</td></tr>
<tr><td>T Test</td><td colspan="3" align="center">p= 0.254 (not significant)</td></tr>
</table>

The fact that there was no significant difference between male and female performance on the written test or the practical test and the fact that as discussed in Section 6.4.1 there were no significant gender-group interactions, suggests that the slightly uneven distribution of males and females across the groups should not have a negative impact on the validity of the results.

6.4.3 Prior Study of Chemistry

Participants were asked to indicate the highest level of chemistry study completed (high school Year 10, Year 11, or Year 12, tertiary study at Charles Sturt University, other tertiary study or other study) and the year in which this study was undertaken. Based on this data, participants' data was grouped into the following chemistry experience levels for analysis purposes:

- Recent highly relevant experience: those who had studied Year 11, Year 12 or tertiary chemistry in the past five years;

- Any other relevant experience: those who were not in the first category, but who had studied any chemistry in the past 10 years; and

- No relevant experience: those who had not studied any chemistry in the past 10 years (under the assumption that chemistry studied prior to 10 years ago would have involved the use of quite different laboratory equipment and would have been very poorly recalled by participants).

There were 28 participants with the highest level of experience, 24 with the second and 28 with no relevant experience. Table 6.11 shows the number of participants with each level of experience in each of the three groups within the investigation. Because the information about the level of chemistry experience was gathered as part of the written spatial test, that is, after participants had explored a version of the virtual laboratory, it was not possible to use this information for grouping purposes. Consequently, the distribution of experience across the three groups was not equal. Due to this unequal distribution of experience, the degree to which chemistry experience affects performance on the spatial tests is an important issue. If chemistry experience does contribute to performance on the tests then those groups with a greater number of participants with substantial chemistry experience may perform better than other groups, which may lead to false conclusions about the effect of the different virtual environment treatments.

	Table 6.11 Chemistry experience levels within each group		
	Recent highly relevant experience (Year 11, Year 12 or tertiary chemistry within last 5 years)	**Other relevant experience (any chemistry experience within last 10 years)**	**No relevant experience (no chemistry experience during last 10 years)**
Static Views	10	9	11
Dynamic Views	13	8	5
User-control	5	7	12

Table 6.12 compares the results on each part of the test for participants with each level of experience. As discussed in Section 6.4.1 there were significant interactions between gender, group and chemistry experience on the recollection of apparatus structure task

within Part B of the test. Consequently, a factorial ANOVA was used to determine if there was a main effect of chemistry experience on this item. For the remaining items, a single factor ANOVA was used to compare performance. For most test items there was no significant difference between the performances of participants with different levels of chemistry experience. For the number of key steps correctly described in Part C of the test an ANOVA indicated that there may have been a difference, and a Post Hoc Tukey's Honestly Significant Difference (HSD) test showed that there was a significant difference between participants with no chemistry experience and those with recent highly relevant experience. Consequently, given that the number of participants with different levels of chemistry experience in the three groups within the study differed, this result limits the validity of comparisons of the performance across groups on this item.

Table 6.12

Performance on spatial learning test by prior chemistry experience

Test Part		Recent highly relevant experience	Any relevant experience	No relevant experience
Part B. Identification of apparatus (Percentage of items of apparatus identified)	n	28	24	28
	mean	85%	82%	81%
	SD	21%	22%	21%
	ANOVA	p=0.774 (not significant)		
Part B. Identification of apparatus (Percentage of items of apparatus identified that were new to this participant)	n	28	24	28
	mean	51%	68%	65%
	SD	39%	35%	35%
	ANOVA	p=0.203 (not significant)		
Part B. Recollection of apparatus structure (Percentage of correct models identified)	n	28	24	28
	mean	69%	75%	67%
	SD	25%	19%	18%
	ANOVA	p=0.997 (not significant)		
Part C. Assembling and using apparatus (Number of steps correctly described, maximum 14)	n	28	24	28
	mean	9.04	8.69	7.57
	SD	3.26	3.19	3.47
	ANOVA	p=0.234 (not significant)		

Table 6.12 (cont.)

Performance on spatial learning test by prior chemistry experience

Test Part		Recent highly relevant experience	Any relevant experience	No relevant experience
Part C. Assembling and using apparatus (Number of key steps correctly described, maximum 4)	**n**	28	24	28
	mean	2.46	2.08	1.48
	SD	1.37	1.40	1.44
	ANOVA	p=0.036 (significant)		
	Post-Hoc Tukey's HSD Tests	Recent highly relevant experience v any other relevant experience p=0.594 (not significant)		
			Any other relevant experience v no relevant experience p=0.278 (not significant)	
		Recent highly relevant experience v no experience p=0.028 (significant)		
Part D. Laboratory plan (Number of correctly positioned items of furniture and landmarks on plan, maximum 41)	**n**	28	24	28
	mean	20.71	23.04	22.89
	SD	10.45	11.28	11.42
	ANOVA	p=0.687 (not significant)		
Part E. Positioning of views (Number of views correctly identified, maximum 6)	**n**	28	24	28
	mean	2.75	2.92	3.04
	SD	1.69	1.25	1.43
	ANOVA	p=0.769 (not significant)		
Part F. Location of apparatus on map (Number of items correctly located, maximum 11)	**n**	28	24	28
	mean	4.59	3.90	3.50
	SD	2.56	2.69	2.46
	ANOVA	p=0.282 (not significant)		

Table 6.13 compares the scores of participants with differing levels of chemistry experience on the parts of the real laboratory test that involved working with apparatus. For each step a score was calculated indicating whether the critical step was carried out immediately (scoring 5), after a delay (4), after experimenting (3), after verbal assistance (2) or never (1). Because these scores are qualitative and non-linear, it was not appropriate to use an ANOVA. Instead the scores were ranked and a Kruskal-Wallis test was used to compare the performance across the experience groups. As suggested by Cramer (1998), Post Hoc comparisons were made using the Mann-Whitney U test with the significance level reduced by a factor of 3 (due to the 3 Post Hoc comparisons performed) to 0.017 for 95% confidence or 0.033 for 90% confidence.

For Steps 1 and 4 of the apparatus manipulation task, the Kruskal-Wallis test indicated that there may have been a difference in performance for students with differing chemistry experience. For Step 1, Post Hoc Mann-Whitney U tests indicated that the difference between participants with recent highly relevant experience and those with no experience was significant at the 90% level. For Step 4, a Post Hoc Mann-Whitney U test indicated that the difference between participants with highly relevant experience and those with no relevant experience was significant at the 90% level. Given that chemistry experience was not spread evenly across groups, this finding suggests that the validity of comparisons of group performance on these parts of the apparatus usage test may be limited.

Table 6.13

Performance on real laboratory apparatus usage test by prior chemistry experience

Critical step		Recent highly relevant experience	Any relevant experience	No relevant experience
1.Closed the burette tap first	n	27	19	24
	mean rank	38.9	38.1	29.6
	Kruskal-Wallis	p=0. 028 (significant)		
	Post-Hoc Mann-Whitney U Tests	Recent highly relevant experience v any other relevant experience p=0.749 (not significant)		
			Any other relevant experience v no relevant experience p=0.064 (not significant)	
		Recent highly relevant experience v no experience **p=0.020 (significant at 90% level)**		
2.Opened the burette tap	n	27	19	24
	mean rank	35.5	35.5	35.5
	Kruskal-Wallis	p=1.000 (not significant)		
3.Lowered plunger on pipette filler first	n	27	19	24
	mean rank	38.9	39.2	28.8
	Kruskal-Wallis	p=0.110 (not significant)		

Table 6.13 (continued)

Table 6.13 (continued)
Performance on real laboratory apparatus usage test by prior chemistry experience

Critical step		Recent highly relevant experience	Any relevant experience	No relevant experience
4. Used dial to lower and/or raise plunger	n	27	19	24
	mean rank	41.8	34.0	29.6
	Kruskal-Wallis	p=0.072 (significant at 90% level)		
	Post-Hoc Mann-Whitney U Tests	Recent highly relevant experience v any other relevant experience p=0.145 (not significant)		
			Any other relevant experience v no relevant experience p=0.401 (not significant)	
		Recent highly relevant experience v no experience p=0.029 (significant at 90% level)		
5. Used dial to lower plunger	n	27	19	24
	mean rank	37.7	35.2	33.3
	Kruskal-Wallis	p=0.617 (not significant)		
6. Used lever to empty all of the liquid	n	27	19	24
	mean rank	38.0	34.4	33.5
	Kruskal-Wallis	p=0.633 (not significant)		

An ANOVA was used to compare the results for participants with each level of chemistry experience on the parts of the real laboratory test involving the location of items of apparatus. Table 6.14 shows a summary of the results and analysis. The results indicate that there was no significant difference between the performances of participants with differing levels of chemistry experience on this part of the test.

Consequently the unequal distribution of experience across the groups will not have a negative impact on the validity of the results on these items.

Table 6.14 Performance on real laboratory apparatus location test by prior chemistry experience				
Score		Recent highly relevant experience	Any relevant experience	No relevant experience
Number of items located (maximum 10)	n	27	18	25
	mean	7.93	7.89	7.12
	SD	1.27	1.45	1.74
	ANOVA	p=0.114 (not significant)		
Total time taken (seconds)	n	27	18	25
	mean	155.37	164.33	174.60
	SD	36.99	42.70	51.91
	ANOVA	p=0.300 (not significant)		

6.4.4 Identification of Apparatus and Recollection of Apparatus Structure

Part B of the test contained 10 questions. In each question, participants were provided with pictures of two models of an item of apparatus, with subtle structural differences. They were asked to identify the item and to indicate which was the correct model, or to specify that neither was correct. The analysis of the results for identification of items is summarised in Table 6.15. There were a total of six items to be identified (two of the items, the pipette filler and the burette, each appeared in three questions, with different features in the incorrect distracter models in each case). User-control participants (with a mean of 90% of items correctly identified) performed better than Dynamic Views participants (86%), who performed better than Static Views participants (73%). An ANOVA indicated that some of the differences may have been significant, and a Post Hoc Tukey's HSD test indicated that the difference between User-control and Dynamic Views participants was not significant, but that the differences between User-control and Static Views and Dynamic Views and Static Views participants were significant.

Table 6.15
Performance on Part B of the test, requiring identification of apparatus
Score is percentage of items correctly identified

	Static Views group	Dynamic Views group	User-control group
n	30	26	24
mean	73%	86%	90%
SD	22%	21%	16%
ANOVA	p=0.005 (significant)		
Post-Hoc Tukey's HSD Tests	Static Views v Dynamic Views p=0.039 (significant)		
		Dynamic Views v User-control p= 0.770 (not significant)	
	Static Views v User-control p= 0.007 (significant)		

The results on total number of items identified would suggest that smooth display of object motion is important for spatial learning. However, recognising that some participants would have already been able to identify some items, they were also asked to indicate whether they would have, prior to the study, been able to name each item. The mean percentage of items already able to be identified was 45%. A second score was calculated, the percentage of unfamiliar items able to be identified, that is, their score as a percentage excluding those items which were both correctly identified and marked as already familiar. Table 6.16 shows a summary of these results and the corresponding analysis. An ANOVA suggested that there were no significant differences between the scores of participants in the three groups. This indicates that the differences in scores in percentage of items able to be identified may have reflected differences in prior knowledge rather than differences due to the three learning conditions (that is, the three virtual laboratory versions). Interestingly, however, as discussed in Section 6.4.3, there was no significant effect of chemistry experience on this item, which implies that if there was a difference in prior familiarity of items across the groups, it was not due to different levels of chemistry experience.

It is difficult to make a clear conclusion from this data. The high number of items already able to be identified by many participants meant that the scores for percentage of unfamiliar items able to be identified were based on a small number of items. The fact that the number of new items differed for each participant also casts some doubt on the validity of the results. For example, one would expect that it would be easier to learn the identity of one or two new items than to learn the identity of six new items. Consequently, the results on this item don't provide a clear indication about whether the smooth display of object animation or object manipulation are important for spatial learning.

	Static Views group	Dynamic Views group	User-control group
Table 6.16 Performance on Part B of the test, requiring identification of apparatus Score is percentage of unfamiliar items able to be identified			
n	30	26	24
mean	62%	61%	61%
SD	28%	40%	44%
ANOVA	p=0.990 (not significant)		

Table 6.17 compares performance on identification of correct models of apparatus for the three groups. There were 10 correct models to identify. The scores were very similar, with the Dynamic Views group performing slightly better than the User-control group who in turn performed slightly better than the Static Views group. As discussed in Section 6.4.1, interactions between gender, group and chemistry experience were found to be significant on this item, and thus a factorial ANOVA was used to examine the significance of the main effect of group. The factorial ANOVA suggested that the differences between groups were not significant. This suggests that smooth display of object motion and object manipulation did not contribute to spatial learning.

Table 6.17
Performance on Part B of the test, requiring identification of correct model of apparatus. Score is percentage of items, for which the correct model was able to be identified.

	Static Views group	Dynamic Views group	User-control group
n	30	26	24
mean	66%	73%	71%
SD	23%	22%	18%
ANOVA	p=0.895 (not significant)		

6.4.5 Recall of Apparatus Usage Procedure

Part C of the test was a new item unlike any included in Investigation 1. It required participants to list the steps required to transfer some liquid from a reagent bottle to a conical flask using the burette and then to measure some liquid from a conical flask to a test tube using the pipette. Participants were asked to include all of the steps required to assemble the apparatus as well as the detailed steps in operating the burette and the pipette filler and were provided with a diagram showing the names of the items of apparatus. The number of correctly described steps was recorded. If a participant's description of a step was partially correct they were awarded half a mark. There were 14 steps to be identified. Table 6.18 shows a summary of the results and analysis. User-control participants (with a mean of 9.85 correct steps) performed better than Dynamic Views participants (mean of 8.75), who performed better than Static Views participants (mean of 6.98). An ANOVA indicated that the differences may have been significant. Post Hoc Tukey's HSD tests indicated that the difference between Static Views and Dynamic Views participants was significant at the 90% level and the difference between Static Views and User-control participants was significant at the 95% level, but the difference between Dynamic Views and User-control participants was not significant.

Table 6.18
Performance on Part C of the test, requiring description of apparatus usage procedure. Score is number of steps correctly described.

	Static Views group	Dynamic Views group	User-control group
n	30	26	24
mean	6.98	8.75	9.85
SD	3.19	3.37	2.83
ANOVA	p=0.005 (significant)		
Post-Hoc Tukey's HSD Tests	Static Views v Dynamic Views p=0.098 (significant at 90% level)		
		Dynamic Views v User-control p= 0.435 (not significant)	
	Static Views v User-control p= 0.004 (significant)		

In addition to recording the total number of steps described correctly, four critical steps, which involved operations using the burette and the pipette filler, were identified and the number of these steps correctly described was also recorded. A summary of the results and analysis based on this result are shown in Table 6.19. Once again User-control participants performed best, followed by Dynamic Views participants and then followed by Static Views participants. Once again an ANOVA indicated that the differences may have been significant. Post Hoc Tukey's HSD tests indicated that the difference between Dynamic Views and User-control participants was not significant but that the Dynamic Views and User-control groups both performed significantly better than the Static Views group (however in the case of the Dynamic Views group only at the 90% level).

The fact that prior study of chemistry was identified as a factor in performance on recall of the critical steps in Part C of the test, and the fact that there was not an even distribution of prior experience across the groups, limit to an extent the validity of this result. Specifically, the Dynamic Views group had only five participants with no previous chemistry experience, whereas the Static Views group had eleven, which may mean that the superior performance of the Dynamic Views group may have been due to their, on average, greater prior experience. However, prior chemistry study was not a significant factor in performance on recall of all steps, and so the differences identified here can be considered to be valid.

Table 6.19
Performance on Part C of the test, requiring description of apparatus usage procedure. Score is number of identified critical steps correctly described.

	Static Views group	Dynamic Views group	User-control group
n	30	26	24
mean	1.38	2.17	2.60
SD	1.23	1.49	1.40
ANOVA	p=0.005 (significant)		
Post-Hoc Tukey's HSD Tests	Static Views v Dynamic Views p=0.086 (significant at 90% level)		
		Dynamic Views v User-control p= 0.509 (not significant)	
	Static Views v User-control p= 0.005 (significant)		

The results on this test item provide limited support for the proposition that smooth display of object motion contributes to spatial learning, but do not provide evidence that object manipulation contributes to spatial learning.

6.4.6 Recall of Laboratory Layout

As with the first investigation, Part D of the test required participants to draw a labelled plan of the laboratory showing furniture, doors and windows, beginning with an outline of the laboratory with the walkway indicated to show the orientation, and given a list of items to include. Scoring was done in an identical way to the first investigation, with a score of one mark for each correctly placed item. Items were scored as correct if they were:

- placed with their centre within 2m of the correct location;

- sized between 50% and 200% of the correct size in each direction;

- sized within 2m of the correct size in each direction;

- placed in the correct room; and

- at the correct orientation.

There were 41 items to include on the plan so the maximum possible score was 41. Table 6.20 shows a summary of the results and analysis.

The mean score for User-control participants was 22.75 marks, which was marginally better than Static Views participants (mean of 22.43 marks), which was marginally better again than Dynamic Views participants (mean of 21.35 marks). An ANOVA comparing the means of the three groups suggested that there was no group effect on performance on this part of the test. This result does not support the proposition that smooth view changes and user control over view contribute to spatial learning.

The results for the two investigations can be compared in percentage terms. Although the mean for the Dynamic Views group on this investigation (52%) was similar to the mean for the corresponding group in the first investigation (53%), the User-control group in this investigation (55%) performed substantially worse than their counterparts in the first investigation (65%). It may be that the task performed by User-control participants directed their attention towards the location of items of apparatus and thus their learning of other aspects of the laboratory structure suffered as a result.

	Table 6.20 **Performance on Part D of the test, requiring the drawing of a plan of the laboratory including all furniture, doors and windows Score is number of correctly positioned items**		
	Static Views group	**Dynamic Views group**	**User-control group**
n	30	26	24
mean	22.43	21.35	22.75
SD	9.63	12.19	11.54
ANOVA	p=0.893 (not significant)		

6.4.7 Positioning of Views

Part E of the test was identical to Part E of the test used in Investigation 1. It required participants to indicate the position and direction of the camera, given photos taken from eight positions within the laboratory, by drawing a line from the camera position to the opposite wall, on an outline of the laboratory. The number of correct views was recorded, where views were marked correct if they were within 4 metres of the correct location in the north-south direction, within 2.5 metres of the correct location in the east-west direction and within 30 degrees of the correct direction. As discussed in Section 5.4.7, the 4 metre by 2.5 metre tolerance for correct answers was chosen so that the tolerance in the north-south and east-west directions were equal relative to the dimensions of the room. Table 6.21 shows a summary of the results and data analysis for this item. The scores for the three groups were very similar, with Dynamic Views participants performing a little better than User-control participants, who were a little better than Static Views participants. An ANOVA indicated that there were no significant differences.

Comparing these results with those in Investigation 1, User-control participants performed slightly worse (with a mean of 3.36 in Investigation 1) and Dynamic Views participants performed substantially better (with a mean of 1.82 in Investigation 1). This may indicate that the greater range of views seen by the Dynamic Views participants in this investigation (428 compared with 210 in Investigation 1) gave them a substantially better spatial model. If this is the case then the significant difference between Dynamic Views and User-control participants in Investigation 1 may have been due to a greater range of views seen by User-control participants rather than an effect of user control on spatial learning.

Table 6.21 Performance on Part E of the test, requiring indication of position and direction of given views of the laboratory		
	Static Views group	**Dynamic Views group**	**User-control group**
n	30	26	24
mean	2.83	3.00	2.88
SD	1.34	1.39	1.73
ANOVA	p=0.911 (not significant)		

6.4.8 Location of Apparatus

Part F of the test required participants to indicate the location in which each of a list of 11 items of apparatus would normally be found, given a plan of the laboratory (including labelled furniture) and a colour photo of each item. The scoring scheme used was the same as in the first investigation, with the number of correctly placed items recorded and half a mark recorded for items in the adjacent storage location to the correct location and within 2.5 metres of the correct location. In this investigation only one location of each item was required, so the maximum score was 11. Table 6.22 shows a summary of the results and analysis for this item.

The mean for User-control participants was 5.63 marks which was greater than the Dynamic Views participants who had a mean of 4.10 marks, which in turn was greater than Static Views participants with a mean of 2.62. An ANOVA comparing the three groups indicated that group was a factor in performance on this test item (p=0.000). Post Hoc analysis using Tukey's HSD test showed that all three of the differences were significant. This provides evidence for both dynamic view changes and user control over view being important for spatial learning.

<table>
<tr><td colspan="4" align="center">Table 6.22
Performance on Part F of the test, requiring recall of apparatus location
Score is number of items correctly placed (maximum 11)</td></tr>
<tr><td></td><td>Static Views group</td><td>Dynamic Views group</td><td>User-control group</td></tr>
<tr><td>n</td><td>30</td><td>26</td><td>24</td></tr>
<tr><td>mean</td><td>2.62</td><td>4.10</td><td>5.63</td></tr>
<tr><td>SD</td><td>1.85</td><td>2.80</td><td>2.17</td></tr>
<tr><td>ANOVA</td><td colspan="3" align="center">p=0.000 (significant)</td></tr>
<tr><td rowspan="3">Post-Hoc Tukey's HSD Tests</td><td colspan="2" align="center">Static Views v Dynamic Views
p=0.048 (significant)</td><td></td></tr>
<tr><td></td><td colspan="2" align="center">Dynamic Views v User-control
p= 0.050 (significant)</td></tr>
<tr><td colspan="3" align="center">Static Views v User-control
p= 0.000 (significant)</td></tr>
</table>

6.4.9 Real Laboratory Apparatus Usage

The apparatus usage task carried out in the real laboratory required participants to carry out a series of operations using a set of apparatus. For each operation a critical step was identified and observation notes were made indicating whether this critical step was carried out and the degree of assistance required. A score was recorded for each critical step, with a score of 5 recorded if the critical step was carried out immediately, 4 if it was carried out after a delay, 3 if it was carried out after experimenting, 2 if it was carried out after verbal assistance, and 1 if it was not carried out. Because these scores are qualitative and non-linear, it was not appropriate to use an ANOVA. Instead the scores were ranked and a Kruskal-Wallis test was used to compare the performance across the experience groups. As suggested by Cramer (1998), Post Hoc comparisons were made using the Mann-Whitney U test with the significance level reduced by a factor of three (due to the three such comparisons to be made) to 0.017 for 95% confidence or 0.033 for 90% confidence. Table 6.23 shows a summary of the results and analysis.

For most of the steps within the task, the Kruskal-Wallis tests indicated that there were no significant differences in the performances of the three groups. For step three, which required participants to lower the plunger on the Pipette Filler prior to extracting liquid into the pipette, the Kruskal-Wallis test indicated that there may have been a difference but a Post Hoc Mann-Whitney U test indicated that none of the differences between pairs of groups were significant.

The results on this item are somewhat surprising because whereas User-control and Dynamic Views participants performed significantly better than Static Views participants on Part C of the test, requiring recall of apparatus usage procedures, there was no such difference on the real laboratory test. It may be that there were aspects of apparatus usage which became clear to participants when they saw and held the items in the real laboratory even if the procedures were not clear after exploration of the virtual laboratory. If this is the case then it may have reduced the size of any difference between the mean performances of participants in each group and thus led to the lack of a significant difference.

In order to explore the difference between written apparatus usage test performance and real laboratory apparatus usage performance further it was seen as desirable to determine the degree of correlation between performance on part C of the test and performance on the apparatus usage real laboratory test. Because the scores for the apparatus usage task are qualitative and non-linear it was necessary to use a non-parametric correlation test, rather than using Pearson's Correlation Coefficient. As suggested by Gravetter and Wallnau (2000) the scores were converted to ranks and the Spearman correlation was used.

The scores for the number of critical steps described in Part C of the written test correlated strongly with scores in the two parts of the real laboratory apparatus usage test, which assessed tasks included in this critical list. Specifically, for Step 1, which was to close the burette tap before commencing, the correlation coefficient was 0.340, which was highly significant (p=0.004). For Step 4, which was to use the dial on the pipette filler to raise the plunger, the correlation coefficient was 0.288, which was also highly significant (p=0.016). It is not clear why there is such a clear correlation between performances in the written test and in the corresponding apparatus usage test, but no significant differences between groups in the usage test, and clear differences in the written test. It is possible that additional cues provided by the real laboratory made the real laboratory task easier than the corresponding written test item, and consequently the scores on the real laboratory task were closer together.

Table 6.23				
Performance on real laboratory apparatus usage test by group				
Critical step		**Static Views group**	**Dynamic Views group**	**User-control group**
1.Closed the burette tap first	n	26	24	20
	mean rank	35.9	37.3	32.8
	Kruskal-Wallis	p=0.514 (not significant)		
2.Opened the burette tap	n	26	24	20
	mean rank	35.5	35.5	35.5
	Kruskal-Wallis	p=1.000 (not significant)		
3.Lowered plunger on pipette filler first	n	26	24	20
	mean rank	34.6	41.8	29.1
	Kruskal-Wallis	**p=0.093 (significant at 90% level)**		
	Post-Hoc Mann-Whitney U Tests	Static Views versus Dynamic Views p=0.178 (not significant)		
			Dynamic Views versus User-control p=0.034 (not significant)	
		Static Views versus User-control p=0.315 (not significant)		
4.Used dial to lower and/or raise plunger	n	26	24	20
	mean rank	37.3	34.6	34.3
	Kruskal-Wallis	p=0.837 (not significant)		

Table 6.23 (cont) Performance on real laboratory apparatus usage test by group				
Critical step		**Static Views group**	**Dynamic Views group**	**User-control group**
5.Used dial to lower plunger	**n**	26	24	20
	mean rank	37.0	30.6	39.4
	Kruskal-Wallis	p=0.156 (not significant)		
6.Used lever to empty all of the liquid	**n**	26	24	20
	mean rank	34.9	36.5	35.1
	Kruskal-Wallis	p=0.943 (not significant)		

6.4.10 Real Laboratory Apparatus Location

The apparatus location task carried out in the real laboratory required participants to walk to the location within the laboratory where they could find each of 10 items of apparatus, after the name of the item was read out. If after 30 seconds they had not located the item they moved on to the next item. The total time taken along with the total number of items located were recorded. Table 6.24 shows a summary of the results and analysis for total number of items located. Table 6.25 shows a summary of the results and analysis for total time taken. For the number of correctly located items, User-control participants performed marginally better than Dynamic Views participants, who were marginally better than Static Views participants. However, an ANOVA indicated that none of the differences were significant. For the total time taken, the performance for User-control participants (with a mean of 154 seconds) was similar to the performance of Dynamic Views participants (with a mean of 156 seconds), but both were substantially better than Static Views participants (with a mean of 181 seconds). An ANOVA indicated that the differences may have been significant however a Post Hoc Tukey's HSD test indicated that none of the differences were significant.

This result was surprising because in Part F of the test, requiring recall of apparatus location, User-control participants performed significantly better than Dynamic Views participants, who in turn performed significantly better than Static Views participants. The scores for apparatus location in the real laboratory were higher for all groups than the corresponding scores on Part F of the test. On Part F of the test Static Views participants had a mean of 2.62 items out of 10, Dynamic Views participants had a mean of 4.10 items and User-control participants had a mean of 5.63. This suggests that the additional cues in the real laboratory (for example labels on cupboards and draws) allowed participants to locate items even if they did not recall where the items were from their experience in the virtual laboratory.

This difference between written test results and real laboratory task performance was explored further by calculating Pearson's Correlation Coefficients (PC) between the scores on Part F of the test and the scores in the apparatus location test in the real laboratory. The PC value for Part F of the test compared with number of items located was 0.445, which is highly significant (p=0.000) and the PC value for Part F compared with time taken was 0.468, which is also highly significant (p=0.000). Once again, a possible reason for the high correlation between scores, but the lack of a significant difference between groups on the real laboratory task where there was a clear difference on the written task, is that additional cues made the real laboratory task easier, resulting in scores that were closer together.

Table 6.24
Performance on real laboratory task requiring location of apparatus
Score is number of items correctly located (maximum 10)

	Static Views group	Dynamic Views group	User-control group
n	26	24	20
mean	7.46	7.58	7.90
SD	1.61	1.44	1.55
ANOVA	p=0.623 (not significant)		

	Table 6.25 Performance on real laboratory task requiring location of apparatus Score is total time taken in seconds (maximum 300)		
	Static Views group	**Dynamic Views group**	**User-control group**
n	26	24	20
mean	180.50	155.83	154.25
SD	42.83	35.28	51.81
ANOVA	p=0.067 (significant at 90% level)		
Post-Hoc Tukey's HSD Tests	Static Views v Dynamic Views p=0.117 (not significant)		
		Dynamic Views v User-control p= 0.992 (not significant)	
	Static Views v User-control p= 0.111 (not significant)		

6.4.11 Spatial Ability

Participants were asked one question designed to gauge their spatial ability. They were asked to indicate the degree to which they agreed or disagreed with the statement "you are good at finding your way around unfamiliar places". Participants' answers were recorded as a number from 0 (very strongly disagree) to 100 (very strongly agree). Table 6.26 shows an analysis of responses to this question by group. An ANOVA indicated that there was no significant difference between responses across groups. These results indicate that, if we can assume that this question was measuring self reported spatial ability, and that self reported spatial ability correlates with actual spatial ability, then spatial ability is distributed evenly across the groups, and thus should not be a factor in any performance differences across groups.

Table 6.26
Responses on question requiring self-report of spatial ability by group

Question		Static Views Group	Dynamic Views group	User-control group
Degree of agreement with statement "you are good at finding your way around unfamiliar places"	n	30	26	24
	mean	58.53	53.35	54.25
	SD	21.42	20.78	22.13
	ANOVA	p= 0.625 (not significant)		

In order to explore whether participants with higher spatial ability did better on the tests, Pearson's Correlation Coefficients were calculated between the spatial ability question and performance on the various test items, and these are shown in Table 6.27. The question correlated with performance only in Part C of the test, which measured ability to recall the steps for assembling and using items of apparatus.

Table 6.27

Pearson's Correlations (PC) between question on spatial ability and performance on spatial tests

Test Part	Pearson Correlation	Significance
Part B. Identification of apparatus (Percentage of items of apparatus identified)	0.102	p=0.370 (not significant)
Part B. Identification of apparatus (Percentage of items of apparatus identified that were new to this participant)	-0.045	p=0.692 (not significant)
Part B. Recollection of apparatus structure (Percentage of correct models identified)	-0.037	p=0.747 (not significant)
Part C. Assembling and using apparatus (Number of steps correctly described, maximum 14)	0.272	**p=0.015 (significant)**
Part C. Assembling and using apparatus (Number of key steps correctly described, maximum 4)	0.270	**p=0.016 (significant)**
Part D. Laboratory plan (Number of correctly positioned items of furniture and landmarks on plan, maximum 41)	0.044	p=0.699 (not significant)
Part E. Positioning of views (Number of views correctly identified, maximum 6)	0.099	p=0.385 (not significant)
Part F. Location of apparatus on map (Number of items correctly located, maximum 11)	0.016	p=0.889 (not significant)

As discussed in Chapter 5, if the question was effective in measuring participants' spatial ability, and if spatial ability was a factor in test performance, a significant correlation with scores on all parts of the test would be expected. Instead, the question correlated significantly with participant scores in only one test item. It would be expected that the aspect of spatial ability that the question asked about (ability to find a way around unfamiliar places) would assist with parts D, E and F of the test. The fact that this was not the case suggests either that self reported spatial ability does not in fact correlate with actual spatial ability, or spatial ability in the real-world does not correlate with corresponding ability in a virtual environment. This is discussed further in Chapter 7.

Spearman Correlation Coefficients were calculated to determine the degree of correlation between responses to the spatial ability question and performance on the real laboratory apparatus usage tasks (using ranked test scores) and these are shown in Table 6.28. There was a significant correlation between reported spatial ability and performance on two of the steps within the apparatus usage task. Pearson's correlation coefficients were also calculated between responses to the spatial ability question and performance on the apparatus location task. These are shown in Table 6.29. There was no significant correlation between self reported spatial ability and performance in the locating apparatus task. These results are somewhat surprising, since it would be expected that participants with the spatial ability described would do better at locating apparatus within the laboratory, but not necessarily at manipulating items of apparatus.

Table 6.28 Spearman Correlations between question on spatial ability and performance on real laboratory apparatus usage task		
Critical step	Spearman Correlation Coefficient	Significance
1.Closed the burette tap first	0.062	p=0.613 (not significant)
2.Opened the burette tap	unable to calculate since all participants scored 5	
3.Lowered plunger on pipette filler first	0.270	p=0.024 (significant)
4.Used dial to lower and/or raise plunger	0.295	p=0.013 (significant)
5.Used dial to lower plunger	0.002	p=0.986 (not significant)
6.Used lever to empty all of the liquid	0.196	p=0.105 (not significant)

Table 6.29 Pearson's Correlations (PC) between question on spatial ability and performance on real laboratory apparatus location task		
Score	Pearson Correlation	Significance
Number of items located (maximum 10)	0.102	p=0.403 (not significant)
Total time taken (seconds)	-0.079	p=0.514 (not significant)

Participants completed a questionnaire about the overall effectiveness of the virtual laboratory as a familiarisation tool, about the ease of use of the virtual laboratory and about their level of enjoyment in using it. In each case participants were asked to indicate the degree to which they agreed or disagreed with a series of statements about the virtual laboratory or their experience of using it, using a 7 point Likert scale from very strongly agree (7) to very strongly disagree (1). Pearson's Correlation Coefficients were calculated to determine whether there was a correlation between self reported spatial ability and perceived effectiveness, ease of use and enjoyment of using the virtual laboratory. Table 6.30 shows a summary of this data. There was no significant correlation between responses to the spatial ability question and either enjoyment or perception of overall effectiveness. However, the correlation between the spatial ability question and perceived ease of use was significant at the 90% level. This suggests that participants who rate their spatial ability as high find it easier to use virtual environments.

Table 6.30
Pearson's Correlations (PC) between question on spatial ability and questionnaire responses

Question	Pearson Correlation	Significance
2. You enjoyed using the virtual lab.	0.130	p=0.284 (not significant)
3. Overall the virtual lab helped you to become familiar with the real lab.	0.132	0.277 (not significant)
5. The virtual lab is easy to use.	0.199	**0.099 (significant at 90% level)**

Table 6.31 shows a comparison of male and female self reported spatial ability. The T-test results indicate that there was no difference between male and female responses. This is consistent with the findings in Investigation 1.

Table 6.31
Responses to question requiring self-report of spatial ability by gender

Background Question		Male	Female
4. Degree of agreement with statement, "You are good at finding your way around unfamiliar places".	n	49	31
	mean	56.67	53.81
	SD	21.66	20.92
	T Test	p=0.561 (not significant)	

6.4.12 Presence

Participants were asked two questions designed to gauge the degree to which they felt immersed or present within the virtual environment. Each question asked them to indicate the degree to which they agreed or disagreed with a statement. The first statement was, "you felt involved in the virtual environment experience". The second statement was, "you felt a compelling sense of moving around inside the virtual environment". Table 6.32 shows a summary of the responses by group and the corresponding analysis.

For the first question, which asked about participants' feeling of involvement in the experience, User-control participants and Dynamic Views participants had very similar levels of agreement (means of 55 and 56 respectively) and both had a greater level of agreement than Static Views participants (mean of 48), however an ANOVA indicated that the differences were not significant. For the second question, which asked about the degree to which participants felt a sense of moving around inside the environment, User-control participants and Dynamic Views participants again had similar levels of agreement (means of 57 and 58 respectively) and again both had greater levels of agreement than Static Views participants (mean of 45). This time an ANOVA indicated that there may have been a significant difference (p=0.069) and a Post Hoc Tukey's HSD test indicated that the difference between the Dynamic Views and Static Views participants was significant at the 90% level.

These results are somewhat surprising and contrast with those of Investigation 1, which suggested that having control over their navigation, rather than following a pre-defined tour, resulted in the User-control participants experiencing a greater sense of presence. These results suggest that having control over view does not contribute to a sense of presence but that dynamic view changes may contribute to a sense of presence.

The scores for the User-control and Dynamic Views groups can be compared with the results on the corresponding questions in Investigation 1. In Investigation 1, the mean response to the statement "you felt involved in the virtual environment experience" for Dynamic Views participants was 70, and for User-control participants was 77. In this investigation the means were 56 and 55 respectively. In Investigation 1, the mean response to the statement, "you felt a compelling sense of moving around inside the virtual environment" for Dynamic Views participants was 66 and for User-control

participants was 78. In this investigation the means were 58 and 57 respectively. The

lower scores in this investigation may be explained by the fact that in Investigation 1,

participants were IT students, who one would expect would have had a greater degree of

interest and experience in playing computer games, and thus may have more readily

allowed themselves to become immersed in the environment.

Table 6.32 Responses to questions on sense of presence by group				
Question		Static Views group	Dynamic Views group	User-control group
Degree of agreement with statement "You felt involved in the virtual environment experience"	n	30	26	24
	mean	47.67	56.19	55.38
	SD	24.75	26.31	25.13
	ANOVA	p= 0.384 (not significant)		
Degree of agreement with statement "You felt a compelling sense of moving around inside the virtual environment"	n	30	26	24
	mean	45.37	57.92	57.04
	SD	23.89	23.68	18.47
	ANOVA	p= 0.069 (significant at the 90% level)		
	Post-Hoc Tukey's HSD Tests	Static Views v Dynamic Views p=0.097 (significant at the 90% level)		
			Dynamic Views v User-control p=0.989 (not significant)	
		Static Views v User-control p=0.143 (not significant)		

Pearson's correlation coefficients were calculated to compare the responses to questions

about sense of presence with performance on the test items. Table 6.33 shows a

summary. Unlike Investigation 1, in which there were no significant correlations

between responses to questions on the sense of presence experienced and test

performance, in this investigation there was a significant correlation with one or both of

the presence questions for six of the eight test scores. This suggests that contrary to the findings of Investigation 1, maximising the degree of presence or engagement may positively influence learning and so may be an appropriate design goal.

<table>
<tr><td colspan="4" align="center">Table 6.33
Pearson's Correlations (PC) between sense of presence and performance on spatial tests</td></tr>
<tr><td>Test Part</td><td></td><td>Correlation with first question (involvement)</td><td>Correlation with second question (sense of moving)</td></tr>
<tr><td rowspan="2">Part B. Identification of apparatus
(Percentage of items of apparatus identified</td><td>Pearson Correlation</td><td>0.220</td><td>0.125</td></tr>
<tr><td>Significance</td><td>p=0.050 (significant)</td><td>p=0.271
(not significant)</td></tr>
<tr><td rowspan="2">Part B. Identification of apparatus
(Percentage of items of apparatus identified that were new to this participant)</td><td>Pearson Correlation</td><td>-0.124</td><td>-0.173</td></tr>
<tr><td>Significance</td><td>p=0.272
(not significant)</td><td>p=0.124
(not significant)</td></tr>
<tr><td rowspan="2">Part B. Recollection of apparatus structure
(Percentage of correct models identified)</td><td>Pearson Correlation</td><td>0.322</td><td>0.195</td></tr>
<tr><td>Significance</td><td>p=0.004 (significant)</td><td>p=0.084 (significant at 90% level)</td></tr>
<tr><td rowspan="2">Part C. Assembling and using apparatus
(Number of steps correctly described, maximum 14)</td><td>Pearson Correlation</td><td>0.254</td><td>0.328</td></tr>
<tr><td>Significance</td><td>p=0.023 (significant)</td><td>p=0.003
(significant)</td></tr>
<tr><td rowspan="2">Part C. Assembling and using apparatus
(Number of key steps correctly described, maximum 4)</td><td>Pearson Correlation</td><td>0.200</td><td>0.291</td></tr>
<tr><td>Significance</td><td>p=0.075 (significant at 90% level)</td><td>p=0.009
(significant)</td></tr>
<tr><td rowspan="2">Part D. Laboratory plan
(Number of correctly positioned items of furniture and landmarks on plan, maximum 41)</td><td>Pearson Correlation</td><td>0.158</td><td>0.097</td></tr>
<tr><td>Significance</td><td>p=0.161
(not significant)</td><td>p=0.391
(not significant)</td></tr>
<tr><td rowspan="2">Part E. Positioning of views
(Number of views correctly identified, maximum 6)</td><td>Pearson Correlation</td><td>0.204</td><td>0.246</td></tr>
<tr><td>Significance</td><td>p=0.070 (significant at 90% level)</td><td>p=0.028
(significant)</td></tr>
</table>

Table 6.33 (continued) Pearson's Correlation (PC) between sense of presence and performance on spatial tests			
Test Part		**Correlation with first question (involvement)**	**Correlation with second question (sense of moving)**
Part F. Location of apparatus on map (Number of items correctly located, maximum 11)	**Pearson Correlation**	0.244	0.251
	Significance	p=0.029 (significant)	p=0.025 (significant)

It was seen as desirable to also determine the degree of correlation between responses to the presence questions and performance on the real laboratory apparatus usage tasks. However, as discussed in Section 6.4.9, because the scores for the apparatus usage task are qualitative and non-linear it was necessary to use a non-parametric correlation test. The scores were converted to ranks and the Spearman correlation was used. Table 6.34 shows these Spearman correlations between performance on the apparatus usage task and presence question responses. There was a significant positive correlation between sense of presence and performance on one of the critical steps in the apparatus usage task undertaken in the real laboratory, that of lowering the plunger on the pipette filler before extracting liquid into it.

Table 6.34

Spearman Correlations between sense of presence and performance on real laboratory apparatus usage tasks

Critical Step		Correlation with first question (involvement)	Correlation with second question (sense of moving)
1.Closed the burette tap first	Spearman Correlation	0.077	0.135
	Significance	p=0.527 (not significant)	0.267 (not significant)
2.Opened the burette tap	Spearman Correlation	Unable to be calculated since all participants scored 5	Unable to be calculated since all participants scored 5
	Significance		
3.Lowered plunger on pipette filler first	Spearman Correlation	0.239	0.247
	Significance	p=0.046 (significant)	p=0.039 (significant)
4.Used dial to lower and/or raise plunger	Spearman Correlation	-0.026	0.074
	Significance	p=0.831 (not significant)	p=0.540 (not significant)
5.Used dial to lower plunger	Spearman Correlation	-0.166	-0.058
	Significance	p=0.170 (not significant)	p=0.632 (not significant)
6.Used lever to empty all of the liquid	Spearman Correlation	0.113	0.013
	Significance	p=0.352(not significant)	p=0.912(not significant)

Pearson's correlation coefficients were also calculated to compare the responses to questions about presence with performance on apparatus location tasks undertaken in the real laboratory. Table 6.35 shows a summary of these correlations. There was a significant positive correlation between both of the presence questions and number of items located in the apparatus location task and a significant negative correlation between both of the presence questions and time taken. This adds further weight to the argument that a greater sense of presence leads to greater learning in a 3D learning environment.

Table 6.35 Pearson's Correlations (PC) between sense of presence and performance on real laboratory apparatus location test			
Score		Correlation with first question (involvement)	Correlation with second question (sense of moving)
Number of items located (maximum 10)	Pearson Correlation	0.220	0.277
	Significance	p=0.068 (significant at 90% level)	p=0.020 (significant)
Total time taken (seconds)	Pearson Correlation	-0.214	-0.217
	Significance	p=0.076 (significant at 90% level)	p=0.071 (significant at 90% level)

Participants completed a questionnaire about the overall effectiveness of the virtual laboratory as a familiarisation tool, about the ease of use of the virtual laboratory and about the participants' level of enjoyment in using it. In each case participants were asked to indicate the degree to which they agreed or disagreed with a series of statements about the virtual laboratory or their experience of using it, using a 7 point Likert scale from very strongly agree (7) to very strongly disagree (1). Pearson's Correlation Coefficients were calculated to determine whether there were correlations between sense of presence experienced and perceived effectiveness, ease of use and enjoyment of using the virtual laboratory. Table 6.36 shows a summary of this data. Responses to the question about involvement in the virtual laboratory experience correlated with enjoyment, perceived effectiveness and perceived ease of use.

Responses to the question about sense of moving through the environment correlated with perceived effectiveness and ease of use (the latter only at the 90% level). This suggests that a greater sense of presence can lead to greater enjoyment. It also suggests that if the use of the environment interface is easier, participants are more likely to experience a sense of presence. And lastly it adds further weight to the proposition that a greater sense of presence leads to greater spatial learning.

Table 6.36 Pearson's Correlations (PC) between sense of presence and questionnaire responses			
Question		Correlation with first question (involvement)	Correlation with second question (sense of moving)
2. You enjoyed using the virtual lab	Pearson Correlation	0.539	0.146
	Significance	p=0.000 (significant)	p=0.229 (not significant)
3. Overall the virtual lab helped you to become familiar with the real lab	Pearson Correlation	0.515	0.347
	Significance	p=0.000 (significant)	p=0.003 (significant)
5. The virtual lab is easy to use	Pearson Correlation	0.364	0.213
	Significance	p=0.002 (significant)	p=0.077 (significant at the 90% level)

Table 6.37 shows a comparison of male and female responses to the background questions on sense of presence experienced. The results suggest that male participants may have experienced a stronger sense of presence than female participants, although a T-test showed a statistically significant difference only on question 5, which asked about the degree to which the participant felt involved in the virtual environment experience. This is consistent with the results in Investigation 1.

Table 6.37

Responses to questions on sense of presence by gender			
Background Question		**Male**	**Female**
5. Degree of agreement with statement, "You felt involved in the virtual environment experience"	**n**	49	31
	mean	58.06	44.35
	SD	23.66	26.08
	T Test	p=0.018 (significant)	
6. Degree of agreement with statement, "You felt a compelling sense of moving around inside the virtual environment"	**n**	49	31
	mean	53.22	52.52
	SD	23.60	21.95
	T Test	p=0.893 (not significant)	

6.4.13 Questionnaire

Participants completed a questionnaire on their perceptions of the value of the virtual laboratory as a tool for familiarising them with the laboratory. The questionnaire was structured as a series of statements and in each case participants were asked to indicate the degree to which they agreed or disagreed, using a seven point Likert scale from very strongly disagree (1) to neutral (4) to very strongly agree (7).

The first two questions asked participants whether they enjoy playing computer games and whether they enjoyed using the virtual laboratory. A Pearson's Correlation Coefficient (PC) was calculated to determine whether enjoyment of computer game play correlated with enjoyment of use of the virtual laboratory. The PC value was 0.347, which is highly significant (p=0.003). This indicates that enjoyment of computer game use is a predictor of enjoyment of the use of 3D learning environments. The fifth question asked about the ease of use of the virtual laboratory. A Pearson's Correlation Coefficient was calculated to determine whether enjoyment of computer game play correlated with ease of use of the virtual laboratory. The PC value was 0.280, which is significant (p=0.019), indicating that participants who enjoyed playing computer games also tended to find the virtual laboratory easy to use.

Pearson's Correlation Coefficients were also calculated to determine if enjoyment of computer game play and enjoyment of use of the virtual environment correlated with sense of presence. The PC value between enjoyment of computer game play and sense of involvement was 0.342 which is highly significant (p=0.004) and the PC value between enjoyment of computer game play and sense of moving around in the environment was 0.203, which was significant at the 90% level (p=0.093). The PC value between enjoyment of using the virtual environment and sense of involvement was 0.539 which is highly significant (p=0.000) and the PC value between enjoyment of using the virtual environment and sense of moving around in the environment was 0.146, which is not significant.

ANOVAs were calculated to determine whether enjoyment of the use of the virtual laboratory and ease of use differed across groups. Table 6.38 shows a summary of the results and analysis. User-control participants were slightly more likely to state that they enjoyed using the virtual environment than Static Views participants, who were more likely than Dynamic Views participants. An ANOVA suggested that enjoyment of the use of the virtual laboratory may have differed across groups. A Post Hoc Tukey's HSD test indicated that User-control participants were significantly more likely than Dynamic Views participants to state that they enjoyed using the environment, but that the other differences were not significant. This is somewhat surprising because one would expect the Static Views participants to enjoy the experience less than Dynamic Views participants.

Participants in the Dynamic Views group were most likely to rate their version of the virtual laboratory as easy to use, followed by participants in the Static Views group and then the User-control group. An ANOVA indicated that there was a difference in ease of use across the versions of the virtual laboratory. Post Hoc Tukey's HSD tests indicated that the Dynamic Views version was significantly easier to use than the User-control version. This is important because it emphasises the importance of being able to demonstrate the learning benefits of 3D learning environments over alternatives such as animations or videos, because the latter tend to be easier to use. Interestingly the Dynamic Views version was also rated as significantly easier to use than the Static Views version. This is somewhat surprising because the Static Views interface was identical to the Dynamic Views interface. Possibly the lack of animated view changes made it difficult for Static Views participants to develop a clear mental model of the layout of the laboratory and this detracted from its ease of use.

These results suggest that a resource that is easiest to use (in this case the Dynamic Views version of the environment) may not be the most enjoyable to use (which in this case was the User-control version). To explore this further a Pearson's Correlation Coefficient was calculated between ease of use and enjoyment. The value was 0.162, which is not significant (p=0.176). This suggests that there is neither a positive nor a negative correlation between enjoyment and ease of use.

Table 6.38 Responses to questions about enjoyment and ease of use of virtual laboratory by group		Static Views group	Dynamic Views group	User-control group
Question		**Static Views group**	**Dynamic Views group**	**User-control group**
2.You enjoyed using the virtual lab.	n	26	24	20
	mean	4.21	3.54	4.40
	SD	0.90	1.32	0.99
	ANOVA	**p=0.024 (significant)**		
	Post-Hoc Tukey's HSD Tests	Static Views versus Dynamic Views p=0.182 (not significant)		
			Dynamic Views versus User-control **p=0.029 (significant)**	
		Static Views versus User-control p=0.829 (not significant)		
5.The virtual lab is easy to use.	n	26	24	20
	mean	5.02	5.92	4.70
	SD	1.00	0.83	1.42
	ANOVA	**p=0. 001 (significant)**		
	Post-Hoc Tukey's HSD Tests	Static Views versus Dynamic Views **p=0.013 (significant)**		
			Dynamic Views versus User-control **p=0.001 (significant)**	
		Static Views versus User-control p=0.588 (not significant)		

The third and fourth question and the sixth to twelfth questions asked participants about their perceptions of the usefulness of the virtual laboratory. As discussed in Section 6.4.1 significant interactions between gender and chemistry experience were detected on responses to question 6 and consequently a factorial ANOVA was used to explore the main effect of group on this question. For all other questions single factor ANOVAs were calculated to determine if responses differed across groups. The results and analysis are summarised in Table 6.39. The results indicate that there was a significant difference in the perceived overall usefulness of the virtual laboratory as a familiarisation tool. Specifically, User-control participants rated it significantly more useful than Dynamic Views participants and than Static Views participants. There was no significant difference between the perceived usefulness by Static Views and Dynamic Views participants. Surprisingly, even though there was a difference in overall perceptions of usefulness, there was not a significant difference in perceptions of its usefulness for specific purposes such as familiarisation with laboratory layout or location of apparatus.

Table 6.39
Responses to questions about usefulness of the virtual laboratory by group

Question		Static Views group	Dynamic Views group	User-control group
3. Overall the virtual lab helped you to become familiar with the real lab.	n	26	24	20
	mean	4.81	4.88	5.65
	SD	0.94	0.99	1.14
	ANOVA	p=0.014 (significant)		
	Post-Hoc Tukey's HSD Tests	Static Views versus Dynamic Views p=0.970 (not significant)		
			Dynamic Views versus User-control p=0.037 (significant)	
		Static Views versus User-control p=0.019 (significant)		
4. The virtual lab is an accurate representation of the real lab.	n	26	24	20
	mean	5.21	5.13	5.45
	SD	1.08	1.15	1.23
	ANOVA	p=0.634 (not significant)		

	Table 6.39 (cont.) Response to questions about usefulness of the virtual laboratory by group			
Question		Static Views group	Dynamic Views group	User-control group
6.The virtual lab helped you to become familiar with the layout of the lab building.	n	26	24	20
	mean	5.06	5.38	5.70
	SD	1.02	0.97	1.03
	ANOVA	p=0.044 (significant)		
	Post-Hoc Tukey's HSD Tests	Static Views versus Dynamic Views p=0.495 (not significant)		
			Dynamic Views versus User-control p=0.525 (not significant)	
		Static Views versus User-control p=0.082 (significant at 90% level)		
7.The virtual lab helped you to be able to identify items of apparatus.	n	26	24	20
	mean	5.23	5.21	5.45
	SD	0.82	1.06	1.36
	ANOVA	p=0.721 (not significant)		
8.The virtual lab helped you to be able to locate items within the lab.	n	26	24	20
	mean	4.96	4.92	5.05
	SD	1.15	1.06	1.39
	ANOVA	p=0.933 (not significant)		
9.The virtual lab helped you to become familiar with the procedure for using a burette.	n	26	24	20
	mean	4.31	4.58	4.73
	SD	1.01	1.10	1.50
	ANOVA	p=0.483 (not significant)		

Table 6.39 (cont.) Response to questions about usefulness of the virtual laboratory by group		Static Views group	Dynamic Views group	User-control group
10.The virtual lab helped you to become familiar with the procedure for using a pipette.	n	26	24	20
	mean	4.31	4.25	4.35
	SD	1.05	1.11	1.76
	ANOVA	p=0.968 (not significant)		
11.In its current form, you would recommend that new students use the virtual lab prior to their first laboratory experiment.	n	26	24	20
	mean	5.08	4.58	5.20
	SD	1.16	1.56	1.61
	ANOVA	p=0.314 (not significant)		
12.If the virtual lab allowed you to carry out virtual experiments, you would use it prior to laboratory sessions to practice the experiments.	n	26	24	20
	mean	5.31	5.33	5.40
	SD	1.05	1.13	1.50
	ANOVA	p=0.967 (not significant)		

Table 6.40 shows a summary of the responses to the questions on enjoyment, effectiveness and ease of use by gender. The results indicate that there was no significant difference between male and female perceptions of ease of use or perceptions of overall effectiveness of the virtual laboratory. However, male participants were significantly more likely to agree with the statement, "you enjoyed using the virtual lab". It is commonly thought that males enjoy playing computer games more than females, and so this result could just reflect this same tendency. However, there was no significant difference in male and female responses to the statement, "you enjoy playing computer games", which suggests that the difference in levels of enjoyment of virtual laboratory use did not just reflect differing degrees of interest in playing computer games.

Table 6.40 Questionnaire responses by gender		Male	Female
1. You enjoy playing computer games.	n	43	27
	mean	4.79	4.48
	SD	1.28	1.34
	T Test	p= 0.338 (significant)	
2. You enjoyed using the virtual lab.	n	43	27
	mean	4.31	3.59
	SD	0.94	1.28
	T Test	**p= 0.008 (significant)**	
3. Overall the virtual lab helped you to become familiar with the real lab.	n	43	27
	mean	5.14	4.96
	SD	0.86	1.34
	T Test	p= 0.505 (not significant)	
5. The virtual lab is easy to use.	n	43	27
	mean	5.38	5.00
	SD	1.18	1.18
	T Test	p= 0.190 (not significant)	

6.5 Summary and Discussion

6.5.1 Summary of results on each test item

The following is a summary of the findings on each of the test items within this investigation:

- There was no significant difference between User-control and Dynamic Views participants on the written test on identification of apparatus, but both performed significantly better than Static Views participants. However, the performance on identification of unfamiliar items suggests that the difference may have been due only to differences in prior knowledge.

- User-control and Dynamic Views participants performed significantly better than Static Views participants on the written test on recall of apparatus usage procedures.

- There were no significant differences between the performances of the three groups on the written test on recall of laboratory layout.

- There were no significant differences between the performances of the three groups on the written test on positioning of views

- User-control participants performed significantly better than Dynamic Views participants who performed significantly better than Static Views participants on the apparatus location written test.

- There were no significant differences between the performances of the three groups on an apparatus manipulation task.

- There was no significant difference between the three groups in the number of items located or the total time taken on the apparatus location real laboratory test.

6.5.2 Discussion of findings in relation to the research questions

6.5.2.1 Question 1. Does smooth display of view changes in a 3D learning environment contribute to spatial learning?

Dynamic Views participants performed significantly better than Static Views participants on the apparatus location written test. Dynamic Views participants also performed better than Static Views participants on the apparatus location test in the real laboratory (higher mean number of items located and lower mean time taken to locate all items), but the differences were not significant. The lack of a significant difference in the real laboratory task may have been due to the fact that additional cues provided in the real laboratory made the apparatus location task substantially easier and resulted in mean group scores that were closer together.

There was no significant difference between Dynamic Views and Static Views participants on the laboratory layout test or the positioning of views test. It may be that because the laboratory environment was structurally quite simple, participants were able to form an accurate spatial model through static views from key positions within the environment. It may be that smooth view changes would be more important in a more complex environment. These results provide some support for the assertion that smooth view changes contribute to spatial learning, but the findings are inconclusive.

6.5.2.2 Question 2. Does smooth display of object motion in a 3D learning environment contribute to spatial learning?

Dynamic Views participants performed significantly better than Static Views participants on identification of apparatus. However, the scores when familiar items were excluded suggested that the difference in identification of apparatus may have been due to differences in prior knowledge. There was no significant difference between Static Views and Dynamic Views participants on recall of apparatus structure. Dynamic Views participants performed better than Static Views participants on recall of apparatus usage procedures (significant at the 90% level), but there was no significant difference between Static Views and Dynamic Views participants on the apparatus usage test in the real laboratory. These results provide some support for the idea that smooth display of object animation contributes to spatial learning, but the results are by no means conclusive. It may be that if the items of apparatus chosen had more complex structure, Dynamic Views participants would have performed better than Static Views participants on identification and recall of structure, because in this case it may have been more difficult to form a clear spatial cognitive model from static views. Similarly, it may be that if the items of apparatus chosen had more complex moving parts and consequently greater complexity to their usage procedures, Dynamic Views participants may have performed significantly better than Static Views participants on apparatus usage tasks.

6.5.2.3 Question 3. Does user control over view position and direction in a 3D learning environment contribute to spatial learning?

User-control participants performed significantly better than Dynamic Views participants on the written test on location of apparatus. In Investigation 1, where User-control participants undertook free exploration rather than a directed task, there was no difference between Dynamic Views and User-control participants on location of apparatus. This suggests that the difference in this investigation resulted from the fact that User-control participants undertook a task requiring knowledge of apparatus location. Consequently it can be concluded that user control over view can contribute to spatial learning but only if the task carried out by User-control participants requires this learning.

Surprisingly, even though there was a significant difference in the written test on apparatus location, there was no significant difference between User-control and Dynamic Views participants on either number of items located or time taken in the apparatus location task within the real laboratory. The high correlation between performance on the written apparatus location test and performance on the real laboratory test suggests that the spatial learning assessed in the written task contributed to performance on the real laboratory task, but this may have been only one factor. It may be that the laboratory provided additional visual cues that helped with this task, and ability to observe these additional cues was another important factor contributing to performance. It may also have been that these additional cues made the task too easy. The high mean scores (7.58 out of 10 for Dynamic Views and 7.9 out of 10 for User-control) on this task compared with the means on the written task (4.1 out of 11 and 5.63 out of 11) suggest that this may have been the case.

User-control participants were more likely than Dynamic Views participants to agree with a statement that the virtual laboratory was useful as a familiarisation tool. This supports the conclusion that where participants undertake a directed task that requires spatial learning, user control over view can contribute to spatial learning.

The lack of a significant difference between User-control and Dynamic Views participants on the positioning of views and laboratory layout written tests can be explained by the fact that the task carried out by the User-control participants did not require them to remember the layout of the laboratory or to recognise given views, and thus user control did not provide an advantage on these items. If they had undertaken a task, for example, where they were given descriptions of the location of apparatus in relation to items of furniture (for example, "the burette is in the fume cupboard near the first door") and had to then find the items of apparatus, User-control participants may have performed better on laboratory layout. Had they undertaken a task, for example, where they were instantly taken to a new position and view direction and had to find their way back where they came from, User-control participants may have performed better than Dynamic Views participants on the positioning of views test.

Alternatively, the lack of a significant difference between User-control and Dynamic Views participants on the laboratory layout written test could be explained by the fact that User-control participants undertook a task requiring them to focus specifically on the location of items of apparatus and this could have had a negative effect on their learning of the layout of the laboratory. A comparison of the results on this test item across the two studies supports this argument, with User-control participants in this second investigation performing substantially worse in percentage terms than User-control participants in the first investigation, whereas participants in the Dynamic Views groups performed similarly across the two investigations.

In Investigation 1, User-control participants scored better than Dynamic Views participants on the positioning of views written test, whereas in this investigation there was no significant difference. This disparity requires further exploration. In this investigation Dynamic Views participants performed substantially better than they did in Investigation 1, whereas the performance of User-control participants was very similar in both investigations. In Investigation 1, Dynamic Views participants were provided with 210 views of the laboratory, which were primarily from viewpoints around the edges of the laboratory, either in a direction along the edges of the laboratory, or away from the centre of the laboratory towards individual items of apparatus or furniture. Five out of six of the views that were included in the test, however, were either from a position away from the edge of the laboratory or were in a direction diagonally across the laboratory. Consequently, the views seen by User-control participants in Investigation 1, who explored the laboratory freely looking for apparatus, would have prepared them better for the test than Dynamic Views participants.

In this investigation, participants of the Dynamic Views groups were provided with 428 views and these included a greater number of views away from the edge of the laboratory and a greater number of views diagonally across the laboratory. Additionally, the views provided to Dynamic Views participants in this investigation showed the collection and assembly of apparatus, and given that this was the same task carried out by User-control participants, there was likely to be a closer match between the views seen by User-control and Dynamic Views participants.

This suggests that the difference between User-control participants and Dynamic Views participants on the positioning of views test in Investigation 1 could have been due to the Dynamic Views participants experiencing an inferior selection of views of the laboratory. When equivalent views were provided in this investigation there was no significant difference between Dynamic Views and User-control participants, possibly due to the fact that the task of searching for apparatus did not require participants to develop an ability to recognise the position of views.

6.5.2.4 Question 4. Does object manipulation in a 3D learning environment contribute to spatial learning?

There was no significant difference between the User-control and Dynamic Views participants on identification of apparatus, recall of apparatus structure or recall of apparatus usage procedure. There was also no significant difference between User-control and Dynamic Views participants on the apparatus usage test in the real laboratory. These results do not support the assertion that object manipulation contributes to spatial learning.

As discussed above it may be that the items of apparatus chosen were relatively simple in both their structure and their usage. Just as this may have meant that Dynamic Views participants did not have a learning advantage over Static Views participants, it may also have prevented User-control participants from performing better than Dynamic Views participants. Additionally, an argument could be made that the tasks carried out by the User-control group did not require substantial object manipulation and the actual object manipulations carried out did not require substantial spatial learning. Further research is required that uses more complex objects, and a greater range of object manipulation tasks, before a conclusive answer to this question can be reached.

6.5.2.5 Question 5. How does the design of the learning task within a 3D environment affect the spatial learning that occurs?

Comparing the relative performance of the User-control and Dynamic Views groups in Investigation 1 and in Investigation 2 allows some conclusions to be reached with regard to the nature of learning tasks required for spatial learning in 3D environments. There was a significant difference between User-control and Dynamic Views participants on location of apparatus in Investigation 2 whereas there was not in Investigation 1. The main difference between these two investigations was that, in Investigation 2, User-control participants, after collecting items of apparatus, were required to return them to their correct location, a task which required these participants to learn the location of apparatus. This suggests that it is important that the learning task undertaken is closely aligned with the desired spatial learning. Just exploring a 3D environment without any task direction will not facilitate spatial learning beyond that achieved by watching an animation.

6.5.3 Other findings

The following were further findings from this investigation, which do not relate directly to the research questions:

- There was no difference between male and female performance on any of the written or practical tests.

- Participants with higher self reported spatial ability performed better on written tests requiring recall of apparatus usage procedures and some practical tests requiring apparatus usage but no other tests.

- Participants with higher self reported spatial ability found the virtual environment easier to use.

- User-control participants enjoyed the experience more than Dynamic Views participants.

- Male participants found the experience more enjoyable than female participants.

- Participants who enjoy playing computer games found the virtual laboratory more enjoyable to use and easier to use, and experienced a stronger sense of presence.

- Dynamic Views participants experienced a stronger sense of presence than Static Views participants.

- Male participants experienced a stronger sense of presence than female participants.

- Sense of presence correlated with performance on most test items.

- Sense of presence correlated with enjoyment, ease of use and perceived effectiveness of the virtual laboratory.

- Dynamic Views participants found their virtual environment easier to use than Static Views and User-control participants.

6.6 Conclusion

This chapter has described the second and final major investigation undertaken in the study. Chapter 7 summarises the results from the two major investigations and discusses the conclusions reached in light of key literature. Possibilities for future research are also identified.

Chapter 7. Conclusions and Discussion

7.1 Overview of the Study

This study has identified a series of distinguishing characteristics of 3D learning environments and has explored the contribution of some of these characteristics to spatial learning. The characteristics identified were:

- Realistic display, including 3D perspective, lighting and occlusion;

- Smooth update of views showing viewer motion or panning;

- Smooth display of object motion;

- Consistency of object behaviour;

- Control of view position and direction;

- Object manipulation; and

- Control of object model and simulation parameters.

An investigation of the contribution of consistency of object behaviour and control of object model and simulation parameters was determined to be outside the scope of the thesis and consequently the main research questions were as follows:

- Question 1. Does smooth display of view changes in a 3D learning environment contribute to spatial learning?

- Question 2. Does smooth display of object motion in a 3D learning environment contribute to spatial learning?

- Question 3. Does user control over view position and direction in a 3D learning environment contribute to spatial learning?

- Question 4. Does object manipulation in a 3D learning environment contribute to spatial learning?

Recognising that in exploring the contributions to learning of a 3D environment, the characteristics of the environment cannot be looked at in isolation from the learning tasks undertaken, the following additional question was identified:

- Question 5. How does the design of the learning task within a 3D environment affect the spatial learning that occurs?

The study consisted of three investigations, a pilot investigation and two major investigations, referred to as Investigation 1 and Investigation 2. In each investigation participants explored versions of a virtual environment modelled on the Charles Sturt University undergraduate chemistry laboratory (referred to as 'the virtual laboratory') and then undertook written or practical tests on their spatial learning. The virtual environment was developed for this study, using the Virtual Reality Modelling Language (VRML), and was delivered on desktop computers.

The pilot investigation provided an opportunity to test the initial versions of the virtual laboratory, learning tasks and written test items. Investigation 1 explored the importance of user control over view and object manipulation, addressing the 3rd and 4th research questions. This was done by comparing the spatial learning of a group who explored a version of the virtual laboratory that provided user control over view and basic object manipulation capability (the 'User-control' group), with that of a group who used a version that provided an animated tour but no user control (the 'Dynamic Views' group). The spatial learning was assessed through written tests. Additionally the spatial learning through undertaking tasks within a 3D learning environment was compared to the learning from undertaking similar tasks in a corresponding real environment, by including a third group who undertook tasks in the real laboratory (the 'Real Laboratory' group).

Investigation 2 further explored the importance of user control over view and object manipulation as well as exploring the importance of smooth display of view changes and smooth display of object motion. This was done by comparing the spatial learning of three groups of participants: one who used a version of the virtual laboratory that allowed full control over view and object manipulation (the 'User-control' group), one who used a version providing an animated tour (the 'Dynamic Views' group), and one who used a version providing a similar tour, but consisting only of still images (the 'Static Views' group). The spatial learning was assessed through both written tests and through practical tests undertaken within the real laboratory. By providing a learning task for User-control participants that was more closely aligned with an aspect of the spatial tests than that used in Investigation 1, the effect of learning task design was also explored. Thus, Investigation 2 addressed all five research questions.

In addition to the written and practical tests designed to gauge participants' spatial learning, a number of other types of data were gathered. These were not central to the research questions, but allowed for the exploration of broader issues related to the use of 3D learning environments. Specifically, the gender and prior chemistry experience of each participant was recorded and participants were asked questions designed to gauge their perceived level of spatial ability and the degree to which they felt present in the environment. In Investigation 2, participants were also asked to rate the effectiveness of the virtual laboratory, its ease of use and the degree to which they enjoyed the experience.

7.2 Main Findings

7.2.1 Question 1. Does smooth display of view changes in a 3D learning environment contribute to spatial learning?

If smooth display of view changes contributed to spatial learning it was expected that Dynamic Views participants would have performed significantly better than Static Views participants on the laboratory layout, positioning of views and apparatus location written tests as well as on the apparatus location test in the real laboratory. These tests were all testing aspects of spatial knowledge of the laboratory environment, as distinct from apparatus within the laboratory. For knowledge of apparatus, it was considered that smooth display of object motion would be more important than smooth display of views.

In fact, Dynamic Views participants performed better than Static Views participants on the apparatus location written test, but there was no significant difference on the laboratory layout test or the positioning of views test. On average, Dynamic Views participants performed better than Static Views participants on the apparatus location test in the real laboratory, but the differences were not significant.

The lack of a difference between Static Views and Dynamic Views participants on the laboratory layout and view recognition tests was surprising. It was expected that Dynamic Views participants would have formed significantly more complete spatial models of the laboratory and thus would have been more able to produce a topographical plan and more able to recognise views. However, due to the relative simplicity of the laboratory structure, it was possible to see large parts of the laboratory from some of the vantage points viewed by Static Views participants. Consequently it appears that Static Views participants were able to form a complete spatial model of the laboratory from these static images.

The superior scores for Dynamic Views participants over Static Views participants on the apparatus location written test and at least in raw terms on the apparatus location real laboratory test were more consistent with expectations. Typically, when viewing apparatus, participants experienced a view from very close to the object and consequently a view that provided less information about the current position within the environment. It could be that the difference reflected the fact that, because Dynamic Views participants viewed animated transitions to these close-up views, they had a clearer idea of where they were in the laboratory at all times than did Static Views participants. Possibly, if a more complex environment was used, so that it was not possible to see large parts of the environment from single vantage points, the Dynamic Views participants would have been able to also score higher on laboratory layout and recognition of view tests.

Finding: Smooth display of view changes can lead to greater spatial learning, but it does not always do so. More research is required to ascertain the circumstances in which it does contribute.

7.2.2 Question 2. Does smooth display of object motion in a 3D learning environment contribute to spatial learning?

If smooth display of object motion contributed to spatial learning it was expected that Dynamic Views participants would have scored significantly higher than Static Views participants on the written tests on identification of apparatus, recall of apparatus structure and recall of apparatus usage procedures, as well as on the real laboratory test of apparatus usage. These tests all test spatial knowledge of apparatus, for which perception of object motion was considered likely to be important. Perception of object motion was considered likely to be more important than perception of smooth view changes for knowledge of apparatus because it was considered that viewing an animation of an item of apparatus rotating would be a more effective way to view the structure of an item than to view an animation showing a change in the view position.

Dynamic Views participants performed better than Static Views participants on the identification of apparatus written test. However, when familiar items were taken out of the results, there was no significant difference, suggesting that the difference may have been due to differences in prior knowledge. Dynamic Views participants scored higher in raw terms than Static Views participants on recall of apparatus structure, but the difference was not significant. These results do not support the proposition that smooth display of object motion leads to greater spatial learning, but they are inconclusive. It may be that the items of apparatus were not complex enough for animated views to make a difference. The structure of many items of apparatus could be clearly determined from one or two static views. Possibly if more complex items of apparatus were used, with structure that could not be determined without multiple views, Dynamic Views participants would have performed significantly better than Static Views participants.

Dynamic Views participants performed better than Static Views participants on the written test on apparatus usage (significant only at the 90% level), but there was no significant difference between Static Views and Dynamic Views participants on the apparatus usage test in the real laboratory. These results are also inconclusive. Possibly, if more complex apparatus were used, which included a greater range of movable components, Dynamic Views participants would have scored significantly better than Static Views participants.

Finding: These results provide little support for the proposition that smooth display of object animation leads to greater spatial learning, however the lack of complexity to the structure of objects used in the study suggests that further research is required.

7.2.3 Question 3. Does user control over view position and direction in a 3D learning environment contribute to spatial learning?

If user control over view position and direction contributed to spatial learning it was expected that User-control participants would have performed significantly better than Dynamic Views participants on the laboratory layout, positioning of views and apparatus location written tests as well as on the apparatus location test in the real laboratory. These tests were all testing aspects of spatial knowledge of the laboratory environment, as distinct from apparatus within the laboratory. For knowledge of apparatus, it was considered that object manipulation would be more important than user control over view.

In Investigation 2, User-control participants performed significantly better than Dynamic Views participants on the written test on location of apparatus, however this was not the case in Investigation 1. The main difference between the two investigations was that in Investigation 2, completion of the task carried out by User-control participants required knowledge of the location of apparatus. Specifically, the task required participants to locate and collect items of apparatus, assemble them and then put them away in their correct location. The fact that participants knew that they would have to put the items away was expected to ensure that they focussed their attention on the location of items, and the fact that it was not possible to put the items away in an incorrect location was intended to ensure that the task could not be completed without acquiring knowledge of apparatus location. In Investigation 1, participants just explored the laboratory and could complete the task without developing knowledge of the location of apparatus. The significantly better performance of User-control participants in Investigation 2 suggests that user control over view contributes to spatial learning only if the task carried out by User-control participants is aligned with or requires the particular desired spatial learning. It suggests that simply providing a 3D environment and allowing the learner to explore it freely without providing any tasks, goals or problems to solve will not result in any learning benefits over equivalent animated views. It also suggests that attention needs to be paid by designers to the learning outcomes that they hope that their learners will achieve, and the tasks that will lead to their achievement, so that appropriate task direction and support can be provided.

On the written tests on laboratory layout there was no significant difference between User-control and Dynamic Views participants in either investigation. It was expected that this test would provide a good indication of the degree to which participants formed a consistent configurational representation of the laboratory. It may have been that the laboratory environment was not complex enough and that most items of furniture and features of the layout could be viewed from single positions within the laboratory. However, it may also have been that the tasks carried out by User-control participants could be completed without knowledge of the laboratory layout and consequently, user control over view did not contribute to this type of spatial learning because neither of the tasks carried out required it.

User-control participants in the second investigation performed worse in absolute terms than User-control participants in the first investigation on the laboratory layout test. This suggests that because participants in the second investigation were so focussed on the task of locating items of apparatus they did not pay as much attention to the layout of the laboratory. If this is the case then it adds further weight to the argument that learning task design is very important in 3D learning environments.

Whereas in Investigation 1, User-control participants scored better than Dynamic Views participants on the positioning of views written test, this was not the case in Investigation 2. The reason for the difference in these two results appears to be related to improved performance of Dynamic Views participants in Investigation 2. In Investigation 2, Dynamic Views participants performed substantially better than they did in Investigation 1, whereas the performance of User-control participants was very similar in both investigations. In Investigation 2 Dynamic Views participants experienced 428 views compared to 210 in Investigation 1, and in Investigation 2 the range of views was comparable to the range likely to have been seen by User-control participants. This indicates that the difference between User-control participants and Dynamic Views participants in Investigation 1 was due to the Dynamic Views participants experiencing inferior views of the laboratory to those experienced by User-control participants.

An explanation for the lack of difference between User-control and Dynamic Views participants in Investigation 2 on the positioning of views test may once again be that the task carried out by User-control participants could be completed without the ability to recognise views of the laboratory. In other words, this knowledge was not developed significantly better by User-control participants because their task did not require it.

In Investigation 2, User-control participants were more likely than Dynamic Views participants to agree with a statement that the virtual laboratory was useful as a familiarisation tool. This adds more weight to the argument that user control over view can contribute to spatial learning if the task is structured in such a way as to require this learning.

Finding: These results suggest that user control over view position and direction leads to greater spatial learning but only if the task carried out by user control participants requires this learning.

7.2.4 Question 4. Does object manipulation in a 3D learning environment contribute to spatial learning?

If object-manipulation contributed to spatial learning it was expected that User-control participants would have scored significantly better than Dynamic Views participants on the written tests on identification of apparatus, recall of apparatus structure and recall of apparatus usage procedures, as well as on the real laboratory test of apparatus usage. These tests all test spatial knowledge of apparatus, for which object manipulation was considered likely to be important.

In fact, there was no significant difference between the User-control and Dynamic Views participants on identification of apparatus, recall of apparatus structure or recall of apparatus usage procedures. It was expected that the fact that in Investigation 2, User-control participants had to directly manipulate the dial and the lever on the pipette filler and the tap on the burette, would have ensured that they were more likely to recall the structure of these items.

On the apparatus usage test in the real laboratory, there was no significant difference between User-control and Dynamic Views participants. Once again it was expected that the direct manipulation of the burette and pipette filler by User-control participants would have led to greater recall of the usage procedures.

These counter-intuitive findings require further exploration. On the surface the findings suggest that object manipulation does not contribute to spatial learning. However, there are a number of alternative explanations. Firstly, the items of apparatus had relatively simple structure and were relatively simple to operate and this may have meant that user control was not necessary to develop a spatial cognitive model of them. Additionally, an argument could be made that the tasks carried out by the User-control group did not require substantial object manipulation and the actual object manipulations carried out did not require spatial learning in order to be completed, which prevented User-control participants from having an advantage over Dynamic Views participants. A follow up study with more complex objects, a greater range of object manipulation tasks and with the use of spatial tests very closely aligned to the structural components manipulated could shed more light on this.

Finding: These results provide little support for the proposition that object manipulation leads to greater spatial learning, however the limited range of object manipulation tasks within the study suggests that further research is required.

7.2.5 Question 5. How does the design of the learning task within a 3D environment affect the spatial learning that occurs?

This question is somewhat open-ended compared with the other questions and consequently it was not expected that a definitive answer would be found. Rather, it was expected that if learning task design was an important contributing factor to spatial learning, then greater learning would occur in Investigation 2 than in Investigation 1, due to the fact that the learning task in Investigation 2 was more detailed and more closely aligned to the measured spatial learning.

In fact, there was a significant difference between User-control and Dynamic Views participants on location of apparatus in Investigation 2 whereas there was not in Investigation 1. The main difference between these two investigations was that in Investigation 2 User-control participants undertook a task that required them to learn the location of apparatus, in order to be able to return the items of apparatus to their correct location. This suggests that the design of the learning task is important for spatial learning in a 3D environment. Specifically, if spatial learning is to occur beyond that which would occur through watching an animation, learning tasks must be identified which are closely aligned with the desired spatial learning, and appropriate task direction or task support must be provided. Just exploring a 3D environment without any task direction will not facilitate spatial learning beyond that achieved by watching an animation.

Finding: These results suggest that the types of learning tasks within a 3D environment that are likely to facilitate spatial learning are those tasks designed in such a way as to require the desired learning to occur in order for the tasks to be completed.

7.3 Additional Findings

The following sections summarise the additional findings that do not relate directly to the research questions.

7.3.1 Gender and Spatial Ability

In Investigation 1 female participants performed significantly better than male participants on one test item, an item that required them to draw a map of the laboratory without being provided with a list of items of furniture to include. This item was not used in Investigation 2. A similar item, used in both investigations, required participants to draw a map of the laboratory given a list of items to include on the map, and there was no difference between male and female performance on this test in either investigation. There was no difference between male and female performance on any of the other written tests in either investigation. There was also no difference between male and female performance in the practical tests undertaken in Investigation 2.

These results can be looked at in light of previous research, which shows clear evidence for differences in spatial ability between males and females. For example McGee (1979) in a meta-analysis of research on spatial skills, discussed numerous studies which found that males performed better than females on both 'spatial visualisation' and 'spatial orientation'. He defines spatial visualisation as "a process of recognition, retention and recall of a configuration in which there is movement among the moving parts" (p. 893). He defines spatial orientation as "the comprehension of the arrangement of elements within a visual stimulus pattern and aptitude to remain unconfused by the changing orientation in which a spatial configuration may be presented" (p. 893).

One would expect that these differences in spatial ability would lead to differences in spatial learning in a 3D environment. In this study, one might have expected gender differences to be found both in tests measuring learning of apparatus structure and in tests measuring learning of laboratory layout. However, studies exploring gender differences in spatial learning in a 3D environment have been inconclusive. Arthur et al. (1997) carried out a study requiring participants to draw a map showing the location of items within a room after either exploring the room, exploring an equivalent virtual environment or viewing an image of the room. They found that males made significantly fewer errors. However, Gillner and Mallot (1998), in a study exploring spatial learning from exploration of a virtual maze, found no significant gender differences. Waller et al. (1998) in a study comparing spatial learning from exploration of immersive, desktop and real environments, found that males out-performed women in the virtual environment groups, but attributed this to differences in ability to operate the virtual environment interface and thus comfortably move around the environment.

In Investigation 1, participants with higher self reported spatial ability performed significantly better on a written test requiring identification of items of apparatus, a test requiring drawing of a map of the laboratory given a list of items to include and a test requiring positioning of apparatus on a panoramic photograph. In Investigation 2, participants with higher self reported spatial ability performed significantly better on written tests requiring recall of apparatus usage procedures and on practical tests requiring apparatus usage but no other tests. In Investigation 2, where participants were surveyed on their perceptions after using the 3D environment, participants with higher self reported spatial ability indicated that they found the virtual environment easier to use.

These results suggest that self reported spatial ability does coincide with abilities that are relevant to some types of learning in 3D environments. However, more research is required to determine the degree to which distinct spatial skills, such as those identified by McGee (1979), contribute to spatial learning in a 3D environment, or whether there are other spatial ability factors specific to 3D environments. The need for such research has also been identified by Durlach et al. (2000). One outcome of such research might be the derivation of questionnaires and pre-tests allowing an individual's level of 3D environment spatial learning skill to be assessed. Such questionnaires would be useful for research studies such as this one as well as being useful for determining the appropriateness of the use of a 3D learning environment for individual learners. Additionally, further research is required to determine the circumstances in which gender differences in spatial skills will result in gender differences in learning in a 3D environment.

7.3.2 Presence, Enjoyment and Ease of Use

In Investigation 1, User-control participants on average experienced a significantly higher sense of presence than Dynamic Views participants but in Investigation 2 there was no significant difference. Witmer and Singer (1998, p. 230) suggest that to "the extent that observers can modify their viewpoint to change what they see…or to search the environment haptically, they should experience more presence". Hendrix and Barfield (1996), in discussing the results of an exploratory study of the sense of presence (or immersion), suggest that "subjects can be further 'pulled into' a virtual environment by giving them a task to perform" and "in the process, result in additional cognitive resources being allocated to the virtual world as compared to the real-world environment" (p. 284). The results of this study do not provide clear evidence that user control over view contributes to a sense of presence nor that a more involved task contributes to a sense of presence. However, Dynamic Views participants on average experienced a higher sense of presence than Static Views participants in Investigation 2. This supports the claim by Witmer and Singer (1998) that the 'degree of movement perception' will contribute to a sense of presence.

In Investigation 1 there was no significant correlation between the sense of presence experienced and performance on written spatial learning tests. However, in Investigation 2, sense of presence correlated with performance on most written test items and on some of the practical test items. Stanney and Salvendy (1998, p. 157) suggest that "the relationship between sense of presence and task performance in VEs is commonly thought to be both positive and causal". However, they suggest that this relationship "has yet to be fully understood and is likely to be highly task dependent". This study supports this view, providing evidence that spatial learning performance can correlate with the sense of presence, but that this is not always the case.

In Investigation 2, where participants were surveyed after their use of the 3D environment, User-control participants were more likely to indicate that they enjoyed the experience than Dynamic Views participants, but there was no difference between the likelihood of enjoyment of Static Views and Dynamic Views participants. Dynamic Views participants found their virtual environment easier to use than Static Views and User-control participants. Additionally ease of use did not correlate (positively or negatively) with enjoyment. These results are interesting because they suggest that a resource that is less easy to use can nevertheless be more enjoyable to use for some participants. The results would probably come as no surprise to computer game developers who sometimes aim to make their interface challenging to use in order to facilitate engagement. Further research is required to explore these parameters so that educational developers can find the right balance, in order that their resources are sufficiently engaging but not so challenging to use that they deter some learners from using them.

In Investigation 2, presence correlated with enjoyment, ease of use and perceived effectiveness of the virtual laboratory. Additionally, participants who enjoyed playing computer games found the virtual laboratory more enjoyable to use and easier to use and were also more likely to experience a sense of presence. These results suggest that there may be a certain class of learner for which the use of 3D environments is particularly appropriate.

Male participants were significantly more likely to state that they found the use of a 3D environment enjoyable. Male participants also indicated through questionnaire responses that they experienced a stronger sense of presence in both investigations. However, in the case of both sense of presence and enjoyment there was substantial variance in the data. In other words, there were many males and many females who did enjoy the experience and many males and females who did not. There were also many males and females who felt present and many males and females who did not. Consequently, it would not be appropriate to conclude that 3D environments should be used for males and not females. A more appropriate conclusion would be that 3D environments should not be used as the only learning resource in any learning context. Some learners may find it effective but some may not. Consequently, wherever possible an alternative resource should be provided for those who do not enjoy the use of a 3D environment, find such environments difficult to use, or find it difficult to achieve spatial learning from the use of such environments.

7.3.3 Interface Design for 3D Learning Environments

The user interface for moving around the environment and manipulating objects evolved over the course of the study with changes made from the version used in the pilot investigation, to the version used in Investigation 1 and again to the version used in Investigation 2. In each case multiple smaller usability tests were undertaken to explore the effectiveness of the successive versions.

Earlier work by the researcher had suggested that some users find it difficult to move around in a 3D environment and in particular the use of the mouse for motion control and the use of modal interfaces can be problematic (Dalgarno and Scott, 2000). Based on these findings, and on the findings of preliminary usability tests, the motion control interface used in the User-control versions of the environment was keyboard based and was made as simple as possible. Specifically, in the versions used in the two major investigations, the arrow keys were used for movement, with the Shift key used in conjunction with the arrow keys to allow the user to 'look' to the left or right or to look up or down, without moving. This interface was able to be mastered with minimal training by all participants in both investigations except for one in Investigation 1. That is, of 36 participants who used the User-control version in the two investigations, 35 were able to master the interface without difficulty.

The provision of an interface for manipulating apparatus was more difficult. To allow an object to be moved in any direction and rotated in any direction requires six degrees of freedom. However, a conventional mouse provides only two degrees of freedom. One possibility was to make use of keys on the keyboard to alter the plane of movement or to switch between moving an object and rotating it. This was considered to be too complex and to be likely to require substantial training. A number of alternatives were considered and trialed.

In the pilot investigation an interface was provided that allowed users to drag an item around within a single plane, normally corresponding with the surface of a bench or a shelf within a cupboard. This presented problems because it was difficult to prevent the objects from being dragged through the walls of cupboards and becoming lost. No mechanism for rotating objects was provided in the pilot investigation.

In Investigation 1, it was not considered necessary for participants to be able to drag objects around, but in order to explore the effect on spatial learning of object manipulation, an interface was required that allowed for objects to be rotated. The interface used allowed participants to 'pick up' an object by double-clicking on it. Once picked up, an object could be rotated about the Y-axis by dragging the object from left to right with the mouse and to be rotated about the X-axis by dragging from top to bottom. Usability studies indicated that some users found this rotation difficult to control and so an additional mechanism was provided, where the object would slowly rotate 360 degrees about the Y-axis when clicked and would do the same about the X-axis when clicked again.

In Investigation 2, it was necessary for users to be able to move objects around in order to assemble items of apparatus. A mechanism for carrying objects was devised, where objects could be dragged and dropped on top of an always visible image of a hand, and then later dragged and dropped to a new location. This interface, which was similar to that used by many first-person computer games was able to be easily mastered by all participants. To avoid items of apparatus becoming lost in the way that they were in the pilot version, objects could only be dropped in pre-determined locations, such as on a bench. A highlight was used to indicate when an item could be dropped. Objects dropped elsewhere returned to the position from where they were picked up.

The provision of an interface for actually assembling the items was more difficult. It was originally intended that users would have to rotate the objects to the correct orientation before connecting them together. An interface which was an extension of that proposed by Chen et al. (1988) was developed. With this interface, when an object was clicked on, a transparent sphere was shown around it, and this sphere could then be dragged left-right, top-bottom or around in a circle to provide for three degrees of rotation. Usability tests suggested that with some training this interface could be mastered. However, it was determined that the apparatus connection tasks would have taken too long if participants had to rotate each item to the correct orientation and thus this interface was not used. Instead a simpler interface, which allowed participants to drag items of apparatus together, with the item automatically being rotated to the correct orientation, was used. Objects could only be connected to specific other objects and once again a highlight was used as a cue to indicate when an item was able to be dropped on another item. This interface proved quite easy to master for all participants. However, the limited capability for manipulating an individual object may have contributed to the lack of a significant difference in learning of object structure between User-control and Dynamic Views participants.

To summarise, then, the results of usability studies carried out as part of the development of the virtual environment used in this study suggest that a keyboard driven motion control interface is easy to use for most users. However, additional research is required to determine the most effective interface for object manipulation in desktop 3D environments.

7.4 Discussion

7.4.1 User control over view and learning task design

The most important finding from this research was that the contribution of user control over view to spatial learning is dependant on alignment between the aspect of spatial learning tested and the tasks undertaken in the 3D environment. That is, user control alone does not contribute to spatial learning. Two other studies have explored the issue of user control for spatial learning in 3D environments, but neither identified task alignment as an important issue. An analysis of these two studies is required in order to determine whether their results are consistent with the conclusions reached in this study.

In the first study, Peruch et al. (1995) concluded that active exploration of a 3D environment leads to greater spatial learning than passive viewing of an equivalent animation. In the other study Christou and Bulthoff (1999) found that active exploration did not lead to greater spatial learning than viewing an animation, but explained this in terms of the additional mental load in using the view control interface. Table 7.1 shows a summary of the methods and findings in these two studies. It also shows a summary of the corresponding methods and findings in Investigations 1 and 2 of this study. In comparing this study to the studies of Peruch et al. (1995) and Christou and Bulthoff (1999), only the results of the apparatus location and positioning of views tests are discussed because these correspond most closely to the tests used in these two studies. Peruch et al. and Christou and Bulthoff referred to their User-control participants as 'active' and their Dynamic Views participants as 'passive'. For simplicity, the terms,

'User-control' and 'Dynamic Views', used in this study have also been used to refer to the groups used in these other two studies.

	This study (Investigations 1 and 2)	Peruch et al. (1995)	Christou and Bulthoff (1999) (Experiment 3)
	Table 7.1 **Contrast of methods and results in this study for exploring user control with those used by Peruch et al. (1995) and Christou and Bulthoff (1999)**		
Overall design	Random allocation of participants to a User-control, a Dynamic Views and a Static Views group In Investigation 1, 34 participants, in Investigation 2, 80 participants	Repeated measures design with 18 participants each exploring three virtual environments, one under a User-control condition, one under a Dynamic Views condition and one under a Static Views condition	Random allocation of 32 participants to a User-control or a Dynamic Views group
Apparatus	Desktop 3D environment, using a keyboard for motion control	Projected 3D environment, using a joystick for motion control	Desktop 3D environment using a "spaceball" six degree of freedom mouse for motion control
Environment Design	Chemistry laboratory, with items of apparatus in cupboards and drawers	Abstract environment consisting of a relatively uncluttered room with partitions obscuring coloured cubes	Attic of a house
Task carried out in active exploration condition	In Investigation 1, free exploration for 40 minutes with focus on learning the structure and the location of items of apparatus In Investigation 2, 60 minute task involving collection of apparatus, assembly of items and return of apparatus to original location	Free exploration of each environment for 4 minutes with focus on learning the location of cubes.	Free exploration for 20-25 minutes with a goal of locating numbered markers.

	Table 7.1 (cont.) Contrast of methods and results in this study for exploring user control with those used by Peruch et al. (1995) and Christou and Bulthoff (1999)		
	This study (Investigations 1 and 2)	**Peruch et al. (1995)**	**Christou and Bulthoff (1999) (Experiment 3)**
Description of animated view condition	Series of animated movements, based on a logical path through the environment, with control over when next movement occurred, and with the ability to go back to previous position, and to repeat the tour	Single animation sequence, based on an optimal path through the environment, with no control over pace.	Single animation sequences, each recorded from one active participant's exploration, with no control over pace
Spatial test	Indication of position and direction of given views, on a topological map Indication of position of items of apparatus on a topological map	Location of cubes within virtual environment	Recognition of familiar and novel views
Main finding	User-control participants performed significantly better than Dynamic Views participants on positioning of views in Investigation 1, but there was no difference in Investigation 2. User-control participants performed significantly better than Dynamic Views participants on apparatus location in Investigation 2, but there was no difference in Investigation 1.	User-control participants performed significantly better than Dynamic Views participants.	There was no significant difference.

Christou and Bulthoff suggested that the reason for the difference between the results obtained by Peruch et al. and their own results was that their participants were subject to additional cognitive load due to usability problems with the operation of the spaceball. However, it is the view of this researcher that although cognitive load was likely to be a factor, an equally important factor likely to have contributed to the difference in outcomes of these two studies was task differences. In Peruch et al.'s study participants were told in advance that they would be tested on their ability to locate coloured cubes, and the focus of their task was exploration to locate these cubes. In Christou and Bulthoff's study participants were told little about how they would be tested, but were instructed to memorise the location of a set of markers. They were then tested on their ability to recognise novel and familiar views of the environment. Thus, their test was not at all aligned with their focus as they explored the virtual environment.

Christou and Bulthoff's results are consistent with the results of the positioning of views tests in Investigations 2, which also found no significant difference between User-control and Dynamic Views participants. However, in Investigation 1, User-control participants performed significantly better than Dynamic Views participants on the positioning of views test, even though the task performed by the User-control group was not aligned with this test. This anomaly can be explained by the fact that the views of the laboratory seen by Dynamic Views participants in Investigation 1 were inferior to those likely to be seen by User-control participants, and in particular, few of the views provided to Dynamic Views participants were from a position or in a direction similar to those included in the test. In Investigation 2, participants of the Dynamic Views groups performed substantially better than the corresponding participants in Investigation 1 on the positioning of views test, and there was no significant difference between User-control and Dynamic Views participants. In this second investigation, a much greater number of views was provided, including a larger number of views similar to those in the test. Additionally, the views provided to Dynamic Views participants in Investigation 2 were much more similar to those likely to be seen by User-control participants.

Because of the limitations in the views provided to Dynamic Views participants in Investigation 1, it is more appropriate to compare the results obtained by Christou and Bulthoff with those obtained in Investigation 2 than those obtained in Investigation 1.

The results obtained in the study carried out by Christou and Bulthoff and in Investigation 2 of this study were very consistent, with no significant difference between User-control and Dynamic Views participants on recall of views in either case. It is argued that the lack of alignment between the task of searching for apparatus and the test requiring positioning of views was a major factor in the lack of a difference between the performance of User-control and Dynamic Views participants in both Christou and Bulhoff's study and in Investigation 2 of this study.

The task carried out by User-control participants in Investigation 1 of this study was similar in some ways to that carried out by User-control participants in Peruch et al.'s study. In both cases participants searched for objects within the environment. The written test on apparatus location could also be considered to be testing the same knowledge as Peruch et al.'s test requiring participants to find objects in the virtual environment. Consequently, the fact that there was no significant difference between User-control and Dynamic Views participants in Investigation 1, but that Peruch et al. found a difference between their User-control and Dynamic Views participants, needs to be explained.

One difference between Investigation 1 of this study and the study carried out by Peruch et al., was that the virtual laboratory used here contained a great deal more detail than the environment used by Peruch et al. Additionally, in Investigation 1, participants were given much less specific information about how they would be tested than Peruch et al.'s participants. They were told that they would be tested on the layout of the laboratory and its furniture and the identity and structure of items of apparatus, but were given no specific information on the types of tests to be used. These instructions, in addition to the more complex layout of the environment, would have made it less likely that participants focussed their attention closely on the location of items of apparatus. Thus, there were clear task differences between Investigation 1 and the study carried out by Peruch et al.

Additionally, the Dynamic Views condition used in Investigation 1 allowed an element of user control not provided to the corresponding participants in Peruch et al.'s study, that is, the ability to control the pace of their animated tour and the ability to go back to a previous step. Peruch et al. (1995, p. 17) suggest that the reason for the superior performance of their User-control participants was that "the active dynamic exploration allowed the observers to construct and to update a more accurate internal representation of space according to their specific needs in specific time". If they are correct in this explanation of their results, then one would expect that the provision of an interface allowing Dynamic Views participants to control the pace of their tour, and to backtrack to view previous parts of the tour again, would lead to improved performance for these participants.

It is argued then, that there were two reasons for the significant difference in Peruch et al.'s study but the lack of such a difference in Investigation 1, namely, differences in the degree to which the learning task was aligned with the test, and differences in the degree of control provided to Dynamic Views participants.

The results of Investigation 2 shed further light on the proposition that, as well as differences in the degree of control provided to Dynamic Views participants, differences in task alignment contributed to the conflict between the results of Investigation 1 and those of Peruch et al. In Investigation 2, Dynamic Views participants had the same degree of control as they did in Investigation 1, but in this case there was a difference between the performance of User Control and Dynamic Views participants on the apparatus location test. It is argued that the reason for this was that the task carried out by User-control participants in Investigation 2 was much more closely aligned to learning of the location of items of apparatus and thus User-control participants were able to perform better than Dynamic Views participants. It is also argued that the degree of alignment between the task performed and the apparatus location test in Investigation 2 was similar to the degree of alignment between the task and the test used by Peruch et al. Consequently, it is argued that the results of this study are consistent with those obtained by Peruch et al.

It could be argued that the degree of control provided to Dynamic Views participants meant that a comparison between the User-control and Dynamic Views participants was not in fact measuring the effect of user control. However, it is important to note that the research question refers to 'user control over view position and direction' not user control in general. Consequently the provision of an interface to Dynamic Views participants that allowed user control over pace, ensured that user control over pace was not a confounding variable.

Additionally, one of the reasons for comparing Dynamic Views and User-control performance was to determine if there is value in the use of a 3D environment rather than an alternative computer-based resource including animation or video. Given that video delivered on a computer allows for very easy pausing and forward and backward movement through the sequence, the provision of an interface to Dynamic Views participants allowing for control over pace, and the ability to backtrack was appropriate.

Much of the literature on spatial perception and cognition comes from an information processing model, which has implicit within it an assumption that the information perceived and the processing that occurs can be treated separately, or factored (Greeno, 1994). Put another way, this model does not consider the task that the learner is attempting to carry out, or their motivations, to be important factors in determining the information that they will perceive. Similarly, the issue of task design has been largely neglected by researchers into 3D environments for spatial learning. For example, Durlach et al. (2000) in proposing a research agenda for spatial learning in virtual environments, identify task design as a factor that can affect the validity of comparisons between different virtual environment systems, but do not advocate it as an important focus of future research.

Constructivist theories of learning, especially those building on Jean Piaget's stage-independent theories consider the learner's activity to be much more important. These theories suggest that learning is a process of a learner actively testing their existing knowledge against their experience (Piaget, 1973; Gruber & Voneche, 1977). It could be argued, then, that a consequence of these theories is that what a learner perceives will depend to a large extent on their activity.

However, Piaget differentiates between figurative knowledge, which is knowledge about the static world, and operative knowledge, which incorporates the dynamic properties of objects and the ways in which they can be manipulated or acted upon (Piaget, 1968). Piaget's focus in explaining the learning process was primarily on operative knowledge, with figurative knowledge considered less important (Campbell, 1997). He saw the role of perception as being responsible for gathering figurative knowledge and of importance only where it contributed to the development of operative knowledge (Piaget, 1969). Consequently, it could be argued that it would be inappropriate to apply Piaget's views on active learning to the perception and recall of laboratory layout and location of objects, because of the figurative nature of this knowledge.

However, an alternative interpretation of Piaget's work is that our "representation of space arises from the coordination and internalisations of actions" and that our understanding and representation of space "results from extensive manipulations of objects and from movement in the physical environment, rather than from any immediate perceptual 'copying' of this environment" (Hart and Moore, 1974, p. 261). Such an interpretation would suggest that the process of collecting and returning items of apparatus to their correct location in the virtual laboratory would be an operative one, and consequently tests of the recall of apparatus location would in fact be testing operative rather than figurative knowledge.

James Gibson's theories, on which the discipline of ecological psychology is based, give perception a higher status than does Piaget. Gibson suggests that perception and action are very heavily intertwined and specifically, that perception is an aspect of a person's interaction with the environment, rather than simply involving encoding of information about the environment (Greeno, 1994; Bickhard & Richie, 1983). Gibson introduced the notion of affordances and suggested that our perception is primarily focussed on identifying the affordances of the objects around us (Gibson, 1979). In other words "in ecological theory, it is assumed that perception exists to facilitate adaptive action" (Stoffregen, 2000, p. 18). Consequently, what we perceive will depend on the activities that we are engaged in at a more general level (Greeno, 1994). The results found in these studies are consistent with this theory in that for the learners in the second investigation perception of the location of items of apparatus was necessary to afford the task of retrieving the items and putting them away again. For the learners in the first investigation perception of apparatus location was not essential to the task that they undertook and so their perception and retention were less.

7.4.2 Static versus animated display of views

The key studies which have explored the contribution of animated display of views to spatial learning in 3D environments were again those carried out by Peruch et al. (1995) and Christou and Bulthoff (1999). Once again the results of these two studies were different. Peruch et al. (1995) found no significant difference between participants who viewed a series of static images of a 3D environment and those who viewed an animated display. Christou and Bulthoff did not directly compare static and animated display but in two separate experiments compared static display to user control and animated display to user control. They found no difference between animated display and user control but found that spatial learning from user control was significantly greater than that from static display, implying that animated display resulted in greater spatial learning than static display.

Table 7.2 shows a summary of the methods used and results obtained in these two studies, along with the corresponding methods used and results obtained in Investigation 2 of this study. Once again, in comparing this study to the studies of Peruch et al. (1995) and Christou and Bulthoff (1999), only the tests on apparatus location and view position are discussed, since these correspond most closely to those used in these studies, and once again this study's terms for the two groups, 'Dynamic Views' and 'Static Views' are used, rather than the terms used in the other studies.

Table 7.2

Contrast of methods and results in this study for exploring static and animated display with those used by Peruch et al. (1995) and Christou and Bulthoff (1999)

	Investigation 2 of this study	Peruch et al. (1995)	Christou and Bulthoff (1999) (Experiment 3)
Description of animated display condition	Series of animated movements, based on a logical path through the environment, with control over when next movement occurred, and with the ability to go back to previous position, and to repeat the tour	Single animation sequence, based on an optimal path through the environment, with no control over pace	Single animation sequences, each recorded from one active participant's exploration, with no control over pace
Description of static display condition	Series of views of environment corresponding with the end points of each animated movement, with control over when next display was shown, and with the ability to go back to previous display, and to repeat the tour 429 views were shown with participants having 60 minutes to explore them.	Series of 60 views of environment corresponding with every 72nd frame of animated sequence, with each display shown for four seconds Total time four minutes No control over the pace	Series of 50 views of the environment chosen specifically so that they did not "result in any spatial-temporal sequence that could give rise to the impression of movement through the scene" (p. 1002) Each view shown for 1.5 seconds with four of the views containing numbered markers and participants able to stop the display to write down the number when these images appeared Displays shown repeatedly for 20-25 minutes
Spatial test	Indication of position and direction of given views, on a topological map Indication of position of items of apparatus on a topological map	Location of cubes within virtual environment	Recognition of familiar and novel views

Table 7.2 (cont.)

Contrast of methods and results in this study for exploring static and animated display with those used by Peruch et al. (1995) and Christou and Bulthoff (1999)

	Investigation 2 of this study	Peruch et al. (1995)	Christou and Bulthoff (1999) (Experiment 3)
Main finding	No significant difference on positioning of views Performance of Dynamic Views participants significantly better than Static Views participants on location of apparatus	No significant difference	Implication that Dynamic Views participants performed significantly better than Static Views participants

The difference between the results of the Peruch et al. study, which found no difference between Dynamic Views and Static Views participants and those of the Christou and Bulthoff study, which found that Dynamic Views participants performed significantly better than Static Views participants can be explained by differences in the Static Views condition. The static images viewed by Christou and Bulthoff's participants did not provide a sequential tour of the environment, making it difficult for participants to form a clear idea of their relationship to each other and thus making it difficult for a clear spatial model to be formed. Peruch et al.'s participants on the other hand viewed a series of images making up a tour of the environment, making it much more likely that the participants would form a consistent cognitive spatial model.

In Investigation 2 of this study, like participants in the Peruch et al. study, participants in the Static Views group viewed a series of images making up a sequential tour of the environment. Consequently, one would expect similar results to the Peruch et al. study, that is, no significant difference between the performance of Static Views and Dynamic Views participants. In fact, on the location of apparatus written test, Dynamic Views participants performed better than Static Views participants. This can be explained by limitations in the views of apparatus locations shown to Static Views participants. Typically, the images showing the positions of apparatus were from viewpoints very close to a cupboard or drawer, with the narrow field of view preventing participants from forming a clear idea of where in the laboratory they were currently located.

Dynamic Views participants would have been much clearer on the position of these locations due to the animated transition between their previous view and this one.

The results of this study and the studies by Peruch et al. and Christou and Bulthoff suggest that static views can be as effective for spatial learning as Dynamic Views if there are sufficient static images provided and if the static images are chosen in such a way that participants can see a clear relationship between the position of one view and the next, and if the field of view is wide enough to identify the location of each view within the nearby parts of the environment. This is interesting because it also suggests that lower frame rates (which essentially bring an animated display closer to a series of static images) may not be an impediment to spatial learning in 3D environments. Further research is required to explore this issue.

7.4.3 Recommendations for Educational Designers

As a result of the findings of this study a number of recommendations can be made for educational designers or developers considering the use of 3D learning environments. These are discussed in this section.

The finding that the contribution to spatial learning of user control over view depends on alignment of the task carried out within the 3D environment with the desired learning, leads to the following recommendations:

- **An important part of the design of a 3D learning environment is the identification of desired learning outcomes and the design of learning tasks aligned with these outcomes.**

- **A 3D environment should be chosen ahead of a video or animation only if learning tasks that require the interactive characteristics of a 3D environment, aligned to the desired learning outcomes, are able to be identified.**

- **Learners should be explicitly advised to undertake these tasks either through guidance provided within the environment or as part of supporting materials.**

The results of the various formative evaluations of the virtual laboratory carried out in the course of this study lead to the following recommendations about user-interface design for desktop 3D environments:

- **A motion control interface based on the use of the arrow keys in conjunction with modifiers such as the Shift and Ctrl keys, will be able to be used by most learners with minimal training.**

- **Developing an easy-to-use interface that allows for flexible manipulation of objects, including movement in any direction and rotation about any axis, is likely to be very difficult; compromising on the range of manipulation possible is likely to result in enhanced ease of use.**

The high variance in test results, along with the range of questionnaire responses, lead to the following recommendation:

- **There are significant individual differences in ability to use a 3D environment, ability to learn from the use of such environments, and enjoyment of the use of such environments, and consequently it may not be appropriate to provide a 3D environment as the primary means for all learners to learn essential concepts.**

- **The use of alternative resources or at the very least a simplified interface allowing for an animated tour rather than user control, would be appropriate to cater for learners, for whom a 3D environment may not be appropriate.**

7.5 Limitations of the Study

7.5.1 Narrow age range of participants

The use of undergraduate on-campus University students as participants in each investigation restricts the degree to which the results can be generalised to an extent because of the narrow age range of such students. In Investigation 2, where the date of birth of participants was recorded, the mean age was 21 with a standard deviation of 4.

Pearson's Correlation Coefficients were calculated between age and immersion, spatial test results and questionnaire responses in Investigation 2. There was a significant correlation between age and results on the real laboratory test on apparatus location, specifically a significant correlation with time and a significant negative correlation with number of items found. This indicates that older participants performed worse than younger participants on this task. There was also a significant negative correlation with sense of presence as measured through responses to the question about involvement in the experience. There was also a highly significant negative correlation with perceived ease of use. This suggests that older participants were less likely to experience a sense of presence and found the virtual laboratory more difficult to use.

These results are consistent with the results of earlier research by this researcher, which found that older users had more difficulty using a 3D environment (Dalgarno and Scott, 2000). As a consequence educational designers and developers should beware of assuming that 3D environments similar to the one used in this study will be as easy to use and will result in similar levels of spatial learning to the one used in this study, if an older group of participants is used.

7.5.2 Lack of control for spatial ability

In both major investigations in this study, participants were randomly assigned to groups and, rather than completing a spatial ability test, were asked to respond to questions designed to gauge their opinion of their own level of spatial ability. Although self reported spatial ability level correlated with performance on a number of tests, it did not correlate with performance on a number of others. The use of a standard spatial ability test, although more time consuming than self-report questions, would have made it easier to determine if the high variance in test results was due to spatial ability differences. If such a test was carried out prior to grouping of participants it may have also allowed for spatial ability to be controlled across groups, which would have added to the validity of the results.

An alternative approach would have been to use a repeated measures design with each participant undertaking tasks in a static views, dynamic views and user control condition with separate tests after each. This would have required the careful development of three separate but equivalent environments, each with user control, dynamic views and static views versions. Such a design would have ensured that spatial ability was not a factor.

7.5.3 Testing only of static aspects of spatial cognition

In Section 2.5 it was postulated that the aspects of a person's spatial cognitive model include knowledge of the properties of objects and structures, knowledge of the dynamic (changeable) properties, and knowledge of the relationships between objects, structures and people within the space. The tests used in this study focussed primarily on structural properties of the apparatus, the laboratory and furniture, with a small number of tests focussing on apparatus usage procedures.

It is recognised that the most important value of 3D learning environments may be in facilitating the learning of more complex spatial knowledge, including the dynamic properties of objects and the way that such objects interact with each other or with people. For example, the 3D environments used in Project Science Space by Salzman et al. (1999) focussed on learning various physics concepts, such as mechanics, electrostatic charge and quantum mechanics. It is likely that consistency of object behaviour and control of object model and simulation parameters would be important characteristics of 3D learning environments for these more dynamic aspects of spatial learning. An exploration of the importance of these characteristics for spatial learning was outside the scope of this research.

However, it could also be argued that user control over view and object manipulation, as well as dynamic view changes and object animation, would also contribute to these more dynamic aspects of spatial learning. Consequently, a limitation of this study was that there were few tests of these dynamic aspects of spatial cognition.

7.5.4 Complexity of the learning process in 3D environments

Although a great deal of effort has been taken to control for natural ability and prior experience through the random allocation of participants to groups, and to control for user-interface differences in the various treatments, it is important to acknowledge that the complexity of the process of learning in 3D environments ensures that the results obtained should be seen as contributions to ongoing research, rather than as final definitive conclusions. As pointed out in Section 3.3.9.3, the complex nature of the human-computer interactions and the cognitive processing involved and the range of potentially relevant participant abilities and prior experiences, means that there is always the possibility that unexpected factors could have affected the results.

Consequently, further research is required to replicate or shed further light on the findings.

7.6 Further Research

The finding that user control over view contributes to spatial learning only if the learning task is aligned to the desired learning outcome, could be further explored through a follow-up study. Such a study could compare learning from free exploration of a 3D environment with learning scaffolded by suggested learning tasks, aligned specifically to the spatial learning to be tested. For example, tasks could be devised that were aligned with view recognition tests and with environment layout tests, in addition to object location tests. Testing of various types of spatial learning as a result of each of these tasks would determine quite clearly whether the conclusions reached in this study are correct.

The limited object manipulation capability provided in this study and the limited range of tasks requiring spatial learning of objects, along with the relatively simple spatial structure of the items of apparatus, suggest that a study focussing on object manipulation alone would be warranted. Such a study could, for example, use a 3D environment with a fixed view, allowing for a more complex range of object manipulation capability, because the learners would not have to also learn how to move around. By including a more complex range of objects, each with greater structural detail and more sophisticated interactive characteristics, the degree to which object manipulation and object animation contribute to spatial learning could be more effectively explored.

Another possible follow-up study would be one that explored the degree to which consistency of object behaviour and control of object model and simulation parameters contribute to spatial learning. These questions were identified as being important in Chapter 2, but were determined to be beyond the scope of this study. Such a study could be carried out using an extension of the virtual laboratory to allow a virtual experiment, such as a titration, to be undertaken, with the ability to switch between a view of the laboratory and a view at the molecular level. As well as allowing the exploration of the degree to which object behaviour and control over simulation parameters contribute to spatial learning, such a study would also allow more complex aspects of spatial learning beyond just the static structure of objects and the space to be explored.

7.7 Conclusion

It is recognised that most educators considering the use of 3D environments as learning resources hope to achieve learning beyond the spatial learning that has been the focus of this study. However, many possible applications of 3D learning environments have implicit within their design the assumption that the learner will form a spatial cognitive representation of the concepts studied. If these resources are to be more effective than alternatives such as multimedia resources incorporating video, animation and static images, it must be established that they are more effective in facilitating the formation of such spatial representations. The results of this study suggest that 3D learning environments can be more effective than other multimedia resources for spatial learning, but only if the design of the environment and the task support are carefully thought out to ensure an alignment with the desired learning. Further research is required to explore these parameters. It is the view of this researcher that this research is necessary as a prerequisite for further research into the wider potential of 3D learning environments.

References

Active Worlds. (2003). *Active Worlds.* Retrieved September 18, 2003, from
http://www.activeworlds.com/

Alberti, M. A., Marini, D., & Trapani, P. (1998). Experimenting web technologies to
access an opera theatre. In T. Ottman, & I. Tomak (Eds), *Proceedings of the World
Conference on Educational Multimedia, Hypermedia and Telecommunications.*
Charlottesville, VA: AACE.

Alias. (2004). *Maya 3D animation and effects software* . Retrieved April 9, 2004, from
http://www.alias.com/eng/products-services/maya/index.shtml

Anooshian, L. J., & Young, D. (1981). Developmental changes in cognitive maps of a
familiar neighborhood. *Child Development, 52,* 341-348.

Antonietti, A., Imperio, E., Rasi, C., & Sacco, M. (2001). Virtual reality and
hypermedia in learning to use a turning lathe. *Journal of Computer Assisted
Learning, 17,* 142-155.

Apple. (2003). *QuickTime VR authoring.* Retrieved October 15, 2003, from
http://www.apple.com/quicktime/qtvr/

Arthur, E. J., Hancock, P. A., & Chrysler, S. T. (1997). The perception of spatial layout
in real and virtual worlds. *Ergonomics, 40*(1), 69-77.

Baddeley, A. (1993). *Your memory: A user's guide.* New York: Avery Publishing
Group.

Ballard, R. D. (1992). The JASON project: Hi-tech exploration promotes students'
interest in science. *T.H.E. Journal, 20*(4), 70-74.

Belingard, L., & Peruch, P. (2000). Mental representation and the spatial structure of
virtual environments. *Environment and Behaviour, 32*(3), 427-442.

Bell, G., Parisi, A., & Pesce, M. (1995). *The Virtual Reality Modelling Language,
version 1.0 specification.* Retrieved January 13, 2004, from
http://www.web3d.org/technicalinfo/specifications/VRML1.0/index.html

Bickhard, M. H., & Richie, M. D. (1983). *On the nature of representation: A case study
of James Gibson's theory of perception.* New York: Praeger.

Bitmanagement. (2004). *BS Contact VRML* . Retrieved May 1, 2004, from
http://www.bitmanagement.de/?page=/products/bs_contact_vrml.html

Blaxxun Technologies. (2004). *Blaxxun Contact 5.1.* Retrieved April 30, 2004, from
http://www.blaxxun.com/en/products/contact/index.html

Bonk, C. J., Medury, P. V., & Reynolds, T. H. (1994). Cooperative hypermedia: The
marriage of collaborative writing and mediated environments. *Computers in the
Schools, 10*(1), 79-119.

Bowman, D. A., Wineman, J., Hodges, L. F., & Allison, D. (1998). Designing animal
habitats within an immersive VE. *IEEE Computer Graphics and Applications,
18*(5), 9-13.

Brna, P. (1999). Collaborative virtual learning environments for concept learning. *International Journal of Continuing Engineering Education and Life-Long Learning, 9*(3/4), 315-327.

Broll, W., & Prinz, W. (1999). Using 3D to support awareness in virtual teams on the Web. P. de Bra, & J. Leggett, (Eds.), *Proceedings of WebNet 99: World Conference on the WWW and Internet* (pp. 137-142). Charlottesville, VA: AECT.

Brown, D. J., Cobb, S. V. G., & Eastgate, R. M. (1995). Learning in virtual environments (LIVE). In R. A. Earnshaw, J. A. Vince, & H. Jones (Eds.), *Virtual Reality Applications* (pp. 245-252). London: Academic Press.

Brown, J. S., Collins, A., & Duguid. (1989). Situated cognition and the culture of learning. *Educational Researcher, 18*(1), 32-42.

Bruce, B. C. (2001). Using Active Worlds technology to build an iUniverse of 3D collaborative learning environments. *Learning Technology Newsletter, 3*(1).

Bryson, S. (1995). Approaches to the successful design and implementation of VR applications. In R. A. Earnshaw, J. A. Vince, & H. Jones (Eds.), *Virtual reality applications*. London: Academic Press.

Bryson, S. (1996). Virtual reality in scientific visualisation. *Communications of the ACM, 39*(5), 62-71.

Bulthoff, H. H., Edelman, S. Y., & Tarr, M. J. (1995). How are three-dimensional objects represented in the brain? *Cerebral Cortex, 3*, 247-260.

Campbell, R. L. (1997). *Jean Piaget's genetic epistemology: Appreciation and critique.* Retrieved July 18, 2003, from http://hubcap. clemson.edu/~campber/piaget.html

Card, S. K., Robertson, G. G., & York, W. (1996). The Web Book and the Web Forager: An information workspace for the world-wide web. *Proceedings of CHI '96* ACM.

Carey, R., & Bell, G. (1997). *The annotated VRML 2.0 reference manual.* Reading, Massachusetts: Addison-Wesley.

Carson, G. S., Puk, R. F., & Carey, R. (1999). Developing the VRML 97 international standard. *IEEE Computer Graphics and Applications, 19*(2).

Chapman, N., & Chapman, J. (2000). *Digital Multimedia.* Chichester, England: John Wiley and Sons.

Chen, M., Mountford, J. S., & Sellen, A. (1988). A study of interactive 3-D rotation using 2-D control devices. *Computer Graphics, 22*(4), 121-129.

Christou, C. G., & Bulthoff, H. H. (1999). View dependence in scene recognition after active learning. *Memory and Cognition, 27*(6), 996-1007.

Christou, C. G., Tjan, B. S., & Bulthoff, H. H. (1999). *Viewpoint information provided by a familiar environment facilitates object identification.* (Report No. 68). Max-Planck Institute for Biological Cybernetics.

Clark, R. E. (1994). Media will never influence learning. *Educational Technology Research and Development, 42*(2), 21-29.

Clark, R. E. (1983). Reconsidering research on learning from media. *Review of Educational Research, 53*(4).

Collings, P. , Richards-Smith, A., & Walker, D. (1995). Groupware support for student project teams: Issues in implementation. In J. M. Pearce, & A. Ellis, (Eds.), *Learning with Technology: Proceedings of the twelfth annual conference of the Australasian Society for Computers in Learning in Tertiary Education* (pp. 72-80). Melbourne: University of Melbourne.

Coors, V., & Jung, V. (1998). Using VRML as an interface to the 3D data warehouse. *Proceedings of VRML 98* (pp. 121-125). ACM.

Cramer, D. (1998). *Fundamental statistics for social research*. New York: Routledge.

Creswell, J. W. (1994). *Research design: Qualitative and quantitative approaches*. Thousand Oaks, CA: Sage.

Crosier, J. K., Cobb, S. V. G., & Wilson, J. R. (2000). Experimental comparison of virtual reality with traditional teaching methods for teaching radioactivity. *Education and Information Technologies, 5*(4), 329-343.

Csikszentmihalyi, M. (1990). *Flow: The psychology of optimal experience*. New York: Harper Collins.

Cutting, J. E., & Vishton, P. M. (1995). Perceiving layout and knowing distances: The integration, relative potency and contextual use of different information about depth. In W. Epstein, & S. Rogers (Eds.), *Perception of space and motion*. San Diego: Academic Press.

Cybertown. (2004). *Cybertown: Civilization for the virtual age*. Retrieved September 4, 2004, from http://www.cybertown.com

Dalgarno, B., & Scott, J. (2000). Motion control in virtual environments: A comparative study. In V.Paelke , & S.Volbracht, (Eds.), *User guidance in virtual environments, workshop on guiding users through interactive experiences: Usability centred design and evaluation of virtual 3D environments* Paderborn, Germany: Shaker Verlag.

Dalgarno, B. (1996). Constructivist computer assisted learning: Theory and techniques. In A. Christie, P. James, & B. Vaughan , (Eds.), *Making new connections, Proceedings of the thirteenth annual conference of the Australasian Society for Computers in Learning in Tertiary Education* (pp. 143-154). Adelaide: Faculty of Health and Biomedical Sciences University of South Australia.

Dalgarno, B. (2001). Interpretations of constructivism and consequences for computer assisted learning. *British Journal of Educational Technology, 32*(2), 183-194.

Dalgarno, B., & Atkinson, J. (1999). Cooperative project work with distance education students using computer-mediated communication. In J. Winn, (Ed.), *Responding to Diversity, Proceedings of the sixteenth annual conference of the Australasian Society for Computers in Learning in Tertiary Education* Queensland: Teaching an Learning Support Services Queensland University of Technology.

Darken, R. P. , & Sibert, J. L. (1996). Navigating large virtual spaces. *International Journal of Human-Computer Interaction, 8*(1), 49-71.

Dede, C. (1995). The evolution of constructivist learning environments: Immersion in distributed virtual worlds. *Educational Technology, 35*(5), 46-52.

Dede, C., Salzman, M., Loftin, R. B., & Ash, K, (1997). Using virtual reality technology to convey abstract scientific concepts. *Learning the sciences of the 21st century: Research, design, and implementing advanced technology learning environments.* Hillsdale: Lawrence Erlbaum.

Dias, J. M. S., Galli, R., Almeida, A. C., Belo, C. A. C., & Rebordao, J. M. (1997). mWorld: A multiuser 3D virtual environment. *IEEE Computer Graphics and Applications, 17*(2), 55-65.

Dickinson, R. R., & Jern, M. (1995). A unified approach to interface design for data visualization using desktop and immersion virtual environments. In R. A. Earnshaw, J. Vince, & H. Jones (Eds), *Virtual Reality Applications* (pp. 307-320). London: Academic Press.

Discreet Software. (2004). *3ds max 6.* Retrieved April 9, 2004, from http://www.discreet.com/3dsmax/

Durlach, N., Allan, G., Darken, R., Garnett, R. L., Loomis, J., Templeman, J. et al. (2000). Virtual environments and the enhancement of spatial behaviour: Toward a comprehensive research agenda. *Presence: Teleoperators and Virtual Environments, 9*(6), 593-615.

Earnshaw, R. A., Vince, J. A., & Jones, H. (1995). *Virtual Reality Applications.* London: Academic Press.

Eidos Interactive. (2004). *Lara Croft tomb raider: The angel of darkness.* Retrieved April 9, 2004, from http://www.eidosinteractive.co.uk/gss/trangel/home.html

Ellis, S. R. (1991). Nature and origins of virtual environments: a bibliographic essay. *Computing Systems in Engineering, 2*(4), 321-347.

Ellis, S. R. (1993). Seeing. In S. R. Ellis, M. K. Kaiser, & A. J. Grunwald (Eds), *Pictorial communication in virtual and real environments* (pp. 419-424). London, UK: Taylor and Francis.

Epic Games. (2004). *Unreal Tournament.* Retrieved September 4, 2004, from http://www.unrealtournament.com/

Ericson, K. A., & Simon, H. (1993). *Protocol analysis: verbal reports as data.* Cambridge, MA: MIT Press.

Feijs, L., & De Jong, R. (1998). 3D visualisation of software architectures. *Communications of the ACM, 41*(12), 73-78.

Fellner, D., & Hopp, A. (1999). VR-LAB: a distributed multi-user environment for educational purposes and presentations. *Proceedings of the fourth symposium on the Virtual reality modeling language* Association of Computing Machinery.

Ferrington, G., & Loge, K. (1992). Virtual Reality: A new learning environment. *The Computing Teacher, 19*(7), 16-19.

Fisher, K. M. (1992). SemNet: A tool for personal knowledge construction. In P. A.M. Kommers, D.H. Jonassen, & J.T. Mayers (Eds.), *Cognitive Tools for Learning .* Berlin: Springer Verlag.

Fisher, S. S. (1990). Virtual interface environments. In B. Laurel (Ed), *The Art of Human Computer Interface Design* (pp. 423-438). Reading, Massachusetts: Addison-Wesley.

Fisher, S. S., Fraser, G., & Kim, A. J. (1998). Real-time interactive graphics in computer gaming. *Computer Graphics, 32*(2), 15-19.

Frohlich, B., & Plate, J. (2000). The cubic mouse: A new device for three-dimensional input. In T. Turner, & G. Szwillus, (Eds.), *Proceedings of CHI 2000, Annual Conference of ACM SIGCHI* ACM Press.

Gabrielli, S., Rogers, Y., & Scaife, M. (2000). Young children's spatial representations developed through exploration of a desktop virtual reality scene. *Education and Information Technologies, 5*(4), 251-262.

Gaines, B. R., & Shaw, M. L. G. (1995). *Concept maps as hypermedia components.* Retrieved April 30, 2004, from http://ksi.cpsc.ucalgary.ca/articles/ConceptMaps/

GarageGames. (2004). *GarageGames home of independent games and game makers: Game engines.* Retrieved April 12, 2004, from http://www.garagegames.com/index.php?sec=mg&mod=resource&page=category&qid=80

Gibson, J. J. (1979). *The ecological approach to visual perception.* London: Houghton Mifflin.

Gillner, S., & Mallot, H. A. (1998). Navigation and acquisition of spatial knowledge in a virtual maze. *Journal of Cognitive Neuroscience, 10*(4), 445-463.

Grantham, C. (1993). Visualization of information flows: virtual reality as an organizational modeling technique. In A. Wexelblat (Ed), *Virtual reality applications and explorations* . Cambridge, MA: Academic Press.

Gravetter, F. J., & Wallnau, L. B. (2000). *Statistics for the Bahavioral Sciences.* Belmont, CA: Wadsworth, Thomson Learning.

Greeno, J. G. (1994). Gibson's affordances. *Psychological Review, 101*(2), 336-342 .

Gruber, H. E., & Voneche, J. J. (1977). *The essential piaget.* London: Routledge and Kegan Paul.

Grudin, J. (1990). Groupware and cooperative work: Problems and prospects. In B. Laurel (Ed), *The Art of Human Computer Interface Design* (pp. 171-185). Reading, Massachusetts: Addison-Wesley.

Hand, C. (1997). A survey of 3D interaction techniques. *Computer Graphics Forum, 16*(5), 269-281.

Harasim, L., Hiltz, S. R., Teles, L., & Turoff, M. (1995). *Learning networks a field guide to teaching and learning online.* Cambridge, Massachusetts: MIT Press.

Harper, B., Hedberg, J., & Brown, C. (1995). Investigating Lake Iluka [computer software]. Wollongong, NSW: Interactive Multimedia Unit University of Wollongong.

Harper, B., & Hedberg, J. (1997). Creating motivating interactive learning environments: a constructivist view. In R. Kevill, R. Oliver, & R. Phillips, (Eds.), *What works and why, proceedings of the 14th annual conference of the Australasian Society for Computers in Learning in Tertiary Education* Perth: Curtin University of Technology.

Hart, R. A., & Moore, G. T. (1974). The development of spatial cognition: A review. In R. M. Downs, & D. Stea (Eds), *Image and environment* (pp. 246-288). London: Edward Arnold.

Hedberg, J., & Alexander, S. (1994). Virtual reality in education: Defining researchable issues. *Educational Media International, 31*(4).

Hendrix, C., & Barfield, W. (1996). Presence within virtual environments as a function of visual display parameters. *Presence, 5*(3), 274-289.

Henry, D., & Furness, T. (1993). Spatial perception in virtual environments: Evaluating an architectural application. *Proceedings of the IEEE virtual reality annual symposium.* Piscataway, NJ.

Hopper, D. G. (2000). Display technology overview. *Human Systems IAC Gateway, XI*(4), 1-8.

Hsiung, P. -K., & Dunn, R. H. P. (1989). Visualizing relativistic effects in spacetime. *Proceedings of the 1989 ACM/IEEE conference on Supercomputing* Reno, Nevada: ACM.

Hunt, E., & Waller, D. (1999). *Orientation and wayfinding: a review (ONR technical report N00014-96-0380).* Arlington, VA: Office of Naval Research.

Id Software. (2004). *Quake III Gold.* Retrieved April 9, 2004, from http://www.idsoftware.com/games/quake/quake3-gold/

Inspiration Software. (1999). *Inspiration visual thinking and learning software.* http://www.inspiration.com/

Jonassen, D. H. (1992a). What are cognitive tools?. In P. A. M. Kommers, D. H. Jonassen, & J. T. Mayes (Eds.), *Cognitive tools for learning* . Berlin: Springer-Verlag.

Jonassen, D. H. (1992b). Cognitive flexibility theory and its implications for designing CBI. In S. Dijkstra, H.P. M.Krammer, & J.G. van Merrienboer (Eds.), *Instructional models in computer-based learning environments* (pp. 385-405). Berlin: Springer-Verlag.

Jonassen, D. H. (1991). Objectivism versus constructivism: Do we need a new philosophical paradigm? *Educational Technology Research and Development, 39*(3), 5-14.

Jonassen, D. H., Campbell, J. P. , & Davidson, M. E. (1994). Learning with media: restructuring the debate. *Educational Technology Research and Development, 42*(2), 31-39.

Kaufmann, H., Schmalstieg, D., & Wagner, M. (2000). Construct3D: A virtual reality application for mathematics and geometry education. *Education and Information Technologies, 5*(4), 263-276.

Kelty, L., Beckett, P. , & Zalcman, L. (1999). Desktop simulation . *Advancing simulation technology and training, proceedings of SimTecT99, The simulation technology and training conference* . Simulation Industry Association of Australia.

Kennedy, R. S., Lane, N. E., Berbaum, K. S., & Lilienthal, M. G. (1993). Simulator sickness questionnaire: An enhanced method for quantifying simulator sickness. *The International Journal of Aviation Psychology, 3*(3), 203-220.

Kerlinger, F. N., & Lee, H. B. (2000). *Foundations of behavioural research*. South Melbourne: Thomson Learning.

Kitchin, R. M. (1994). Cognitive maps: What are they and why study them? *Journal of Environmental Psychology, 14*, 1-19.

Kourtzi, Z., & Nakayama, K. (2002). Distinct mechanisms for the representation of moving and static objects. *Visual Cognition, 9*, 248-264.

Kozak, J. J., Hancock, P. A., Arthur, E. J., & Chrysler, S. T. (1993). Transfer of training from virtual reality. *Ergonomics, 36*(7), 777-784.

Kozlowski, L. T., & Bryant, K. J. (1977). Sense of direction, spatial orientation and cognitive maps. *Journal of Experimental Psychology: Human Perception and Performance, 3*(4), 590-598.

Kozma, R. B. (1994). Will media influence learning? Reframing the debate. *Educational Technology Research and Development, 42*(2), 7-19.

Krueger, M. W. (1993). An easy entry artificial reality. In A. Wexelblat (Ed.), *Virtual reality applications and explorations* (pp. 147-161). Cambridge, MA: Academic Press.

Lapointe, J.F., & Robert, J.M. (2000). Using VR for efficient training of forestry machine operators. *Education and Information Technologies, 5*(4), 237-250.

Lawton, C. A., Charleston, S. I., & Zieles, A. S. (1996). Individual and gender-related differences in indoor wayfinding. *Environment and Behavior, 28*(2), 204-219.

Leach, G., Al-Qaimari, G., Grieve, M., Jinks, N., & McKay, C. (1997). Elements of a three-dimensional graphical user interface. In S. Howard, J. Hammond, & G. Lindgaard, (Eds.), *Human-Computer Interaction: Proceedings of INTERACT '97* Sydney, Australia: Chapman and Hall.

Leahey, T. H., & Harris, R. J. (1993). *Learning and Cognition*. Englewood Cliffs, New Jersey: Prentice-Hall.

Lefcowitz, E. (2003). *Welcome to the Retrofuture*. Retrieved October 15, 2003, from http://www.retrofuture.com/

Levine, M., Marchon, I., & Hanley, G. (1984). The placement and misplacement of you-are-here maps. *Environment and Behaviour, 16*(2), 139-157.

Lindberg, E., & Garling, T. (1983). Acquisition of different types of location information in cognitive maps: Automatic or effortful processing? *Pschological Research, 45*, 19-38.

Lohr, L., Ross, S., & Morrison, G. R. (1995). Using a hypertext environment for teaching process writing: An evaluation study of three student groups. *Educational Technology Research and Development, 43*(2), 33-51.

Mackinlay, J. D., Card, S. K., & Robertson, G. G. (1990). Rapid controlled movement through a virtual 3D workspace. *Computer Graphics, 24*(4), 171-176.

Macpherson, C., & Keppell, M. (1998). Virtual reality: What is the state of play in education? *Australian Journal of Educational Technology, 14*(1), 60-74.

Massie, T. H., & Salisbury, J. K. (1994). The PHANTOM haptic interface: A device for probing virtual objects. *Proceedings of the ASME winter annual meeting, symposium on haptic interfaces for virtual environment and teleoperator systems.* Chicago, IL, Nov 1994.

Matthews, M. H. (1987). Sex differences in spatial competence: the ability of young children to map 'primed' unfamiliar environments. *Educational Psychology, 7*(2), 77-90.

McAtamney , H. (2000). *National gallery of Ireland virtual environment.* Retrieved April 9, 2004, from http://www.dmc.dit.ie/guests/eirenet/eirenet/pages/vrart.htm

McGee, M. G. (1979). Human spatial abilities: Psychometric studies and environmental, genetic, hormonal and neurological influences. *Psychological Bulletin, 86*(5), 889-917.

McGreevy, M. W. (1993). Virtual reality and planetary exploration. In A. Wexelblat (Ed), *Virtual reality applications and explorations* . Cambridge, MA: Academic Press Professional.

McInerney, D., & McInerney, V. (1994). *Educational psychology constructing learning.* Sydney: Prentice Hall.

McKnight, C., Dillon, A., & Richardson, J. (1991). *Hypertext in context.* Cambridge: Cambridge University Press.

McLellan, H. (1996). Virtual realities. In D. H. Jonassen (Ed), *Handbook of research for educational communications and technology* (pp. 457-490). New York: Simon and Schuster.

Mertens, D. M. (1998). *Research methods in education and psychology: integrating diversity with quantitative and qualitative approaches.* Thousand Oaks, CA: Sage Publications.

Microsoft. (2004). *Microsoft DirectX.* Retrieved April 9, 2004, from http://www.microsoft.com/windows/directx

Miles, G. E., & Howes, A. (1999). Using 3D for electronic commerce on the web: A psychological perspective. In P. De Bra, & J. J. Leggett, (Eds.), *Proceedings of Web-Net 1999: World conference on the WWW and Internet* (pp. 745-750). Charlottesville, VA: Association for the Advancement of Computing in Education (AACE).

Mohageg, M., Myers, R., Marrin, C., Kent, J., Mott, D., & Isaacs, P. (1996). A user interface for accessing 3D content on the World Wide Web. In R. Bilger, S. Guest, & M. J. Tauber, (Eds.), *Proceedings of CHI'96* Vancouver, British Columbia: Association for Computing Machinery.

Moloney, J. (2001). 3D game software and architectural education . In G. Kennedy, M. Keppell, C. McNaught, & T. Petrovic, (Eds.), *Meeting at the crossroads: Short paper proceedings of the 18th annual conference of the Australasian Society for Computers in Learning in Tertiary Education* (pp. 121-124). Melbourne, Australia: University of Melbourne.

Moore, G. T., & Golledge, R. G. (1976). Environmental knowing: Concepts and theories. In G. T. Moore, & R. G. Golledge (Eds), *Environmental Knowing* (pp. 3-24). Stroudsberg, PA: Dowden, Hutchinson, Ross.

Moore, P. (1995). Learning and teaching in virtual worlds: Implications of virtual reality for education. *Australian Journal of Educational Technology, 11*(2), 91-102.

Moore, W. E., & Curry, B. (1998). The application of VRML to cave preservation. *VSMM98: Future vision - application realities for the virtual age* (pp. 606-611). Gifu, Japan: IOS Press.

Moshman, D. (1982). Exogenous, endogenous and dialectical constructivism. *Developmental Review, 2*, 371-384.

Neider, J., Davis, T., & Woo, M. (1993). *OpenGL programming guide: The official guide to learning OpenGL, release 1.* Reading, Massachusetts: Addison-Wesley.

Norris, B. E., Rashid, D. Z., & Wong, B. L. W. (1999). Wayfinding/navigation within a QTVR virtual environment: Preliminary results. In A. Sasse, & C. Johnson, (Eds.), *Human Computer Interaction - Proceedings of INTERACT'99* IOS Press, IFIP TC.14.

O'Malley, C. (1995). *Computer supported collaborative learning.* Berlin: Springer-Verlag.

Orey, M. A., & Nelson, W. A. (1993). Development principles for intelligent tutoring systems: Integrating cognitive theory into the development of computer-based instruction. *Educational Technology Research and Development, 41*(1), 59-72.

Osberg, K. (1997). *Spatial cognition in the virtual environment.* (Report No. R-97-18). Seattle, Washington: Human Interface Technology Lab, University of Washington.

Papert, S. (1993). *Mindstorms, children, computers and powerful ideas.* NewYork: Harvester and Wheatsheaf.

Parallel Graphics. (2004). *Cortona VRML client.* Retrieved May 1, 2004, from http://www.parallelgraphics.com/products/cortona/

Park, I., & Hannafin, M. J. (1993). Empirically-based guidelines for the design of interactive multimedia. *Educational Technology Research and Development, 39*(3), 63-85.

Patrick, E., Cosgrove, D., Slavkovic, A., Rode, J. A., Verratti, T., & Chiselko, G. (2000). Using a large projection screen as an alternative to head-mounted displays for virtual environments. In T. Turner, G. Szwillus, M. Czerwinski, & F. Paterno, (Eds.), *CHI 2000 Conference Proceedings.* New York: ACM Press.

Perkins, D. N. (1991). Technology meets constructivism: Do they make a marriage? *Educational Technology, 31*(5), 18-23.

Peruch, P. , Vercher, J. L., & Gauthier, G. M. (1995). Acquisition of spatial knowledge through visual exploration of simulated environments. *Ecological Psychology, 7*, 1-20.

Phillips, D. C. (1995). The good, the bad, and the ugly: The many faces of constructivism. *Educational Researcher, 24*(7), 5-12.

Piaget, J. (1968). *Genetic epistemology.* New York: Columbia University Press.

Piaget, J. (1969). *The mechanisms of perception.* London: Routledge and Kegan Paul.

Piaget, J. (1973). *To understand is to invent: The future of education.* New York: Grossman Publishers.

Psotka, J. (1995). Immersive training systems: Virtual reality and education and training. *Instructional Science, 23,* 405-431.

Rafey, R. A., Gibbs, S., Hoch, M., Le Van Gong, H., & Wang, S. (2001). Enabling custom enhancements in digital sports broadcasts. In *Proceedings of* Web 3D '2001 Paderborn, Germany: Association for Computing Machinery.

Ramires-Fernandes, A., Pires, H., & Rodrigues, R. (1998). Building virtual interactive 3D galleries. *VSMM98: Future vision - application realities for the virtual age* (pp. 60-65). Gifu, Japan: IOS Press.

Reeves, T. C. (1995). *Questioning the questions of instructional technology research, invited Peter Dean lecture presented for the division of learning and performance environments (DLPE) at the 1995 national convention of the Association for Educational Communications and Technology (AECT), Anaheim, CA, USA. February 8-12, 1995.* Retrieved December 17, 2003, from http://www.gsu.edu/~wwwitr/docs/dean/index.html

Reinhart, B. (1999). *Mod authoring for Unreal Tournament.* Retrieved April 12, 2004, from http://unreal.epicgames.com/UTMods.html

Richardson, A. E., Montello, D. R., & Hegarty, M. (1999). Spatial knowledge acquisition from maps and from navigation in real and virtual environments. *Memory and Cognition, 27*(4), 741-750.

Rieber, L. P. (1992). Computer-based microworlds: A bridge between constructivism and direct instruction. *Educational Technology Research and Development, 40*(1), 93-106.

Rieber, L. P. (1994). *Computers, graphics and learning.* Debuque, I.A: Brown and Benchmark.

Riecke, B. E., van Veen, H. A. H. C., & Bulthoff, H. H. (2002). Visual homing is possible without landmarks: a path integration study in virtual reality. *Presence, 11*(5), 443-473.

Riva, G. (1999). From technology to communication: Psycho-social issues in developing virtual environments. *Journal of Visual Languages and Computing, 10.*

Robertson, G., van Dantzich, M., Robbins, D., Czerwinski, M., Hinckley, K., Risden, K. et al. (2000). The task gallery: A 3D window manager. In T. Turner, G. Szwillus, M. Czerwinski, & F. Paterno (Eds), *Proceedings of CHI 2000* (pp. 494-501). ACM.

Robertson, G. G., Card, S. K., & Mackinlay, J. D. (1993). Nonimmersive virtual reality. *Computer, 26*(2), 81-83.

Rollings, A., & Adams, E. (2003). *Andrew Rollings and Ernest Adams on game design.* Indianapolis: New Riders.

Romano, D. M., & Brna, P. (2000). ACTIVE World: manipulating time and point of view to promote a sense of presence in a collaborative virtual environment for training in emergency situations. In *Proceedings of the 3rd international workshop on presence.* Delft: Delft University of Technology.

Ross, S. M., & Morrison, G. R. (1989). In search of a happy medium in instructional technology research: issues concerning external validity, media replication, and learner control. *Educational Technology Research and Development, 37*(1), 1042-1629.

Rossano, M. J., Warren, D. H., & Kenan, A. (1995). Orientation specificity: How general is it? *American Journal of Psychology, 108*(3), 359-380.

Rouse, R. (1998). Do computer games need to be 3D? *Computer Graphics, 32*(2), 64-66.

Ruddle, R. A., Payne, S. J., & Jones, D. M. (1997). Navigating buildings in "desk-top" virtual environments: Experimental investigations using extended navigational experience. *Journal of Experimental Psychology: Applied, 3*(2), 143-159.

Ruddle, R. A., Payne, S. J., & Jones, D. M. (1999). Navigating large-scale virtual environments: What differences occur between helmet-mounted and desk-top displays. *Presence, 8*(2), 157-168.

Ruddle, R. A., Savage, J. C. D., & Jones, D. M. (2002). Symmetric and asymmetric action integration during cooperative object manipulation in virtual environments. *ACM Transactions on Human Computer Interaction, 9*(4), 285-308.

Ruzic, F. (1999). The future of learning in virtual reality environments. In M. Selinger, & J. Pearson (Eds), *Telematics in Education: Trends and Issues.* Amsterdam: Pergamon.

Ryan, M., & Hall, L. (2001). *eLearning, teaching and training: A first look at principles, issues and implications.* Charlottesville, VA: Association for the Advancement of Computing in Education.

Saar, K. (1999). VIRTUS: A collaborative multi-user platform. In *Proceedings of VRML'97, the fourth symposium on the Virtual Reality Modelling Language* Paderborn, Germany: Association for Computing Machinery.

Salomon, G. (1991). Transcending the qualitative-quantitative debate: The analytic and systemic approaches to educational research. *Educational Researcher, 20*(6), 10-18.

Salomon, G. (1994). *Interaction of media, cognition and learning.* Hillsdale, New Jersey: Lawrence Erlbaum Associates.

Salzman, M. C., Dede, C., Loftin, B. R., & Chen, J. (1999). A model for understanding how virtual reality aids complex conceptual learning. *Presence: Teleoperators and Virtual Environments, 8*(3), 293-316.

Sanchez, A., Barreiro, J. M., & Maojo, V. (2000). Design of virtual reality systems for education: a cognitive approach. *Education and Information Technologies, 5*(4), 345-362.

Scardamalia, M., & Bereiter, C. (1996). Student communities for the advancement of knowledge. *Communications of the ACM, 39*(4), 36-37.

Schmitt, G. N. (1993). Virtual reality in architecture. In N. M. Thalmann, & D. Thalmann (Eds.), *Virtual Worlds and Multimedia .* Chichester, England: John Wiley and Sons.

Schultz, D. P. , & Schultz, S. E. (1992). *A history of modern psychology.* Fort Worth: Harcourt Brace Jovanovich.

Simpson, J. (2002). *Game engine anatomy 101*. Retrieved April 12, 2004, from http://www.extremetech.com/article2/0,1558,594,00.asp

Slater, M., Usoh, M., & Steed, A. (1995). Taking steps: The influence of a walking technique on presence in virtual reality. *ACM Transactions on Computer-Human Interaction, 2*(3), 201-219.

Slavin, R. E. (1994). *Educational psychology, theory and practice*. Boston: Allyn and Bacon.

Spiro, R. J., Feltovich, P. J., Jacobson, M. J., & Coulson, R. L. (1991). Cognitive flexibility, constructivism and hypertext: Random access instruction for advanced knowledge acquisition in ill-structured domains. *Educational Technology, 31*(5), 24-33.

Stanney, K., Salvendry, G., Deisinger, J., DiZio, P. , Ellis, S., Ellison, J. et al. (1998). After-effects and sense of presence in virtual environments: Formulation of research and development agenda. *International Journal of Human Computer Interaction, 10*(2), 135-187.

Stella. (1996). Stella (Version 3) [computer software]. Hanover, NH: High Performance Systems.

Stevens, S. M. (1989). Intelligent interactive video simulation of a code inspection. *Communications of the ACM, 32*(7), 832-842.

Stevenson, D., Smith, K., Veldkamp, P., McLaughlin, J., O'Hagan, R., Smith, D. et al. (1997). Virtual environments for industrial applications. In S. Howard, J. Hammond, & G. Lindgaard (Eds.), *Human-Computer Interaction: Proceedings of INTERACT '97*. Chapman and Hall: IFIP.

Stoffregen, T. A. (2000). Affordances and events. *Ecological Psychology, 12*(1), 1-28.

Sweller, J., van Merrienboer, J. J. G., & Paas G. W. C. (1998). Cognitive architecture and instructional design. *Educational Psychology Review, 10*(3), 251-296 .

Tarr, M. J., & Pinker, S. (1989). Mental rotation and orientation-dependence in shape recognition. *Cognitive Psychology, 21*, 233-282.

Thorndyke, P. W., & Golden, S. E. (1983). Spatial learning and reasoning skill. In H. L. Pick, & L. P. Acredolo (Eds.), *Spatial orientation: Theory, research and application*. New York: Plenum.

Thorndyke, P. W., & Hayes-Roth, B. (1982). Differences in spatial knowledge acquired from maps and from navigation. *Cognitive Psychology, 14*, 560-589.

Thurman, R. A. (1993). Instructional simulation from a cognitive psychology viewpoint. *Educational Technology Research and Development, 41*(4), 75-89.

Thurman, R. A., & Mattoon, J. S. (1994). Virtual reality: Towards fundamental improvements in simulation-based training. *Educational Technology, 34*(October), 56-64.

Vince, J. (1995). *Virtual Reality Systems*. Wokingham, UK: ACM Press.

Von Glasserfeld, E. (1984). An introduction to radical constructivism. In P.W. Watzlawick (Ed), *The Invented Reality* (pp. 17-40). New York: W. Norton and Company.

Vygotsky, L. S. (1978). *Mind in society, the development of higher psychological processes*. Cambridge, Massachusetts: Harvard University Press.

Waller, D., Hunt, E., & Knapp, D. (1998). The transfer of spatial knowledge in virtual environment training. *Presence, 7*(2), 126-139.

Wallis, G. (2002). The role of object motion in forging long-term representations of objects. *Visual Cognition, 9*(1/2), 233-247.

Wallis, G., & Bulthoff, H. H. (1999). Learning to recognise objects. *Trends in Cognitive Sciences, 3*, 22-31.

Wang, M. (2003). *Morten's JavaScript Tree Menu*. Retrieved April 12, 2004, from http://www.treemenu.com/

Wann, J., & Mon-Williams, M. (1996). What does virtual reality NEED?: human factors issues in the design of three-dimensional computer environments. *International Journal of Human-Computer Studies, 44*, 829-847.

Ware, C. (1995). Dynamic stereo displays. In *Proceedings of CHI 1995, Conference on Human Factors in Computing Systems* Denver, Colorado: Association for Computing Machinery.

Ware, C., & Osborne, S. (1990). Exploration and virtual camera control in virtual three dimensional environments. In *Proceedings of the 1990 symposium on interactive 3D graphics* Snowbird, Utah: Association for Computing Machinery.

Web3D Consortium. (1997). *The Virtual Reality Modelling Language International Standard ISO/IEC 14772-1:1997*. Retrieved January 13, 2004, from http://www.web3d.org/technicalinfo/specifications/ISO_IEC_14772-All/index.html

Whitelock, D., Brna, P., & Holland, S. (1996). What is the value of virtual reality for conceptual learning? Towards a theoretical framework. In *Proceedings of EuroAIED, European Conference on AI in Education* . Lisbon, Portugal.

Whitelock, D., Romano, D., Jelfs, A., & Brna, P. (2000). Perfect presence: What does this mean for the design of virtual learning environments. *Education and Information Technologies, 5*(4), 277-289.

Wild, M., & Kirkpatrick, D. (1996). Multimedia as cognitive tools: Students working with a performance support system. C. McBeath, & R. Atkinson, (Eds.), *The Learning Superhighway, New World? New Worries? Proceedings of the 3rd International Interactive Multimedia Symposium* (pp. 412-417). Perth: Promaco Conventions.

Williamson, K., Burstein, F., & McKemmish, S. (2002). The two major traditions of research. In K. Williamson (Ed), *Research methods for students, academics and professionals: Information management and systems* (2nd ed.,). Wagga Wagga, Australia: Centre for Information Studies.

Wilson, J. R. (1997). Virtual environments and ergonomics: needs and opportunities. *Ergonomics, 40*(10), 1057-1077.

Wilson, P. N., Foreman, N., & Tlauka, M. (1997). Transfer of spatial information from a virtual to a real environment. *Human Factors, 39*(4), 526-531.

Winn, W. (1993). *A conceptual basis for educational applications of virtual reality.* (Report No. R-93-9). Seattle, Washington: Human Interface Technology Lab, University of Washington.

Winn, W. (1997). *The impact of three-dimensional immersive virtual environments on modern pedagogy.* (Report No. R-97-15). Seattle, Washington: Human Interface Technology Lab, University of Washington.

Winn, W. (2002). What can students learn in artificial environments that they cannot learn in class? *First International Symposium, Open Education Faculty, Anadolu University, Turkey* .

Winn, W., & Jackson, R. (1999). Fourteen propositions about educational uses of virtual reality. *Educational Technology, 39*(4), 5-14.

Witmer, B. G., Bailey, J. H., & Knerr, B. W. (1996). Virtual spaces and real world places: transfer of route knowledge. *International Journal of Human-Computer Studies, 45*, 413-428.

Witmer, B. G., & Kline, P. B. (1998). Judging perceived and traversed distance in virtual environments. *Presence, 7*(2), 144-167.

Witmer, B. G., & Singer, M. J. (1998). Measuring presence in virtual environments: A presence questionnaire. *Presence, 7* (3), 225-240.

Wright, W. (1989). SimCity [computer software]. Moraga, California: Maxis.

Xiao, D., & Hubbold, R. (1998). Navigation guided by artificial force fields. *Proceedings of CHI 98* (pp. 179-186).

Zeltzer, D. (1992). Autonomy, interaction and presence. *Presence: Teleoperators and Virtual Environments, 1*(1), 127-132.

Zhai, S., Kandogan, E., Smith, B. A., & Selker, T. (1999). In search of the 'magic carpet': Design and experimentation of a bimanual 3D navigation interface. *Journal of Visual Languages and Computing, 10*, 3-17.

Appendix A. Laboratory Structures and Apparatus Included in Virtual Laboratory

Buildings and external features

Chemistry laboratory and entrance ramp
Pharmacology laboratory
Computer centre
Lecture theatre
Library
Miscellaneous buildings
Trees
Lampposts
Whiteboard
Paths
Steps
Hills
Communications tower

Furniture

Student lab benches, each containing glassware lockers
Wooden drawers
Laminex cupboards and drawers
Metal drawers
Shelves
Fume cupboards
Sinks
Service hatch
Miscellaneous benches and tables
Air-conditioning ducts

Apparatus

Top loading balance
Analytical balance
Beakers, 30ml, 50ml, 100ml, 250ml
Bunsen burner
Burette
Burette funnel
Burette stand
Clamp
Clay triangle
Conductivity meter
Crucible (evaporating dish)
Conical Flasks, 100ml, 250ml
Eye droppers

Funnel
Gauze
Glass stirrer
Graduated cylinders, 50ml, 250ml
5ml Pipette
Pasteur Pipette
Pipette filler
Reagent bottle
Rubber stopper
Spatula
Test tube
Test tube rack
Tongs
Tripod

Other equipment

Eye wash
Fire blanket
Fire extinguisher
Waste bin
Glass bin
Taps
Gas taps
Power points
Paper towel holder
Clocks
Safety glasses
Incubator
Oven
Atomic Absorption Spectrometer
Refrigerator

Appendix B. Pilot Study Training Tasks

Chemistry Lab Familiarisation
3D Environment Learning Worksheet

Screen Layout

The screen is organised as follows

menus	3D environment
	information

Using the view menus/hide menus options you can enlarge the 3D environment and hide the menus and vice versa

Moving around the lab

You can move around the lab in any of the following ways:

- Using the Viewpoint menu in the left frame;

- Using the Locate options in the Objects or Apparatus menu in the left frame;

- By clicking and dragging your mouse within the environment;

- By using the arrow keys (you may have to click within the environment with your mouse first)

You can switch between Walk, Pan and Jump movement modes using the options at the lower left of the screen.

- Walk mode (the default) allows you to walk at ground level.

- Pan mode allows you to look around without moving.

- Jump mode allows you to click on an object and jump up close to it.

Actions within the laboratory

If your mouse pointer turns into a finger you have found an interactive object. There are two types of interactive objects.

The first type is doors and drawers, which will open or shut when clicked.

The second type is items of apparatus, which allow the following actions:

- If you click on the item, information will be shown in the text area of the screen, and a list of actions for that item will be shown in the menu to the left of the screen

- If you hold the mouse down on the item and drag it around you can drag the object around.

- If you double-click on the item you can pick it up. It will then move around the lab with you, sitting in an area to the bottom left of your view. When you double-click on it again it will be put down, provided that there is a defined position for the object in view at the time.

Practice Tasks

1. Hide menus and try moving around the environment. Try using the mouse and then try using the arrow keys.

2. Show menus and use the Viewpoint menu to move around.

3. Locate the fire blanket using the Objects menu and try dragging it and picking it up.

4. Try carrying the fire blanket to the end of the hall and dropping it.

Appendix C. Pilot Study Virtual Laboratory Task Worksheet

Chemistry Lab Familiarisation
Virtual Lab Task Worksheet

Name_____

As you complete the listed tasks, place a tick to the left of each.

Using the *Lab Procedures* menu at the left of the environment, find out what to wear in the laboratory and write a short statement about each of the following:

Footwear

_____

Protective clothing

_____

Eyewear

_____

First *hide menus* and then complete the following tasks using either the arrow keys or your mouse to control your movement. If you get stuck, view menus and use the Viewpoints menu to go to the desired location, then hide the menus again.

Move to the ramp at the right hand end of the walkway in front of the lab

Walk along the ramp until you get to a door into the lab

Open the door by clicking on it

Walk into the lab

Walk around the lab and into and out of the rooms at either end of the lab.

***View menus* again, and use the *Viewpoints* menu to carry out the following tasks:**

Go to your bench

Go to your locker, open it and look at the contents inside

Go to the service hatch

Go to the preparation room

Go to the equipment room

Go to the fume cupboards (fume hoods)

Locate each of the following items of apparatus, look up close at it using the *Jump* movement mode and experiment with dragging it around, picking it up and putting it down again. Read the information about each.

Hints: A quick way to locate an item of apparatus is to use the *Locate* options in the *Apparatus* menu in the left frame. To pick up an object, double-click on it. To put it down, move so that you can see the location where you want to put it down and then double-click on it again.

5ml Pipette

Reagent bottle

Eye wash

Locate each of the following items and look up close at it. Read the information about each.

Fire extinguisher

Fire blanket

Glass bin

Waste bin

Explore your locker

Explore the contents of your locker. Look up close at each item and read the information about it.

Use the *Lab Procedures* menu to investigate the following. Write down the key points about each.

Lab behaviour

_____

_____

Fire procedures

_____

_____

Chemical spill procedures

_____

_____

Explore the burette

Locate the burette, assemble and disassemble it and explore its components. Read the procedures for using the burette and write down the key points.

_____

_____

Explore the pipette

Locate the pipette and explore its components. Read the procedures for using the pipette and write down the key points.

_____

_____

Explore the balances

Locate the two balances (top loading balance and analytic balance) and look up close at each. Read the procedure for using the balances and write down the key points.

_____

_____

Assemble a Bunsen burner, tripod and gauze

Locate the Bunsen burner, tripod and gauze. Carry each to your bench.

Hint: you will need to use *Pan* mode to look inside the gauze drawer in order to pickup the gauze.

Place some glassware on your bench

Try to place some items of glassware from your locker onto your bench.

Appendix D. Pilot Study Laboratory Manual Task Worksheet

Chemistry Lab Familiarisation
Lab Manual Worksheet

Please read the lab manual extract before your first CHM 104 practical session on Tuesday 19th February at 2.00pm. As you do so, complete this worksheet. You should aim to spend 30 minutes on this. Spend longer if you need to. Please record the time you commenced and finished.

Name...

Date and time commenced ....

Time finished...

Write one statement about the safety issues associated with each of the following:

Chemical spills on eyes or skin

Supervision in the laboratory

Footwear

Lab coats

Safety glasses

Disposal of broken glass

Please turn over

Write one statement about each of the following items of apparatus and equipment:

Types of balances

Graduated cylinder

Pipette

Burette

Appendix E. Pilot Study Test

Chemistry Lab Familiarisation Test

Name_____

Answer the following multiple-choice questions, by circling a, b, c, d, or e.

1. Which of the following statements best describes the rules about footwear in the lab:

   a. Everybody must wear footwear that encloses the feet. Thongs and sandals may not be worn.
   b. Everybody must wear footwear that encloses the feet. Sandals may only be worn with socks.
   c. Everybody must wear hard shoes that enclose the feet. Thongs, sandals, sand shoes and running shoes may not be worn.
   d. Everybody must wear some sort of footwear. Hard shoes that enclose the feet are recommended.

2. Which of the following statements best describes the rules about protective clothing in the lab:

   a. Everybody must wear clothing that covers their arms and legs.
   b. Everybody must wear clothing that covers their arms, legs and hair.
   c. Everybody must cover their clothes and their hair while in the lab. You must wear a protective coat over your clothes and either a hat or hair net over your hair.
   d. Everybody must wear a protective coat to cover their clothes, preferably a white lab coat.
   e. Everybody must wear a white lab coat to cover their clothes.

3. Which of the following statements best describes the rules about eye protection in the lab:

   a. Everybody must wear safety glasses, prescription glasses or sunglasses
   b. Everybody must wear safety glasses or prescription glasses
   c. People who normally wear prescription glasses must wear safety glasses to protect their lenses
   d. Everybody must wear safety glasses. People who wear prescription glasses must wear safety glasses that fit over the top of their prescription glasses
   e. Safety glasses are recommended but not compulsory

4. Which of the following statements best describes the rules about undertaking experiments within the lab:

   a. While undertaking experiments, critical actions, such as mixing chemicals or turning on a burner, may only be undertaken by a member of the teaching staff.
   b. While undertaking experiments, critical actions, such as mixing chemicals or turning on a burner, should only be undertaken when a member of the teaching staff is standing nearby and watching.
   c. Only the experiment specified in the laboratory module may be undertaken and only once a member of the teaching staff is in the laboratory.
   d. Students are encouraged to explore the characteristics of chemicals through their own experimentation, but only after first completing the experiment specified in the laboratory module.

5. Which of the following statements best describes the procedure for using a top-loading balance or an analytic balance:

   a. Always weigh chemicals directly in the pan of the balance so that the weight of a beaker or other container is not included. Make sure that you wash the pan thoroughly after use.
   b. Always place chemicals in a beaker or flask before placing on the balance and subtract the mass of the beaker or flask to obtain the correct mass. The standard mass of various types of beakers and flasks can be found in booklets near the balances.
   c. Always place chemicals in a beaker or flask before placing on the balance and subtract the mass of the beaker or flask to obtain the correct mass. You should weigh the empty beaker or flask on the same balance.
   d. Always place chemicals in a beaker or flask before placing on the balance and subtract the mass of the beaker or flask to obtain the correct mass. To save time get another member of your group to weigh a similar beaker or flask on another balance.

6. Which of the following statements best describes a situation where a burette should be used:

   a. When an approximate volume is required, such as 100ml plus or minus 10ml.
   b. When a reasonably accurate volume is required, such as 100ml plus or minus 1ml.
   c. When a very accurate volume is required, such as 5ml plus or minus 0.01ml.
   d. When the volume required is not known in advance, but instead small quantities of liquid are to be added until some condition (such as a colour change) occurs and the volume added is to be recorded.

7. Which of the following statements best describes a situation where a pipette should be used:

   a. When an approximate volume is required, such as 100ml plus or minus 10ml.
   b. When a reasonably accurate volume is required, such as 100ml plus or minus 1ml.
   c. When a very accurate volume is required, such as 5ml plus or minus 0.01ml.
   d. When the volume required is not known in advance, but instead small quantities of liquid are to be added until some condition (such as a colour change) occurs and the volume added is to be recorded.

8. Which of the following statements best describes a situation where a graduated cylinder should be used:

   a. When an approximate volume is required, such as 100ml plus or minus 10ml.
   b. When a reasonably accurate volume is required, such as 100ml plus or minus 1ml.
   c. When a very accurate volume is required, such as 5ml plus or minus 0.01ml.
   d. When the volume required is not known in advance, but instead small quantities of liquid are to be added until some condition (such as a colour change) occurs and the volume added is to be recorded.

On the desk in front of you there are 5 items of apparatus. Write down their names.

9. Item 1 (leftmost item)

_____

10. Item 2

_____

11. Item 3

_____

12. Item 4

_____

13. Item 5 (rightmost item)

_____

Indicate the position of the following locations, by writing down the number of the item on the laboratory map provided.

- 14. Your current position

- 15. The fume cupboard

- 16. The service hatch

- 17. Your nearest sink with a safety shower and eye wash

- 18. Your nearest exit (that is, the exit you would take in the case of a fire)

- 19. The equipment room

- 20. The preparation room

Indicate where you would find the following items of apparatus or equipment, by writing down the number of the item on the laboratory map provided. If you don't know what an item of apparatus or equipment is, instead write **unknown** next to it:

- 21. A Bunsen burner

- 22. A 100ml beaker

- 23. A top-loading electronic balance

- 24. A tripod stand

- 25. Your nearest glass bin

- 26. Your nearest waste bin

27. Draw a labelled diagram to show the apparatus components involved in the use of a burette and the correct procedure for using it.

28. Draw a labelled diagram to show the apparatus components involved in the use of a pipette and the correct procedure for using it.

29. Describe the procedure to be followed in the event of a fire within the lab. If you mention items of equipment or locations indicate on the laboratory map provided where they are.

30. Describe the procedure to be followed in the event of a chemical spill on either skin or eyes. If you mention items of equipment or locations indicate on the laboratory map provided where they are.

Laboratory Map

Name_____

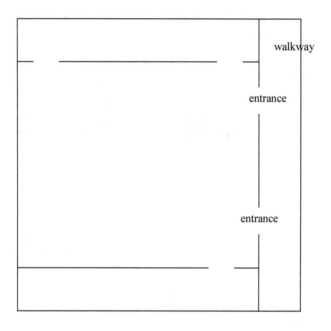

walkway

entrance

entrance

Appendix F. Pilot Study Questionnaire

Chemistry Lab Familiarisation Questionnaire

A. Name ....

B. Group..

C. Date of birth ....

D. Highest level of prior study of chemistry..

E. Gender ....

The current version of the virtual chemistry lab has been designed to familiarise students with the lab, including its contents, appropriate behaviour and safety procedures in preparation for laboratory experiments.

For each of the following statements indicate the degree to which you agree or disagree.

	7. very strongly agree	6. strongly agree	5. agree	4. neutral	3. disagree	2. strongly disagree	1. very strongly disagree
1. You enjoy playing computer games							
2. You enjoyed using the virtual lab							
3. Overall the virtual lab helped you to become familiar with the real lab.							
4. The use of the virtual lab alone was sufficient to prepare you for your first laboratory experiment.							
5a. The virtual lab was more helpful for familiarising you with the lab than the lab manual.							
5b. The virtual lab was more helpful for familiarising you with the lab than the verbal introduction in the first practical session.							
6. The virtual lab is an accurate representation of the real lab.							
7. The information accessible from within the virtual lab is accurate and consistent with the information provided in the lab manual.							
8. The information accessible from within the virtual lab is accurate and consistent with the information provided by your lecturers.							
9. The virtual lab is easy to use.							

	7. very strongly agree	6. strongly agree	5. agree	4. neutral	3. disagree	2. strongly disagree	1. very strongly disagree
10. The training exercise using the national gallery of Ireland environment was sufficient to allow you to use the virtual lab easily.							
11. The virtual lab helped you to become familiar with the layout of the lab building.							
12. The virtual lab helped you to be able to identify items of apparatus.							
13. The virtual lab helped you to be able to locate items within the lab.							
14. The virtual lab helped you to become familiar with the procedure for using a burette.							
15. The virtual lab helped you to become familiar with the procedure for using a pipette.							
16. The virtual lab helped you to become familiar with the procedure for using a laboratory balance.							
17. The virtual lab helped you to become familiar with safety procedures in the lab.							
18. You are more likely to remember procedures if you read about them while carrying out related tasks in the virtual lab than if you read about them in the lab manual away from the lab.							
19. In its current form, you would recommend that new students use the virtual lab prior to their first laboratory experiment.							
20. In its current form, you would use the virtual lab prior to laboratory sessions to practice setting up the apparatus.							
21. If the mechanisms for manipulating apparatus were improved and if all required apparatus were available in the virtual lab, you would use it prior to laboratory sessions to practice setting up the apparatus.							
22. If the virtual lab allowed you to carry out virtual experiments, you would use it prior to laboratory sessions to practice the experiments.							
23. You would prefer to prepare for laboratory sessions using a virtual lab than reading the lab manual							

24. Comment on aspects of the virtual lab that you found useful in familiarising you with the real lab.

25. What information or skills did you need to help you with your first laboratory experiment that were not provided in the virtual lab?

26. Comment on learning from your use of the virtual lab that was not assessed in the test.

Indicate which of the following apparatus you would have already been able to identify prior to coming to CSU:

27.   Burette

28.   Pipette

29.   Beaker

30.   Conical Flask

31.   Graduated Cylinder

32.   Bunsen Burner

33.   Analytic Balance

34.   Top Loading Balance

Indicate which of the following procedures you were already familiar with prior to coming to CSU:

35.   Procedure for using a burette

36.   Procedure for using a pipette

37.   Procedure for using some type of electronic balance

Indicate the degree to which you agree or disagree with the following statements about the existing version of the virtual lab

	7. very strongly agree	6. strongly agree	5. agree	4. neutral	3. disagree	2. strongly disagree	1. very stron disag
38. The menus at the left of the screen were useful.							
39. The use of the menus at the left of the screen was clear and worked as expected							
40. The three movement modes (walk, pan and jump) were useful							
41. The use of the three movement modes was clear and worked as expected							
42. The ability to click on objects to find out information about them was a useful feature							
43. The ability to drag objects around was a useful feature							
44. The mechanism for dragging objects around was clear and worked as expected							
45. The ability to pickup objects and carry them to a new location was a useful feature							
46. The mechanism for picking up and carrying objects was clear and worked as expected							
47. The ability to move some objects to a specific location by choosing an option in the menus was a useful feature							
48. The options provided by right-clicking or double-clicking in the environment window were useful							
49. Using the arrow keys to move around (when they worked) was easier than using the mouse							
50. Using the mouse to move around was easier than the arrow keys (when the arrow keys worked)							
51. The ability to hide the menus and expand the size of the virtual lab on the screen was a useful feature							
52. The ability to locate items of apparatus using the options in the menu was a useful feature							
53. The options in the help menu were useful							

Indicate the degree to which you agree or disagree with the following proposed changes to the virtual lab, with a particular focus on your own learning

	7. very strongly agree	6. strongly agree	5. agree	4. neutral	3. disagree	2. strongly disagree	1. very strongly disagree
54. Adding missing furniture, such as brown draws and sinks, as well as missing door.							
55. Making a greater number of items in the lab clickable, with information about them available							
56. Fixing the arrow keys so that they can always be used for movement							
57. Restricting where an object can be dragged, so that objects can't be dragged through surfaces							
58. Providing a list of choices of where objects can be dropped if you try to drop an object							
59. Changing the locate option so that it locates the current object position rather than the original position							
60. Providing a menu option to return an object to its original location in case it becomes lost							
61. Providing a "see myself" option to help avoid getting stuck behind desks							
62. Making you automatically slide along or around objects if you run into them							
63. Providing viewpoints for accessing each draw, so that moving and panning isn't required							
64. Providing more menu options to place objects in specific locations (eg. on desk)							
65. Providing a transparent overlay map showing your current position within the lab							
66. Providing an animated demonstration of the procedures for using apparatus (eg. burette)							
67. Providing options allowing you to use items of apparatus in a similar way to how you would use them in the real laboratory (eg. burette)							
68. Providing options allowing you to simulate experiments including chemical reactions							
69. Starting you in a virtual bedroom and requiring you to collect everything you need before the prac (labcoat, glasses, footwear, calculator, lab manual, pre-lab exercises)							

70. Comment on additional features of the virtual lab that you think would improve it as a resource for familiarising students with the real lab.

71. List any additional inconsistencies between the virtual lab and the real lab that you noticed.

72. List any additional inconsistencies between the information contained in the virtual lab and the information provided in the lab manual or the information provided by your lecturers.

73. Comment on any additional aspects of using the virtual lab that you found were unclear or didn't work as expected.

74. Comment on any additional improvements to the design of the virtual lab that would make its use clearer and easier.

75. Comment on any improvements to the training exercise using the national gallery of Ireland environment that would have helped you to be able to use the virtual lab.

Appendix G. Pilot Study Information Statement and Consent Form

VIRTUAL CHEMISTRY LAB RESEARCH PROJECT
INFORMATION STATEMENT

Read this information before completing the consent form and retain for your records. **On page 2 you will find the dates, times and venues for your evaluation sessions.**

Title of Project:

Desktop Virtual Environments as Navigation Tools for Locating Information within Educational Web Sites

Purpose of the Research:

To investigate the potential of 3D virtual environments as educational resources.

Researchers:

Principal Investigator:
Barney Dalgarno, School of Information Studies, Charles Sturt University, Wagga Wagga

Contact:
Barney Dalgarno,
email: bdalgarno@csu.edu.au,
phone: (02) 6933 2305,
office: building 4 room 219

Project Summary

This project looks at the potential of virtual environments as educational resources. A 3D virtual chemistry laboratory is under development and will be subjected to formal user evaluation. The analysis of data gathered during evaluation will lead to guidelines for educational developers.

Initially, a pilot evaluation will be carried out, looking at the effectiveness of the virtual lab as a resource to help Chemistry 1A students to become familiar with the real chemistry lab. This pilot will involve twelve students. These students will be divided into two groups, and will carry out the tasks indicated in the following tables.

Project Outcomes

At the completion of the project, papers will be published in journals and at conferences. These papers will include guidelines for developers of web sites incorporating Virtual Environments.

Requirements of Participants

While using the virtual chemistry laboratory participants will be observed and notes will be taken to help improve the design of the environment. Participants will be encouraged to ask questions and make suggestions as they use the virtual lab.

In order to evaluate the effectiveness of the laboratory as an orientation tool, participants will be tested on their familiarity with the lab after using the virtual lab and after the normal lab orientation process that occurs in the first Chemistry 1A practical session.

Ethical Considerations

Participants will be closely observed as they use the software. The investigators will attempt to minimise any stress involved by making this process as informal as possible. It should be noted that it is the characteristics of the software that are being analysed not the participant's skill. Ergonomic guidelines including the use of appropriate furniture and the provision of appropriate rest breaks will be followed to minimise physical or mental stress.

Confidentiality

Participants' names will not be recorded with any of the data gathered. Participants' identities will not be reported in any of the resultant publications.

Withdrawal

Participation in the project is entirely voluntary, and participants may withdraw at any stage without any penalty.

NOTE: Charles Sturt University's Ethics in Human Research Committee has approved this project. If you have any complaints or reservations about the ethical conduct of this project, you may contact the Committee through the Executive Officer:

The Executive Officer
Ethics in Human Research Committee
The Grange
Charles Sturt University
Bathurst NSW 2795

Tel: (02) 6338 4628
Fax: (02) 6338 4194

Any issues you raise will be treated in confidence and investigated fully and you will be informed of the outcome.

VIRTUAL CHEMISTRY LAB RESEARCH PROJECT
CONSENT FORM

This form is to be completed and brought along to your first evaluation session, which is Friday 15th February 1.00pm in Computer Centre room 261 for group 1 or Tuesday 19th February 2.00pm in the Chemistry Laboratory for group 2. The completion of a consent form is part of the University's research ethics requirements.

Name of Research Project	Desktop Virtual Environments as Navigation Tools for Locating Information within Educational Web Sites
Name, Address and Phone No of Principal Investigator(s)	Barney Dalgarno School of Information Studies Charles Sturt University Wagga Wagga NSW Phone: (02) 6933 3205 Email: bdalgarno@csu.edu.au

1.

I, ...

consent to my participation in the research project titled *Desktop Virtual Environments as Navigation Tools for Locating Information within Educational Web Sites.*

2. I understand that I am free to withdraw my participation in the research at any time.

3. The purpose of the research has been explained to me, including the potential risks/discomforts associated with the research. I have read and understood the written explanation given to me

4. I understand that any information or personal details gathered in the course of this research about me are confidential and that neither my name nor any other identifying information will be used or published without my written permission.

5. Charles Sturt University's Ethics in Human Research Committee has approved this study. I understand that if I have any complaints or concerns about this research I can contact:

Executive Officer
Ethics in Human Research Committee
The Grange
Charles Sturt University
Bathurst NSW 2795
Phone: *(02) 6338 4628*
Fax: (02) 6338 4194

Signed by:...

Date ....

Appendix H. Investigation 1 User-control Command Summary

Virtual Chemistry Lab Evaluation
User Control Group - Command Summary

Moving around

Use the keyboard **arrow keys**

If no response, first click somewhere in the environment

Looking around

Hold down the **shift key** while using the keyboard arrows

Interactive objects

Your mouse pointer will turn into a **finger** when placed over an interactive object.

Opening doors, cupboards, drawers

Click on the door, cupboard or drawer

Identifying objects

Click on the object. The object's name will be shown at the bottom of the screen.

Examining objects

To pick up an object **double-click** on it.

Once picked up, to make it **rotate** left-right, **click** on it. Click again to rotate up-down.

You can also **drag** it to rotate it yourself.

To put it down, **double-click** on it again.

Appendix I. Investigation 1 Task Worksheet

Virtual Chemistry Laboratory Evaluation
Exploration Worksheet

Laboratory Layout

You will be tested on your recall of the layout of the laboratory and its furniture. Make sure that you explore the whole laboratory and the adjacent rooms at each end of the laboratory. The following are some of the items of furniture that you will encounter. Place a tick next to each item once you have located it.

Brown drawers	Incubator	Service hatch
Cream cupboards	Lab benches	Shelves
Doors	Metal drawers	Sinks
Fume cupboards	Oven	Whiteboard
General glassware locker	Refrigerator	Windows

Apparatus

You will also be tested on your recall of the names and structure of a series of items of apparatus. Make sure that you have located and examined each of the following items of apparatus. Place a tick next to each item once you have located and examined it.

Analytical Balance	Evaporating Dish	Retort Stand
Atomic Absorption Spectrometer	Eye Wash	Safety Glasses
Beaker	Fire Blanket	Sodium Solutions
Bunsen Burner	Fire Extinguisher	Spatula
Burette	Gauze Mat	Test Tube
Burette Funnel	Glass Bin	Brass Tongs
Clamp	Graduated Cylinder	Top Loading Balance
Clay Triangle	Pasteur Pipette	Tripod
Conductivity Meter	Pipette	Waste Bin
Conical Flask	Pipette Filler	

Other Notes

Write down any other notes that you think will help you to recall the layout of the lab and its apparatus. (You **will not** be able to refer to these notes while doing the test.)

Appendix J. Investigation 1 Test

Virtual Chemistry Laboratory Evaluation
Laboratory Familiarity Test

Background Questions

1. What is the highest level of chemistry study that you have completed?

a) Year 10
b) Year 11
c) Year 12
d) Tertiary level
e) Other (please specify)_____

What year did you last study chemistry?_____

Indicate the degree to which you agree or disagree with each of the following statements, by placing a stroke on the line (eg. _____|_____)

	very strongly agree		very strongly disagree
2. You have a good sense of direction			
3. When you use a street directory or a map you normally turn it around to match the direction you are going			
4. You felt involved in the virtual environment experience			
5. You felt a compelling sense of moving around inside the virtual environment			
6. You were involved in the task to the extent that you lost track of time			

Part A. Identification of Apparatus (7 minutes)

The following is a list of the items of apparatus you have explored.

Analytical Balance	Evaporating Dish	Retort Stand
Atomic Absorption Spectrometer	Eye Wash	Safety Glasses
Beaker	Fire Blanket	Sodium Solutions
Bunsen Burner	Fire Extinguisher	Spatula
Burette	Gauze Mat	Test Tube
Burette Funnel	Glass Bin	Brass Tongs
Clamp	Graduated Cylinder	Top Loading Balance
Clay Triangle	Pasteur Pipette	Tripod
Conductivity Meter	Pipette	Waste Bin
Conical Flask	Pipette Filler	

Write down the names of the 10 items of apparatus shown in the photos provided online.
Please also indicate whether you would have already been able to identify this item before
participating in this study. If you are completely unsure leave the item blank.

Already
able to
identify

1. _____

2. _____

3. _____

4. _____

5. _____

6. _____

7. _____

8. _____

9. _____

10. _____

Part B. Recollection of Apparatus Structure (7 minutes)

Look at the images online, which show four different models of a particular item of apparatus, viewed from various angles. For each item of apparatus, indicate which of the models shown is the correct one.

Item	Circle correct model number			
1. Analytical Balance	I	II	III	IV
2. Bunsen Burner	I	II	III	IV
3. Burette	I	II	III	IV
4. Clay Triangle	I	II	III	IV
5. Conductivity Meter	I	II	III	IV
6. Eye Wash	I	II	III	IV
7. Fire Extinguisher	I	II	III	IV
8. Pipette Filler	I	II	III	IV

Part C. Laboratory Plan (7 minutes)

On the laboratory outline below sketch a plan of the laboratory showing all fixed furniture (benches, shelves, cupboards etc), doors and windows. Label each item of furniture with one distinguishing feature (eg. colour or material)

walkway

Part D. Laboratory Plan (7 minutes)

On the laboratory outline below sketch a plan of the laboratory showing only the items of furniture listed. Photographs of each item have been provided online. Label each item of furniture with a number to indicate which is which.

Items of furniture

1. Lab Benches (6)
2. Metal drawers 2)
3. Fume cupboards (5)
4. Brown drawers (2)
5. Cream cupboards(8)
6. Sinks (5)
7. Service hatch (1)
8. Whiteboard (1)
9 Set of shelves (2)
10. Doors (5)
11. Windows (6)

walkway

Part E. Positioning of Views (6 minutes)

The photographs provided online show the laboratory from 6 different positions. Indicate where each photo was taken from and the direction the camera was pointed, by **ruling** a line from the camera position to the wall. The place where your line reaches the wall should be at the centre of the photo. Place a number next to each line to indicate which photo is represented by each.

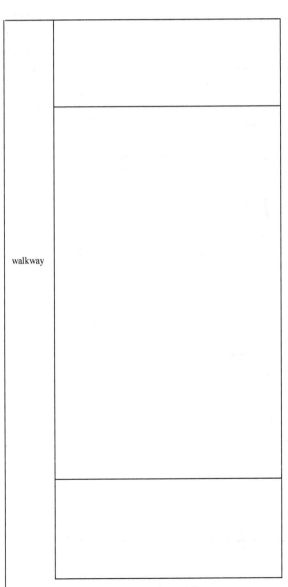

walkway

Part F. Location of Apparatus (5 minutes)

Indicate on the following laboratory plan where the 10 listed items can be found. If an item can be found in more than one location indicate **all of the locations** where it can be found (however assume that all lockers are empty except the one you explored). Photos of each item have been provided online. Use a cross and a number to indicate each position.

Items to Locate

1. Atomic Absorption Spectrometer
2. Beaker
3. Bunsen Burner
4. Burette
5. Conductivity Meter
6. Sodium Solutions
7. Fire Blanket
8. Graduated cylinder
9. Pasteur pipette
10. Safety glasses

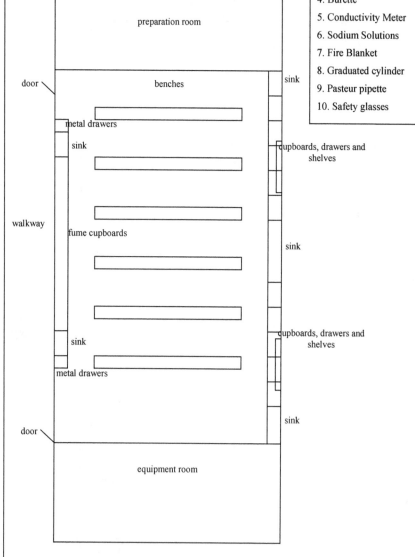

Part G. Location of Apparatus (5 minutes)

The following photos make up a 360 degree panorama taken from a single position in the lab. For each item of apparatus listed, indicate **one place** in the laboratory where it can be found, by marking a position on one of the photos. Use a cross and a number to indicate the position. Photos of each item of apparatus as well as the panorama have been provided online.

1.

Items to locate:

1. Burette	6. Gauze mat
2. Clay triangle	7. Pipette
3. Conductivity meter	8. Pipette filler
4. Evaporating dish	9. Test tube
5. Burette Funnel	10. Brass tongs

2.   **3.**   **4.**

5.   **6.**   **7.**

8.   **9.**   **10.**

Appendix K. Investigation 1 Information Statement and Consent Form

VIRTUAL CHEMISTRY LAB RESEARCH PROJECT
INFORMATION STATEMENT

Read this information before completing the consent form and retain for your records.

Title of Project:

Desktop Virtual Environments as Navigation Tools for Locating Information within Educational Web Sites

Purpose of the Research:

To investigate the potential of 3D virtual environments as educational resources.

Researchers:

Principal Investigator:
Barney Dalgarno, School of Information Studies, Charles Sturt University, Wagga Wagga

Contact:
Barney Dalgarno,
email: bdalgarno@csu.edu.au,
phone: (02) 6933 2305,
office: building 4 room 219

Project Summary

This project looks at the potential of virtual environments as educational resources. A 3D virtual chemistry laboratory is under development and will be subjected to formal user evaluation. The analysis of data gathered during evaluation will lead to guidelines for educational developers.

Earlier in the year a pilot evaluation was carried out with 12 Chemistry students. This current phase of evaluation will look at the effectiveness of the virtual lab as a resource to help students to become familiar with the real chemistry lab. It will also look at the importance of interaction in virtual environments. This phase will involve between 30 and 60 students, divided into three groups. One group will be taken on a tour of the real lab. A second group will explore the virtual laboratory. A third group will also explore the virtual laboratory but with reduced interaction capability. All participants will then be tested on their knowledge of the laboratory.

A further phase of evaluation of the virtual laboratory will be carried out in 2003.

Project Outcomes

At the completion of the project, papers will be published in journals and at conferences. These papers will include guidelines for developers of Virtual Environments.

Requirements of Participants

1. Complete the contact details form including an indication of which session times you are available.

2. Read this information statement and complete the consent form. **If you decide not to participate please contact Barney Dalgarno as soon as possible** (bdalgarno@csu.edu.au or 69332305).

3. Attend the session time you indicated as you first preference (or an alternative session if contacted) in week 12 and **bring along the consent form.**

The exploration of the virtual lab or tour of the real lab, and the knowledge test will be carried out during the indicated session times during week 12 (the week beginning 27th May). **You should attend the session time that you indicated as your first preference by marking with a 1 on the contact details form unless you have been contacted and asked to attend an alternative session.**

It is suggested that you also mark this time in the following table:

Session Time	First preference indicated on contact details form
Monday 27th 9.00am to 11.00am JCC 227	
Monday 27th May 1.00pm to 3.00pm JCC 242	
Tuesday 28th May 9.00am to 11.00am JCC 225	
Tuesday 28th May 3.00pm to 5.00pm JCC 225	
Wednesday 29th May 9.00am to 11.00am JCC 244	
Thursday 30th May 9.00am to 11.00am JCC 225	

It is anticipated that the exploration plus the test will take **no longer than one hour and forty minutes.**

Participants in the two virtual laboratory groups will begin with a 10-minute training session on using a virtual environment. Participants in the real lab group will be shown to the laboratory to begin their tour.

All participants will then be provided with a worksheet to complete while in either the real laboratory or the virtual laboratory. On this worksheet participants will list all apparatus that they encounter and any other information that they think will help them recall information about the laboratory.

Participants will then either explore the virtual laboratory or be taken on a tour of the real laboratory. During this exploration or tour participants will open draws and cupboards and pick up and examine items of apparatus. This exploration or tour will take about 40 minutes.

In order to evaluate the effectiveness of exploring each of the two versions of the laboratory against touring the real laboratory, participants will be tested on their familiarity with the lab. This test will take place in the computer lab and will take about 45 minutes to complete. The questions will be delivered on computer, and the answers will be recorded on paper. For example participants will be asked to identify items of apparatus and locations within the laboratory given a colour photograph.

Ethical Considerations

Participants will be closely observed as they use the software. The investigator will attempt to minimise any stress involved by making this process as informal as possible. It should be noted that it is the characteristics of the software that are being analysed not the participant's skill. Ergonomic guidelines including the use of appropriate furniture and the provision of appropriate rest breaks will be followed to minimise physical or mental stress.

Confidentiality

Participants' names will not be recorded with any of the data gathered. Participants' identities will not be reported in any of the resultant publications.

Withdrawal

Participation in the project is entirely voluntary, and participants may withdraw at any stage without any penalty.

> **NOTE:** Charles Sturt University's Ethics in Human Research Committee has approved this project. If you have any complaints or reservations about the ethical conduct of this project, you may contact the Committee through the Executive Officer:
>
> > The Executive Officer
> > Ethics in Human Research Committee
> > The Grange
> > Charles Sturt University
> > Bathurst NSW 2795
> >
> > Tel: (02) 6338 4628
> > Fax: (02) 6338 4194
>
> Any issues you raise will be treated in confidence and investigated fully and you will be informed of the outcome.

VIRTUAL CHEMISTRY LAB RESEARCH PROJECT
CONSENT FORM

This form is to be completed and brought along to your ITC 161 week 12 practical session, when you will explore the real or virtual chemistry laboratory and then complete a test. The completion of a consent form is part of the University's research ethics requirements.

Name of Research Project   Desktop Virtual Environments as Navigation Tools for Locating Information within Educational Web Sites

Name, Address and Phone No of   Barney Dalgarno
Principal Investigator(s)   School of Information Studies
                                   Charles Sturt University Wagga Wagga NSW
                                   Phone: (02) 6933 3205
                                   Email: bdalgarno@csu.edu.au

1.   I, ...
consent to my participation in the research project titled *Desktop Virtual Environments as Navigation Tools for Locating Information within Educational Web Sites.*

2.   I understand that I am free to withdraw my participation in the research at any time.

3.   The purpose of the research has been explained to me, including the potential risks/discomforts associated with the research. I have read and understood the written explanation given to me

4.   I understand that any information or personal details gathered in the course of this research about me are confidential and that neither my name nor any other identifying information will be used or published without my written permission.

5.   Charles Sturt University's Ethics in Human Research Committee has approved this study. I understand that if I have any complaints or concerns about this research I can contact:

Executive Officer
Ethics in Human Research Committee
The Grange
Charles Sturt University
Bathurst NSW 2795
Phone: *(02) 6338 4628*
Fax: (02) 6338 4194

Signed by:...

Date ....

Appendix L. Investigation 2 User-control Command Summary and Practice Exercises

Laboratory Familiarisation - User Control Group
Control Summary

Moving around

Use the keyboard **arrow keys**. If no response, first click somewhere in the environment.

Undoing a move

To undo a move and jump back to the previous position press the **Home** key.

Looking around

Hold down the **shift key** while using the keyboard arrows.

Zooming in closer

Hold down the **F3** key and click on the object you want to zoom into. To undo the zoom, press the **Home** key before pressing any other keys.

Interactive objects

Your mouse pointer will turn into a **finger** when placed over an interactive object.

Opening doors, cupboards, drawers

Click on the door, cupboard or drawer

Identifying objects

Click on the object. The object's name will be shown at the bottom of the screen.

Movable objects

Next to the name of some objects at the bottom of the screen will be the words **movable object**. These objects can be picked up, carried, placed in other locations and connected to other objects, as explained below.

Carrying objects

Movable objects can be carried, by first dragging them to the hand. As you move around the object will remain in the hand. To release the object drag it to a target location or back to its original location. Target locations will be highlighted in yellow as you drag the object.

Moving objects

You can also drag objects directly from one location to another nearby location without first placing them in the hand.

Connecting objects together

When dragging an object, possible target objects will be highlighted in yellow. When you release an object on a target object the two objects will stay together until you drag the first somewhere else.

Practice

Try the following tasks in the training environment:

- explore the foyer area and click on any objects you find.
- move to the end of the corridor and back.
- look in the draws in the foyer for a small container.
- pick up the container and carry it to the desk.
- place the container on the desk.
- zoom up close to it using F3 and then undo the zoom with the Home button.

Appendix M. Investigation 2 User-control Task Worksheet

Laboratory Familiarisation - User Control Group
Task List

Time allowed 1 hour.

1. Enter the lab, have a look around to familiarise yourself with the layout, and locate the bench containing your **work area** and the **general glassware locker** near the service hatch. You won't need to explore the rooms at either end of the lab (the equipment room and the preparation room).

2. Find the items of apparatus listed below and carry each item to your work area. Tick each item off the list as you go. **Remember where you found each because you will have to put them back away.**

   As you search for the items of apparatus, notice the location of the lab features and furniture listed below and again tick off each as you find it.

   Try to build up a mental image of the lab and its contents.

   You will be tested on your knowledge of the layout of the lab and the location of apparatus and furniture as well as their names or labels.

Apparatus	Lab features and furniture
reagent bottle	The service hatch
250ml conical flask	The whiteboard
250ml beaker	6 lab benches
burette	2 sets of metal drawers
burette stand	5 fume cupboards
clamp	2 sets of brown drawers
burette funnel	8 cream cabinets (each containing cupboards and drawers)
pipette	5 sinks
pipette filler	5 doors
test tube rack	7 windows
test tube	

After 20 minutes your demonstrator will show you where to find the remaining items of apparatus.

3. Carry out the following tasks using the apparatus.

   You will be tested on your knowledge of how to assemble and use the apparatus, and also on your knowledge of the structure of individual items of apparatus.

- Attach the clamp to the stand and the burette to the clamp
- Place the funnel in the burette and the conical flask at the base of the burette.
- Drag the reagent bottle to the beaker to pretend that you are pouring liquid into it.
- Place the reagent bottle back on the shelf.
- Zoom in close to the burette tap using F3 and then turn the tap to pretend that you are making sure that it is shut (use Home to zoom out again).
- Drag the beaker to the funnel to pretend that you are pouring liquid into the burette.
- Place the beaker back on the bench.
- Turn the tap on the burette to pretend that you are releasing liquid from the burette into the conical flask (you may need to zoom in close again using F3).
- Place the conical flask back in its original position on the bench.
- Connect the pipette filler to the pipette
- Place the pipette in the conical flask
- Zoom in close to the pipette filler using F3 and then press the **lever** to lower the plunger and then turn the **wheel** upwards to raise the plunger to pretend that you are extracting liquid from the conical flask to the pipette (use Home to zoom out again).
- Place the test tube in the test tube rack
- Place the pipette in the test tube.
- Press the **lever** on the pipette filler to pretend you are emptying liquid into the test tube (you may need to zoom in close again using F3).

4. Disassemble the apparatus as follows:

- Take the pipette filler off the pipette and place it on the bench
- Take the pipette out of the test tube and place it on the bench
- Take the test tube out of the test tube rack and place it on the bench
- Take the burette funnel out of the burette and place it on the bench
- Take the burette out of the clamp and place it on the bench
- Take the clamp off the burette stand and place it on the bench

5. Return each item of apparatus to its correct location in the lab. (Note that normally you would wash up the glassware before putting it away).

6. In the time left explore the lab further and ensure that you have located all of the lab features and furniture listed in the table above. Take notes or draw pictures if you think it will help you remember the layout of the lab.

Appendix N. Investigation 2 Dynamic Views and Static Views Task Worksheet

Laboratory Familiarisation - Dynamic Tour and Static Tour Groups
Task List

Time allowed 1 hour. Take your time and pay close attention as you go.

You will take a tour of the lab and view the assembly and disassembly of apparatus. To move through the tour keep clicking on **Next**. If you want to go back a step click **Previous**. **Don't click in the virtual environment or try to manipulate the objects in any way.**

1. You will enter the lab, have a look around so you can familiarise yourself with the layout. Take a mental note of the location of the bench containing your **work area** and the **general glassware locker**. Don't worry too much about the contents of the rooms at either end of the lab (the equipment room and the preparation room).

2. You will go to the location of each of the items of apparatus listed below and carry each item to your work area. Tick each item off the list as you go. **Remember where each was found.**

   As you view the items of apparatus, notice the location of the lab features and furniture listed below and again tick off each as you see it.

   Try to build up a mental image of the lab and its contents.

   You will be tested on your knowledge of the layout of the lab and the location of apparatus and furniture as well as their names or labels.

Apparatus	Lab features and furniture
reagent bottle	The service hatch
250ml conical flask	The whiteboard
250ml beaker	6 lab benches
burette	2 sets of metal drawers
burette stand	5 fume cupboards
clamp	2 sets of brown drawers
burette funnel	8 cream cabinets (each containing cupboards and drawers)
pipette	5 sinks
pipette filler	5 doors
test tube rack	7 windows
test tube	

3. You will then see the following tasks carried out using the apparatus (tick each step as you see it):

- Attach the clamp to the stand and the burette to the clamp
- Place the funnel in the burette and the conical flask below.
- Drag the reagent bottle to the beaker to pretend that you are pouring liquid into it.
- Place the reagent bottle back on the shelf.
- Turn the tap on the burette to pretend that you are making sure that it is shut.
- Drag the beaker to the funnel to pretend that you are pouring liquid into the burette.
- Place the beaker back on the bench.
- Turn the tap on the burette to pretend that you are releasing liquid from the burette into the conical flask.
- Place the conical flask back in its original position on the bench.
- Connect the pipette filler to the pipette
- Place the pipette in the conical flask
- Press the lever on the pipette filler to lower the plunger then turn the wheel upwards to raise the plunger to pretend that you are extracting liquid from the conical flask to the pipette.
- Place the test tube in the test tube rack
- Place the pipette in the test tube.
- Press the lever on the pipette filler to pretend you are emptying liquid into the test tube.

  You will be tested on your knowledge of how to assemble and use the apparatus, and also on your knowledge of the structure of individual items of apparatus.

4. You will see the apparatus disassembled as follows (again tick each step as you see it):

- Take the pipette filler off the pipette and place it on the bench
- Take the pipette out of the test tube and place it on the bench
- Take the test tube out of the test tube rack and place it on the bench
- Take the burette funnel out of the burette and place it on the bench
- Take the burette out of the clamp and place it on the bench
- Take the clamp off the burette stand and place it on the bench

5. You will see each item of apparatus returned to its correct location in the lab. (Note that normally you would wash the glassware before putting it away).

6. In the time you have left go through the tour again this time more slowly taking special notice of the lab features and furniture listed in the table above and trying to develop a complete mental image of the lab. Take notes or draw pictures if you think it will help you remember the layout of the lab.

Appendix O. Investigation 2 Test

Laboratory Familiarity Test

Part A. Background Questions (3 minutes)

1. What is the highest level of chemistry that you have studied?

   a) Never studied chemistry
   b) Year 10
   c) Year 11
   d) Year 12
   e) Previously attempted CHM 108 or another chemistry subject at CSU
   f) Tertiary level at another university
   g) Other (please specify)_____

2. What year did you last study chemistry? ....

3. Have you ever been in the CSU chemistry lab? yes - no

   If yes, when (what year?)...........................

Indicate the degree to which you agree or disagree with each of the following statements, by placing a stroke on the line (eg. _____|_____)

	very strongly agree	very strongly disagree
4. You are good at finding your way around unfamiliar places		
5. You felt involved in the virtual environment experience		
6. You felt a compelling sense of moving around inside the virtual environment		

Part B. Identification of Apparatus (8 minutes)

The following is a list of the items of apparatus you may have encountered in the virtual laboratory.

Analytical Balance	Conical Flask	Reagent Bottle
Atomic Absorption Spectrometer	Evaporating Dish	Safety Glasses
Beaker	Eye Wash	Sodium Solutions
Brass Tongs	Fire Blanket	Spatula
Bunsen Burner	Fire Extinguisher	Test Tube
Burette	Gauze Mat	Test Tube Rack
Burette Funnel	Glass Bin	Top Loading Balance
Burette Stand	Graduated Cylinder	Tripod
Clamp	Pasteur Pipette	Waste Bin
Clay Triangle	Pipette	
Conductivity Meter	Pipette Filler	

Look at the images online, which show some of these items of apparatus. In each case there are two images of the item with slightly different structure. You need to do the following:

- Name the item;
- Indicate which (if any) of the images matches the corresponding item in the virtual laboratory; and
- Indicate whether you were already familiar with the item and thus would have been able to name the item prior to exploring the virtual lab.

	Correct Image (circle)	Already able to name (yes or no)
1.	A B neither	
2.	A B neither	
3.	A B neither	
4.	A B neither	
5.	A B neither	
6.	A B neither	
7.	A B neither	
8.	A B neither	
9.	A B neither	
10.	A B neither	

Part C. Assembling and Using Apparatus (8 minutes)

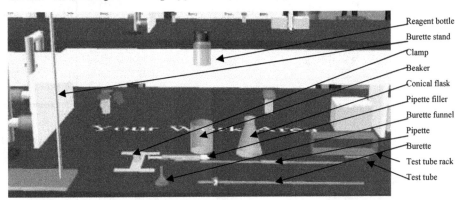

Reagent bottle
Burette stand
Clamp
Beaker
Conical flask
Pipette filler
Burette funnel
Pipette
Burette
Test tube rack
Test tube

List the steps required to transfer some liquid from the reagent bottle to the conical flask using the burette and to then measure some liquid from the conical flask to the test tube using the pipette. Include all of the steps required to **assemble the apparatus** as well as the **detailed steps in operating the burette and the pipette filler**.

The diagram above shows the names of the items of apparatus that you will use, in case you have trouble recalling some of their names. The diagram is also available in colour online.

Part D. Laboratory Plan (8 minutes)

On the laboratory outline below sketch a plan of the laboratory showing the laboratory features and items of furniture listed. Photographs of each item have been provided online. Label each item of furniture with a number to indicate which is which.

Items of furniture

1. Lab Benches (6)
2. Metal drawers (2)
3. Fume cupboards (5)
4. Brown drawers (2)
5. Cream cabinets (8)
6. Sinks (5)
7. Whiteboard (1)
8. Doors (5)
9. Windows (7)

preparation room

service
hatch

walkway
outside lab

equipment room

Part E. Positioning of Views (7 minutes)

The photographs provided online show the laboratory from 6 different positions. Indicate where each photo was taken from and the direction the camera was pointed, by **ruling** a line from the camera position to the wall. The place where your line reaches the wall should be at the centre of the photo. Place a number next to each line to indicate which photo is represented by each.

preparation room

service
hatch

walkway
outside lab

equipment room

Part F. Location of Apparatus (6 minutes)

Indicate on the following laboratory plan where the 11 listed items can be found. If an item can be found in more than one location indicate **one of the locations** where it can be found. A labelled diagram of all items is available online. Use a cross and a number to indicate each position.

Items to Locate

1. Reagent bottle
2. 250ml Beaker
3. 250ml Conical flask
4. Burette
5. Burette stand
6. Clamp
7. Burette funnel
8. Pipette
9. Pipette filler
10. Test tube
11. Test tube rack

preparation room

service hatch

door

benches

sink

metal drawers

sink

cupboards, drawers and shelves

walkway outside lab

fume cupboards

sink

sink

cupboards, drawers and shelves

metal drawers

sink

door

equipment room

Appendix P. Investigation 2 Laboratory Task Observation Notes

Laboratory Familiarisation
Observation Notes for Apparatus Manipulation Task

Name...

Gender...

Task	Critical step	5 immediately	4 after delay	3 after experimenting	2 after verbal assistance	1 never
Pipette some water into the burette using Pasteur pipette without letting any out into the conical flask	Closed the burette tap first					
Empty some water from the burette into the conical flask	Opened the burette tap					
Extract some water from the conical flask using the pipette	Lowered plunger on pipette filler first					
	Used dial to lower and/or raise plunger					
Empty some of the water from the pipette into the test tube	Used dial to lower plunger					
Empty all of the remaining water from the pipette back into the beaker	Used lever to empty all of the liquid					

Appendix Q. Investigation 2 Questionnaire

Chemistry Lab Familiarisation Questionnaire

A. Name ....

B. Date of birth ....

For each of the following statements indicate the degree to which you agree or disagree.

	7. very strongly agree	6. strongly agree	5. agree	4. neutral	3. disagree	2. strongly disagree	1. ver stron disag
1. You enjoy playing computer games							
2. You enjoyed using the virtual lab							
3. Overall the virtual lab helped you to become familiar with the real lab.							
4. The virtual lab is an accurate representation of the real lab.							
5. The virtual lab is easy to use.							
6. The virtual lab helped you to become familiar with the layout of the lab building.							
7. The virtual lab helped you to be able to identify items of apparatus.							
8. The virtual lab helped you to be able to locate items within the lab.							
9. The virtual lab helped you to become familiar with the procedure for using a burette.							
10. The virtual lab helped you to become familiar with the procedure for using a pipette.							
11. In its current form, you would recommend that new students use the virtual lab prior to their first laboratory experiment.							
12. If the virtual lab allowed you to carry out virtual experiments, you would use it prior to laboratory sessions to practice the experiments.							

13. Comment on aspects of the virtual lab that you found useful in familiarising you with the real lab.

14. Comment on any aspects of using the virtual lab that you found were unclear or didn't work as expected.

15. Comment on additional features or improvements to the design of the virtual lab that you think would improve it as a resource for familiarising students with the real lab.

Appendix R. Investigation 2 Information Statement and Consent Form

SPATIAL LEARNING IN 3D ENVIRONMENTS
RESEARCH PROJECT INFORMATION STATEMENT

UNIVERSITY OF WOLLONGONG
AND
CHARLES STURT UNIVERSITY

Summary of the Research

The project investigates spatial learning from exploration of a 3D virtual learning environment using a standard desktop computer. The main purpose of the research is to investigate whether the specific characteristics of 3D environments are important for spatial learning, or whether photographs or video images might be equally effective. A 3D virtual chemistry laboratory, modelled on the undergraduate teaching laboratory at Charles Sturt University will be used as the research instrument. Participants will explore a version of this virtual environment and then undertake a written test on their spatial learning. Participants will also carry out a timed task in the chemistry laboratory, one week later.

Researchers

The research is being undertaken by Barney Dalgarno, School of Information Studies, Charles Sturt University, Wagga Wagga (bdalgarno@csu.edu.au, 6933 2305) as part of a PhD degree in the Faculty of Education at the University of Wollongong, supervised by Professor John Hedberg (John_Hedberg@uow.edu.au, 4221 3310) and Professor Barry Harper (Barry_Harper@uow.edu.au, 4221 3961).

Project Outcomes

At the completion of the project, the results will be included in Barney Dalgarno's PhD thesis and published as part of journal articles and conference papers. It is hoped that the results will be used by educational developers considering the use of 3D environments or videos for teaching spatial concepts.

Benefits for Participants

Participants will learn the layout of the Chemistry Laboratory and will learn the identity of various items of apparatus. This will be helpful in laboratory sessions later in the semester.

Requirements of Participants

All participants will:

- Be given 10 minutes to explore a virtual environment for training purposes with guidance on the user interface.
- Be given 60 minutes to carry out a series of tasks, as specified on a worksheet, within one of three versions of the virtual chemistry laboratory.

- Have a 10 minute rest.
- Be given 50 minutes to complete a test on the chemistry laboratory and its apparatus involving written answers to questions delivered on a computer screen.

One week later participants will:

- Carry out a task in the actual chemistry laboratory while being timed. It is expected that this task will take about 5 minutes to complete.

Ethical Considerations

Some participants may find the use of the virtual environment difficult, especially if they have limited experience with computers. Prior studies have suggested that the degree of difficulty will not be so great that it will place stress on the participants. Nevertheless participants will be free to withdraw from the study at any time.

As with any use of computers there are ergonomic issues to consider, relating to the computer hardware, the furniture and the need for appropriate rest breaks. Computer hardware to be used will consist only of a standard monitor, keyboard and mouse. During the study participants will use ergonomic chairs and they will be asked to adjust the chairs appropriately before commencing the use of the virtual environment. A 10 minute rest break will be scheduled after completion of the learning phase and before commencing the test phase.

Confidentiality

The participants' identities will not be reported in any of the resultant publications. Test results will be recorded using participant numbers rather than names. All data gathered will be stored securely and will be accessible only to the researcher.

Withdrawal

Participation in the project is entirely voluntary, and participants may withdraw at any stage without penalty. The decision to participate or not to participate in the study will not be recorded in any student records and will not have an effect on assessment in any CSU subjects.

More Information

Please don't hesitate to contact Barney Dalgarno (contact details provided above) if you have any additional questions about the project. The project has been approved by the University of Wollongong Human Research Ethics Committee. Any concerns or complaints regarding the way in which the research is or has been conducted, may be directed to the Secretary of the University of Wollongong Human Research Ethics Committee on 42214457.

SPATIAL LEARNING IN 3D ENVIRONMENTS
RESEARCH PROJECT CONSENT FORM

UNIVERSITY OF WOLLONGONG
AND
CHARLES STURT UNIVERSITY

I have been given information about the research project titled *Spatial Learning in 3D Environments* and have had the opportunity to discuss the project with *Barney Dalgarno* who is conducting this research as part of a *PhD* supervised by *John Hedberg and Barry Harper* in the Faculty of Education at the University of Wollongong.

I understand that, if I consent to participate in this project the results of my tests on knowledge of the chemistry laboratory and its apparatus will be used for research purposes.

I have been advised of the potential risks and burdens associated with this research, which include *possible difficulty in using the virtual environment and possible discomfort through use of a computer for a total of 2 hours*, and have had an opportunity to ask *Barney Dalgarno* any questions I may have about the research and my participation.

I understand that my participation in this research is voluntary, I am free to refuse to participate and I am free to withdraw from the research at any time. My refusal to participate or withdrawal of consent will not affect *my treatment in any way as a student at Charles Sturt University.*

If I have any enquiries about the research, I can contact *Barney Dalgarno (bdalgarno@csu.edu.au, 69332305), John Hedberg (John_Hedberg@uow.edu.au, 42213310) or Barry Harper (Barry_Harper@uow.edu.au, 42213961)* or if I have any concerns or complaints regarding the way the research is or has been conducted, I can contact the Complaints Officer, Human Research Ethics Committee, University of Wollongong on 42214457.

By signing below I am indicating my consent to participate in the research entitled *Spatial Learning in 3D Environments,* conducted by *Barney Dalgarno* as it has been described to me in the information sheet. I understand that the data collected from my participation (without any individual participant identification) will be used for *the purpose of Barney Dalgarno's PhD thesis and ensuing publications in journals and conference proceedings* and I consent for it to be used in that manner.

☐   I give my consent for the results of my test to be used for research purposes

☐   I do not give my consent for the results of my test to be used for research purposes

Signed   Date

..../......./......

Name (please print)

....

Appendix S. Contents of CD-ROM and Installation Instructions

Obtaining the CD-ROM

A CD-ROM containing each version of the virtual environment used in this study has been developed but may not be provided with all published versions of the thesis. If a copy of the CD-ROM has not be included with your copy of the thesis, the contents may be downloaded from http://silica.csu.edu.au/vcl/cdrom.html

Contents of the CD-ROM

Pilot Investigation version of Virtual Laboratory (virtual_lab_pilot.zip)
Pilot Investigation version of Training Environment (training_environment_pilot.zip)
Investigation 1 version of Virtual Laboratory (virtual_lab_investigation1.zip)
Investigation 1 version of Training Environment (training_environment_investigation1.zip)
Investigation 1 version of Support Materials for Test (investigation1_test.zip)
Investigation 2 version of Virtual Laboratory (virtual_lab_investigation2.zip)
Investigation 2 version of Training Environment (training_environment_investigation2.zip)
Investigation 2 version of Support Materials for Test (investigation2_test.zip)
Blaxxun Contact VRML Browser (blaxxunContact51.exe)

Installation Instructions

Each version of the virtual laboratory, training environment and test support materials has been provided as a .zip file. The .zip files can be extracted using a tool like WinZip, which has also been provided. When extracting the files ensure that you keep the directory structure contained within the .zip file by choosing the Use Folder Names option.

To use the virtual laboratory or the training environment you need Internet Explorer 5 or later, Blaxxun Contact 5.1 (provided) and Windows 98, Me, NT, 2000 or XP.

Appendix T. VRML Prototypes

Prototype	Purpose	Filename
movingObject	Definition of objects that can be dragged and carried	movingObject.wrl
interactiveObject	Definition of objects that can be dragged, carried and connected together	interactiveObject.wrl
labDoors	Definition of door that is able to be opened by clicking	labDoors.wrl
openableLocker	Definition of locker that is able to be opened by clicking	openableLocker.wrl
openableDraw	Definition of drawer that is able to be opened by clicking	openableDraw.wrl
viewableObject	Definition of object, which when clicked is viewed from a specific position	viewableObject.wrl

VDM

Verlag
Dr. Müller

Wissenschaftlicher Buchverlag bietet
kostenfreie
Publikation
von
wissenschaftlichen Arbeiten

Diplomarbeiten, Magisterarbeiten, Master und Bachelor Theses
sowie Dissertationen, Habilitationen und wissenschaftliche Monographien

Sie verfügen über eine wissenschaftliche Abschlußarbeit zu aktuellen oder zeitlosen
Fragestellungen, die hohen inhaltlichen und formalen Ansprüchen genügt,
und haben **Interesse an einer honorarvergüteten Publikation**?

Dann senden Sie bitte erste Informationen über Ihre Arbeit per Email
an info@vdm-verlag.de. Unser Außenlektorat meldet sich umgehend bei Ihnen.

VDM Verlag Dr. Müller Aktiengesellschaft & Co. KG
Dudweiler Landstraße 125a
D - 66123 Saarbrücken

www.vdm-verlag.de

www.ingramcontent.com/pod-product-compliance
Lightning Source LLC
Chambersburg PA
CBHW071356050326
40689CB00010B/1660